P

HOT, FL.... ~wDED

'Friedman's voice is compelling and will be widely heard'
David Victor, *The New York Times*

'Unlike so many books about the changing environment he hopes
for the best … its persuasiveness lies in the absence of hair-shirt
rhetoric' Ben Macintyre, *The Times*

'America needs a forceful advocate like Friedman to make this
case for change' Richard Lambert, *Guardian*

'Friedman is always worth reading . . . In *Hot, Flat, and Crowded*
he aims to reclaim "greenness" from the liberal, tree-hugging,
sissy and unpatriotic ghetto into which it has been forced by critics,
adopting instead a realistic and economically literate position'
Philip Stott, *Sunday Telegraph*

'A compelling read' *The Times Educational Supplement*

'Lively, sympathetic . . . Friedman has a gift for weaving anecdotes
and examples from around the world into his broader tapestry . . .
will get people talking' Chrystia Freeland, *Financial Times*

Thomas L. Friedman has been awarded the Pulitzer Prize three times for his work with *The New York Times*, where he serves as the foreign affairs columnist. Read by everyone from small-business owners to President Obama, *Hot, Flat, and Crowded* was an international bestseller. Friedman is also the author of *From Beirut to Jerusalem* (1989), which won both the National Book Award and the Overseas Press Club Award, *The Lexus and the Olive Tree* (1999), *Longitudes and Attitudes* (2002), and *The World Is Flat* (2005), which won the first *Financial Times*/Goldman Sachs Business Book of the Year Award. He lives in Bethesda, Maryland.

THOMAS L. FRIEDMAN

Hot, Flat, and Crowded

WHY THE WORLD NEEDS A GREEN
REVOLUTION – AND HOW WE CAN
RENEW OUR GLOBAL FUTURE

RELEASE 2.0

UPDATED AND EXPANDED

PENGUIN BOOKS

PENGUIN BOOKS

Published by the Penguin Group
Penguin Books Ltd, 80 Strand, London WC2R 0RL, England
Penguin Group (USA), Inc., 375 Hudson Street, New York, New York 10014, USA
Penguin Group (Canada), 90 Eglinton Avenue East, Suite 700, Toronto, Ontario, Canada M4P 2Y3
(a division of Pearson Penguin Canada Inc.)
Penguin Ireland, 25 St Stephen's Green, Dublin 2, Ireland (a division of Penguin Books Ltd)
Penguin Group (Australia), 250 Camberwell Road, Camberwell, Victoria 3124, Australia
(a division of Pearson Australia Group Pty Ltd)
Penguin Books India Pvt Ltd, 11 Community Centre, Panchsheel Park, New Delhi – 110 017, India
Penguin Group (NZ), 67 Apollo Drive, Rosedale, North Shore 0632, New Zealand
(a division of Pearson New Zealand Ltd)
Penguin Books (South Africa) (Pty) Ltd, 24 Sturdee Avenue, Rosebank, Johannesburg 2196, South Africa

Penguin Books Ltd, Registered Offices: 80 Strand, London WC2R 0RL, England

www.penguin.com

First published in the United States of America by Farrar, Straus and Giroux 2008
First published in Great Britain by Allen Lane 2008
Published in Penguin Books 2009

1

Printed in Great Britain by Clays Ltd, St Ives plc

A CIP catalogue record for this book is available from the British Library

978-0-141-03666-3

www.greenpenguin.co.uk

For Ann, again

Contents

Preface to the Release 2.0 Edition

Welcome to the Release 2.0 paperback edition of *Hot, Flat, and Crowded*. I have always viewed my books the way computer programmers view software—as works in progress that should be updated whenever possible. Technology today makes that easier than ever to do, and so, as with my previous books, I have taken advantage of that opportunity here.

I want to thank the readers who took the time to share their thoughtful ideas and feedback on my Web site during the past year. The quality and scope of the comments enriched my understanding of the subject and helped me to think about how to push my arguments forward. My original plan to make readers' comments part of a new chapter 18, however, was overtaken by events—particularly the global financial crisis that emerged in full bloom just three weeks after this book was originally published in September 2008. I have substantially rewritten the first three chapters for this new edition to show how the crisis in the financial marketplace and the crisis in our natural world are actually rooted in the same kind of flawed accounting and thinking about risk. Elsewhere, I have used the past year to sharpen certain arguments, update facts, and, I hope, make an even more compelling case that the forces making our world hot, flat, and crowded pose the greatest challenge for our generation—and that rising to that challenge could actually be our greatest economic opportunity. We cannot afford to miss either one.

Thomas L. Friedman
Bethesda, Maryland
September 2009

PART I

When the Market and Mother Nature Hit the Wall

Why Citibank, Iceland's Banks, and the Ice Banks of Antarctica All Melted Down at the Same Time

On June 15, 2005, as the global economy was booming, the satirical newspaper *The Onion* carried the following story about Chinese workers and all the stuff they make for Americans. Though a fake story, like many in *The Onion* it actually spoke some essential truths:

FENGHUA, CHINA—*Chen Hsien, an employee of Fenghua Ningbo Plastic Works Ltd., a plastics factory that manufactures lightweight household items for Western markets, expressed his disbelief Monday over the "sheer amount of [crap] Americans will buy."*

"Often, when we're assigned a new order for, say, 'salad shooters,' I will say to myself, 'There's no way that anyone will ever buy these,'" Chen said during his lunch break in an open-air courtyard. "One month later, we will receive an order for the same product, but three times the quantity. How can anyone have a need for such useless [crap]?"

Chen, 23, who has worked as an injection-mold operator at the factory since it opened in 1996, said he frequently asks himself these questions during his workweek, which exceeds 60 hours and earns him the equivalent of $21.

"I hear that Americans can buy anything they want, and I believe it, judging from the things I've made for them," Chen said. "And I also hear that, when they no longer want an item, they simply throw it away. So wasteful and contemptible."

*Among the items that Chen has helped create are plastic-bag
dispensers, microwave omelet cookers, glow-in-the-dark page mag-
nifiers, Christmas-themed file baskets, animal-shaped contact-lens
cases, and adhesive-backed wall hooks.*

*"Sometimes, an item the factory produces resembles nothing I've
ever seen," Chen said. "One time, we made something that looked
like a ladle, but it had holes in its cup and a handle that bent down
90 degrees. The foreman told us that it was a soda-can holder for an
automobile. If you are lucky enough to own a car, sit back and enjoy the journey. Save the soda beverage for later."*

Chen added: "A cup holder is not a necessary thing to own."

*Chen expressed similar confusion over the tens of thousands of
pineapple corers, plastic eyeshades, toothpick dispensers, and dog
pull-toys that he has helped manufacture.*

*"Why the demand for so many kitchen gadgets?" Chen said. "I
can understand having a good wok, a rice cooker, a tea kettle, a hot
plate, some utensils, good china, a teapot with a strainer, and
maybe a thermos. But all these extra things—where do the Americans put them? How many times will you use a taco-shell
holder? . . ." Chen added that many of the items break after only a
few uses.*

*"None are built to last very long," Chen said. "That is probably
so the Americans can return to buy more . . ."*

The Onion's satire captured in caricature form the most important
engine pulling up living standards across the planet for the last three
decades—the intimate relationship between American consumers and
Chinese savers and producers. At its core, the China-America growth engine worked like this: We in America built more and more stores, to sell
more and more stuff, made in more and more Chinese factories, powered by more and more coal, and all those sales produced more dollars,
which China used to buy more and more U.S. Treasury Bills, which allowed the Federal Reserve to extend more and more easy credit to more
and more banks, consumers, and businesses so that more and more Americans could purchase more and more homes, and all those sales drove
home prices higher and higher, which made more and more Americans
feel like they had more and more money to buy more and more stuff
made in more and more Chinese factories powered by more and more

coal, which earned China more and more dollars to buy more and more T-bills to be recirculated back to America to create more and more credit so more and more people could build more and more stores and buy more and more homes . . .

This relationship, so critical in inflating the post–Cold War credit bubble, was so intimate that when Americans suddenly stopped buying and building in the fall of 2008, thousands of Chinese factories went dark and whole Chinese villages found themselves unemployed. Consider the Chinese artist colony Dafen, north of Hong Kong. Dafen's roughly nine thousand art academy graduates have made the colony the world's center for mass-produced artwork and knockoffs of masterpieces—the oil paintings that hang in motel rooms and starter homes across America. Some 60 percent of the world's cheap oil paintings are produced within Dafen's four square kilometers. "A reasonably skillful copy of Van Gogh's 'Sunflowers' sells for $51," *Spiegel Online* reported (August 23, 2006). "Buy 100 and the price goes down to $33 . . . The 100 paintings, guaranteed to have been produced by art academy graduates, ship within three weeks." Not surprisingly, Dafen was devastated by the bursting of the U.S. credit bubble. "American property owners and hotels were usually the biggest consumers of Dafen's works," Zhou Xiaohong, deputy head of the Art Industry Association of Dafen, told Hong Kong's *Sunday Morning Post* (December 14, 2008). "The more houses built in the United States, the more walls that needed our paintings." And we in America sure did create a lot of new walls for a lot of Chinese watercolors. Overconsuming, overbuilding, overborrowing, and overlending all became the new normal during our post–Cold War credit bubble.

One of my favorite examples comes from my own hometown of Minneapolis. I was visiting there in the spring of 2009 and talking about the problem of runaway consumption with my childhood friend Ken Greer when he said to me, "There is something I have to show you." We drove out to a small strip mall off Shady Oak Road and the Crosstown Highway. "OK, look at this," Ken said as we turned in to the entrance. This "something" was hard to miss. On both sides of the entrance were Caribou Coffee shops, the Minnesota version of Starbucks.

How could one small strip mall need two Caribou Coffees?

We went into the one to the right of the entrance. I ordered my skim latte and asked the barista: "Explain something to me. You're Caribou Coffee and there's another one right over there. I can see it from here.

Why are there two Caribou Coffees here less than a hundred yards apart?" Well, she explained, it was very simple. "There were long lines here every morning, so we needed another one."

"I see," I said to myself. Because people had to wait in line a little longer at rush hour in the morning, the Caribou Coffee folks couldn't just add another coffee machine and a couple more baristas. They had to build a whole carbon copy coffee shop on the other side of the mall entrance. Hey, why not? Money was cheap, resources were available. Why not have two of the same coffee shop in the same strip mall . . .

With all due respect to Dafen and Caribou Coffee, I hope that we never return to the days of Americans just borrowing more and more money to buy more and more stuff with more and more credit fueling more and more Chinese factories or more and more coffee shops powered by more and more coal. Of course, I am not against global trade and economic growth, but our growth needs to be more balanced— economically and ecologically. We cannot just be the consumer and China the producer, and neither of us can allow the goods produced and consumed to be made or used in ways that harm the environment on the scale that we have been. This way of growing standards of living is simply unsustainable—economically unsustainable and ecologically unsustainable.

And that is why the Great Recession that began in 2008 was not your grandmother's standard recession. This was not just a deep economic slowdown that we can recover from and then blithely go back to our old ways—with just a little less leverage, a little less risk, and a little more regulation. No, this Great Recession was something much more important. It was our warning heart attack.

Fortunately, it was not fatal. But we must not ignore what it told us: that we have been growing in a way that is not healthy for either our markets or our planet, for either our banks or our forests, for either our retailers or our rivers. The Great Recession was the moment when the Market and Mother Nature got together and said to the world's major economies, starting with the United States and China: "This cannot continue. Enough is enough."

Indeed. The way we were creating wealth had built up so many toxic assets in both the financial world and the natural world that by 2008/9 it shook the very foundations of our markets and ecosystems. That's right, while they might not appear on the surface to have been related, the destabilization of both the Market and Mother Nature had the same root causes. That is why Bear Stearns and the polar bears both faced extinction at the same time. That is why Citibank, Iceland's banks, and the ice banks of Antarctica all melted down at the same time. The same recklessness undermined all of them. I am talking about a broad breakdown in individual and institutional responsibility by key actors in both the natural world and the financial world—on top of a broad descent into dishonest accounting, which allowed individuals, banks, and investment firms to systematically conceal or underprice risks, privatize gains, and socialize losses without the general public grasping what was going on.

Of course, not all growth in America or elsewhere was fraudulent in these ways—far from it. We did improve productivity and create new companies, like Amazon.com and Google; new products, like the iPod and the iPhone; and new services, like online advertising and open source software, which collectively made people's lives better, easier, more enjoyable, and more productive. But, in America at least, too much of our economic growth was borrowed from our children's piggy banks and from Mother Nature's reserves, not invented. Therefore, we as a society wound up living beyond our collective means.

It all lasted—until it didn't. Or as my friend Rob Watson, the environmental consultant who founded EcoTech International, likes to say: "You know, if you jump off the top floor of an eighty-story building, you can actually feel like you're flying for seventy-nine stories. It's the sudden stop at the end that gets you."

The Great Recession was our sudden stop. The question is: Can we learn from it? As the Stanford economist Paul Romer has said: "A crisis is a terrible thing to waste." I believe we can learn from this crisis and we must learn from this crisis, and the purpose of this book is to provide one pathway for doing so.

This is a revised edition. The hardcover version of this book was first published in September 2008. In it, I argued that America had a problem and the world had a problem. America, I insisted, had "lost its groove" after the end of the Cold War and particularly after 9/11. We had turned inward and begun to export our fears more than our hopes, and we seemed intent on postponing dealing with every big problem weakening our society—from education to Social Security to health care to the deficit to immigration to energy. I argued that we needed to get back to nation-building at home—and I believe it was that sentiment, shared by a majority of Americans, that propelled Barack Obama to the presidency.

But the world also had a problem, I argued. It was getting hot (global warming), flat (the rise of high-consuming middle classes all over the world), and crowded (on track to adding roughly a billion people every thirteen years.) My thesis then, which remains my thesis here, is that America could get its groove back by taking the lead in developing the technologies and policy solutions to address the world's biggest problems—the energy and environmental stresses growing out of a planet getting hot, flat, and crowded.

What has changed? The first thing that has changed is that America's problems and the planet's problems have become more acute. As noted above, the system of growth we have fallen into has destabilized both the Market and Mother Nature to a degree that can no longer be finessed or ignored. The collision of acute financial and ecological distress that made the Great Recession "great" enabled me to see something that was hiding in plain sight—that the problems destabilizing the Market and Mother Nature were rooted in the exact same kind of dishonest accounting, mispricing of risk, privatizing of gains, and socializing of losses.

So I have revised the opening three chapters to explain how and why the Market and Mother Nature hit a wall at the same time. After that, I pick up the narrative of the original book. The remainder of the first half looks at the impact that our reckless behavior has had on the planet, at a time when it is already becoming hot, flat, and crowded. The second half explains how we can use this crisis to reinvigorate and retool America, whose leadership—technological, financial, ethical, and ecological—will be vitally necessary for the whole planet to meet the unique challenges of this moment.

If I had to sum up what this challenging moment means to us, I would put it like this: Our parents were the Greatest Generation, building for us in America a world of freedom, abundance, and opportunity to a degree that no generation in history had ever enjoyed. My generation (I was born in 1953), the baby boomers, turned out to be the "Grasshopper Generation," a term inspired by the writer Kurt Andersen, who in a *Time* essay devoted to our recent age of excess (March 26, 2009) argued that Americans in the past thirty years let out our inner "grasshopper" and gorged on the savings and natural world that had been bequeathed to us—leaving our children huge financial and ecological deficits. We cannot afford to be grasshoppers any longer. And therefore we and our children are going to have to be the "Re-Generation," and summon the will, energy, focus, and innovative prowess to regenerate, renew, and reinvent America in a way that will show the world a new model for growing standards of living and interacting with nature that is truly sustainable, renewable, healthy, safe, fair, and creative of more opportunities for more people in more places than ever before.

The green revolution is not about the whales anymore. And it is not about "our children's children," a generation so distant it is really hard to get energized about it. This is about us. This is about the world we and our children will inhabit for the rest of our lives and whether we can find a way to create wealth—because everyone wants to live better—without creating toxic assets in the financial world or the natural world that overwhelm us. This is an urgent project, because the way of life we lapsed into in recent years cannot be passed on to another generation without catastrophic consequences. It is a tall order, a great challenge—one that our children did nothing to deserve but now can do nothing to escape.

As I said, the Market and Mother Nature hit the wall at the same time for basically the same core reasons, which we need to understand if we are going to avoid a repeat. I am going to focus on three: the systematic obscuring and underpricing of the true costs and risks of what we were doing; the pervasive application of the worst sort of business and ecological values, embodied by the catchphrase IBG/YBG—do whatever you like now, because "I'll be gone" or "You'll be gone" when the bill comes due; and the privatizing of gains and the socializing of losses.

Underpricing Risk

The meltdown that occurred in the market was triggered by subprime mortgages, which allowed people with low incomes and tarnished or no credit histories to buy homes. At the height of the subprime craze, one Los Angeles mortgage broker told me, mortgages were being handed out by banks and mortgage providers to anyone who could "fog up a knife." People with incomes of $15,000 to $20,000, with no credit ratings, or in some cases without even a steady job or citizenship papers were granted mortgages to buy $300,000 and $400,000 homes—with nothing down. What is staggering is precisely how much we and others binged on these "subprime" mortgages, as though they were U.S. savings bonds, not hugely risky financial instruments. How did this happen?

According to Peter J. Wallison, an expert in financial policy and co-director of the American Enterprise Institute's project on financial policy, as of September 2008, there were roughly twenty-five million subprime and other nonprime mortgages outstanding, with an unpaid principal balance of over $4.5 trillion. Subprime mortgages, Wallison explained, are mortgages made to people with blemished credit and low scores on the standard measures used to estimate credit quality. Other nonprime mortgages—also known as Alt-A loans—"are mortgages that have adjustable rates, no or low down payments, and were made to people who did not have to state their income or their income was not verified," he added. These were often referred to as "liar loans," because you could cover up your financial weaknesses, still get a loan for little or nothing down and little to pay at first, and then the big payments would only kick in—or "reset"—later, in a year or two. In other words, the term "subprime loans" referred to the quality of the borrower—people known to be at risk of default from day one. "Alt-A loans" referred to the quality of the loan itself: the borrower may have a good or bad credit record, but these loans themselves were inherently risky because they were extended with little or nothing down, or with little or no credit history, or would reset at a much higher rate in the future, so there was always a good chance the buyer would not be able to meet the mortgage payments as a result of one or more of these conditions. As long as housing prices were going up, though, those holding Alt-A loans could just flip the house when the rate reset, as many speculators riding the boom did, and earn more than the original mortgage value. And brokers were not above telling people: "No worries: Buy now and if you can't meet your mortgage payments, just sell the house. Prices will only go up. It will be worth more tomorrow than it is today—for sure." When housing prices started to go backward, though, and the Alt-A or subprime payments really kicked in, many people holding them were crushed by debt. Their mortgages went up and their home values went down, so they could not escape.

It is stunning how many people got caught up in this. According to Wallison, the twenty-five million subprime and Alt-A loans amounted to almost 45 percent of all single-family mortgages in the United States in 2009.

Not so long ago, this was the norm: Your parents saved long and hard to make a 10 or 20 percent down payment on their home and took out a thirty-year mortgage for the balance from a bank or a credit union, and that institution held the mortgage for its life. You were tethered together. There was a sense of mutual accountability. The new system introduced a new norm: These subprime mortgages were extended by banks and mortgage brokers and then immediately sold to bigger financial firms, like Citibank, Merrill Lynch, or Fannie Mae and Freddie Mac—the government-sponsored institutions set up to work with primary mortgage bankers and brokers to help ensure they had funds to lend to home buyers at afford-able rates. These investment banks and securities firms earned big fees by bundling thousands of these mortgages together into bonds—known as mortgage-backed securities—and then selling them to buyers all over the world. It seemed to make sense to take a bunch of home mortgages that had a predictable cash flow and package them together into a single bond offering that collected all the monthly mortgage payments and then used that cash flow to pay the interest and principle on the bond to the person who bought it. Presto—you have just created an asset-backed security. Fund managers all over the world bought these bonds. Why not? They were paying interest rates better than your average T-bill, and this fattened the balance sheets of those banks or funds that held them, and they seemed as secure as any AAA corporate bond. After all, the rat-ing agencies gave them good marks and Americans—at least our parents' generation—had a long track record of paying off their mortgages.

"This was certainly true when almost all mortgages were prime—made to people with jobs and down payments and at fixed interest rates for thirty years," said Wallison. "Even in the worst downturns, foreclosure rates rarely reached 4 percent." The boom in subprime mortgages was something entirely new, though, he added. Subprimes had always ex-isted, but were traditionally a small part of the total mortgage pool. There was good reason for this—they are very risky. Some projections of total foreclosure rates in the current downturn are 30 percent, he said. Then why did we go on such a binge? A key factor, said Wallison, was a delib-erate United States government policy to foster homeownership and to encourage quasi-government entities that had access to endless cheap capital, particularly home-lending entities like Fannie Mae and Freddie Mac, to make mortgages available to more and more people through "flexible underwriting standards."

"Fannie and Freddie were the enablers," said Wallison. They first stimulated the development of a subprime and Alt-A market on Wall

Street by buying huge amounts of AAA tranches of subprime mortgages from different investment banks, and holding the bonds. Then, in late 2004, they began to buy these primary junk loans in large amounts and bundled them into bonds themselves, competing for product with Wall Street. "The fight between Wall Street and Fannie and Freddie," said Wallison, "drove down the price of junk mortgages, drove up the housing bubble, and filled it with unprecedentedly low quality mortgages . . . This is a story about how a well-intended government policy caused a substantial decline in the quality of U.S. mortgages and ultimately the financial crisis we are living with today."

By the way, what are AAA tranches? This is important. Imagine that you had a pile of dishes in your sink and each of those dishes represented a group of mortgages of different qualities that were all being packaged into one bond offering. The worst BBB and CCC dishes were at the bottom of the sink and paid the highest interest because they were the riskiest. The best, with the most secure borrowers—AAA—were at the top. Then you started to fill the sink with water—the Great Recession of 2008/9. The riskiest tranches of mortgage-backed securities quickly went under water. The best, the AAA tranche, would normally remain above water. Usually, those tranches of mortgage-backed securities never got wet. But this Great Recession was not usual and today many of those AAA tranches are also under water and worth either nothing or only a fraction of their original value.

This subprime frenzy, though, was abetted by more than just a U.S. government desire to promote homeownership and construction. It was also abetted by a broader easing of credit and low interest rates—too low for too long—under the Federal Reserve leadership of Alan Greenspan in the early 2000s. This easing of credit by the Fed, in turn, was enabled by the massive amount of dollars sloshing around the global economy from all the high-saving countries, particularly the Asian Tigers, Middle East oil exporters, and China. Many economists now believe that it was this huge pool of Asian savings and Middle Eastern petrodollars—managed by sovereign wealth funds in all these different countries and reinvested back in America—that depressed interest rates on U.S. Treasury securities and spurred investment bankers and financial wizards to come up with "innovations" that would produce higher yields. This led them to offer more and more subprime mortgages and more and abstruse and exotic derivatives and insurance products surrounding them.

I like the way Sherle R. Schwenninger, director of the Economic Growth Program at the New America Foundation, summarized the situation. Writing in *The Nation* (December 23, 2008), he noted: "The root cause of this unbalanced world economy was the enormous pool of excess savings generated by China, Japan and, more recently, the petrodollar states of the Persian Gulf. This global savings glut, as Federal Reserve chairman Ben Bernanke called it, helped fuel a succession of asset bubbles in the United States, culminating in the expansion of easy credit and the rapid run-up of housing prices following the collapse of the tech-stock bubble," notes Schwenninger. "These housing and credit bubbles in turn helped inflate consumption by enabling households to take on more debt; household debt as a percentage of disposable income rose from 90 percent in the late 1990s to 133 percent in 2007."

To put it in simple terms, the banks and sovereign wealth funds holding Mrs. Tanaka's savings in Japan, Mr. Zhou's savings in China, and Mr. Abdullah's savings in Kuwait shipped them to Wall Street, where some of America's best rocket scientists designed financial products to get them a higher rate of return—without greater risks, or so they were told. With all that money chasing all that yield, it was inevitable that the financial houses managing all that money would lobby Washington to give them more and more "flexibility" to design investment instruments that could produce higher and higher yields. And Washington accommodated. With the end of the Cold War and the intensification of globalization, market-friendly presidents (Ronald Reagan, George H. W. Bush, Bill Clinton, and George W. Bush), along with congressmen and senators whose palms had been greased by Wall Street through campaign donations, rolled back banking regulations that had limited risk-taking. Some of these regulations had been on the books since the Great Depression.

So more and more money flowed into a less and less regulated financial system, and the banks took greater and greater risks with it—not just on subprimes but on all kinds of instruments—in more and more places using more and more exotic instruments and greater and greater leverage, making transactions that fewer and fewer people understood and were less and less transparent.

Consider one example—derivatives. In December 2000, the U.S. Congress passed, and then President Clinton signed, legislation spurred by the financial services industry that exempted derivatives from most oversight. Derivatives are financial instruments that "derive" their value from the price of some real stock, bond, service, or good. "Typically, the seller receives money in exchange for an agreement to purchase or sell some good or service at some specified future date," according to Wisegeek.com. So a bank or insurance company could earn money selling derivatives that insured mortgage-backed securities against default. These are called credit-default swaps. The poster child for this sort of innovation turned out to be the American International Group, the insurance giant.

Gretchen Morgenson and Don Van Natta Jr. described AIG's misadventures into risky global finance in *The New York Times* (May 31, 2009): "After the 2000 legislation was passed, derivatives trading exploded, helping the biggest traders earn immense profits. The market now represents transactions with a face value of $600 trillion, up from $88 trillion a decade ago. JPMorgan, the largest dealer of over-the-counter derivatives, earned $5 billion trading them in 2008, according to Reuters, making them one of its most profitable businesses. Among the companies that expanded rapidly was A.I.G. Straying from its main business of providing property and life insurance, A.I.G. wrote a type of contract known as credit-default swaps that protected holders of mortgage securities against defaults. When millions of subprime borrowers stopped paying their mortgages, A.I.G. had to provide cash collateral that it did not have to clients that had bought its insurance."

AIG completely underpriced, and in some ways hid, the risks it was taking. AIG owned a savings and loan operation, so its banking business was regulated at the federal level. It also sold insurance, so its insurance business was regulated by insurance commissioners in every state. But its derivatives business was run out of a hedge fund it created in its London office—AIG Financial Products, or AIGFP, which was part of the vast forest of *unregulated* hedge funds and private equity groups that had grown up in the last two decades and today accounts for about 50 percent of global credit, dwarfing the traditional banking sector. No one global institution regulates this sector. Even though AIGFP accounted for only 1 percent of the insurance behemoth's total revenues, the risks it took on literally brought the house down when they went bad. And because this universe is very nontransparent and unregulated, few people inside AIG or outside were aware of how big the dice it had rolled were.

"Before the crisis," noted Morgenson and Van Natta, "few market participants knew the size of A.I.G.'s exposure. Some derivatives transactions occur on exchanges, where the value and nature of the contracts are disclosed, but many do not. Credit-default swaps trade privately. This kept risk in these trades under wraps, leaving regulators unaware of how dangerously stretched and poorly managed the market was."

How could sophisticated global finance firms get so crazy and take on so much risk? I'd point to two reasons. First, their math wizards came up with models that told them it was not that risky. In a special report about some of those financial nerds, known as "quants," who built these mathematical models underlying all these mortgage-backed securities, *Newsweek* (June 8, 2009) recalled Warren Buffett's dictum: "Beware of geeks bearing formulas." The magazine then went on to tell the story of über-geek David X. Li, "who, while working at JPMorgan, created the Gaussian copula function, a formula for determining the correlation between the default rates of different securities." In theory, if one mortgage-backed security defaulted, the model gave bankers an estimate of how many others would default as well. "The apparent genius of the Gaussian copula is its abstraction," said *Newsweek*. "Rather than relying on the immense amount of data used to figure the odds that a [subprime bundle of mortgages and collateralized debt obligations] might default, Li appeared to have discovered a law of correlation. That is, you didn't need the data; the correlation was just there. Armed with it, quants could price these much faster, and traders could buy and sell them at record speeds. Gaussian was rocket fuel for the CDO market. The global volume of CDO deals went from $157 billion in 2004 to $520 billion in 2006. As more banks got in on the game, the once-large profit margins started to shrink. In order for banks to make the same kind of returns, they had to pack more and more loans into a CDO, essentially making bigger bombs." Needless to say, Li's benign predictions about the correlation between defaults quickly proved wrong in the subprime crisis, when subprime mortgages and their bonds toppled together like dominoes. As *Newsweek* put it: "Li was on his way to a Nobel Prize when the world blew up."

The second reason they so underpriced the risk was simpler. It is something that happens in every bubble: people who are apparently smart turn out to be really dumb—in large numbers. They buy into a notion that nothing can go wrong. In this case the notion was that housing prices in America would never go down again. As Michael Lewis pointed out in a piece on AIGFP in *Vanity Fair* (August 2009), the AIG unit was originally used by Wall Street investment banks to insure piles of loans to

IBM and GE. Then, in the early 2000s, AIGFP started insuring "messier piles": securities backed by credit card debt, student loans, auto loans, and prime mortgages—anything that generated a cash flow. As Lewis noted, these loans were of such a diverse nature and to so many different parties that the usual risk logic applied: they couldn't all go bust at once. Originally, there were very few subprime mortgages in these piles. But that changed toward the end of 2004. "From June 2004 until June 2007," wrote Lewis, "Wall Street underwrote $1.6 trillion of new subprime-mortgage loans and another $1.2 trillion of so-called Alt-A loans." This expansion was made possible, in part, because AIGFP was ready to insure many of these piles of loans—and made billions of dollars doing it.

Why not? These different piles of loans all seemed so diversified that nothing really big could go wrong. And so AIG gorged on them, but without noticing that these piles of consumer loans it was insuring were changing, said Lewis. After 2005, subprime mortgages went from 2 percent to 95 percent of the consumer loan packages that AIGFP was guaranteeing, without maintaining anywhere near the capital required to cover them if there were widespread defaults. No problem. AIGFP officials were confident that housing prices, even if they fell, could never fall everywhere at once and thereby trigger massive defaults requiring the insurance giant to fork over cash to all the holders of subprime bonds at once. Lewis quotes Joe Cassano, who headed AIGFP at the time, on an investor conference call in the summer of 2007, as the subprime crisis was just starting to unfold: "It is hard for us, without being flippant, to even see a scenario within any kind of realm of reason that would see us losing $1 on any of those transactions."

A few months later, housing prices across the land started falling like dominoes and AIGFP's bets were on their way to bankrupting the entire company. That, ladies and gentlemen, is what you call massively under-pricing risk.

IBG/YBG

It is a lot easier to underprice risk when you can take your percentage quickly and then pass off the bad loan to someone else. All that global capital that flowed into Wall Street in search of higher returns in the early 2000s arrived not only at a time of a loosening of credit and a loosening of traditional regulatory constraints in America, but also at a time of a loosening of ethics. Actually, it was worse than that. The Great Recession was caused in part by a broad-based breakdown in ethics by key players—bankers, rating agencies, investment houses, mortgage brokers, and consumers. You can have all the regulations in the world, but when greed tempts large numbers of people to lose sight of any kind of long-term thinking and sense of accountability, regulations won't help you. It was not the illicit behavior that caused the Great Recession. It was all the stuff going on in plain sight by people who should have known better but suspended their beliefs and values and norms and skepticism to get in on the party. Yes, they had "principles." Unfortunately, the whole credit bubble that destabilized the global economy was built on the "principles" known in the banking world as IBG/YBG—"I'll be gone" or "You'll be gone" when things go bad.

Here's how it worked. The mortgage broker who first sold a family a mortgage and then passed it off to a bigger financial institution, like Fannie Mae or Citibank, knew that he would be "gone" if and when the family holding the mortgage defaulted: He would no longer own the mortgage—Fannie or Freddie or some investment bank would. So there was no risk for him personally in the high-risk deal. And he told the family that the same was true for them. There would be no problem if it turned out they couldn't make the payments because "you'll be gone"—because housing prices would always go up, they could just flip the house for more than they paid for it, or just walk away. The rating agencies, whose fees and revenues depended on how many of these bonds of subprime mortgages they got to rate, had a great incentive to give them high ratings so they would sell more easily and therefore more investment houses and banks would want to use their rating services. And if those bonds blew up, well, said the raters, IBG—"I'll be gone." The investment banks had a great incentive to bundle more and more mortgages into bonds and sell them around the world, because the fees were huge, and as long as they didn't hold too many on their own balance sheets, if they blew up, who cared? IBG—"I'll be gone."

To put it another way, the whole system depended upon people who originated the risk profiting from that origination, then transferring that risk to someone else and never having to be responsible for it afterward. So people who never should have been taking out mortgages took them out, people who never should have granted them granted them, people who never should have bundled them bundled them, people who never should have rated them AAA rated them AAA, people who never should have sold them to pension funds and other financial institutions world-wide sold them. And companies that never should have been insuring them, like AIG, insured them, without setting aside sufficient assets to cover a massive default. Everyone just assumed they could profit person-ally in the short term and never have to worry what happened in the long term after they passed the bond along.

President Obama, in unveiling his own plan to regulate markets after the 2008 crash, put it well when he pointed out that Wall Street devel-oped a "culture of irresponsibility," which involved one person passing on risk to another until a risky financial product was finally bought by someone who didn't understand either the risk or even how the bond or derivative actually worked. "Meanwhile," said the president, "execu-tive compensation—unmoored from long-term performance or even reality—rewarded recklessness rather than responsibility."

Privatizing Gains and Socializing Losses

If the true risks involved in these subprime mortgages or default insur-ance had been priced into these products, they never would have been rated the way they were. Investors would have been much more wary and demanded much higher yields before buying them, which would have forced the mortgage brokers to be more careful in deciding to whom to give these mortgages and the banks to be much more careful in choosing which ones to bundle. But the money was just too good, the temptation to underprice the risk and privatize the gains just too tempting for every-one involved. And rare was the banker who could resist joining the party. As the former Citigroup CEO Charles Prince told the *Financial Times* on July 9, 2007, just weeks before the credit markets started nosediving: "as long as the music is playing, you've got to get up and dance." Share-holders, board members, and market analysts were all saying to these fi-nancial houses and bosses: Why are you not as aggressive as the other guy? Why are you not bundling mortgages and CDOs? Why are you not bringing in these big returns? All the incentives for CEOs pushed them to take more risk. And boy, were there incentives. In December 2007, with the credit markets already badly shaken, Goldman Sachs Group Inc.'s chief executive officer, Lloyd Blankfein, was granted a $67.9 mil-lion bonus, the biggest ever awarded to the CEO of a Wall Street firm.

And if things later went bad for a CEO's firm? No problem. Typically the CEOs' contracts, written in the seven fat years, ensured that the worst they would get were golden parachutes. On November 1, 2007, Merrill Lynch CEO Stan O'Neal quit and received a golden parachute worth $161.5 million, despite the fact that his firm's subprime investments would eventually result in over $2 billion of losses.

Some of our biggest financial firms got away from their original purpose—to fund innovation and to finance the process of "creative destruction," whereby new technologies that improve people's lives replace old ones, said the Columbia University economist Jagdish Bhagwati. Instead, he added, too many banks got involved in exotic and incomprehensible financial innovations that ended up as "destructive creation."

Only when the whole edifice cracked in September 2008 with the collapse of Lehman Brothers, which forced Congress to establish a $700 billion emergency fund for the Treasury to prevent the financial system from melting down, did people grasp what had happened: TWG—"They were gone"—the bankers who piled up these risks and privatized the gains, but WWSH—"We were still here." We had allowed Wall Street investors and executives to underprice risks and privatize their gains, but then force taxpayers to bail them out when the losses threatened a systemic breakdown.

Why were We the People left holding the bag? Because the economy depended on it. Key financial services companies had become too big to fail, and had we let them go down, we all would have gone down with them. You and I would have gone to our ATMs to withdraw money from our banks and nothing would have come out. That actually happened for a while to depositors in America's oldest money market, Reserve Primary. The $64.8 billion fund held $785 million in short-term commercial paper, issued by Lehman Brothers. When Lehman filed for bankruptcy in September 2008, Reserve Primary couldn't pay back its customers in full—$1 for every $1 they had on deposit—and had to close its doors for a period. "When the balance sheet of a company does not capture the true costs and risks of its business activities, and when that company is too big to fail, you end up with them privatizing their gains and socializing their losses," Nandan Nilekani, a founder of the Indian technology company Infosys, said to me. That is exactly what played out. Thanks to its huge losses in the derivatives market, AIG alone required more than $170 billion in taxpayer support of one kind or another to stay afloat, as of summer 2009.

Alas, though, we Americans were not alone in thinking that we could fly. Other countries quickly copied us. It was inevitable. In a flat world, where connectivity is getting tighter and faster every day, and where the electronic herd of capital is moving around everywhere and anywhere looking for higher and higher returns, lots of people wanted in on this game. And it did not matter how small you were; anyone could open a global casino in their garage. Just ask Iceland.

Iceland's Banks and Melting Ice

Iceland turned itself into a hedge fund with glaciers. The government, together with the country's biggest banks, in which it had a large stake, saw the phenomenal returns to be gained from investment banking and decided to get a piece of the action by radically deregulating its economy in order to attract huge sums of foreign capital. For a short time, Iceland, with its 300,000 people and its traditional economy, became one big wild offshore bank. Michael Lewis vividly described what happened in *Vanity Fair* (April 2009):

> An entire nation without immediate experience or even distant memory of high finance had gazed upon the example of Wall Street and said, "We can do that." For a brief moment it appeared that they could. In 2003, Iceland's three biggest banks had assets of only a few billion dollars, about 100 percent of its gross domestic product. Over the next three and a half years they grew to over $140 billion and were so much greater than Iceland's G.D.P. that it made no sense to calculate the percentage of it they accounted for. It was, as one economist put it to me, "the most rapid expansion of a banking system in the history of mankind . . . From 2003 to 2007, while the U.S. stock market was doubling, the Icelandic stock market multiplied by nine times. Reykjavík real-estate prices tripled. By 2006 the average Icelandic family was three times as wealthy as it had been in 2003, and virtually all of this new wealth was one way or another tied to the new investment-banking industry."

The country's entire economy got warped. Students fled from traditional careers in fishing or engineering for the economics of making money from money. When the laws of gravity finally kicked in, and Iceland's three brand-new global-size banks collapsed in October 2008, said Lewis, "Iceland's 300,000 citizens found that they bore some kind of responsibility for $100 billion of banking losses—which works out to roughly $330,000 for every Icelandic man, woman, and child."

How did little Iceland get in so deep? Basically a small group of people in key financial positions drank the same Kool-Aid that bankers in London and on Wall Street drank. They adopted the same model of excessive leverage and nothing-can-go-wrong risk-taking and grafted it onto their little country. You know the old saying: When you are in a poker game and you don't know who the sucker is, it's probably you. It was probably Iceland. Or as Lewis put it, citing an analysis by the Danske Bank, Iceland both spawned and was driven by "this incredible web of cronyism: bankers buying stuff from one another at inflated prices, borrowing tens of billions of dollars and re-lending it to the members of their little Icelandic tribe, who then used it to buy up a messy pile of foreign assets. 'Like any new kid on the block,' says Theo Phanos of Trafalgar Funds in London, 'they were picked off by various people who sold them the lowest-quality assets—second-tier airlines, sub-scale retailers. They were in all the worst [leveraged buyouts].'"

But along the way, naive little Iceland took in and took down a lot of other naive people as well. One way Icelandic banks imported so much capital was by creating online savings accounts, the most popular of which was called Icesave.com, which attracted savers from all over the world because of the high rates of interest they offered—including some 300,000 savers from Great Britain alone. And it wasn't just individuals who got taken in. Indeed, when Iceland's banks collapsed, London's *Daily Telegraph* reported (October 14, 2008) that, according to an official government analysis, more than a hundred British municipal governments, as well as universities, hospitals, and charities, had deposits totaling well over $1.1 billion stranded in blocked Icelandic bank accounts. This included, the *Telegraph* said, "more than a quarter—116—of the 411 local councils in England and Wales [who had] at least £858 million in Icelandic banks. They include some of the largest authorities in the country, among them Kent County Council with £50 million, Nottingham City Council, at £42 million, and Norfolk County Council with £32.5 million." Cambridge University alone had about $20 million deposited there, while fifteen British police forces—

from places like Kent, Surrey, Sussex, and Lancashire—had roughly $170 million frozen in Iceland. Yes, even the bobbies were banking in Iceland! So was the bus company. Transport for London, which runs London's famous bus and tube services, reportedly had some $60 million on deposit with Kaupthing Singer & Friedlander, a UK subsidiary of Iceland's bankrupt Kaupthing bank.

Iceland's story ended the same way as America's—and for the same reasons: the bankers in charge failed to understand what could go wrong and how much they could lose if the markets turned against them. After dramatically underpricing the risks of what they were doing, and then privatizing the gains, Iceland's biggest banks socialized the losses. Iceland's taxpayers and government had to nationalize the country's three biggest banks. And, to keep them operating after massive losses that threatened to bring down the country's entire financial system, Iceland's government secured a $2.1 billion loan from the International Monetary Fund and a $2.5 billion loan from a consortium of Nordic countries. According to CNN.com (November 20, 2008), "The IMF move marks the first time the international lender has had to funnel money to a Western European country in 25 years." Iceland's taxpayers will be paying this off for a long, long time.

What is striking, though, is how the same fraudulent accounting that brought down Iceland's banks also brought down one of the biggest banks of ice in Antarctica—in the same year. Just as the Icelandic economy was melting down, the Wilkins Ice Shelf in the western Antarctic Peninsula, a huge bank of ice that had been stable for most of the last century, began to crumble. According to Reuters (January 19, 2009), the Wilkins—"a flat-topped shelf of ice jutting 65 feet out of the sea off the Antarctic Peninsula"—once covered six thousand square miles, but in the last decade and a half had lost a third of its area under the pressure of global warming. "Researchers believe it was held in place by an ice bridge linking Charcot Island to the Antarctic mainland. But that 127-square-mile bridge lost two large chunks in 2008 and then shattered completely on April 5, 2009," Reuters added in a later report (April 30, 2009). This sent the Wilkins Ice Shelf collapsing into the sea. The report continued:

Icebergs the shape and size of shopping malls already dot the sea around the shelf as it disintegrates. Nine other shelves have receded or collapsed around the Antarctic peninsula in the past 50 years, often abruptly like the Larsen A in 1995 or the Larsen B in 2002. The trend is widely blamed on climate change caused by heat-trapping gases from burning fossil fuels. "This ice shelf and the nine other shelves that we have seen with a similar trajectory are a consequence of warming," said David Vaughan from the British Antarctic Survey. In total about 25,000 sq km of ice shelves have been lost, changing maps of Antarctica. Ocean sediments indicate that some shelves had been in place for at least 10,000 years . . . Temperatures on the Antarctic Peninsula have warmed by about 3 degrees Celsius (5.4 Fahrenheit) since 1950, the fastest rise in the southern hemisphere.

Same meltdown, same risky business. Just as Citibankers and Icelandic bankers got to engage in wild financial practices that did not reflect the real risks of massive defaults or losses, developers, oil companies, coal companies, auto companies, and electric utilities sold energy, mobility, lighting, heating, and cooling based on hydrocarbons at prices that did not reflect the real costs to the planet from all the climate-changing carbon dioxide molecules we were building up in the atmosphere. And every one of us who enjoyed using these underpriced carbon-emitting energy sources got to privatize the gains as well. The losses, however—the long-term impact of all this carbon building up in the atmosphere—we have socialized. We charged all of this on our children's Visa cards to be paid by them and their children's children far into the future, because that carbon will remain in the atmosphere affecting the earth's climate for several thousand years. Maybe we'll be gone, but our children and their children will be here. This is the only home we have and, as environmentalists are fond of saying, Mother Nature doesn't do bailouts. So we better find a better way to grow.

"We have created a way of raising standards of living that we could not possibly pass on to our children," said Joseph Romm, the physicist and climate expert who writes the blog Climateprogress.org. "We have been getting rich by depleting all our natural stocks—water, hydrocarbons, forests, rivers, fish, and arable land—and not by generating renewable flows. You can get this burst of wealth that we have created from this rapacious behavior. But it has to collapse, unless adults stand up and say, 'This is a Ponzi scheme. We have not generated real wealth, and we are destroying a livable climate . . .' Real wealth is something you can pass on in a way that others can enjoy."

Mother Nature's Dow

The sudden loss of an ice shelf that has been around for thousands of years should get our attention. But many other less dramatic warning signs are indicating that our risky business is ravaging the natural world as much as the financial one. We know very well how to measure the costs of reckless economic behavior. When the market hits a wall, it shows up in red numbers on the Dow Jones Industrial Average, which fell sharply during the Great Recession. But no one has devised a Dow that with one simple number tells us how Mother Nature is doing. If we did, though, it would be safe to say that in recent years Mother Nature's Dow hit new scientific lows.

If you just sample the climate and biodiversity research in 2008 and 2009, what is striking is how insistently some of the world's best scientists have been warning that climate change and biodiversity loss are happening faster with bigger impacts than they anticipated just a few years ago. Many of the key estimates about the speed and breadth of climate change offered by the UN's Intergovernmental Panel on Climate Change, which were made as recently as 2007, are now considered woefully out of date. I will discuss this in more detail later, but just a couple of examples:

Consider MIT's Joint Program on the Science and Policy of Global Change. In 2009 the program quietly updated its Integrated Global System Model, which tracks and predicts climate change from 1861 to 2100. Its revised projection indicates that if we stick with business as usual, in terms of carbon dioxide emissions, average surface temperatures on earth by 2100 will hit levels far beyond anything humans have ever experienced.

Or consider the Millennium Ecosystem Assessment, first produced by the United Nations in 2005. This comprehensive, peer-reviewed scientific analysis by 1,300 experts "assessed the consequences of ecosystem change for human well-being." The report concluded that the ability of the earth's ecosystem to absorb our impacts is rapidly diminishing: "At the heart of this assessment is a stark warning. Human activity is putting such strain on the natural functions of Earth that the ability of the planet's ecosystems to sustain future generations can no longer be taken for granted." The MEA spelled out the many "services," or benefits, that human beings derive from nature—from forests that maintain watersheds, prevent silting, and provide timber for building and filtration for the air we breathe, to oceans that provide habitats for fish that we depend upon for food, to coral reefs that keep those oceans and their inhabitants healthy. The National Oceanic and Atmospheric Administration estimates that there may be millions of undiscovered species of organisms living in and around reefs. According to the report, "Many drugs are now being developed from coral reef animals and plants as possible cures for cancer, arthritis, human bacterial infections, viruses, and other diseases." Yet because most nations do not put a price on these services, they too are "underpriced" and therefore easily overexploited—with the profits privatized and the losses socialized. This has been particularly true in the last fifty years. The MEA report noted that 60 percent of the world's ecosystems have now been degraded; more land was converted to agriculture since 1945 than in the eighteenth and nineteenth centuries combined; between 10 and 30 percent of the mammal, bird, and amphibian species on earth are currently threatened with extinction. More than a billion people today already suffer from water scarcity; deforestation in the tropics alone destroys an area the size of Greece every year—more than twenty-five million acres; more than half the world's fisheries are overfished or fished at their limit.

No wonder the World Wildlife Fund's Living Planet 2008 Report concluded that we are already operating 25 percent above the planet's biological capacity to support life. And that is before we add another billion people by the early 2020s. "The world is currently struggling with the consequences of over-valuing its financial assets, but a more fundamental crisis looms ahead—an ecological credit crunch caused by undervaluing the environmental assets that are the basis of all life and prosperity," said WWF International Director-General James Leape, in the foreword to the report. "Most of us are propping up our current lifestyles, and our economic growth, by drawing—and increasingly overdrawing—on the ecological capital of other parts of the world."

Indeed, when you look at them side by side, the parallels between what has been happening in the Market and what is happening in Mother Nature are eerie. In both realms, what used to be once-in-a-century events—unusually powerful storms, heat waves, or global financial crises—are now happening with greater and greater frequency, with greater and greater virulence, and the costs of the cleanups are going higher and higher. In both realms industries that benefited from the underpricing of risks—whether they are credit-default swaps or carbon emissions—quietly lobbied the political authorities to keep loosening regulations so they could continue to reap large private gains at the expense of the greater public good. In both realms, companies and lobbyists funded and diffused "research" that muddied the waters and confused the public about the real dangers that were building up as a result of this widespread underpricing of risks. Eventually, even the terminology merged: We began to speak about "predatory lending" and "financial tsunamis" and "financial perfect storms" and "market meltdowns." Finally, just as a few farsighted financial experts warned us that the market could experience an extreme meltdown—one much worse than the models predicted—if we continued inflating the credit bubble, so a few farsighted scientists have been warning us about the same thing happening to the natural world if we continue inflating the carbon bubble.

"AIG and other companies like them failed because they discounted to zero the very small, remote risk of simultaneous defaults in their investment or insurance portfolios," noted Reid Detchon, the vice president for energy and climate, at the United Nations Foundation. "The risk in fact was probably less than 1 percent, perhaps a great deal less—but it happened nonetheless. We are acting like AIG in our approach to climate change. We are weighing the risks and benefits of action on the assumption that climate change will unfold predictably as temperatures rise. In doing so, we are discounting to zero two risks—the risk of a much greater increase in temperature than we now anticipate and the risk of a non-linear response by the climate system at some point along the way." A nonlinear response means radical change—a sudden drying up of the Amazon, for instance, due to a chain of unpredicted and unpredictable developments in the climate system. "Yet these risks—unlike the AIG case—are not small and remote," added Detchon. "The risk of a catastrophic increase in temperature is more like 50 percent than 5 percent if we follow a business-as-usual course. The risk of a non-linear response is simply unknowable—but we do know that the planet has experienced sudden shifts in the past."

It is for all these reasons that we absolutely must take our planet's warning heart attack seriously. There is no longer a "normal" for us to go back to. That "normal" high-energy and high-nature-consuming diet is what got us here. Mother Nature and the Market hit the wall because our normal became excessive and unsustainable.

The Australian Paul Gilding, a former head of Greenpeace who is now a leading environmental business expert, put it this way: We have been taking "a system operating past its capacity and driving it faster and harder," he observed. "No matter how wonderful the system is, the laws of physics and biology still apply." And those laws are telling us that we, as a species, cannot continue on the growth path we are on. We need a new normal—one that is much more sustainable and healthy for the Market and Mother Nature. The problem, he argues, is that it is very difficult to get human beings to appreciate and undertake the scale of change and innovation we now need without an even bigger crisis than the one we are experiencing. "History indicates that we don't accept large-scale change easily, especially when this change challenges our accepted beliefs," noted Gilding. "It generally takes a crisis to overcome our resistance. The challenge of sustainability, particularly climate change, has characteristics that make our normal resistance to change both deeper and longer lasting. It is an enormous system-wide challenge that affects every person and every country. It requires sweeping change in every aspect of our lives and our society. It also questions many fundamental beliefs about growth and the market economy and threatens some very powerful interests. All this deepens our resistance. Unfortunately this means the crisis will have to be very large and completely undeniable before we respond. This problem is also unusual in that the impacts lag the causes. Current global warming, for example, is caused by CO_2 emissions from decades ago. So when the crisis is big enough to force change, it will also have great and unstoppable momentum. As a result it will be far more damaging, because the impacts will continue to worsen long after we act on the causes."

That is why it is doubly urgent for our leaders and We the People to heed our warning heart attack and develop a more sustainable way of creating wealth in harmony with our natural world—and to begin doing it now, while we have a chance to do it in a reasonably orderly way. If we wait for a climate Pearl Harbor, to make the scale of the problem obvious to all, it will be too late. The impacts and disruptions by then will likely be unmanageable. "This is no longer just an environmental issue," argues Gilding. "How we respond now will decide the future of human civilization. We are the people we've been waiting for. There is no one else. There is no other time. It's us and it is now."

TWO

Dumb As We Wanna Be

German engineering, Swiss innovation, American nothing.
—Advertising slogan used on a billboard in South Africa by Daimler to promote
its Smart "forfour" compact car

How did we get into this fix?

The answer involves more than just the mispricing of risk and the fudging of ethics. Speaking as an American, I would say that we got here as a result of a period of excess, slough, and loss of focus by the baby boomer generation that reached its nadir during the period of American history from 11/9 to 9/11.

November 9, 1989, was the day the Berlin Wall fell, which heralded the collapse of the Soviet Union, America's only real global military and ideological competitor. The years to follow were as schizophrenic as any in American history. It was a period of enormous innovation around personal computers, fiber optics, and networking, in which America produced many of the tools that I later described as flattening the world. And yet the fact that we also lost our main geopolitical competitor in this period made us a little complacent, a little fat, a little dumb, and a little lazy. The events of September 11, 2001, brought on another fit of American schizophrenia. On the one hand, those events pulled us together as a nation, for a while, and on the other hand they disconnected us from the world and from some of our core instincts as a nation. September 11 knocked us off our game, prompted us to pull in, to export more fear than hope, to build walls rather than windows, and to devote enormous amounts of money and energy to homeland security rather than nation-building at home.

On balance, I suspect this period from 11/9 to 9/11 will be remembered as a period of triumph for American ingenuity but a period of crisis for the American spirit. We stood astride the world with unrivaled power, yet in many ways we lost our focus, we lost our groove; we binged on credit and carbon and lost touch with some of the bedrock values that made our nation wealthy, powerful, respected, trusted, and inspiring to others. You know how sometimes you have a friend who, over just a few years, puts on a lot of weight and you say to yourself, "Wow, she really let herself go." That was America after the end of the Cold War. Lots more gadgets and much bigger houses, but we really let ourselves go . . .

Kurt Andersen described this period well in his *Time* essay:

In the early 1980s, around the time Ronald Reagan became President and Wall Street's great modern bull market began, we started gambling (and winning!) and thinking magically . . . It's as if we decided that Mardi Gras and Christmas are so much fun, we ought to make them a year-round way of life. And we started living large literally as well as figuratively. From the beginning to the end of the long boom, the size of the average new house increased by about half. Meanwhile, the average American gained about a pound a year, so that an adult of a given age is now at least 20 lb. heavier than someone the same age back then. In the late '70s, 15% of Americans were obese; now a third are . . . Delayed gratification itself came to seem quaint and unnecessary. So what if every year since the turn of the century the U.S. economy grew more slowly than the global economy? Stuff at Wal-Mart and Costco and money itself stayed super cheap! Even 9/11, which supposedly "changed everything," and the resulting Iraqi debacle came to seem like mere bumps in the road. Even if deep down everyone knew that the spiral of overleveraging and overspending and the prices of stocks and houses were unsustainable, no one wanted to be a buzz kill.

Our parents, God bless them, were indeed the Greatest Generation. They fought and sacrificed so that Americans, men and women, could live free of tyranny from abroad—by defeating fascism in World War II and Communism in the Cold War—and so that their fellow citizens of whatever color, gender, and creed could live with full freedom at home thanks to the civil rights and women's rights movements. Hardened by the deprivation imposed by the Great Depression and inspired by the heroism required to simultaneously defeat Germany and Japan in a world war, they were indeed a special cohort. As my friend John Dernbach, an environment expert at Widener University Law School, said to me one day, "When my mother's parents died, their only son, my uncle Jim—whose B-17 was shot down over Germany in the spring of 1945 and who lived to tell the story—had this statement put on their gravestone: 'They gave their today for our tomorrow.' My maternal grandparents were hardscrabble people—they knew war, poverty, and unemployment firsthand. Yet that statement on their gravestone speaks volumes about the values we seem to have lost." Indeed, the members of the Greatest Generation, while they did not decry the wealth they generated, tended to shun excess. The Greatest Generation believed in hard work, saving to make a down payment on a home, and paying a mortgage, and raised both their children and their standards of living according to those core values. Generally speaking, they ate what they killed and lived within their means.

That certainly described my parents and many others in our Minneapolis neighborhood. Our parents' generation had to be the Greatest Generation "because the threats they faced were real, overwhelming, immediate, and inescapable—the Great Depression, the Nazis, and the nuclear-armed Soviet Communists," said the Johns Hopkins foreign policy expert Michael Mandelbaum. "That generation was ready to fight the Korean War and mobilize for the Cold War, precisely because it had been through the Depression and World War II. That generation understood how bad things could get."

Alas, though, we, their children, the baby boomers, took that freedom and ran with it, presiding over an amazing age of technological and financial innovation but also incredible excess. We have turned out to be that "Grasshopper Generation"—we let loose the locust in us all and in the process we ate through a staggering amount of our national wealth and our natural world in a very short period of time, leaving the next generation a massive economic and ecological deficit. As Kurt Andersen put it, "The grasshopper is the embodiment of the baby-boomer generation's profligate and hedonistic approach to economic life." Sure, we had our

heroic moments in the 1960s with the antiwar and civil rights movements. Those were big initiatives that spanned the Greatest Generation
and the baby boomers. And, post-9/11, we launched quixotic campaigns
to bring democracy to Afghanistan and Iraq, the costs of which have
been huge and the outcomes uncertain. But for the most part, our adult
years, *as a generation*, were devoted not to great national goals, like putting a man on the moon or expanding freedom, but instead to more private preoccupations and consumption. Everyone was encouraged to save
less, borrow more, and live beyond their means—whether it was poor
people who were plied with subprime mortgages or rich people who
were plied with time slots on NetJets. And the globalization of finance,
which enabled Americans to use the savings of the Chinese, combined
with the "innovations" in financial services, enticed many more people
to live beyond their means, without any sense of the risks involved. MIT's
best engineers went to Wall Street to design derivatives rather than to
Detroit to design cars or to NASA to design rockets. Getting rich quick
from a dot-com IPO or the flip of a house, making money from money
rather than from creating new goods and services, became the order of
the day for too many Americans. As Jeffrey Immelt, the CEO of General
Electric, put it in a speech (June 26, 2009) to the Detroit Economic
Club entitled "An American Renewal," "Throughout my career, America has seen so much economic growth that it was easy to take it as a
given. We prospered from the productivity of the information age. But
we started to forget the fundamentals, and lost sight of the core compe-
tencies of a successful modern economy. Many bought into the idea that
America could go from a technology-based, export-oriented powerhouse
to a services-led, consumption-based economy—and somehow still expect to prosper."

Indeed, there was a sense after the end of the Cold War that we were
somehow "entitled" to live large—as large as we wanted, without regard
to the consequences for the financial realm or the natural realm. The
world was our oyster—and we ate it.

All these trends really ramped up after the end of the Cold War,
when we lost our main competitor. You had to be serious when facing a
nuclear-armed foe like the Soviet Union, with a holistic competing ideology to our free-market system. Every good company or university or
newspaper needs a competitor. *The New York Times* is better because of
The Washington Post and *The Wall Street Journal*. What would Harvard

be without Yale? Microsoft without Apple? Competitors keep you sharp. But with the disappearance of the Red Menace, we lost our main competitor, and with it we lost some urgency and edge as well. It made us complacent and lazy, observed Fareed Zakaria, author of *The Post-American World*.

At the same time, the election of Ronald Reagan in 1980 ushered in an age in which we told ourselves that we did not have to sacrifice anymore for a better way of life. Reaganism, which coincided with the slow erosion of America's mortal enemy, ushered in a period of our history in which more and more public officials denigrated government and offered painless bromides for prosperity. The market was always right. Government was always wrong. The market was the solution. Government was the problem. And any policy proposal that involved asking the American people to do something hard—to save more, pay higher taxes, drive more fuel-efficient cars, study longer—fell into a new zone: "off the table." The age of sacrifice was over. Reacting to the Vietnam War, the failure of the Great Society to end poverty, the cynicism of Watergate, and the hyperinflation and geopolitical fecklessness of the Jimmy Carter years, Reagan argued that excessive government regulation and taxes threatened the American way of life and that the country's economic prowess needed to be unshackled. There was a lot about Ronald Reagan and Margaret Thatcher's parallel free-market economic policies that made sense when first introduced. We and others in the West did need to unlock more talent, energy, and entrepreneurship, which had been bottled up in our economies thanks to overregulation of certain market sectors and government ownership of key industries. And that loosening the Reagan-Thatcher revolution inspired around the world did lead to more wealth creation, albeit unevenly, as well as to technological innovation and global collaboration. Let us not forget how many tens of millions of people in India and China alone escaped poverty as a result of the deregulation of their financial markets and their movement to more market-based economics and the lowering of global trade barriers. As Niall Ferguson, the Harvard University historian, noted in an interview with *Barron's* (June 1, 2009): "Deregulation can't be all bad because lots of good things happened in the world economy after 1980."

But all good things have their limits, and we crossed some. Reagan's revolution swung America to another extreme—which led not only to what turned out to be imprudent deregulation in the financial sector, but also to a culture of excessive leveraged risk-taking at both the corporate and individual levels. The fiscal prudence our parents learned from the Great Depression gave way to a gambler's mentality and the celebration of get-rich-quick. My *New York Times* colleague, the Nobel laureate Paul Krugman, argued in a column (May 29, 2009) that

> Reagan-era legislative changes essentially ended New Deal restrictions on mortgage lending—restrictions that, in particular, limited the ability of families to buy homes without putting a significant amount of money down. These restrictions were put in place in the 1930s by political leaders who had just experienced a terrible financial crisis, and were trying to prevent another. But by 1980 the memory of the Depression had faded. Government, declared Reagan, is the problem, not the solution; the magic of the marketplace must be set free. And so the precautionary rules were scrapped. Together with looser lending standards for other kinds of consumer credit, this led to a radical change in American behavior. We weren't always a nation of big debts and low savings: in the 1970s Americans saved almost 10 percent of their income, slightly more than in the 1960s. It was only after the Reagan deregulation that thrift gradually disappeared from the American way of life, culminating in the near-zero savings rate that prevailed on the eve of the great crisis. Household debt was only 60 percent of income when Reagan took office, about the same as it was during the Kennedy administration. By 2007 it was up to 119 percent.

Indeed, the Reagan era lasted far too long for our own good. Reagan, though, at least raised some taxes when the consequences of his actions for the government's balance sheet became inescapable, and he was willing to tolerate a recession to cure inflation. As Joshua Green noted in a review of Reagan biographies in the January/February 2003 *Washington Monthly*, "One year after his massive tax cut, Reagan agreed to a tax increase to reduce the deficit that restored fully one-third of the previous year's reduction. (In a bizarre bit of self-deception, Reagan, who never came to terms with this episode of ideological apostasy, persuaded himself that the three-year, $100 billion tax hike—the largest since World War II—was actually 'tax reform' that closed loopholes in his earlier cut and therefore didn't count as raising taxes.) Faced with looming deficits, Reagan raised taxes again in 1983 with a gasoline tax and once more in

1984, this time by $50 billion over three years, mainly through closing tax loopholes for business." George Bush Sr. also raised taxes, as did Bill Clinton, to keep the federal budget from ballooning out of control. Clinton, in particular, also benefited from the "peace dividend" of lower defense spending after the end of the Cold War.

George W. Bush, however, took Reaganism to its logical extreme—and beyond. Empowered by majorities in the House and Senate, and the temporary national mandate given him in the wake of 9/11, George W. Bush radically lowered taxes and kept them low, and, instead of reaping a peace dividend, undertook two extremely expensive wars that he refused to pay for with new taxes. He made up the difference by getting the Chinese to lend us their savings. It marked the first time America has cut taxes during a war, an act of utter fiscal recklessness. During George W. Bush's presidency, the U.S. national savings rate plummeted to near zero, and consumer debt climbed from $8 trillion to $14 trillion. In essence, under George W. Bush, the traditional Republican Party disappeared in the early twenty-first century; America no longer had a party truly dedicated to fiscal responsibility. We had a government that basically banned recessions. In his book *The Price of Loyalty*, Ron Suskind relates a story of how George W. Bush's treasury secretary Paul O'Neill was making the case at a White House meeting that the country could not afford another round of tax cuts and tried to warn Vice President Dick Cheney that growing budget deficits could undermine the economy, but Cheney cut him off. "You know, Paul, Reagan proved deficits don't matter," he said. They don't matter as long as the economy is growing fast enough to absorb them and keep them relatively small, but when it isn't, living year after year beyond your means matters a lot.

As the Cold War receded further and further into our rearview mirrors, a kind of "dumb as we wanna be" attitude took over our political elite, a mood that said we can indulge in petty red state–blue state catfights, can postpone shoring up our health care system and our crumbling infrastructure, can postpone transforming our energy systems, can postpone addressing immigration reform, can postpone fixing Social Security and Medicare or dealing comprehensively with our environmental excesses—as long as we want. Partisan divides all but guaranteed that we could not solve any of these big multigenerational problems anymore, and post–Cold War lassitude told us we didn't really need to care. Add to all this a permanent presidential campaign, a twenty-four-hour cable news cycle that encouraged short-term tactical responses by both parties to anything the other said, and, lately, a blogosphere that can instantaneously ignite forest fires of passion or indignation—sometimes bogus, sometimes real—capable of tying politicians in knots, and you had a prescription for acting and thinking small. It became political suicide for any politician to advocate what every responsible person in the country knew we needed—higher taxes, lower spending, and a reduction in entitlements. "America and its political leaders, after two decades of failing to come together to solve big problems, seem to have lost faith in their ability to do so," observed the *Wall Street Journal* columnist Gerald Seib. "A political system that expects failure doesn't try very hard to produce anything else."

The underlying attitude on so many big issues became: We'll get to it when we feel like getting to it, and it will never catch up to us, because we're America and we have no competitors.

9/11

And then came 9/11. What happened after that day could have and should have been our wake-up call. The country was ready to be enlisted for a great national rebuilding. We were ready to be a new Greatest Generation. We were ready for a "Patriot Tax" on gasoline that could have been our generation's victory garden to help make us independent of the very people who had attacked us. And when the bugle sounded we heard the call: "Go shopping."

As things turned out, the terrorist attacks on September 11, 2001, only encouraged our loss of focus, diverting enormous energy, money, and attention to the war against al-Qaeda and installing security equipment in every airport, train station, and federal building, as opposed to rebuilding our air travel, railroad, and government infrastructure. I was caught up in this post-9/11 insecurity as much as anyone. So I understand and sympathize with those who were responsible for the nation's security—after a surprise attack on our financial center and our military headquarters—insisting that we put up that extra wall or barrier to entry. We did need to react, we did need to tighten our borders, we did need to improve our intelligence, we did need to retaliate, we did have real enemies who wanted to wreak havoc on our country. But we also needed to rebuild our country. It is all about finding the right balance, and we got out of balance after 9/11. We are not, and surely must never become, the

"United States of Fighting Terrorism." Don't get me wrong, I am happy to go through as many metal detectors as the experts say we need whenever I fly out of Washington, D.C.—on one condition: that on the other side of the last metal detector is a great project worthy of the innovative and inspirational prowess of the United States of America. Let us never forget: *They* are the people of 9/11. *We* are the people of 7/4. We are the people of the Fourth of July. That is my national holiday—not 9/11. I weep for all who died that day. We must honor them, learn from their loss, and protect ourselves from a repeat. But we must never let that terrible day define us—especially now.

But just when we needed to be investing in our homeland to make possible a new America of 9/12, we overinvested in homeland security, looking backward at 9/11. We built a higher fence around a decaying infrastructure—and the cracks have started to show. I was particularly troubled by the sudden collapse of the bridge on Interstate 35W in my home state of Minnesota, because it was a bridge I'd crossed hundreds of times in my youth. But that was just the tip of an iceberg.

In December 2008, I visited Hong Kong. One day I went out to Kau Sai Chau, an island off the city, where I stood on a rocky hilltop overlooking the South China Sea and talked to my wife back in Maryland, static-free, using a friend's Chinese cell phone. A few hours later, I took off from Hong Kong's ultramodern airport after riding out there from downtown on a sleek high-speed train—with wireless connectivity that was so good I was able to surf the Web the whole way on my laptop. Landing at Kennedy Airport a day later from Hong Kong was like going from the Jetsons to the Flintstones. The ugly, low-ceilinged arrival hall was cramped, and access to a simple luggage cart then cost $3. The next day I went to Penn Station in Manhattan, where the escalators down to the tracks are so narrow that they seemed to have been designed before suitcases were invented. The disgusting trackside platforms look as if they have not been cleaned since the Nixon administration. I took the Acela, America's sorry excuse for a bullet train, from New York to Washington. Along the way, I tried to use my cell phone to conduct an interview with someone in Washington, D.C., and the call was dropped three times within one fifteen-minute span. All I could think to myself was: If we're so smart and powerful, why are other people living so much better than we are?

Maybe the reason is that we're not as smart as we used to be. Warren Buffett once famously quipped that "only when the tide goes out do you find out who is not wearing a bathing suit." Credit bubbles are like the tide. They can cover up a lot of rot. In our case, the excess consumer demand and jobs created by America's credit and housing bubbles masked not only our weaknesses in manufacturing and other economic fundamentals, but something worse: how far we had fallen behind in K-12 education and how much it is now costing us, according to a study by the consulting firm McKinsey & Co. (April 2009) titled "The Economic Impact of the Achievement Gap in America's Schools."

In the 1950s and 1960s, McKinsey noted, the United States dominated the world in K-12 education. We also dominated economically. In the 1970s and 1980s, we still had a lead, albeit smaller, in educating our population through secondary school, and America continued to lead the world economically, albeit with other big economies, like China, closing in. Today, we have fallen behind in both per capita high school graduates and their quality. Consequences to follow. For instance, in the 2006 Program for International Student Assessment, which measured the applied learning and problem-solving skills of fifteen-year-olds in thirty industrialized countries, the United States ranked twenty-fifth out of the thirty in math and twenty-fourth in science. That put our average youth on par with those from Portugal and the Slovak Republic, "rather than with students in countries that are more relevant competitors for service-sector and high-value jobs, like Canada, the Netherlands, Korea, and Australia," McKinsey noted. Actually, our fourth graders compare well on such global tests with, say, Singapore. But our high school kids really lag, which means that "the longer American children are in school, the worse they perform compared to their international peers," said McKinsey.

Maybe it is good, then, that American kids are also in school only six and a half hours a day, or 32.5 hours a week. "By contrast," *The Economist* reported (June 13, 2009), "the school week is 37 hours in Luxembourg, 44 in Belgium, 53 in Denmark and 60 in Sweden. On top of that, American children do only about an hour's worth of homework a day, a figure that stuns the Japanese and Chinese."

There are millions of kids who are in modern American suburban schools "who don't realize how far behind they are," said Matt Miller, one of the McKinsey experts. "They are being prepared for $12-an-hour jobs—not $40 to $50 an hour."

And way too many of those who did have the brainpower we need had their IQs diverted to financial engineering. As Jeffrey Immelt put it in his June 26 speech: "You know something is wrong when a mortgage broker is pulling down $5M a year while a Ph.D. chemist is earning $100K. Average real weekly wages have declined since 1980, meaning that we have been unable to provide a rising standard of living for the majority . . . In 2000, the U.S. had a positive trade balance of high-tech products. By 2007, our trade deficit of the same products reached $50B. We have already lost our leadership in many growth industries, and other new opportunities are at risk." Vivek Wadhwa is a senior research associate at the Labor & Worklife Program at Harvard Law School and an executive in residence at Duke University. He is also an entrepreneur who founded two technology companies. In an essay in *BusinessWeek* (November 14, 2008), he noted that "when I joined the Pratt School of Engineering at Duke University in August 2005, more than one-third of the masters of engineering management students from the outgoing class told me they were taking jobs in financial services. From the class of 2007, 22% went into finance." Fortunately, he noted, the 2008/9 market meltdown has shifted those numbers back in favor of real engineering. Still, the damage has been done.

Remember: a dollar is a dollar is a dollar. A dollar made from a hedge fund is worth the same as a dollar made from manufacturing, a dollar made from a kickback, a dollar made from selling services, or a dollar made from innovation. People are always adjusting their imagination and entrepreneurial energy to where the best opportunities lie, or, to put it more crassly, to where the most money can be made the most easily. Beginning in the 1980s, and lasting right up to the Great Recession, we created an economy where an increasing number of people made their money the easy way. It was easier to flip a house than to save money for a bigger one, and it was a lot easier to make money by flipping bonds than by investing in the underlying innovation of new manufactured products and services that the bonds were originally designed to finance.

The Real Reason for the Great Recession

When you add all this up, you start to see that the Great Recession was not just the product of financial chicanery, subprime mortgages, and ethical breakdowns. They were all huge drivers, to be sure. But there is actually a deeper problem that is the root cause: a certain connection between educational achievement, hard work, and prosperity got broken. We became a subprime nation that thought it could just borrow its way to riches—that promised the American dream with nothing down and nothing to pay for two years. We didn't need to upgrade our public schools or massively increase our funding of basic research to propel new industries—at a time when the world was getting flat and technology was enabling more people than ever to compete, connect, and collaborate with us. No, the bank around the corner or online would just borrow the money from China and lend it to us—with a credit check no more intrusive than the check you get at the airport when they make sure the name on your airline ticket matches the one on your driver's license.

While our parents' generation earned the American dream by leveraging their own hard work and education, the Grasshopper Generation tried to secure the American dream with financial leverage—by borrowing more and more money and making bigger and bigger bets with it. You saw it with investment banks, which earned incredible returns in their good years by leveraging thirty to one, and you saw it with consumers who bought homes out of line with their incomes. When you secure a mortgage for a $400,000 home on a $25,000 income, with little or nothing down, you are leveraging every bit as wildly as Merrill Lynch was.

I attended a lecture by Michelle Rhee, the chancellor of the District of Columbia public schools, in Aspen, Colorado, in the summer of 2009. Just before the lecture started a man came up, introduced himself as Todd Martin, and whispered to me that what Rhee was about to talk about—the decline of public school education in America's biggest cities and the need to reform it—was the real reason for the Great Recession. I told him that jibed with my own thinking and that he should send me his thoughts, which he did. I think they hit the nail right on the head.

"This education failure is the largest contributing factor to the decline of the American worker's global competitiveness, particularly at the middle and bottom ranges," argued Martin, a former global executive with PepsiCo and Kraft Europe and now an international investor based in Dallas. This loss of competitiveness has weakened the American worker's production of wealth, precisely when technology brought global competition much closer to home. So over a decade the American worker has maintained his or her standard of living by borrowing and overconsuming vis-à-vis his or her real income. When the Great Reces-

sion wiped out all the credit and asset bubbles that made the overconsumption possible, it left many American workers not only deeper in
debt than ever, but out of a job and lacking the skills to compete globally.
Here's why, says Martin:

"America Inc." is the sum collection of all our businesses and all
our workers. Each worker is just like a business, selling his or her
services to another business. America Inc. has an income statement and a balance sheet. Most of the fuss lately has been around
the balance sheet—debt, assets, write-downs, foreclosures, net
worth, capital adequacy, etc. But the income statement feeds the
balance sheet, and that is where America Inc.'s underlying problems lie. Prosperity at the worker and business level is determined
by what we can produce times what we can sell it for, less what it
costs us to produce. Today, that means vis-à-vis global competitors. Over the last three decades we have seen, and abetted, the
fall of Communism, the emergence of new huge functional
economies, and within them the emergence of hundreds of millions of increasingly competent workers who are absolutely delighted to produce what the American middle and lower classes
can at a fraction of the price. Technology—the Internet, fiber op-
tic communications, hardware, software, distribution systems—
has not only enabled dramatically greater global competition for
the average U.S. worker, it has actually forced American employ-
ers to shift sourcing—if they don't go to the lowest cost, then their
competitor will, and they will be forced out of business. This has
eroded the earning power and jobs of American workers; particularly those whose skills are overpriced [relative to] global competition. This is a massive problem for the U.S. economy, as those
same workers consume 70 percent of GDP. If they have a problem with their productive competitiveness, wage growth, and
keeping their job [in the face of] increasingly tougher competition—and they clearly do today—then the entire economy—
America Inc.—has a problem growing. The problem only gets
"cured" when the decline in worker competitiveness reverses, i.e.,
we have enough jobs which are worth $40+ an hour [compared
to] global alternatives. This requires a turnaround in the productivity of U.S. education—in fact we must improve faster than
China et al. are improving, and we must shift/churn our economy

to producing products, services, and jobs which can't be produced cheaper elsewhere. This is very likely to be a combination of a knowledge economy, knowledge products, knowledge jobs, and knowledge workers produced by a dramatically better education system. Technology and innovation will likely be at the root of all of these businesses. This clearly is going to take decades of focused effort led vigorously from the top to both enable this innovation and dramatically improve the skills of American workers; most fundamentally via fixing education at all levels.

Our parents' generation mortgaged their future so our generation could get educated. In too many cases our generation mortgaged its future to buy homes we could not afford and possessions we did not need. Our parents said higher education is the key to the American dream. Too many in our generation said getting a cheaper subprime mortgage — with the money behind it actually borrowed from China — was the key to the American dream.

So the biggest danger America faces today is not so much that it will suddenly nosedive as a country. The danger is that it will undergo a gradual but very real erosion of its strengths and assets as a society. We will slowly choke off the immigration that is our lifeblood of new talent, slowly give up our commitment to free trade, slowly allow the budgets for research in science to decline, slowly let our public schools slide into mediocrity, and slowly let a well-educated generation give way to one without the problem-solving skills to thrive in today's world. The danger, said Newsweek's Fareed Zakaria, "is that it will be just slow enough so we can be complacent and in denial about it." Things will just go along and go along, until we wake up one day and look around and find that as a country we really have fallen behind.

Energy as a Metaphor

I can think of no better example of America's lack of sustained focus to take on a big challenge than the way we dealt with our energy crises over the last thirty-five years. It is a sad but highly revealing tale. In the wake of the 1973–74 Arab oil embargo, the Europeans and Japanese responded by raising gasoline taxes and, in Japan's case particularly, by launching a huge drive toward energy efficiency. France invested espe-

cially heavily in nuclear energy as a state project, with the result that
today France gets 78 percent of its electricity from nuclear plants, and
much of the waste is reprocessed and turned into energy again. Even
Brazil, a developing country, launched a national program to produce
ethanol from sugarcane to make itself less dependent on imported oil.
Today, between Brazil's domestic oil production and its ethanol industry,
it doesn't need to import crude oil.

America's initial response was significant. Urged on by Presidents
Gerald Ford and Jimmy Carter, the United States implemented higher
fuel economy standards for American cars and trucks. In 1975, Congress
passed the Energy Policy and Conservation Act, which established corporate average fuel economy (CAFE) standards that required the gradual doubling of passenger vehicle efficiency for new cars—to 27.5 miles
per gallon—within ten years.

Not surprisingly, it all worked. Between 1975 and 1985, American
passenger vehicle mileage went from around 13.5 miles per gallon to
27.5, while light truck mileage increased from 11.6 miles per gallon to
19.5—all of which helped to create a global oil glut from the mid-1980s
to the mid-1990s, which not only weakened OPEC but also helped to
unravel the Soviet Union, then the world's second-largest oil producer.

So what happened next? Did we keep our focus on the long term?
No. After the original congressional mandate of 27.5 miles per gallon
took full effect in 1985, President Reagan, rather than continuing to increase the fuel economy standard to keep reducing our dependence on
foreign oil, actually rolled it back to 26 miles per gallon in 1986. Reagan
also slashed the budgets of most of President Carter's alternative energy
programs, particularly the Solar Energy Research Institute and its four
regional centers, which were just getting off the ground. Reagan's White
House and the Democratic Congress also teamed up to let the tax incentives for solar and wind start-ups lapse, and several of these companies and their technologies, which were originally funded by American
taxpayers, ended up being bought by Japanese and European firms—
helping to propel those countries' renewable industries. Reagan even
stripped off the solar panels Carter had put on the White House roof.

They were eventually given away to a college in Maine, which later
sold them in an online auction to history buffs. The Associated Press
story (October 28, 2004) about that auction recalled: "The 32 panels
were put on the presidential mansion during a period [when] the country was reeling from the effects of an Arab oil embargo. After calling for a

nationwide campaign to conserve energy, President Jimmy Carter ordered the panels erected in 1979 to set an example for the country, according to the White House Historical Association. The solar heating
panels were installed on the roof of the West Wing, but removed during
Ronald Reagan's presidency in 1986, after the energy crisis and worries
about dependence on foreign oil had subsided."

In backing away from fuel economy standards, Reagan apparently
thought he was giving America's then sagging domestic oil and auto
industries a boost. The result: We quickly started to get readdicted to
imported oil. While the Reagan administration was instrumental in
bringing down the Soviet Union, it was also instrumental in building our
current dependence on Saudi Arabia.

The Reagan administration was an environmental turning point in
another way. We forget, because it was so long ago, that there was a time
when Washington had a bipartisan approach to the environment. It was
a Republican, Richard Nixon, who signed into law the first wave of major environmental legislation in the United States, which addressed our
first generation of environmental problems—air pollution, water pollution, and toxic waste. But Reagan changed that. Reagan ran not only
against government in general but against environmental regulation in
particular. He and his interior secretary, James Watt, turned environmental regulation into a much more partisan and polarizing issue than
it had ever been before. It has been so ever since. (One noteworthy exception: It was Secretary of State George P. Shultz's team that enthusiastically negotiated the Montreal Protocol on Substances That Deplete
the Ozone Layer—a landmark international agreement designed to protect the stratospheric ozone layer that shields the planet from damaging
UV-B radiation.)

In 1989, the elder Bush's administration at least moved the fuel economy standard back up to the 1985 level of 27.5 miles per gallon. It also
passed substantial improvements in building standards and new appliance standards, introduced a production tax credit for renewable energy,
and elevated the Solar Energy Research Institute to the status of a national institution as the National Renewable Energy Laboratory. But after Bush liberated Kuwait from Saddam Hussein, and oil prices went
back down, he did nothing strategic to liberate America from dependence on Middle East oil.

When the Clinton administration came into office, it looked into
raising fuel economy standards further, just for light trucks. But to make

sure there would be none of that, Congress, spurred on by the Michigan congressional delegation—which was a wholly owned subsidiary of the Big Three automakers and the United Auto Workers—literally gagged and blindfolded the government when it came to improving mileage standards. Specifically, Congress inserted a rider into the fiscal year 1996–fiscal year 2001 Department of Transportation appropriations bill that expressly prohibited the use of appropriated funds for any rulemaking by the National Highway Traffic Safety Administration to tighten fuel economy standards for American cars and trucks—thereby freezing the whole process. Congress effectively banned the NHTSA from taking any steps to improve mileage standards for American cars!

This move blocked any mileage improvements until 2003, when the younger Bush's administration made a tiny adjustment upward in the mileage standard for light-duty trucks. In 2003, even China leaped ahead of the United States, announcing fuel economy standards "for new cars, vans and sport utility vehicles to get as much as two miles a gallon of fuel more in 2005 than the average required in the United States, and about five miles more in 2008" (*The New York Times*, November 18, 2003). Only in late 2007—thirty-two years after Congress ordered mileage improved to 27.5 miles per gallon—did America once again act. It moved the U.S. fuel economy standard up to 35 miles per gallon— roughly where Europe and Japan are already—by 2020. That's eleven years away.

One result of all this nonsense, according to a study by the Pew Foundation, was that in America "the average car and truck sold at the end of the [1990s] went about a mile less on each gallon of gas than it did 10 years earlier." All this had a direct effect on our oil consumption—and on our foreign policy. According to Amory Lovins, the experimental physicist who heads the Rocky Mountain Institute, if the United States had continued into the 1990s to conserve oil at the rate it did in the period from 1976 to 1985, thanks in large part to the improved mileage standards, it would no longer have needed Persian Gulf oil after 1985. "When Reagan rolled back CAFE standards," said Lovins, "it was the equivalent of 'undiscovering' one Arctic National Wildlife Refuge's worth of oil. It wasted as much oil as is believed to exist under the Refuge."

Meanwhile, the 1979 accident at the Three Mile Island nuclear power station ended any hopes of expanding our nuclear industry. Then Detroit introduced the sport-utility vehicle and successfully lobbied the government to label these as light trucks so they would not have to meet the 27.5 miles per gallon standard for cars, but only the light truck standard of 20.7. So we became even more addicted to oil. When I asked Rick Wagoner, the last chairman and CEO of General Motors before it declared bankruptcy, why his company didn't make more fuel-efficient cars, he gave me the standard answer: that GM has never succeeded in telling Americans what cars they should buy. "We build what the market wants," he said. If people want SUVs and Hummers, you have to give them what they want. (Toyota was always eager to point out that it doesn't talk about "the market" but about many markets, and tries to build something for each of them. As a member of that part of the market that wanted to get good gasoline mileage and not spend time on car maintenance, I appreciated that. Had GM done more of that, it might have noticed that my end of the market was growing larger every year.)

But what the Detroit executives never told you was that one big reason the public wanted SUVs and Hummers all those years was that Detroit and the oil industry consistently lobbied Congress against raising gasoline taxes, which would have shaped public demand for something different. European governments imposed very high gasoline taxes and taxes on engine size—and kept imposing them—and guess what? Europeans demanded smaller and smaller cars. America wouldn't impose more stringent gasoline and engine taxes, so American consumers kept wanting bigger and bigger cars. Big Oil and Big Auto used their leverage in Washington to shape the market so people would ask for those cars that consumed the most oil and earned their companies the most profits—and our Congress never got in the way. It was bought off for more than two decades.

These were the years the locust ate—brought to a filling station near you by a bipartisan alliance of special interests, with Democrats supporting the auto companies and their unions and Republicans supporting the oil companies, while the groups representing the broad national interest were marginalized and derided as part of some eco-fringe. That is "dumb as we wanna be." When the public is engaged, as it was after 1973, when people were waiting in lines for gasoline, it can override the entrenched interests of the auto and oil lobbies. But the minute—and I mean the minute—the public takes its eye off the ball, those special interest lobbyists barge back into the cloakrooms of Congress, passing out political donations and calling the shots according to their needs, not the nation's. What was good for General Motors was not always good for America, or even for General Motors, but few Democrats or Republicans in high office were ready to lead the country on a different energy path. In the end, after protecting General Motors for so many years from pressures to innovate around mileage and energy efficiency, they protected General Motors right into bankruptcy.

Contrast this with how one small European country, Denmark, behaved after 1973. "We decided we had to become less dependent on oil," Connie Hedegaard, Denmark's minister for climate and energy, explained to me. "We had a huge debate on nuclear, but in 1985 we decided against it. We decided to go instead for energy efficiency and renewable energy. We decided to use taxation, so energy was made relatively expensive and [therefore] people had an incentive to save and do things in their homes to make them more efficient . . . It was a result of political will."

Premium gasoline in Denmark in 2008 was about $9 a gallon. On top of that, Denmark has a CO_2 tax, which it put in place in the mid-1990s to promote efficiency, even though it had discovered offshore oil by then. "When you get your electricity bill you see your CO_2 tax [itemized]," the minister said. Surely all of this killed the Danish economy, right? Guess again. "Since 1981 our economy has grown 70 percent, while our energy consumption has been kept almost flat all those years," she said. Unemployment remained low. And Denmark's early emphasis on solar and wind power, which now provide 16 percent of its total energy consumption, spawned a whole new export industry.

"It has had a positive impact on job creation," said Hedegaard. "For example, the wind industry—it was nothing in the 1970s. Today, one-third of all terrestrial wind turbines in the world come from Denmark. Industry woke up and saw that this is in our interest. To have the first-mover advantage, [when we know] the rest of the world will have to do this, will be to our benefit." Two of the world's most innovative manufacturers of enzymes for converting biomass to fuel—Danisco and Novozymes—also come from Denmark. "In 1973 we got 99 percent of our energy from the Middle East," said Hedegaard. "Today it is zero." I know: Denmark's a small country and it is a lot easier to make change there than across a huge economy like ours. Nevertheless, it's hard to look at Denmark and not see the road not taken.

George W. Bush's tenure was the perfect capstone to this abdication of any serious attempt to grapple with America's energy excesses. The younger Bush came into office bound and determined not to ask the

American people to do anything hard when it came to new challenges, particularly on the issue of energy consumption. On May 7, 2001, then White House spokesman Ari Fleischer was asked the following question at the daily press briefing: "Does the President believe that, given the amount of energy Americans consume per capita—how much it exceeds any other citizens in any other country in the world—does the President believe we need to correct our lifestyles to address the energy problem?"

Fleischer responded: "That's a big no. The President believes that it's an American way of life, and that it should be the goal of policy makers to protect the American way of life. The American way of life is a blessed one."

Fleischer went on to add that of course the president encourages energy efficiency and conservation, but he reiterated that the president believes "the American people's use of energy is a reflection of the strength of our economy—of the way of life the American people have come to enjoy." And that was not going to change.

Robert Hormats, the vice chair of Goldman Sachs (International), notes in his book *The Price of Liberty*—about how America has paid for its wars since 1776—that George Washington, in his farewell address, warned against "ungenerously throwing upon posterity the burden which we ourselves ought to bear." But that is exactly what we, the Grasshopper Generation, were doing.

Donald Rumsfeld, George W. Bush's defense secretary, once answered a U.S. soldier who asked him why he and his comrades were sent to battle in Iraq without proper equipment—"You go to war with the army you have, not the army you might want or wish to have at a later time." In too many ways, Rumsfeld's answer applied to the whole country. We were behaving as if we thought we could just march into the future with the government we had, not the one we wanted to have or needed to have.

My fellow Americans: We are not who we think we are. Our political system seems incapable of producing long-range answers to big problems or big opportunities. We are the ones who need a better-functioning democracy—more even than the Iraqis and Afghans. We are the ones in need of nation-building. It is our political system that is not working. I believe that the main force propelling Barack Obama to the presidency was an unstated but widely shared intuition by many Americans that we had lost our groove as a country, and to get it back we needed a president who could bring out the best in us again. There was a widespread understanding that we could not just march into the future with the government we had, because, as the French poet Paul Valéry famously said, "The trouble with our times is that the future is not what it used to be." The age we are entering is at once much more dangerous than it looks and much more opportune than it looks. To thrive in this age, America will have to be at its best. And to be our best we now need nation-building at home.

When I think of our situation, I am reminded of the movie *The Leopard*, based on the novel of the same name by Giuseppe Tomasi di Lampedusa. It is set in nineteenth-century Italy, at a time of enormous social, political, and economic turmoil. The main character is the Sicilian prince Don Fabrizio of Salina (played by Burt Lancaster). Don Fabrizio understands that he and his family will have to adapt if they want the House of Salina to retain its leadership in a new era, where social forces from below are challenging the traditional power elites. Nevertheless, Prince Salina is bitter and uncompromising—"We were the leopards, the lions; those who take our place will be jackals and sheep." The wisest advice he gets comes from his nephew Tancredi (played by Alain Delon), who marries a wealthy shopkeeper's daughter from the new moneyed middle class, and along the way cautions his uncle: "If we want things to stay as they are, things will have to change."

And so it is with America. Alas, we are not just the people we've been waiting for. We are the people we have to overcome. We have been consuming too much, saving too little, studying too laxly, and investing not nearly enough. And our political institutions are also the institutions we have to overcome. As long as our political system and Congress and Senate seem incapable of producing the right answers to big problems, as long as our politicians can only behave like Santa Claus and give things away, and never like Abraham Lincoln and make the really hard calls, the greatness that America is capable of will elude it in this generation.

Have no doubts. The era we have entered is one of enormous social, political, and economic change—driven in part by the Market and in part by Mother Nature. If we want things to stay as they are—that is, if we want to maintain our technological, economic, and moral leadership, and a habitable planet, rich with flora and fauna, leopards and lions, and human communities that can grow in a sustainable way—things will have to change around here, and fast.

THREE

The Re-Generation

In the spring of 2009, I delivered the commencement address at Grinnell College in Iowa. I thought long and hard about what to say. After all, what do you tell young men and women who are about to enter the workforce in the middle of the Great Recession?

I started by describing a picture I had just seen: "My wife is a board member of the Seed Foundation in Washington, D.C.," I explained. "It runs a charter college prep boarding school that aspires to help African Americans and other disadvantaged minorities from Washington's most depressed neighborhoods get the quality education they need to enter a four-year college. It is a wonderful institution. And the other day President Barack Obama and First Lady Michelle Obama paid a visit to the school and met with the students and staff. Several days later I got to see the pictures that were taken of their visit. And there is one that really stuck in my mind. It was a picture of Michelle Obama from the back. She was going down a receiving line of girls, probably seventh graders. And all you see in this picture is the first lady's back—and two delicate, slender black arms wrapped around her waist, hugging her tight. It was one of the Seed girls, who had obviously done this spontaneously. I thought to myself: 'Wow, how amazing must it be for an African American girl to have as a role model today a first lady like Michelle Obama, graduate of Princeton and Harvard Law School. Who can know what such a role model will inspire in so many other African American girls?' But those two slender arms hugging the first lady around the waist told me: 'It's a lot more than I will ever know.'"

I relate that story, I told the graduates, because it is easy to look around America and say, "What a lousy time to be graduating." Indeed, it is a lousy economic time. But it is an amazing political time. The election of Barack Obama as president was one of those rare moments when America reminds itself and the world how crazy radical it can be sometimes—radical enough to take a chance on an inspiring young African American junior senator from Illinois, born of a Muslim father, raised by a single mother in Hawaii, to lead us out of the Great Recession. It is way too early to predict how President Obama's administration will turn out. But it is not too soon to say that his mere election is hugely important. It represents America's extraordinary capacity for renewal. It says that our country still has the ability to change course, to start afresh, to begin anew—to literally reinvent itself to a degree that most other nations can only dream about.

And that is why I am hopeful that while our parents really were the Greatest Generation, and while we lapsed into being the Grasshopper Generation, we and our children can together become the "Re-Generation." I first heard that term from Michael Dell, the founder of Dell, Inc. It was coined by one of his marketing experts, who used the concept in some Dell ads to refer to people of all ages who share an interest in renewable resources, recycling, and other ways of sustaining the natural world.

I would take it a step further, though. For me, the Re-Generation's task is to do nothing less than help repair both the Market and Mother Nature by bringing the concept and the values of "sustainability" to both realms. This is not a job we can leave for our grandchildren. This is our problem. We lapsed into a set of behaviors that have endangered our economic well-being and made us an endangered species. Our good fortune as Americans, though, is that we live in the country that has the technological prowess and the radical temperament to change course.

"Democracy has to be reinvented and reconstructed every generation from new materials and new fabrics," said the Hebrew University political scientist Yaron Ezrahi. "With the election of Barack Obama, the whole world is now watching again the American experiment—as it did at the end of the eighteenth century—to see whether America will come up with a model of coexistence between politics, economics, and freedom that could be inspiring for the rest of the world." The concept of sustainability will be central to that.

Indeed, what the struggle for freedom was to our parents' generation, the struggle for "sustainability" has to be for the Re-Generation. Sustainability is today's freedom crusade, because the next generation will not live free—will not have the freedom to pursue its economic dreams or to delight in all that nature has to offer—if our approach to the financial world and the natural are not grounded in sustainable values. That lack of sustainability will constrict everything in our lives. It will limit everything we might want to do. Unless we become less dependent on hydrocarbons, and unless we find a balance between the need for markets to be free enough to reward innovation and risk-taking but not so free as to reward recklessness that can destabilize the whole global economy, our lives will be reduced, redacted, and restricted. We will be overwhelmed by all the toxic assets we will produce in the Market and in Mother Nature. It will feel worse than had the Soviet Union won the Cold War, because we and our children will be enslaved by our financial debts and constricted by our ecological debts.

That is why I am convinced that sustainability is to the Re-Generation what the freedom campaigns—from World War II to civil rights—were to the Greatest Generation. It is the campaign against the forces most likely to make us unfree—a radically changing climate, environmental disasters that create millions of refugees, financial markets that produce sudden and steep losses of wealth, and a worldwide struggle over scarce resources that sparks wars and fosters authoritarianism.

We live in a world in which globalization is now a fact: More people are connecting and competing with more other people in more ways on more days than ever before. But when you have this many people on the planet connecting and competing through free markets, the effects can be staggering. Their consumption can devour forests, rivers, and ocean life so swiftly as to change the climate and the landscape at unprecedented speeds. And when you have such an interconnected world, where financial contagions can spread so quickly and capsize dozens of economies at once, it is obvious that our overarching goal has to be "sustainable globalization." That is a concept I first argued for in 1999 in my book *The Lexus and the Olive Tree*. I feel we need it now more than ever.

Why? Because a world defined by the values of sustainability is not just a greener world, noted David Rothkopf: "It is a safer world, it is a more just world, and it is a politically more stable world." A world of sustainable markets and environments is a world of abundance, and a world of abundance always favors freedom and democracy. It is much easier to give people the freedom to choose when there is plenty to choose from.

"A world of scarcity always favors authoritarianism—someone will have to go around rationing," said the climate expert and physicist Joseph Romm. If climate change and environmental degradation ever get the better of our planet, he added, "we will have to ration where we live, how we live and how much we can use."

That is why I agree with John Dernbach, who argued in his book *Agenda for a Sustainable America* that "sustainable development is among the most important ideas to come out of the 20th century." It should be right up there, he said, with "democracy promotion," "human rights protection," "free markets," "collective security," and the need to "combat poverty on a world-wide basis." Sustainable development, or simply "sustainability," deserves to be up there, wrote Dernbach, "because it provides a framework for humans to live and prosper in harmony with nature rather than . . . at nature's expense. Everything we care about—a growing economy, human well-being and security—is compromised, undermined or lessened by environmental degradation."

In short, promoting the ethic of sustainability is precisely how we can prevent Citibank, Iceland's banks, and the ice banks of Antarctica from all melting down any further, and it is how we prevent another Bear Stearns and another family of polar bears from going extinct at the same time.

Sustainability: You Know It When You See It

Now that we have established how important sustainability is, we need to establish what exactly it means—what are the values that underpin sustainable behavior, whether in the financial world or the natural world? When you talk about environmental or ecological sustainability, says Dernbach, the definition is pretty clear: "Something is environmentally or ecologically sustainable when it protects, restores, or regenerates the environment rather than degrades it."

The same could be said in the financial realm: a market is financially sustainable when it fosters practices, investments, and innovations that promote the *long-term* growth of the economy, companies, and jobs, rather than reckless, short-term thinking that can undermine them all overnight.

But what are the values you need to inspire in citizens, business executives, and community leaders to ensure that they understand sustainability and implement it? I posed that question to Dov Seidman, the CEO of LRN, which helps companies build sustainable ethical cultures, and the author of the book *How*.

Seidman said he wanted to begin by establishing what "sustainability" isn't. In too many cases, he explained, "we equated sustainability in the financial world with size and scale, as measured by profits, market caps, number of customers, and historical growth rates." We wrongly thought that an institution's becoming really big would make it too big to fail—and therefore sustainable. "But being big does not, as we've painfully seen, make something sustainable," said Seidman.

AIG's motto was "The strength to be here." But AIG got disconnected from the values and long-term thinking that would make it a sustainable company. AIG, though enormous in size, could not sustain itself. It took the U.S. Treasury and the Federal Reserve to keep it upright.

What actually makes an institution sustainable is not the scale and size it reaches, "but *how* it does its business"—how it relates to its employees, shareholders, customers, and suppliers, insisted Seidman. Has it built its business like a house of cards—with superficial and one-night-stand relationships like those between mortgage buyers, brokers, rating agencies, bankers, and pension funds that led to the whole subprime mess—or has it built its business one brick at a time by nurturing sustainable relationships with customers, suppliers, bankers, shareholders, and employees? Sustainability as a value is the opposite of "I'll be gone." Sustainability says instead that I will behave as if I will always be here and always be held accountable for what took place on my watch.

There are no "seven habits of highly sustainable people," said Seidman. "Acting with sustainable values cannot be reduced to a simple checklist. Sustainability is about the disposition, the mind-set, and behaviors which shape and sustain relationships—relationships with family, friends, customers, investors, employees, borrowers, fellow citizens, the community, the environment, and with nature." In both the natural world and the financial world, it means that you think and then behave in a way that literally sustains—sustains the natural world around you, sustains business relationships, sustains personal relationships, sustains your community, sustains your country, sustains the planet, and sustains your relationships with your grandchildren and with generations to come. And that mind-set automatically leads you, said Seidman, "to the values that connect us deeply as people to other people and as people to institutions, to communities, and to the environment—values such as transparency, integrity, honesty, and shared responsibility." This mind-set also always leads you to think about the impact your actions will have over the long term.

Don't get me wrong: Free markets are about raw and naked competition. There are and always will be winners and losers. Sustainability is not a euphemism for charity work or socialism. It is an essential ingredient for winning. Practicing sustainable values not only helps a company survive, it helps it thrive over the long term. "Sustainable values do double duty," Seidman explained. They preserve, restore, and enhance companies, while simultaneously generating renewable resources, innovation, advantage, and prosperity. "There is real value in sustainable values," he added.

In other words, sustainability is both the end and the means. Sustainability is an outcome—we want our best institutions and companies, and as much as possible of our natural world, to be sustained. And sustainability is a practice—a set of principles for growing companies and ecosystems so they will endure. When we act with sustainable values we make it more likely that our natural world and the institutions and companies that undergird our lives and improve our standards of living will also stick around. Practicing an ethic of sustainability, in other words, produces institutions that are *too good to fail* and *too strong to fail*—not institutions that are too big to fail.

America's best companies, the companies that have been built to last, understand this—but too many others have forgotten. As Jeffrey Immelt of GE put it: We must "build competitive companies that win over the long term in every corner of the world. Business must shake off the short-term mind-set that brought on so many problems. If we want to see our country back in the lead, we have to start thinking like leaders again, and take the long-term view. We can't blame Wall Street. We must have the courage to invest . . . It is time to think big again. And time to make things again that work and last." It is a measure of how off track we got as a country in the early twenty-first century, how steeped in short-term, instant-gratification thinking we got, that one of our leading executives had to exhort us to have "the courage to invest."

As Seidman sees it, there are really only two kinds of business relationships: situational and sustainable. "Situational relationships are all about what I can get out of the here and now—right now. They're all about pragmatically exploiting short-term opportunities rather than consistently living the principles that create long-term success."

The upside of what I like to call the "flattening" of the world is that so many more people are connected today by networks and high-speed travel that they can meaningfully collaborate. The downside, though, is that so many more people can be connected situationally rather than sustainably. Whoever thought that British savers, with the click of a mouse, could deposit funds in online banks in Iceland? But in the flat world they could. And precisely because they were connected with technology, but without sustainable values regarding risk management and proper finance, those British savers were exposed to so much more financial peril than they ever realized.

The same is true in the natural world. Today an unprecedented number of people have access to capital, computers, labor, and technologies to spur growth and development. But if all these people act on nature with just situational values and not sustainable ones, the earth will be turned into a Florida strip mall faster than ever.

"That is why we need to inspire more and more people to embrace sustainable values and then to live those values with sustainable behaviors," said Seidman. "Laws and regulations tell you what you *can* do, but values tell you what you *should do*. There is a difference between doing that which you have a right to do and doing what is right to do."

Regulatory agencies tell you what you can and cannot do, but leaders, teachers, religious figures, philosophers, and parents inspire in us the values that tell us what you should and should not do. "In that way values are very efficient," Seidman concluded. "A handful of values can inspire an infinite amount of sustainable behaviors that would take a thousand pages of regulations to accomplish."

Your bank in Iceland, in a flat world, can—situationally speaking—turn itself into a hedge fund and draw savings from all over the world by offering ridiculous returns, but should it? Sustainable values will tell you no. You can today strip and clear forest in the Amazon to plant more soybeans that will reap a great profit when sold to China, but should you? Sustainable values will tell you no. A few years ago, you could have gotten a $500,000 mortgage with nothing down and no payments for two years on a $20,000 a year salary, but should you? Sustainable values will tell you no. Sustainability requires us to be more than just situational. But if you are not in the grip of values, you will only act situationally. Of course, regulations are better than anarchy, and you need them to govern a society. But you need values of sustainability to go along with regulations. Otherwise, the regulations tell you not to put your feet on the couch, so you will just put them on the chair. Values would tell you that you should never put your feet on furniture anywhere; otherwise the furniture won't last. No doubt we need smarter regulations and more regulators to prevent a repeat of the 2008/9 economic crisis. But we can't lose sight of the fact that the Great Recession was also caused in many ways by people doing what they could do, but should never have done. (Do we really need to pass a law that says banks can lend money only to people who have a good chance of being able to pay it back? Every banker should have the values to answer that question without a new law.) Precisely what combination of new banking regulations, limits on leverage, requirements for transparency, and values of sustainability we need to make our financial system more sustainable, so we do not keep lurching from economic crisis to economic crisis, are beyond the scope of this book. That is for experts in business and finance to devise, and I will leave it to them. I will be focusing on the laws, regulations, prices, and values that are required to enhance and broaden sustainability in the natural world. And that leads me to the core argument of this book.

The Core Argument

If you take these first three chapters together, the argument I am making is very simple: America has a problem and the world has a problem. America's problem is that it has lost its way in recent years—partly because of 9/11 and partly because of some bad habits, lazy thinking, and financial recklessness that we have let build up, particularly since the end of the Cold War, which together have weakened our society's ability and willingness to take on big challenges and realize our full potential.

The world also has a problem, as I will explain in detail in the coming chapters: It is getting hot, flat, and crowded. And as we try to grow everyone's standard of living in such a world, we are rapidly depleting our natural resources, intensifying the extinction of plants and animals, deepening energy poverty, strengthening petrodictatorship, and accelerating climate change—all at unprecedented rates. I am convinced that the best way for America to solve its big problem—the best way for America to get its groove back—is for us to take the lead in solving the problems of a hot, flat, and crowded planet. And that means creating the tools, strategies, energy sources, and values that will allow the world as a whole to grow in cleaner, more sustainable ways.

But this challenge is also an opportunity for America. Rising to this challenge "is not simply a new form of generating electric power," said Rothkopf. "It is a new form of generating national power—period." Rising to these challenges and opportunities will revive America at home, reconnect America abroad, and retool America for tomorrow. And given how big these challenges are, it is impossible for me to imagine us meeting them globally without America really stepping up and saying, "Follow me," not "After you."

"We are either going to be losers or heroes—there's no room anymore for anything in between," says Rob Watson, the CEO of EcoTech International and one of the best environmental minds in America. Either we are going to rise to the level of leadership, innovation, and collaboration that is required, or everybody is going to lose—big. Just coasting along and doing the same old things is not an option any longer. We need a whole new approach.

The simple name for the new project I am proposing is "Code Green." What "red" was to America in the 1950s and 1960s—a symbol of the overarching Communist threat, the symbol that was used to mobilize our country to build up its military, its industrial base, its highways, its railroads, ports, and airports, its educational institutions, and its scientific capabilities to lead the world in defense of freedom—we need "green" to be for today's America.

Unfortunately, after 9/11, instead of replacing red with green, President George W. Bush replaced red with "Code Red" and all the other crazy colors of the Department of Homeland Security's warning system. It's time to scrap them all and move to Code Green. For me, going Code Green means making America the world's leader in innovating clean power and energy-efficiency systems and inspiring an ethic of sustainability in relation to both the Market and Mother Nature.

"The hallmark of those companies and countries that continually thrive is that they continually reinvent themselves," noted Rothkopf. "We reinvented ourselves as a continental industrial power in the nineteenth century, and we reinvented ourselves as a global industrial power in the twentieth century and then as a global information society in the twenty-first century." Now we have to—for our own sake and the world's—reinvent ourselves one more time. Making America the world's greenest country, the world's most sustainable country, is not a selfless act of charity or naive moral indulgence. It is now a core national security and economic interest. It is how we will survive and how we will thrive.

There is a Chinese proverb that says, "When the wind changes direction, there are those who build walls and those who build windmills." Well, the wind has definitely changed direction, and we need to build the kind of windmills that can sustainably harness it. The old ways will not suffice any longer. The era we are heading into will be an era in which our lives, our ecosystems, our economies, and our political choices will be constrained if we do not find a cleaner way to power our future, a more sustainable way to manage our finances, and a better way to protect our natural world. So I say we build windmills. I say we lead and that we lead under the banner of sustainable development.

In such an America, our air will be cleaner, our environment will be healthier, our young people will see their idealism mirrored in their own government, and our industries will have more tools to do good for themselves and the planet at the same time. In such an America we will have our groove back. We will be respected, trusted, and inspiring to others, because we will again be leading the world on the most important strategic mission and values issue of the day.

Most important, in such an America we will be acting every day the way we act on our best days. Never forget, we have it in us to think and act sustainably. We have it in us to think and act for the long term. We have it in us to pull together for great nation-building projects. After all, we are not just the people of 7/4—the people who proclaimed that our country would be propelled by great values and ethics about freedom and human dignity and that by adhering to these ideals we would progress as a nation. We are also the people of 7/20, who pulled together and put a man on the moon within a decade of proclaiming that goal. We are the people of 12/8, who, faced with the overwhelming threat of fascism after the attack on Pearl Harbor, completely reconfigured our economy and mobilized the whole country to meet that threat to our way of life. And we are the people of 9/12, who, in the wake of an attack on our mainland, put aside our political differences, red states and blue states, and united to defend the nation and quickly rebuild our Pentagon and our economy. Precisely because we did all those things on those dates and beyond, we know we have it in us. But now we have to be our best for more than just a few days. That is why we don't just need a bailout from a Great Recession. We need a reboot by the Re-Generation. We have been living for far too long on borrowed time and borrowed dimes. We need to get back to work on our country and on our planet. The hour is late, the stakes couldn't be higher, the project couldn't be harder, and the payoff couldn't be greater.

The rest of this book is about how to make it happen.

PART II

Where We Are

FOUR

Today's Date: 1 E.C.E.
Today's Weather: Hot, Flat, and Crowded

So what is this new era we're heading into, which makes it so necessary, so relevant, and so opportune for America to take the lead in
developing a clean-tech, low-carbon, net-zero energy economy?
The short answer is that we're entering the "Energy-Climate Era."

In *The World Is Flat* (2005), I argued that the technological revolution leveling the global economic playing field and enabling so many
more people around the world to compete, connect, and collaborate was
ushering in a new phase of globalization that would have a huge impact
on economics, politics, and military and social affairs. The more I travel,
the more I see the effects of the flattening of the world.

But events of the past few years have made it clear to me that two
other enormously powerful forces are impacting our planet in fundamental ways: global warming and soaring global population growth. As I
absorbed these into my own analysis, it became obvious that it's actually
the convergence of global warming, global flattening, and global crowding that is the most important dynamic shaping the world we live in today. My shorthand for this convergence is the title of this book—*Hot,
Flat, and Crowded*—and my shorthand for the historical epoch this convergence is giving birth to is the Energy-Climate Era.

This book focuses on five key problems that a hot, flat, and crowded
world is dramatically intensifying. They are: the growing demand for
ever scarcer energy supplies and natural resources; a massive transfer of
wealth to oil-rich countries and their petrodictators; disruptive climate
change; energy poverty, which is sharply dividing the world into electricity haves and electricity have-nots; and rapidly accelerating biodiversity
loss, as plants and animals go extinct at record rates. I believe that these

problems—and how we manage them—will define the Energy-Climate Era. Because they are no ordinary problems, any one of them, if not managed properly, could cause sweeping, nonlinear, irreversible disruptions that might affect multiple generations. If we are going to solve these problems, we will need new tools, new infrastructure, new ways of thinking, and new ways of collaborating with others—the stuff of great new industries and scientific breakthroughs and the stuff that propels one nation forward and leaves another behind.

So we had better understand this new era we're heading into. The operative word here is "new." We need to stop thinking of ourselves as "post" something—postcolonial, postwar, post–Cold War, post-post–Cold War. Those eras are meaningless today. Wash them out of your mind. They explain nothing about where we are now.

"I don't think we're post-anything anymore—I think we're pre–something totally new," said David Rothkopf, the energy consultant. And the thing we are entering is the Energy-Climate Era.

"I think we are at one of those bright-line moments in history when things could change in ways that we can hardly imagine and across a very broad number of areas simultaneously," added Rothkopf. "We have seen such moments before—the democratic revolutions of the Enlightenment or the Industrial Revolution, and in our own time, the information technology revolution. One thing they all had in common is that when things started changing, people could not initially grasp their full significance. Another thing they had in common was that with all these great changes came great challenges. And it was rising to those challenges that defined the new eras, drove progress, gave birth to new institutions, and separated the winners from the losers."

Indeed, the countries that inspired and invented the big solutions to the big problems of the past led the eras that followed. And those countries that failed to adapt fell by the wayside. In this new Energy-Climate Era, America has to make sure it is among the former.

L et's start by examining the engine of this new era—this convergence of hot, flat, and crowded—beginning with *crowded*.

Here is a statistic I find staggering. I was born on July 20, 1953. If you go to the Web site Infoplease.com and put in your date of birth, you can find out roughly how many people were living on planet earth the day you were born. I did that and the number that popped up was 2.681 billion. God willing, if I keep biking and eating yogurt, I might live to be one hundred. By 2053, the United Nations projects that there will be more than 9 billion people on the planet, thanks to improvements in health care, disease eradication, and economic development. That means that in my lifetime the world's population will have more than tripled, and roughly as many people will be born between now and 2053 as were here when I was born.

Specifically, the United Nations Population Division issued a report (March 13, 2007) stating that "the world population will likely increase by 2.5 billion over the next 43 years, passing from the current 6.7 billion to 9.2 billion in 2050. This increase is equivalent to the total size of the world population in 1950, and it will be absorbed mostly by the less developed regions, whose population is projected to rise from 5.4 billion in 2007 to 7.9 billion in 2050. In contrast, the population of the more developed regions is expected to remain largely unchanged at 1.2 billion, and would have declined, were it not for the projected net migration from developing to developed countries, which is expected to average 2.3 million persons annually."

So if you think the world feels crowded now, just wait a few decades. In 1800, London was the world's largest city with one million people. By 1960, there were 111 cities with more than one million people. By 1995 there were 280, and today there are over 300, according to UN Population Fund statistics. The number of megacities (with ten million or more inhabitants) in the world has climbed from 5 in 1975 to 14 in 1995 and is expected to reach 26 cities by 2015, according to the UN. Needless to say, these exploding populations are rapidly overwhelming infrastructure in these megacities—nineteen million people in Mumbai alone—as well as driving loss of arable land, deforestation, overfishing, water shortages, and air and water pollution.

In 2007, the United Nations Population Fund's executive director, Thoraya Ahmed Obaid, issued a report stating that in 2008, more than half of humanity will be living in cities, and "we are not ready for them." The Associated Press reported from London (June 27, 2007) that by 2030 the number of city dwellers is expected to climb to five billion. Obaid said smaller cities will absorb the bulk of urban growth: "We're focusing on the megacities when the data tell us most of the movement will be coming to smaller cities of 500,000 or more," which often lack the water and energy resources and governing institutions to deal with rising migrant populations.

This growth has come on so big, so fast that Michael V. Hayden, the director of the Central Intelligence Agency, stated that his analysts now believe the most worrying trend in the world is not terrorism but demographics.

"Today, there are 6.7 billion people sharing the planet," said General Hayden in a speech at Kansas State University (April 30, 2008). "By mid-century, the best estimates point to a world population of more than 9 billion. That's a 40 to 45 percent increase—striking enough—but most of that growth is almost certain to occur in countries least able to sustain it, and that will create a situation that will likely fuel instability and extremism—not just in those areas, but beyond them as well. There are many poor, fragile states where governance is actually difficult today, where populations will grow rapidly: Afghanistan, Liberia, Niger, the Democratic Republic of the Congo. Among that group the population is expected to triple by mid-century. The number of people in Ethiopia, Nigeria, and Yemen is likely to more than double. Furthermore—just beyond the raw numbers—all those countries will therefore have, as a result of this, a large concentration of young people. If their basic freedoms and basic needs—food, housing, education, employment—are not met, they could be easily attracted to violence, civil unrest, and extremism."

This is what I mean by *crowded*. What about *flat*? When I wrote that the world is flat I wasn't suggesting, of course, that it was getting physically flat or that we were all becoming economically equal. What the book argued was that a combination of technological, market, and geopolitical events at the end of the twentieth century had leveled the global economic playing field in a way that was enabling more people than ever, from more places than ever, to take part in the global economy—and, in the best of cases, to enter the middle class.

This flattening was a product of several factors. The first was the invention and proliferation of the personal computer, which enabled individuals—*individuals*—to become authors of their own content in digital form. For the first time in history, individuals could create words, data, spreadsheets, photos, designs, videos, drawings, and music on their own PCs in the form of bits and bytes. Once an individual's content was in digital form, it could be shaped in many more ways and distributed to many more places.

Another big flattener was the emergence of the Internet, the World Wide Web, and the Web browser—a set of tools that enabled individuals to send their digital content anywhere in the world virtually for free and to easily display or access that content via Web pages.

The third flattener was a quiet revolution in software and transmission protocols, which I call the "work flow revolution" because of how it made everyone's computer and software interoperable—thus enabling work to flow farther and faster through internal company networks, the Internet, and the World Wide Web. Suddenly, so many more people could work together on so many different things. So Boeing could hire airplane designers in Moscow and integrate them with airplane builders in Wichita, and Dell could design computers in Austin and Taiwan and have them built in China and Ireland and serviced by technicians in India.

The big geopolitical flattener was the collapse of Communism and the fall of the Berlin Wall. The demise of the Soviet Union and its iron curtain was like the elimination of a huge physical and political roadblock on the global economic playing field. In the wake of that collapse, market economics became the norm in virtually every country in the world, and even the likes of Cuba and North Korea began to dabble in capitalism.

Put all these flatteners together and what you have is a much more seamless, unobstructed global marketplace. In this global agora, millions and millions of new consumers and producers were able to buy or sell their goods and services—as individuals or companies—and were able to collaborate with more people in more places on more things with greater ease for less money than ever before. That is what I meant by a flat world.

The good news is that the end of Communism and the flattening of the world helped to lift 200 million people out of abject poverty in the 1980s and 1990s in China and India alone, according to the International Monetary Fund—and moved tens of millions more higher up the economic ladder into the middle class. But as they've come out of poverty, which usually is associated with a rural and agricultural way of life, these several hundred million new players have begun earning wages that enabled them to consume more things and produce more things. And all these consumers walked onto the global economic playing field with their own versions of the "American dream"—a car, a house, an air conditioner, a cell phone, a microwave, a toaster, a computer, and an iPod—creating a huge new demand for "things," all of which devour lots of energy, natural resources, land, and water and emit lots of climate-changing greenhouse gases from the time they are produced to when they are discarded.

This process, of course, is stoking an unprecedented competition for energy, minerals, water, and forest products, as rising (and growing) nations like Brazil, India, and China pursue comfort, prosperity, and economic security for more and more of their people. The combination of flat and crowded—more and more people who are able to live a modern high-energy and high-resource-consuming lifestyle—is what poses the most dangerous threat to the global environment in the long run.

And we're just at the beginning. Within the next fifteen years, the world's population is expected to swell by roughly another billion people, and in the years to follow many of them will become new consumers and producers. When that happens, the law of large numbers starts to kick in and everything starts to add up to huge, noted David Douglas, chief sustainability officer for Sun Microsystems: huge appetites for resources, huge development projects, huge cities, huge energy demands, huge pressures on the environment. Douglas called me one day with a small example of what happens when flat meets crowded. What if, he asked, once the next billion people are all here, we gave each of them just one small gift—a sixty-watt incandescent lightbulb? "Each bulb doesn't weigh much—roughly 0.7 ounces with the packaging—but a billion of them together weigh around 20,000 metric tons, or about the same as 15,000 Priuses," explained Douglas. "Now let's turn them on. If they're all on at the same time, it'd be 60,000 megawatts. Luckily, [these billion people] will only use their bulbs four hours per day, so we're down to 10,000 megawatts at any moment. Yikes! Looks like we'll still need twenty or so new 500-megawatt coal-burning power plants"—just so the next billion people can turn a light on!

W hat about *hot*? The broad scientific understanding today is that our planet is experiencing a warming trend—over and above natural and normal variations—that is almost certainly due to human activities associated with large-scale manufacturing. The process began in the late 1700s with the Industrial Revolution, when manual labor, horsepower, and water power began to be replaced by or enhanced by machines. This revolution, over time, shifted Britain, Europe, and eventually North America from largely agricultural and trading societies to manufacturing ones, relying on machinery and engines rather than tools and animals.

The Industrial Revolution was at heart a revolution in the use of energy and power. Its beginning is usually dated to the advent of the steam engine, which was based on the conversion of chemical energy in wood or coal to thermal energy and then to mechanical work—primarily the powering of industrial machinery and steam locomotives. Coal eventually supplanted wood because, pound for pound, coal contains twice as much energy as wood (measured in BTUs, or British thermal units, per pound) and because its use helped to save what was left of the world's temperate forests. Coal was used to produce heat that went directly into industrial processes, including metallurgy, and to warm buildings, as well as to power steam engines. When crude oil came along in the mid-1800s, still a couple of decades before electricity, it was burned, in the form of kerosene, in lamps to make light—replacing whale oil. It was also used to provide heat for buildings and in manufacturing processes, and as a fuel for engines used in industry and propulsion.

In short, one can say that the main forms in which humans need and use energy are for light, heat, mechanical work and motive power, and electricity—which can be used to provide any of the other three, as well as to do things that none of those three can do, such as electronic communications and information processing. Since the Industrial Revolution, all these energy functions have been powered primarily, but not exclusively, by fossil fuels that emit carbon dioxide (CO_2).

To put it another way, the Industrial Revolution gave a whole new prominence to what Rochelle Lefkowitz, president of Pro-Media Communications and an energy buff, calls "fuels from hell"—coal, oil, and natural gas. All these fuels from hell come from underground, are exhaustible, and emit CO_2 and other pollutants when they are burned for transportation, heating, and industrial use. These fuels are in contrast to what Lefkowitz calls "fuels from heaven"—wind, hydroelectric, tidal, biomass, and solar power. These all come from above ground, are endlessly renewable, and produce no harmful emissions.

The early years of the twentieth century also brought a transportation revolution with the invention of the internal combustion engine and its use to power cars and trucks. Gasoline-powered motorcars were invented in Germany in the late nineteenth century, but, according to Ideafinder .com, "the first automobile to be produced in quantity was the 1901

Curved Dash Oldsmobile, which was built in the United States by Ransom E. Olds. Modern automobile mass production, and its use of the modern industrial assembly line, is credited to Henry Ford of Detroit, Michigan, who had built his first gasoline-powered car in 1896. Ford began producing his Model T in 1908, and by 1927, when it was discontinued, over 18 million had rolled off the assembly line." The internal combustion engine transformed commerce, made crude oil hugely valuable for powering automobiles, and greatly increased demand for iron, steel, and rubber. A steam engine worked by external combustion, with coal, oil, or wood burning outside and creating the steam that actually powered the engine; the internal combustion engine created the combustion process internally, which was more efficient, required less fuel, and allowed for smaller engines and motors.

Meanwhile, industrialization promoted urbanization, and urbanization eventually gave birth to suburbanization. This trend, which was repeated across America, nurtured the development of the American car culture, the building of a national highway system, and a mushrooming of suburbs around American cities, which rewove the fabric of American life. Many other developed and developing countries followed the American model, with all its upsides and downsides. The result is that today we have suburbs and ribbons of highways that run in, out, and around not only America's major cities, but China's, India's, and South America's as well. And as these urban areas attract more people, the sprawl extends in every direction.

And why not? All the coal, oil, and natural gas inputs for this new economic model seemed relatively cheap, relatively inexhaustible, and relatively harmless—or at least relatively easy to clean up afterward. So there wasn't much to stop the juggernaut of more people and more development and more concrete and more buildings and more cars and more coal, oil, and gas needed to build and power them. Summing it all up, Andy Karsner, the Department of Energy's assistant secretary for energy efficiency and renewable energy, once said to me: "We built a really inefficient environment with the greatest efficiency ever known to man."

After the publication of books like Rachel Carson's *Silent Spring* in 1962, people became more aware of the toxic effects of pesticides. This early environmental awareness gradually expanded to embrace concerns about urban air pollution, industrial waste emitted into lakes and rivers, and the rapidly increasing loss of green spaces due to urban sprawl. In

America, these concerns set in motion an environmental movement, which eventually produced legislation designed to protect or restore clean air and clean water, and to stem the worst water pollution, toxic waste dumping, smog, ozone depletion, acid rain, and roadside litter. Building on a century of wilderness conservation dating back to the naturalist John Muir, the modern environmental movement also brought about passage of the Endangered Species Act and other conservation legislation to safeguard America's natural wonders and biodiversity.

But there was no time to rest. Beginning in the second half of the twentieth century, a scientific understanding began to emerge that an excessive accumulation of largely invisible pollutants—called greenhouse gases—was affecting the climate. The buildup of these greenhouse gases had been under way since the start of the Industrial Revolution in a place we could not see and in a form we could not touch or smell. These greenhouse gases, primarily carbon dioxide emitted from human industrial, residential, and transportation sources, were not piling up along roadsides or in rivers, in cans or empty bottles, but, rather, above our heads, in the earth's atmosphere. If the earth's atmosphere was like a blanket that helped to regulate the planet's temperature, the CO_2 buildup was having the effect of thickening that blanket and making the globe warmer.

To visualize this process, the California Institute of Technology energy chemist Nate Lewis offers the following analogy: "Imagine you are driving in your car and every mile you drive you throw a pound of trash out your window. And everyone else on the freeway in their cars and trucks is doing the exact same thing, and people driving Hummers are throwing two bags out at a time—one out the driver-side window and one out the passenger-side window. How would you feel? Not so good. Well, that is exactly what we are doing; you just can't see it. Only what we are throwing out is a pound of CO_2—that's what goes into the atmosphere, on average, every mile we drive."

Those bags of CO_2 from our cars float up and stay in the atmosphere, along with bags of CO_2 from power plants burning coal, oil, and gas, and bags of CO_2 released from the burning and clearing of forests, which releases all the carbon stored in trees, plants, and soil. In fact, many people don't realize that deforestation in places like Indonesia and Brazil is responsible for more CO_2 than all the world's cars, trucks, planes, ships, and trains combined—that is, about 20 percent of all global emissions.

And when we're not tossing bags of carbon dioxide into the atmosphere, we're throwing up other greenhouse gases, like methane (CH_4) released from rice farming, petroleum drilling, coal mining, animal defecation, solid waste landfill sites, and yes, even from cattle belching.

Cattle belching? That's right—the striking thing about greenhouse gases is the diversity of sources that emit them. A herd of cattle belching can be worse than a highway full of Hummers. Livestock gas is very high in methane, which, like CO_2, is colorless and odorless. And like CO_2, methane is one of those greenhouse gases that, once released into the atmosphere, also absorb heat radiating from the earth's surface. "Molecule for molecule, methane's heat-trapping power in the atmosphere is twenty-one times stronger than carbon dioxide, the most abundant greenhouse gas," reported *Science World* (January 21, 2002). "With 1.3 billion cows belching almost constantly around the world (100 million in the United States alone), it's no surprise that methane released by livestock is one of the chief global sources of the gas, according to the U.S. Environmental Protection Agency . . . 'It's part of their normal digestion process,' says Tom Wirth of the EPA. 'When they chew their cud, they regurgitate [spit up] some food to rechew it, and all this gas comes out.' The average cow expels 600 liters of methane a day, climate researchers report."

What is the precise scientific relationship between these expanded greenhouse gas emissions and global warming? Experts at the Pew Center on Climate Change offer a handy summary in their report "Climate Change 101." Global average temperatures, notes the Pew study, "have experienced natural shifts throughout human history. For example, the climate of the Northern Hemisphere varied from a relatively warm period between the eleventh and fifteenth centuries to a period of cooler temperatures between the seventeenth century and the middle of the nineteenth century. However, scientists studying the rapid rise in global temperatures during the late twentieth century say that natural variability cannot account for what is happening now." The new factor is the human factor—our vastly increased emissions of carbon dioxide and other greenhouse gases from the burning of fossil fuels such as coal and oil, as well as from deforestation, large-scale cattle-grazing, agriculture, and industrialization.

"Scientists refer to what has been happening in the earth's atmosphere over the past century as the 'enhanced greenhouse effect,'" notes the Pew study. By pumping man-made greenhouse gases into the atmosphere, humans are altering the process by which naturally occurring greenhouse gases, because of their unique molecular structure, trap the sun's heat near the earth's surface before that heat radiates back into space.

"The greenhouse effect keeps the earth warm and habitable; without it, the earth's surface would be about 60 degrees Fahrenheit colder on average. Since the average temperature of the earth is about 45 degrees Fahrenheit, the natural greenhouse effect is clearly a good thing. But the enhanced greenhouse effect means even more of the sun's heat is trapped, causing global temperatures to rise. Among the many scientific studies providing clear evidence that an enhanced greenhouse effect is under way was a 2005 report from NASA's Goddard Institute for Space Studies. Using satellites, data from buoys, and computer models to study the earth's oceans, scientists concluded that more energy is being absorbed from the sun than is emitted back to space, throwing the earth's energy out of balance and warming the globe."

A variety of data reinforces this conclusion. The composition of the earth's atmosphere "has been relatively unchanged for twenty million years," noted Caltech's Nate Lewis, but in the last hundred years "we have begun to dramatically transform that atmosphere and change the heat balance between the earth and the sun in ways that could profoundly affect the habitats of every plant, animal, and human on this planet." On the eve of the Industrial Revolution—according to ice core samples that have trapped air bubbles from previous eras and can provide us with a snapshot of climate conditions going back thousands of years—the level of carbon dioxide in the atmosphere stood at roughly 280 parts per million by volume. "And it had been stable around that level for about ten thousand years before that," Lewis added. It started to surge in the 1950s, tracking the broad global surge in energy consumption, led by the Western industrial powers after World War II. Despite all the talk about the need to mitigate climate change, the rate at which we humans are pumping carbon dioxide into the atmosphere is still accelerating. In 2007, the CO_2 level in the atmosphere stood at 384 parts per million by volume and appeared to be climbing at a rate of 2 parts per million a year.

The general agreement among climate experts is that the earth has already warmed on average by 0.8 degrees Celsius (1.44 degrees Fahrenheit) above its level in 1750, with the most rapid rise occurring since 1970. Changes over the different continents and altitudes have been much greater than just these averages. A one-degree change in the global average temperature may not sound like much, but it is telling you something is amiss with the state of the climate—just as small changes in your body temperature tell you that something is amiss with your body.

"Your body temperature is normally 98.6 degrees Fahrenheit, and when it goes up just a few degrees to 102 Fahrenheit, it is a big deal—it tells you something is wrong," says John Holdren, who is professor of environmental policy at Harvard, director of the Woods Hole Research Center, and former president of the American Association for the Advancement of Science. "The same is true with changes in the global average surface temperature."

From our ice core samples, Holdren explained, we know that the difference in global average temperature between an ice age and an interglacial period like we are in now—that is, the difference between the earth being an ice ball and being very comfortable for human development and agriculture—is a mere five to six degrees Celsius. So a small difference in that global average temperature can lead to very big changes, which is why this 0.8-degree Celsius rise is telling us, as Al Gore likes to say, that planet earth has "a fever." According to the World Meteorological Organization, the ten hottest years since thermometer records became available in 1860 all occurred between 1995 and 2005.

CNN founder Ted Turner is not a scientist, but in his own blunt way he summed up what it means when the world gets hot, flat, and crowded. "We're too many people—that's why we have global warming," he said in an interview with Charlie Rose (April 2, 2008). "Too many people are using too much stuff."

As I indicated, though, the story of the Energy-Climate Era doesn't stop with the perfect storm of hot, flat, and crowded. The convergence of global warming, global flattening, and global crowding is driving those five big problems—energy supply and demand, petrodictatorship, climate change, energy poverty, and biodiversity loss—well past their tipping points into new realms we've never seen before, as a planet or as a species. Here is a brief look at each one:

ENERGY AND NATURAL RESOURCES SUPPLY AND DEMAND: From the beginning of the Industrial Revolution right up to the late twentieth century, most Americans, and most people around the world, lived under the happy illusion that the fossil fuels we were using to generate mechanical power, transportation power, building heat, cooking heat, industrial processes, and electricity were largely inexhaustible, inexpensive, politically benign, and (though nasty if you lived in Newcastle) climatically benign as well.

As we enter the Energy-Climate Era, that changes: We now understand that these fossil fuels are exhaustible, increasingly expensive, and politically, ecologically, and climatically toxic. That's the line we've crossed.

What changed? The simple answer is that flat met crowded: So many more people were suddenly able to improve their standards of living so much faster. And when the crowding of the world and the flattening of the world converged around the year 2000, the world went onto a track where global demand for energy, natural resources, and food all started to grow at a much accelerated pace—as the Western industrialized countries still consumed considerable amounts of energy and natural resources and big emerging countries got to join them at the middle-class dinner table.

If you want to have a graphic image of what is happening, you couldn't do better than the one offered by Richard Richels from the Electric Power Research Institute. It's as if the world were a bathtub that America and other developed countries, with their own growth, filled to the brim, he told me. And then along came India and China and others, and they turned on the shower. Now all this demand is just overflowing onto the bathroom floor.

The energy economist Philip K. Verleger, Jr., notes that global energy consumption grew by 5 percent per year from 1951 to 1970. "This rapid growth occurred simultaneously with the economic reconstruction in Europe and Japan after World War II, as well as the postwar growth in the United States," Verleger wrote in *The International Economy* (September 22, 2007). "History may well repeat from 2001 to 2020 as China, India, and other countries move from developing to developed nations. Consumption can be expected to increase at a pace close to the rate of the economic growth in these nations, just as it did in Europe, Japan, and the United States following the Second World War."

While these countries may, through efficiency measures, be able to produce more GDP growth with less energy, the fact is, they are now involved in building massive amounts of new infrastructure, and "that infrastructure is energy-intensive," said Verleger. That is why Royal Dutch Shell's energy scenario team predicted in its 2008 report that global consumption of all forms of energy will at least double between now and 2050, because of the combination of population growth and greater wealth driven by the globalization of markets.

That is what's new about the forces propelling the Energy-Climate Era: They are demand-driven, as so many more people suddenly are, can, or will be living a middle-class lifestyle.

The pivotal year that told us we were in a new era in terms of global energy supply and demand was 2004, says Larry Goldstein, an oil expert at the Energy Policy Research Foundation. "What happened in 2004 was the world's first demand-led energy shock." Here's what he means: In 1973, 1980, and 1990, we saw sudden oil price spikes because of wars and revolution in the Middle East, which sharply limited the supply of oil. What happened in 2004, said Goldstein, was a price shock that was simply the product of long-term trends that pushed demand well ahead of supply, spurred in large part by a sudden leap in demand from China.

Historically, outside of wars, whenever the crude oil market got tight, said Goldstein, shortages could be eased either by "spare usable crude oil capacity, spare refining capacity, or spare discretionary oil product inventories." These three reserves were the shock absorbers for the world oil market. And year after year, as oil demand continued to increase at about 1 percent a year, these shock absorbers would absorb that gradual increase and ensure that prices went up only gradually—until 2004.

Two things happened that year. All the shock absorbers, all that spare crude, product, and refining capacity, disappeared, and demand for energy took a great leap forward, due to China's growth. At the start of 2004, the International Energy Agency predicted that global demand for crude oil would grow by 1.5 million barrels a day that year, said Goldstein. "Instead, it grew by three million barrels a day, and [demand in] China alone grew by over one million barrels a day," he said. And because all three of the traditional shock absorbers were gone, that extra demand could not be cushioned.

Why not? Normally, high prices would prompt more investment, more drilling, and more oil. It has been slow to happen this time around, though, for several reasons, said Goldstein. First, there was a broad shortage of equipment in the oil industry—from skilled petroleum engineers to drilling rigs to tankers—to expand production. Second, countries like Russia began retroactively changing the drilling rules in their fields, squeezing out foreign producers in order to pump more oil themselves;

what this did was discourage more professional and experienced global oil companies from operating there, and this in turn reduced production. Finally, America and other Western nations continued to limit the amount of acreage they were ready to offer for oil drilling for conservation reasons. So not only did the market tip in 2004, but it kept tipping and tipping and tipping, which is why prices skyrocketed by 2008 as demand continued to rise, until the Great Recession finally cooled things down—for the moment.

Soaring oil and gas prices, though, are only one of the things that happen when global flattening meets global crowding. What else happens? You get a world in which there are still about 2.4 billion people living on $2 a day or less, according to the World Bank, but in which millions of them are striving and succeeding to get onboard the flat world platform, which creates enormous new demand for other natural resources—a blessing for world stability but a challenge for ecology and climate.

"Everything today is in shortage—steel, bauxite, construction equipment, engineers, contractors, ships," said Klaus Kleinfeld, president of Alcoa, the global aluminum manufacturer. "You run into bottlenecks now everywhere you turn."

Take aluminum, he explained. First of all, there are more people on the planet every day and, particularly in the developing world, more of them are moving to urban areas, where they live in high-rise buildings, drive cars or motor scooters, ride buses, fly on airplanes, and start to drink Coke from cans. All of that increases demand for aluminum. Companies like Alcoa then go out and try to acquire more bauxite. That requires more mines and smelters, and that requires more ships and more steel and more energy, and that requires more engineers and more contractors. When you try to do every one of those things today—build a new ship, build a new smelter, hire a global contracting firm—he said, everyone tells you the same thing: "We will put you on the waiting list. Can you wait three years?"

This pattern is not going away. The Great Recession has slowed down the growth trend, but rising demand for energy and natural resources is the new normal.

When fuel prices around the world increased, the costs of farming around the world also increased, and therefore the cost of food increased. It also encouraged more and more countries to allocate land for biofuels such as ethanol, so they wouldn't be so dependent on oil, which adds to grocery prices by reducing the acreage devoted to food crops. And, finally, the higher crude oil prices went, the less acreage farmers in the developing world could afford to plant. The BBC reported (April 22, 2008) that in Kenya's Rift Valley farmers were planting a third less of their land than last year, because petrochemical fertilizer had more than doubled in price.

Why didn't the market respond beforehand through the natural laws of supply and demand? In part, say World Bank experts, it is because spiking demand was not immediately translated into higher prices for consumers, owing to years of massive subsidies for energy and food around the world. In 2007, according to the World Bank, the governments of India, China, and the Middle East alone spent $50 billion subsidizing gasoline for their motorists, and cooking and heating oil and electricity for homes and factories: importing energy at global prices, selling it to their people at discounted prices, and eating the difference in their national budgets. This kept prices artificially low and demand artificially high. Had prices been allowed to rise with the global market, demand would have dropped. But that was not permitted. In 2007, Indonesia spent 30 percent of its budget on energy subsidies and only 6 percent on education. At the same time, the Western industrial countries spent roughly $270 billion subsidizing agriculture, so their farmers got rich, their consumers got cheap food, and Third World farmers had a hard time competing. This helped to keep some food supplies artificially low even as worldwide demand was growing and there were more and more middle-class mouths to feed. Bottom line: The markets were distorted.

What changed, say the World Bank experts, is that in the past few years demand from a world becoming flat and crowded reached a point where it just burst through all these distortions and cushions in the market, like a volcano blowing its top.

"For the last ten years, every year, we would look at the growth statistics from China or India and say, 'Wow, they grew 8 or 9 or 10 percent this year,'" a World Bank energy expert remarked to me. "Well, guess what," he said, "the emerging markets have emerged."

PETRODICTATORSHIP: The big geopolitical redline that is being crossed as we enter the Energy-Climate Era involves the massive transfer of wealth—hundreds of billions of dollars a year—from energy-consuming countries to energy-producing countries, as the price of oil and gas has soared and stayed high. This unprecedented financial transfer is strengthening nondemocratic actors and trends in many oil-producing countries. It's giving power to leaders who have not earned it by actually building their economies or educating their people. And it's strengthening the most conservative hard-line clerics all across the Muslim world, who tend to get their financing from Saudi Arabia, Iran, and other oil-rich Persian Gulf states.

There are many developments that illustrate this power shift, but for me one of the most vivid took place in early 2006, when then Russian president Vladimir Putin briefly shut down Russia's gas pipeline to Central and Western Europe to intimidate the newly elected Western-oriented government of Ukraine. Here is how *The New York Times* described the incident (January 2, 2006):

> Russia cut off the natural gas intended for Ukraine on Sunday as talks over pricing and transit terms unraveled into a bald political conflict that carried consequences for Ukraine's recovering economy and possibly for gas supplies to Western Europe. The dispute comes a year after the Orange Revolution brought a pro-Western government to power in Ukraine . . . Sunday's early-winter cut in gas supplies to Ukraine came as an unsettling reminder that *promises* [italics mine] of energy exports are not Russia's only method of using oil and gas to further its foreign policy goals—it can also turn off the valve of energy exports.

Russia, in the space of just a few years, has gone from the sick man of Europe, begging to be invited to meetings of the club, to the rich man of Europe, able to club any of its neighbors by turning off the natural gas should they get a little too frisky, a little too democratic, or a little too independent of Russia's interests. Russia did not get better educated, more productive, or more efficient at manufacturing. Europe simply got more dependent on Russia's natural resources and Russia got more aggressive about exploiting that dependence.

CLIMATE CHANGE: As the earth's average temperature has risen, the change has begun to play havoc with the climate, and because CO_2 stays in the atmosphere for several thousand years, the effects will only build as more CO_2 gets poured into Mother Nature's operating system. So as we enter the Energy-Climate Era, we are leaving an era in which whatever effects we were having on the climate and environment were perceived to be manageable and reversible—acid rain, ozone depletion, conventional pollution, for instance—and entering an era in which our effects on the climate and earth's natural systems are becoming potentially unmanageable and irreversible.

The flashing red lights that told us we were entering this new era were Hurricane Katrina and a report of the United Nations–sponsored Intergovernmental Panel on Climate Change, issued in 2007, after a review of the impact of climate change since 1990. Katrina gave us a sample of what unmanageable climate change could look like, when on August 29, 2005, that hurricane smashed New Orleans with a ferocity that many climatologists believe was fed by the warmer waters in the Gulf of Mexico attributable to global warming. The IPCC report told us that the broadest consensus of climate experts in the world, drawing on some tens of thousands of peer-reviewed scientific studies, concluded that the reality of global warming is "unequivocal" and that there is strong evidence that this increase in temperature since 1950 is directly attributable to greenhouse gas emissions from human activity.

The IPCC further concluded that without a dramatic reduction in human-induced CO_2 emissions, climate change may bring "abrupt or irreversible" effects on air, oceans, glaciers, land, coastlines, and species. The panel's chairman, Rajendra Pachauri, told reporters at the issuance of the final summary that "if there's no action before 2012, that's too late. What we do in the next two to three years will determine our future. This is the defining moment."

How bad could things get? At the request of the United Nations, the scientific research society Sigma Xi also convened its own international group of climate scientists and produced a report in February 2007, "Confronting Climate Change," in which it noted that even the relatively small rise in global average temperature, 0.8 degrees Celsius, that we have seen so far since 1750 has been "accompanied by significant increases in the incidence of floods, droughts, heat waves and wildfires . . . There have also been large reductions in the extent of summer sea ice in the Arctic, large increases in summer melting on the Greenland Ice Sheet, signs of instability in the West Antarctic Ice Sheet, and movement in the geographic and altitudinal ranges of large numbers of plant and animal species."

Since we can't stop CO_2 emissions cold, if they continue to grow at just the mid-range projections, "the cumulative warming by 2100 will be between 3 and 5 degrees Celsius over preindustrial conditions," says the

Sigma Xi report, which could trigger sea level rises, droughts, and floods of a biblical scale that will affect the livability of a range of human settlements. And these are just the mid-range projections. Many climatologists think things will get much hotter.

Now that we know this, our challenge as a civilization in the Energy-Climate Era is to manage those effects that are already "unavoidable," already baked into our future, and to avoid those effects that would be truly "unmanageable," as Sigma Xi put it so well. Indeed, if there is a bumper sticker for the Energy-Climate Era, it is surely that suggested by Sigma Xi: Avoid the unmanageable and manage the unavoidable.

"There are degrees of screwed," says Peter Gleick, cofounder and president of the Pacific Institute for Studies in Development, Environment, and Security in Oakland. "And no matter how bad it is, it could be worse or less worse. There is a huge difference between a two-foot sea level rise and a ten-foot. There is a big difference between a two-degree temperature rise and a five-degree temperature rise—and that is why thinking about manageable and unmanageable comes into play, because one scenario might kill ten million and one might kill a hundred million."

ENERGY POVERTY: It has long been vitally important to have access to electricity, but when the world gets hot, flat, and crowded, it is even more important. Because today, in an increasingly flat world, if you don't have electricity you cannot get online and you cannot compete, connect, and collaborate globally, and, increasingly, even locally. And in a hotter world, where the computer models forecast that climate change will exacerbate weather extremes—heavier rains, stronger floods, longer droughts—those with the least shelter and fewest tools to adapt will suffer the most. If you don't have the power tools to build a higher wall, or electricity to drill a deeper well or desalinate water, your ability to adapt will be radically diminished. And in a crowded world, more and more people are falling into that category—into the category of out of grid and out of luck.

For me, that point was highlighted by a little news item carried by Bloomberg.com (January 24, 2008): "In the third quarter of 2007, South Africans imported 44,590 generators, according to the South African Reserve Bank. That compares with 790 in the third quarter of 2003."

Behind that little news item is a big story: In the last quarter of 2007, South Africa and Zimbabwe, which depends on neighboring South Africa for a portion of its electric power, experienced widespread blackouts as the poorly maintained South African electricity grid was overwhelmed by rising demand. This triggered not only a stampede to buy home and office generators, but also talk of a long-term economic slowdown because people will just not have enough juice to run their businesses.

That same Bloomberg story noted: "Workers at Johannesburg's Tre Gatti Cucina restaurant spent peak business hours last week wiping down tables and folding napkins by candlelight, their kitchen idled by South Africa's worst-ever blackouts. With the country's power monopoly, Eskom Holdings Ltd., predicting shortages until at least 2013, the six waiters and kitchen workers may soon be out of work. 'If it continues like this we will have to sell,' said Dee Kroon, who opened the Italian restaurant in the Johannesburg neighborhood of Craighall Park in 2005. 'Who is going to buy a business if there are power cuts all the time?'"

For those who already are energy-poor and never had electricity, extended power cuts won't matter much. But for those who now have it, and whose aspirations have increased with every kilowatt, suddenly losing it could become politically explosive.

BIODIVERSITY LOSS: The flattening and crowding of the world is driving economic development, commerce, road building, natural resource extraction, overfishing, and urban sprawl at a pace that is devouring open lands, coral reefs, and tropical forests, disrupting ecosystems, despoiling rivers, and driving species extinctions across the planet at an unprecedented pace.

"For all the material blessings economic progress has provided, for all the disease and destitution avoided, for all the glories that shine in the best of our civilization, the costs to the natural world, the costs to the glories of nature, have been huge and must be counted in the balance as tragic loss," wrote James Gustave Speth, dean of the School of Forestry and Environmental Studies at Yale and the author of *The Bridge at the Edge of the World*. "Half the world's tropical and temperate forests are now gone. The rate of deforestation in the tropics continues at about an acre a second. About half the wetlands and a third of the mangroves are gone. An estimated 90 percent of the large predator fish are gone . . . Twenty percent of the corals are gone, and another 20 percent severely threatened. Species are disappearing at rates about a thousand times faster than normal."

There are many events one could point to that tell us that we passed a biodiversity tipping point as the world got hot, flat, and crowded. For me, the most potent symbol was when, in 2006, we humans lost a relative. We are large mammals, and for the first time in many decades human hands brought a large mammal to extinction—the baiji, or river dolphin. Also known as the Yangtze River dolphin, the baiji lived only in China's Yangtze River and was one of the few freshwater dolphins in the world.

The reason the baiji was such a painful loss to our global heritage is that it represented a genus, not just a species. Species are being lost with increasing regularity, and each loss is a tragedy. But when you lose a genus, which potentially includes many species, you lose a much bigger slice of the history of life. Think of biodiversity as the tree of life. When a species goes extinct, it is as if we cut a twig off the tree. When a genus goes extinct, we are cutting an entire branch off the tree. The baiji was a big branch.

The Baiji.org Foundation reported (December 13, 2006) that the baiji was probably extinct, as a search expedition concluded.

> During the six-week expedition scientists from six nations desperately searched the Yangtze in vain. The scientists were traveling on two research vessels almost 3,500 kilometers from Yichang nearby the Three Gorges Dam to Shanghai into the Yangtze Delta and back, using high-performance optical instruments and underwater microphones. "It is possible we may have missed one or two animals," said August Pfluger, head of Swiss-based baiji.org Foundation and co-organizer of the expedition in Wuhan. Regardless, these animals would have no chance of survival in the river. "We have to accept the fact, that the Baiji is functionally extinct. It is a tragedy, a loss not only for China, but for the entire world," said Pfluger in Wuhan.

The Guardian followed up the next year (August 8, 2007) with an article also noting the historic significance.

> The Yangtze river dolphin, until recently one of the most endangered species on the planet, has been declared officially extinct following an intensive survey of its natural habitat. The freshwater marine mammal, which could grow to eight feet long and weigh up to a quarter of a tonne, is the first large vertebrate forced to extinction by human activity in 50 years, and only the fourth time

an entire evolutionary line of mammals has vanished from the face of the Earth since the year 1500. Conservationists described the extinction as a 'shocking tragedy' yesterday, caused not by active persecution but accidentally and carelessly through a combination of factors including unsustainable fishing and mass shipping. In the 1950s, the Yangtze river and neighbouring watercourses had a population of thousands of freshwater dolphins, also known as Baiji, but their numbers have declined dramatically since China industrialized and transformed the Yangtze into a crowded artery of mass shipping, fishing and power generation.

All five of these key problems—energy supply and demand, petropolitics, climate change, energy poverty, and biodiversity loss—have been building for years. But they all reached a critical mass some time shortly after the year 2000. Two thousand years ago, the world went from B.C.E. to C.E. Well, I have a gut feeling that one day historians will look back and conclude that December 31, 1999, was not simply the end of a century, not simply the end of a millennium, but the end of the period we called the common era—and that January 1, 2000, was actually the first day of a new era.

It was day one, year one, of the Energy-Climate Era.

It was 1 E.C.E.

Yes, we're somewhere new. Human beings have never faced this intense combination of energy-driven and climate-driven problems before. When I think about what it means—in the deepest sense—to have entered the Energy-Climate Era, I am reminded of something Bill Collins, one of the top climate modelers at the Lawrence Berkeley National Laboratory in California, said to me after showing me a supercomputer-aided simulation of climate change over the next century. It is a shocking animation to watch. The warm parts of the planet appear in red and they just keep getting redder and redder as the century unfolds on the computer-generated planet—reaching average temperature levels by 2100 that no humans have ever lived through before. Collins summed it all up like the good scientist he is: "We're running an uncontrolled experiment on the only home we have."

FIVE

Our Carbon Copies
(or, Too Many Americans)

ENERGY AND RESOURCE SUPPLY AND DEMAND

Affluenza is a term used by critics of consumerism, a portmanteau of affluence and influenza. Sources define this term as follows:

affluenza, n. a painful, contagious, socially transmitted condition of overload, debt, anxiety and waste resulting from the dogged pursuit of more. (de Graaf)

affluenza, n. 1. The bloated, sluggish and unfulfilled feeling that results from efforts to keep up with the Joneses. 2. An epidemic of stress, overwork, waste and indebtedness caused by the pursuit of the American Dream. 3. An unsustainable addiction to economic growth. (PBS)

—Wikipedia

In the fall of 2007, I visited two cities you may have never heard of—Doha and Dalian. They are two cities you should know about if you want to understand how and why the meeting of flat and crowded has helped tip us over into the Energy-Climate Era. Doha is the capital of Qatar, a tiny peninsular state off the east coast of Saudi Arabia. Population: around 450,000. Dalian is in northeast China and is known as China's Silicon Valley, because of its software parks, verdant hillsides, and tech-savvy mayor, Xia Deren. Population: around six million. I have gone to both cities several times, so I knew them pretty well, but I had not been to either one for over three years when I happened to visit them two weeks apart.

I barely recognized them.

In Doha, since I had been there last, a skyline that looked like a mini-Manhattan had sprouted from the sands like a big desert wildflower after a flash rainstorm. Whatever construction cranes were not working in Shanghai and Dubai must have been working in Doha. In fact, there were so many cranes poking up through the city skyline, it looked like Doha needed a haircut. This once-sleepy Persian Gulf port had given birth to a whole extended family of glass-and-steel skyscrapers, in various states of construction, thanks to a sudden massive injection of oil and gas revenues.

The Dalian I knew already had a mini-Manhattan. But when I returned, I saw that it had given birth to another; this one included a gleaming new convention complex built on a man-made peninsula: the Dalian Xinghai Convention & Exhibition Center, said to be the biggest in Asia. It was, indeed, bigger, more luxurious, and more whiz-bang modern than any convention center I've ever visited, and it is located in just one of the forty-nine cities in China with over one million people — forty-seven of which you've probably never heard of.

But this, alas, is not a tale of tourism. It's a tale of energy consumption in a flat world, when so many more people are starting to prosper, consume energy, and emit carbon dioxide at the same levels as Americans. Seeing Doha and Dalian made me worry that we'll never get our collective arms around climate change. Can you imagine how much energy all these new skyscrapers in just two cities you've never heard of are going to consume and how much CO_2 they, and the vehicles going to and from them, are going to emit? I hardly can.

I'm glad that many people in the United States and Europe have switched from incandescent lightbulbs to long-lasting compact fluorescent lightbulbs in their homes. That has saved a lot of kilowatts of energy. But the recent growth in Doha and Dalian just ate all those energy savings for breakfast. I'm glad that many people are buying hybrid cars. But Doha and Dalian devoured all those gasoline savings before noon. I'm glad that the U.S. Congress decided to boost U.S. mileage-per-gallon requirements up to European levels by 2020. But Doha and Dalian will have those energy savings for lunch — maybe just as the first course. I'm glad that solar and wind power are "soaring" toward 2 percent of U.S. energy generation, but Doha and Dalian will guzzle all those clean electrons for dinner. I am thrilled that people are now doing the "twenty green things" to save energy suggested by their favorite American magazine. But Doha and Dalian will snack on all those good intentions like popcorn before bedtime.

Doha and Dalian show what happens when flat meets crowded. Not only will the world's population grow from around three billion in 1955 to a projected nine billion by 2050, but—much, much more important—we will go from a world population in which maybe one billion people were living an "American" lifestyle to a world in which two or three billion people are living an American lifestyle or aspiring to do so. Remember: the metric to watch is not the total number of people on the planet—it's the total number of "Americans" on the planet. That is the key number and it has been steadily rising.

I certainly don't blame the citizens of Doha or Dalian for aspiring to an American lifestyle or for opting to build it on the same cheap-fossil-fuel foundation that we did. We invented that system. We exported it. Others are entitled to it every bit as much as we are, if not more, since we've been enjoying this kind of growth and consumption for decades and others are just getting their first taste of it. Growth is not negotiable, especially in a flat world where everyone can see how everyone else is living. To tell people they can't grow is to tell them they have to remain poor forever.

As an Egyptian cabinet minister remarked to me: It is like the developed world ate all the hors d'oeuvres, all the entrees, and all the desserts and then invited the developing world for a little coffee "and asked us to split the whole bill." That's not going to happen. The developing world will not be denied.

We Americans are in no position to lecture anyone. But we are in a position to know better. We are in a position to set a different example of growth. We are in a position to use our resources and know-how to invent the renewable, clean power sources and energy efficiency systems that can make growth greener. Both Europe and Japan have demonstrated that it is possible to live a middle-class lifestyle with much less consumption. In a world that is both flat and crowded, if we, as Americans, do not redefine what an American middle-class lifestyle is—and invent the tools and spread the know-how that enable another two or three billion people to enjoy it in a more sustainable fashion—we will need to colonize three more planets. Because we are going to make planet earth so hot, and strip it so bare of resources, that nobody, including us, will be able to live like Americans one day.

"It took all of human history to build the seven-trillion-dollar world economy of 1950; today economic activity grows by that amount every decade," notes Yale's James Gustave Speth in *The Bridge at the Edge of the World*. "At current rates of growth, the world economy will double in size in a mere fourteen years."

"Americans" are popping up all over now—from Doha to Dalian and from Calcutta to Casablanca to Cairo, moving into American-style living spaces, buying American-style cars, eating American-style fast food, and creating American levels of garbage. The planet has never seen so many Americans.

Cities all over the world have caught America's affluenza—surely one of the most infectious diseases ever known to man. Tom Burke, a founding director of E3G—Third Generation Environmentalism, a nonprofit green consultancy—has invented a whole new unit of measure to illuminate the problem. He calls it the "Americum." Yes, think of America as a unit of energy. So one "Americum," as Burke puts it, "is any group of 350 million people with a per capita income above $15,000 and a growing penchant for consumerism." For many years, there were only two Americums in the world, says Burke—one in North America and another in Europe, with small pockets of Americum-style living in Asia, Latin America, and the Middle East.

"Today," he notes, "there are Americums taking shape all over the planet." China has given birth to one Americum and is pregnant with a second, which is due in 2030. India has one Americum now and also has another on the way, also due by 2030. Singapore, Malaysia, Vietnam, Thailand, Indonesia, Taiwan, Australia, New Zealand, Hong Kong, Korea, and Japan constitute another Americum. Russia and Central Europe are nurturing another Americum, and parts of South America and the Middle East still another. "So, by 2030," says Burke, "we will have gone from a world of two Americums to a world of eight or nine."

These are America's carbon copies.

While in Dalian, I met up with my friend Jack Hidary, a young New York–based Internet and energy entrepreneur. He told me about a tour he had just taken, with his official Chinese hosts, to the nearby port of Dayao, Dalian's gateway to the Pacific. He toured the new port complex built by the Chinese government with help from Norway and Japan. It included China's largest crude oil terminal—a stainless-steel forest of oil and gas pipelines, storage tanks, and oil tankers flying Middle East flags.

"I just looked at that and turned to my Chinese hosts and said, 'Oh my God, you've copied us—why have you copied us?'" Hidary recalled.

"'You didn't do it with telephony. You leapfrogged us with cell phones. There's only 5 percent landline penetration in China. So why did you copy us here?' I was so depressed. They saw what we did and they could have taken a detour around our pothole and they didn't."

There is still time for China and others to adopt a different approach, but, again, it is unlikely to happen unless we show them the way. This is more urgent than you might imagine, because if the currently developing world locks in American-style consumption, building, and transportation patterns, we will be living with, and limited by, the energy and climate implications for decades.

We have been limited before in history by the logic of disease or hunger or war, but never by "the ecological logic of capitalism," argues Jeff Wacker, the futurist for Electronic Data Systems Corporation. You know that you are in the Energy-Climate Era when the eco-logic of capitalism becomes an important, if not the most important, restraint on our growth.

"Our prosperity is now threatened by the very foundation of that prosperity"—the nature of American capitalism, said Wacker. "We have to fix the foundation before we can live in the house again. China's foundation cannot be the same foundation we built America on. And America's foundation can no longer be the same. We have reached the physical limits of building on this foundation. It has to be a different foundation."

The problem is that we have not invented that new foundation yet.

W hat exactly does it look like when crowded meets flat? It looks like the arrival terminal at Shanghai airport when I landed there in 2006 on a reporting trip and had to wait in the passport line for almost ninety minutes to get my passport stamped and visa checked. I stood in that line, crushed between traveling Chinese citizens and visiting foreign business types, many of whom seemed barely able to wait to get into the country and start engaging in extreme capitalism. Every other person on the passport line was already on his or her cell phone or PDA. I felt naked without one, as if I had arrived at summer camp without my toothbrush. Not only is China not a Communist country anymore—it may now be the world's *most capitalist* country in terms of the sheer determination and enthusiasm of the people there.

Indeed, I believe history will record that it was Chinese capitalism that put the last nail into the coffin of the postwar European welfare state. France can no longer sustain a thirty-five-hour workweek or Europe its lavish social safety nets, because of the rising competition from low-wage, high-aspiration China and India. It is hard for France to maintain a thirty-five-hour workweek when China and India have invented a thirty-five-hour workday.

When you unleash that much capitalist energy from so many people, the effect on our natural resources can be staggering. In the southern Chinese city of Shenzhen, a single Sam's Club, part of the Walmart family of stores, sold roughly 1,100 air conditioners in one hot weekend in 2006. I would bet that is more than some Sears stores in the United States sell during a whole summer.

And it is not just the numbers that have gotten big. I play a mental game with myself now whenever I am stuck in traffic in Beijing. I look at the office buildings out the car window—which are both enormous and often architecturally stunning—and I count the ones that would be tourist attractions if they were in Washington, D.C., but are just lost in the forest of giant buildings that is Beijing today. No exaggeration: Beijing must have thirty office buildings today that are so gigantic, so supersized, and so laden with ultramodern design features that if they were in Washington, you would insist on taking your out-of-town guests to see them on Thanksgiving weekend, along with the White House and the Washington Monument.

And now that trend is moving to private homes. Consider this story from *The Wall Street Journal* (October 19, 2007): "Let 100 McMansions Bloom," by Geoffrey A. Fowler.

BEIJING—On a tour of the model homes in Palais De Fortune, sales manager Cai Siyu points out features one might expect in any French-style chateau. There are sculptures of cherubs adorning the front gate, a Swarovski crystal chandelier hanging above a sweeping central staircase, and a maid in a lace-ruffled uniform waiting at the front door. Next door, just 33 feet away, another miniature Versailles rises out of the Beijing smog, and down the road there are 172 more just like it. The sight is a jarring reminder that this gated community, where houses cost about $5 million and measure approximately 15,000 square feet, isn't in France. It's one of the most exclusive, if architecturally incongruous, neighborhoods in China . . . Today, two decades after the post-Mao economic reforms that transformed the country—there are 106 Chinese billionaires, according to the Hurun Report rich list— many Chinese still don't like to talk about their wealth. But they're not ashamed to show it off. The lavish, granite-clad homes in the 82-acre Palais De Fortune embody new China's infatuation with foreign lifestyles, or, at least, its image of them. "Our developers went to France to study the style," Mr. Cai says. During the model-home tour, he shows off the gleaming white "Western style" kitchen, which features a coffee maker, a wine rack, an oven and other appliances, plus a bowl of plastic fruit. Palais De Fortune, notes the marketing brochure, "represents the lifestyle of top rich families around the world."

In August 2007, the Venetian hotel on the Chinese island of Macau, the world's biggest casino, opened its doors and was flooded by gamblers eager to get to its tables. *The Economist* (September 1, 2007) described the new casino this way:

The enormous building, Asia's largest, required 20,000 construction workers and 3m sheets of gold leaf. Running it takes 16,000 employees and enough power for 300,000 homes . . . The Venetian has 870 tables and 3,400 slot machines in the world's largest gambling hall, which is encircled by 350 shops, more retail space than any Hong Kong mall . . . [all aimed to attract] enthusiastic Chinese punters.

And remember, we are just at the beginning of the meeting of flat and crowded. Wait until China grows a little richer—and the law of large numbers starts to kick in on the tourism side. In *Foreign Affairs* (September 7–October 7, 2007), Elizabeth C. Economy, an expert on China's environment, offered a quick catalog of where our Chinese carbon copy is headed:

Chinese developers are laying more than 52,700 miles of new highways throughout the country. Some 14,000 new cars hit China's roads each day. By 2020, China is expected to have 130 million cars, and by 2050—or perhaps as early as 2040—it is expected to have even more cars than the United States . . .

China's grand-scale urbanization plans will aggravate matters. China's leaders plan to relocate 400 million people—equivalent to well over the entire population of the United States—to newly developed urban centers between 2000 and 2030. In the process, they will erect half of all the buildings expected to be constructed in the world during that period. This is a troubling prospect considering that Chinese buildings are not energy efficient—in fact, they are roughly two and a half times less so than those in Germany. Furthermore, newly urbanized Chinese, who use air conditioners, televisions, and refrigerators, consume about three and a half times more energy than do their rural counterparts.

In 2006, more than thirty-four million Chinese traveled abroad, a 300 percent increase from the year 2000, according to *Foreign Policy* (July–August 2007). By 2020, 115 million Chinese are expected to vacation overseas, which will make them the largest bloc of tourists in the world and will certainly drive more airplane travel, hotel bookings, gasoline use, and CO_2 emissions. On February 22, 2008, the Salon.com aviation expert Patrick Smith noted that "in countries like China, India and Brazil, emerging middle classes have spawned the birth of scores of new airlines. China alone intends to construct more than forty large airports over the next several years. In the United States, the number of annual airline passengers, already approaching a billion, is anticipated to double by 2025. Greenhouse gases from planes could rise to as much as five times current levels."

Again, we can hardly blame the Chinese people for wanting to enjoy the same smorgasbord of life's treats that Americans and other Westerners have. I simply share these stories to underscore the consumption volcano that is erupting in the former Communist and socialist worlds after people's desires were artificially suppressed for so many years.

Communism and socialism were systems of restraint—both by design and through their inefficiency. By design, Communist governments substituted planned economic development for growth through a market-incentive system. In the red old days, there were basically just three stores in Moscow—bread, milk, and meat—and virtually no private automobiles. As a result, it was a relatively low-impact society in terms of energy consumption. By implementation, Communist economies were corrupt, inefficient, and not very productive, and this also restricted everything from their people's energy consumption to their caloric intakes. While it is true that state-owned Soviet and Chinese industries paid little heed to the environment, and their dirty, energy-gulping factories did enormous damage to their air, land, forests, and water, the damage was relatively—*relatively*—mild because their overall pulse of economic activity and development was limited compared to the West's. Anyone who has visited Moscow regularly over the years can tell you that. When I went there for the first time as a student back in 1977, I was struck by the contrast between the incredibly wide boulevards in Moscow, especially around Red Square in the center of town, and the virtual absence of cars. Not anymore. When I visited Moscow in 2007, thirty years later, there were so many cars on those wide boulevards that you could barely move. A city that was built for 30,000 cars, and which ten years ago had 300,000 cars, today has 3,000,000 cars and a ring of new suburbs that Muscovites commute to and from every day. The day I left town on my last visit, my colleagues in the Moscow bureau told me to depart my hotel near Red Square "four hours" before my flight to London was due to take off. How could that be, I thought, when it had always taken me only thirty-five minutes to go by car from Red Square to Sheremetyevo Airport?

Just in case, I took their advice. I left the Marriott hotel at 4:20 p.m. for the 8:25 flight. The road to the airport, which, when I first visited in the 1970s, and even into the early 1990s, was largely undeveloped, now looked almost indistinguishable from the road to any American airport—lined with McDonald's outlets, big-box stores like Ikea, and shopping centers, and jammed with cars heading for the suburbs. I arrived at the airport at 7:10 p.m.—almost three hours later—just barely enough time to get through customs and board the flight. And here's the kicker: There wasn't even a traffic accident along the route. There was just one long traffic jam.

Even a country like India is now groaning under a powerful new growth trend. After independence, from about 1950 to 1980, India's leaders instituted a socialist-style planned economy, with a dose of free-market capitalism on the side, persuaded that what came to be called the "Hindu rate of growth"—3.5 percent a year—was sufficient. They did so even though that rate of growth barely kept ahead of India's 2.5 percent annual population growth rate, and didn't leave much in the way of rising living standards for most of its people.

Although India, as a democracy, has been slower to take advantage of the collapse of socialist ideology and the flattening of the world than China has, it is catching up fast. India has almost tripled the old Hindu rate of growth and is now motoring along at around 9 percent a year. The impact this is having on both the buying power and building power of the Indian economy is staggering, as illustrated through some revealing comparisons by the Indian economics writer Salil Tripathi on the *Guardian Unlimited* Web site (June 13, 2006):

> To put Indian growth in perspective: when it grew at 7.5% last year, India's income rose by an amount higher than the total income of Portugal ($194 billion), Norway ($183 billion), or Denmark ($178 billion) that year. It was the equivalent of adding a rich country's economy to a very poor one . . . What it also means is that even though India added 156 million more people to its population during that decade—a figure combining the total populations of Britain, France and Spain put together—during that period, the number of poor people in India actually fell by 37 million, or the size of Poland. Had the poverty level remained the same, there would have been 361 million poor in India. Instead, the Indian economy had lifted 94 million people out of absolute poverty during that period—that's 12 million more people than the entire population of Germany, the most populous state in the European Union.

Ho-hum: add a Germany here, a Poland there—all in fifteen years . . .

When you visit India today, you can literally see and touch the rise in living standards happening around you, which is beautiful—as long as you're not in a car caught in traffic. In Hyderabad in October 2007, I was going by car through the city's busy downtown when we passed a group of about fifty men sitting cross-legged at the foot of what looked to be a new bridge. A Hindu priest in a colorful outfit was walking among them, swinging a lantern with burning coconut shells and reciting some chants (an Indian friend in the car with me explained) to bring good tidings to the people who would travel on that bridge. Local politicians had also gathered around the ceremony for a photo op. They were dedicating a just-completed overpass that would lift traffic off the streets of Hyderabad and ease the gridlock. The overpass was two years in the making. I was happy to see the progress. Over breakfast at my hotel the next morning, I was flipping through the *Sunday Times of India* (Hyderabad edition, October 28, 2007) when my eye caught a color photograph of totally gridlocked traffic—motor scooters, buses, cars, and yellow three-wheeled motorized rickshaws, all knotted together.

The headline over the picture read: "No flying over, only snarls." The caption read: "Traffic ends in bottleneck on the Greenlands flyover which was opened in Hyderabad on Saturday. On day one, the flyover was chock-a-block with traffic, raising questions over the efficacy of the flyover in reducing vehicular congestion."

That was my overpass! In one day, an overpass that had taken two years to build was devoured by India's growth without a burp. Now that India's Tata Group has started mass-producing a $2,500 four-passenger car I shudder to think what that bridge looks like today.

Sheila Dikshit, chief minister of the Indian capital territory of Delhi, once told a conference of the World Economic Forum and the Confederation of Indian Industry about what it was like to try to run a city of sixteen million inhabitants that attracts 500,000 new migrants every year: "Each one of them, when they live in Delhi, they want more water, more power, they want more wages, more oil." The article went on to say that no Indian politician dared to deny their people cheap fuel, noting that in the fiscal year 2007, "the Indian government will spend an estimated $17.5 billion, or 2 percent of national output, on fuel subsidies—because it refuses to pass on the greatly increased world price of energy to its citizens" out of fear of a political backlash (*The Financial Times*, December 6, 2007).

Don't think this phenomenon is confined to just the hot economies of China, Russia, and India. In June 2008, I visited the thousand-acre olive farm owned by Khalil Nasrallah and Sarah Gauch, located on the Cairo-Alexandria highway, about thirty miles from the Pyramids. Khalil, a Lebanese entrepreneur, had bought this property in 1991. He later met Sarah, an American freelance writer and journalist, and they married and had children, setting up homes both in Cairo and out on the farm.

"This is what it looked like when we first came here," said Khalil, opening a photo album to a page with a view from their roof. What I saw was the green swatch of his olive farm surrounded by empty desert on both sides. There wasn't even a water well here when they arrived. Khalil bought the land on spec and discovered the water later—abundant water. "We were really out here alone," he says wistfully.

When you go up to the roof of their desert home today, "alone" is not the word that comes to mind.

Khalil and Sarah are now basically surrounded by gated communities filled with McMansions on quarter-acre lots—gated communities with names like Moon Valley, Hyde Park, Richmont, Riviera Heights, and Beverly Hills. The one immediately to his right has a ninety-nine-hole golf complex. There is a French-based Carrefour big-box store and modern supermarket around the corner. Over the horizon to the left is another gated community and beyond that another golf course. They are all populated by Egyptians who have worked hard and made money in the Gulf or who are part of the globalized business class in Cairo. They are entitled to their golf courses and McMansions as much as Americans living in Palm Desert, California, are. But the energy and water implications of all these new gated communities is one reason the Middle East is increasingly consuming, rather than exporting, so much of its own oil.

What Khalil is worried about is the water. A ninety-nine-hole golf complex drinks a lot of H_2O. "I am worried about the day when my engineer is going to call me up and say we have a problem with the well and don't have enough water," said Khalil. "So far the drop is only one meter."

It used to be dead quiet at night out here in the desert, he added, but not anymore. "Sometimes at night we are sleeping here and we are kept up by people having parties at four a.m.," said Khalil. "We are four kilometers away but [in the open desert] we now hear it."

Sarah came to the Middle East, like so many journalists of my generation, attracted by the unique sights, sounds, people, and dramas of the region. She never anticipated that America would follow her—to Cairo, maybe, but not out into the desert. "The last thing I would want to live in is an American suburb in the Egyptian desert," she mused.

When I put all these stories and numbers together, the image that comes to mind is a monster truck. That is today's global economy: a monster truck with the gas pedal stuck, and we've lost the key. Nobody can turn it off. Yes, in India and China some 200 million people have emerged from poverty in the last thirty years, most of them moving from low-impact village life to middle-class life in urban areas. But, as economists point out, there are still 200 million behind them, and another 200 million behind them . . . all waiting their turn. Their governments will not be able to deny them, and they will not deny themselves, an American style of life.

In a flat world, where every country has some form of market economy and everyone can see how everyone else is living, "no one can turn off the growth machine," said Nandan Nilekani, co-chairman of Infosys, the Indian technology giant. "It would be political suicide, and why would any politician commit suicide? So because no one wants to commit individual suicide, we are all committing collective suicide."

The energy, food, and natural resource implications of so many people becoming "Americans" are simply staggering. James Kynge, the author of *China Shakes the World: The Rise of a Hungry Nation*, tells this wonderful story:

> For me, this new trend [the rise of China] reached its crescendo in the several weeks beginning in mid-February 2004, when, slowly at first but with mounting velocity, manhole covers started to disappear from roads and pavements around the world. As Chinese demand drove up the price of scrap metal to record levels, thieves almost everywhere had the same idea. As darkness fell, they levered up the iron covers and sold them to local merchants who cut them up and loaded them onto ships to China. The first displacements were felt in Taiwan, the island just off China's southeast coast. The next were in other neighbors, such as Mongolia and Kyrgyzstan. Soon the gravitational pull of a resurgent "Middle Kingdom" . . . was reaching the farthest places. Wherever the sun set, pilferers worked to satisfy China's hunger. More than 150 covers disappeared during one month in Chicago. Scotland's "great drain robbery" saw more than a hundred vanish in a few days. In Montreal, Gloucester and Kuala Lumpur, unsuspecting pedestrians stumbled into holes.

Amusing as it is, this story reflects one of the most fundamental forces driving us into the Energy-Climate Era: "This is the first time in human history that economic growth has become the prerogative of most people on the planet," said Carl Pope, executive director of the Sierra Club.

"That was not the case until ten years ago. This is an utterly new phenomenon." As the geographer and historian Jared Diamond has pointed out, for a long time it was simply assumed that rising population was the main challenge facing humanity. But now we understand that the effect of rising population depends on how much people consume and produce, and as the world gets flat, more and more people are going to be consuming and producing more and more.

"If most of the world's 6.5 billion people were in cold storage and not metabolizing or consuming, they would create no resource problem," Diamond noted in an essay in *The New York Times* (January 2, 2007):

> What really matters is total world consumption, the sum of all local consumptions, which is the product of local population times the local per capita consumption rate. The estimated one billion people who live in developed countries have a relative per capita consumption rate of 32. Most of the world's other 5.5 billion people constitute the developing world, with relative per capita consumption rates below 32, mostly down toward 1. The population especially of the developing world is growing, and some people remain fixated on this. They note that populations of countries like Kenya are growing rapidly, and they say that's a big problem. Yes, it is a problem for Kenya's more than 30 million people, but it's not a burden on the whole world, because Kenyans consume so little. (Their relative per capita rate is 1.) A real problem for the world is that each of us 300 million Americans consumes as much as 32 Kenyans. With 10 times the population, the United States consumes 320 times more resources than Kenya does . . . People who consume little want to enjoy the high-consumption lifestyle. Governments of developing countries make an increase in living standards a primary goal of national policy. And tens of millions of people in the developing world seek the first-world lifestyle on their own, by emigrating, especially to the United States and Western Europe, Japan and Australia. Each such transfer of a person to a high-consumption country raises world consumption rates, even though most immigrants don't succeed immediately in multiplying their consumption by 32. Among the developing countries that are seeking to increase per capita consumption rates at home, China stands out. It has the world's fastest growing

economy, and there are 1.3 billion Chinese, four times the United States population. The world is already running out of resources, and it will do so even sooner if China achieves American-level consumption rates. Already, China is competing with us for oil and metals on world markets.

Diamond points out that "per capita consumption rates in China are still about 11 times below ours," but if they just rise to our level, and no other country increases its consumption, and all national populations (including China's) remain unchanged in size and immigration ceases, the simple fact of the Chinese consuming the way we do "would roughly double world consumption rates. Oil consumption would increase by 106 percent, for instance, and world metal consumption by 94 percent. If India as well as China were to catch up, world consumption rates would triple. If the whole developing world were suddenly to catch up, world rates would increase elevenfold. It would be as if the world population ballooned to 72 billion people (retaining present consumption rates)."

Larry Brilliant, the first head of Google.org, Google's charitable foundation, worked for years in India as a medical doctor. He said he is struck by the contrast between how the older and younger generations in India think about food consumption. "You talk to the old people in India today and ask them: 'Are your kids going to be vegetarians?' They say, 'Yes.' And then you talk to the kids and they say, 'No way—we're going to eat Mc-Donald's.' Everything we are talking about is per capita, so if we have more capita—and a 40 to 50 percent increase in population is pretty much baked into the cake already—we're going to have a lot more pressure on resources." And, if present health trends continue, many of these new mouths are going to live ten years longer—so you will have more people living like Americans and living longer than ever. The Associated Press ran a story from Mexico City (March 24, 2008) about rising global food prices, which included the following anecdote: "In China . . . per capita meat consumption has increased 150 percent since 1980, so Zhou Jian decided six months ago to switch from selling auto parts to pork. The price of pork has jumped 58 percent in the past year, yet every morning housewives and domestics still crowd his Shanghai shop, and more customers order choice cuts. The twenty-six-year-old now earns $4,200 a month, two to three times what he made selling car parts."

All of this raises a simple but profound question, argues the editor of *Foreign Policy*, Moisés Naím. "Can the world afford a middle class?" he asked in the March–April 2008 issue of the magazine. "The middle class in poor countries," he noted,

> is the fastest-growing segment of the world's population. While the total population of the planet will increase by about 1 billion people in the next 12 years, the ranks of the middle class will swell by as many as 1.8 billion . . . While this is, of course, good news, it also means humanity will have to adjust to unprecedented pressures . . . Last January, 10,000 people took to the streets in Jakarta to protest skyrocketing soybean prices. And Indonesians were not the only people angry about the rising cost of food . . . The debate about the Earth's "limits to growth" is as old as Thomas Malthus's alarm about a world where the population outstrips its ability to feed itself. In the past, pessimists have been proven wrong. Higher prices and new technologies, like the green revolution, always came to the rescue, boosting supplies and allowing the world to continue to grow. That may happen again. But the adjustment to a middle class greater than what the world has ever known is just beginning. As the Indonesian and Mexican protesters can attest, it won't be cheap. And it won't be quiet.

And food isn't the half of it. The McKinsey Global Institute projects that from 2003 to 2020 average residential floor space in China will increase 50 percent and energy demand will grow 4.4 percent annually.

After China, the Arab nations and Iran have the highest rate of growth in energy usage in the developing world, largely because their abundant resources allow them to keep their domestic oil and gas prices low, and therefore their citizens use energy very profligately. The oil producers are becoming increasingly thirsty consumers. Some experts predict that the soaring rates of domestic energy usage, for consumption and industry, by Russia, Mexico, and the OPEC countries could force those nations to reduce their crude exports by between two million and three million barrels a day by the end of the decade—which in a tight global oil market will only drive prices up further.

As a World Bank expert in Iraq observed to me while I was on a visit there in August 2007: "Here, energy is taken for granted—conservation is not even on the agenda, and when you look at the planning here, there is very little critique on the environmental side. You are almost speaking a foreign language with them when you bring up environmental standards and controls. They are burning all sorts of [stuff] in all sorts of machines and putting all sorts of shit in the air and water, and nobody cares."

I don't know when we will hit the wall. But the steady rise in energy, food, and other commodity prices since 2000 is surely a sign that the world, at present levels of science and technology, is straining to supply all the raw materials for the growth of so many Americums. Without a dramatic improvement in sustainable energy and resource productivity, China, India, and the Arab world's strategy of just aping the resource-wasting development model of America is unviable. The old way is not replicable on the China-India scale in a flat world, without irreparable harm to planet earth.

"Every previous economic spurt and takeoff in history by one country or a region was nurtured by an unexploited biological commons," argues Carl Pope, referring to a region of vast untapped natural resources. "Northern Europe was taken into capitalism by the cod fishermen of the North Atlantic in the seventeenth century. Europe at the time did not have many sources of protein, until it discovered the Grand Banks fishing grounds. It was how they provided protein for all the people who left farms and moved to cities to engage in industry, textiles, and trade. Britain's fleet, by the way, was made possible by the virgin pine forests of North America and hardwood forests of India."

The Industrial Revolution in the eighteenth and nineteenth centuries, added Pope, was fed, in part, "by the American Midwest, an unexploited commons for producing grain, and by Britain exploiting India to grow tea that was shipped to China to obtain Chinese silver and silks. Parts of Africa were exploited for slaves to grow sugar in the Caribbean. [The Japanese] in the early twentieth century stoked [their] growth with tungsten from Indonesia, rubber from Malaysia, rice from China. When that failed after [Japan lost World War II], they fueled their postwar industrial revolution by harvesting all the fisheries in the world to feed the Japanese salarymen making Toyotas."

The bad news for today's rising economic powers and new capitalists is that there are few virgin commons left to fuel their takeoff into capitalism. "That is why China is now reduced to stealing manhole covers," said Pope. "Yes, it is unfair, but it's the reality."

Either they will devour themselves, or they will use globalization like a straw to suck every drop of resources out of the last corners of Africa, Latin America, and Indonesia, or, ideally, we will find a more sustainable growth model for a world that is hot, flat, and crowded.

"The good news is that there is another way to grow," argues Carl Pope. "Today we can substitute knowledge for raw materials in so many more ways." No, you can't build a building with computer bits and bytes like cement bricks and mortar, but with smarter materials and smarter designs you can build a building with a lot fewer bricks and a lot less mortar. You can build a building with tighter windows and a lot better insulation. You can make steel with so much less iron ore and so much less heat. You can make buildings that retain heat or cooling so much more efficiently. You can grow more food per acre. *All it takes is knowledge*. Innovation around sustainable energy and resource productivity is our only way out of this problem. China and India have to become much more knowledge-intensive in everything they produce much faster than the West did in its day, so they can grow with fewer resources. They are trying. But they cannot afford a 150-year learning curve, and neither can we—not when so many of them are going to be living like Americans. If they take even fifty years to get around to the best practices, said Pope, "it's all over."

So how can we encourage economic growth in a world in which natural resources are limited, not growing? One of the most innovative ways to think about this challenge is the "cradle to cradle" concept the architect William McDonough and the chemist Michael Braungart describe in their book *Cradle to Cradle: Remaking the Way We Make Things*. They argue that our current approach to recycling is that we take bigger and higher quality computers, electronics, boxes, and cars and turn them into lower quality, less sophisticated products—and then we throw them away. It is not really recycling, they say, but "downcycling"—just slow-motion waste and resource depletion. In *Cradle to Cradle*, they argue that we can and must make every TV set, chair, carpet, piece of furniture, and computer screen out of materials that can be either completely reusable in other products or completely biodegradable, so that they can be used as fertilizer. All product components, they insist, can be designed for continuous recovery and reutilization as biological or technical nutrients—"eliminating the concept of waste."

I visited McDonough in his office near the University of Virginia and he elaborated on the concept, pointing to the chair in which I was sitting: "Cradle to cradle means, in counterdistinction to cradle to grave, that we close all the cycles, so we don't just send things to landfills and incinerators, we put them into closed cycles so that we can use them over and over again . . . Like this chair you're sitting on is aluminum and fabric. The fabric goes back to soil. The aluminum goes back to industry, so nothing is ever wasted. We eliminate the concept of waste—everything is in a closed cycle . . . We look at all these materials, [and] instead of worrying about where they're going to end up in a landfill or incinerator, we design them to be completely safe, so they go back to nature or back to industry forever. And importantly, this creates a massive new opportunity for job creation—in our own country, because in the future, as labor costs begin to level out, logistics will be the most expensive thing and the local will become not only the most cost-beneficial but the necessary. So imagine, today there are 4.5 billion pounds of carpet that get thrown away every year in America. Instead of throwing it away to a landfill, shipping it to China, or incinerating it, what if it all could become carpet again because you designed a cradle-to-cradle product. Not only would you be able to change your carpet as often as you wanted without guilt, but you would be producing massive amounts of jobs in America."

One day, McDonough suggested, all appliances could be leased— refrigerators, microwaves, television sets, even all cars—and returned to their manufacturers to be completely recycled, over and over and over: not cradle to grave, but cradle to cradle. Some variation of this approach is the only viable solution for economic growth in a flat world.

Unfortunately, instead of rethinking and redesigning what it means to be an American, in many areas we Americans are still intensifying, expanding, and plain old doubling down on our old energy-guzzling model.

In November 2006, I made a documentary about energy for the Discovery Times channel. One of the sites we decided to film was Walmart's experimental "green" store in McKinney, Texas, which has its own wind turbine in the parking lot, a solar-energy system on the building's exterior, high-efficiency lighting, waterless urinals, and even a system for taking the used cooking oil from the fryers in the food department and mixing it with used automotive oil from the Tire & Lube Express for a biofuel boiler that fuels the store's radiant floor heating systems. When I asked the producer where McKinney was, she answered, "It's a suburb of Dallas." No problem squeezing in a visit, I thought. So we flew into Dallas, late in the evening, and rented a van for our whole film crew to drive out to the "suburb" of McKinney. And we drove and we drove and we drove—thirty miles north of Dallas, to be exact.

The producer was right: It was a suburb of Dallas (actually what would now be called an exurb). But it wasn't the kind of suburb I grew up in, a few minutes from downtown Minneapolis. It was a suburb in the sense that it was connected by an umbilical cord of development all the way back to Dallas. We spent much of the journey on a service road, because the highway was being expanded. But the commercial enterprises that would decorate the expanded highway were already well in place, a nightmarish neon blur of McDonald's, Pizza Huts, KFCs, Burger Kings, gas stations, motels, new apartments and town houses, more McDonald's, shopping centers, strip malls, more McDonald's—even a non-green Walmart—before we got to the experimental green one in McKinney. It was anywhere and everywhere U.S.A.

The next day—after filming Walmart's environmentally friendly store—we drove back to the airport. I spent the whole trip just staring out the window at the sprawl and thinking to myself: "We're on a fool's errand. Whatever energy this green Walmart store might save, or even a thousand green Walmarts might save, will be swamped by this tidal wave of development," which looked like it was destined to rumble all the way to the border of Oklahoma.

For all the talk about India and China's rising energy and resource use, Americans need to remember that we are still the world's greatest energy hogs by far. Our national overall energy use is accelerating, even if we are getting more productivity from each unit of energy. Take a look at the 2007 InterAcademy Council report on energy, entitled "Lighting the Way," produced by a group of scientists from a variety of disciplines.

"The amount of energy needed to keep a human being alive varies between 2000 and 3000 kilocalories per day," the study noted.

By contrast, average per capita energy consumption in the United States is approximately 350 billion joules per year, or 230,000 kilocalories per day. Thus, the average American consumes enough energy to meet the biological needs of 100 people, while the aver-

age citizen in [the other developed economies] uses the energy required to sustain approximately 50 people. By comparison, China
and India currently consume approximately 9–30 times less energy per person than the United States. The worldwide consumption of energy has nearly doubled between 1971 and 2004, and is
expected to grow another 50 percent by 2030, as developing countries move—in a business-as-usual scenario—toward an economic
prosperity deeply rooted in increased energy use.

No wonder *The New York Times* (November 9, 2007) reported that
"while demand is growing fastest abroad, Americans' appetite for big cars
and large houses has pushed up oil demand steadily in this country, too.
Europe has managed to rein in oil consumption through a combination
of high gasoline taxes, small cars and efficient public transportation, but
Americans have not." Demand for oil has grown 22 percent in the U.S.
since 1990, Margo Oge, director of the Environmental Protection
Agency's Office of Transportation and Air Quality, said in 2007. The International Energy Agency in Paris predicts that world oil demand will
grow to 116 million barrels a day by 2030—up from 86 million in 2007.
About two-fifths of the increase will come from China and India. *The
New York Times* also reported in that 2007 article that "if the Chinese and
Indians consumed as much oil for each person as Americans do, the
world's oil consumption would be more than 200 million barrels a day,
instead of the 85 million barrels it is today. No expert regards that level of
production as conceivable."

And then there is what goes on inside our bigger and bigger homes: a
chicken in every pot, an iPod in every pocket, a computer and flat-screen
TV in every other room. Peter Bakker is the CEO of TNT, one of the
biggest express-delivery companies in Europe. In 2007, the Dow Jones
Sustainability Indexes named TNT the world's number-one industrial
goods and services company in terms of energy and environmental practices. But for all the environmentally sensitive practices his company has
instituted, it might as well be running in place when you look at the current levels of growth, just in the West. When I met Bakker in China in
September 2007, just after his company won the sustainability award, he
told me this story:

"We operate 35,000 trucks and forty-eight aircraft in Europe. We just
bought two Boeing 747s, which, when fully operational, will do nine

round-trips every week between our home base in Liège [Belgium] and Shanghai. They leave Liège only partly full and every day fly back to Europe as full as you can stuff them with iPods and computers. By our calculations, just these two 747s will use as much fuel each week as our forty-eight other aircraft combined and emit as much CO_2."

All this "stuff" is starting to pile up. I was visiting my mother in Minnesota when I came across this story on the front page of the *Minneapolis Star Tribune* (November 17, 2007):

A three-day effort at the Mall of America to collect electronics for recycling was cut short Friday because of the overwhelming public need to jettison old stuff. More than 1 million pounds were collected before the company decided it was all they could handle, said an official with Materials Processing Corp. (MPC) of Eagan. The collection filled 86 trucks. The event dramatized the pent-up need for free and easy ways to discard old TV sets and computers piling up in people's basements and garages, now that it's illegal to put them in the garbage. The pressure can only build as newer and faster computers and state-of-the-art TVs prompt consumers to upgrade. "People don't know what to do with their stuff," said David Kutoff, CEO for [Materials Processing Corp.].

So guess where it ends up? The very next morning (November 18, 2007), I noticed this Associated Press report from Guiyu, China:

The air smells acrid from squat gas burners that sit outside homes, melting wires to recover copper and cooking computer motherboards to release gold. Migrant workers in filthy clothes smash picture tubes by hand to recover glass and electronic parts, releasing as much as 6.5 pounds of lead dust. For five years, environmentalists and the media have highlighted the danger to Chinese workers who dismantle much of the world's junked electronics. Yet a visit to this southeastern Chinese town regarded as the heartland of "e-waste" disposal shows little has improved. In fact, the problem is growing worse because of China's own contribution. China now produces more than 1 million tons of e-waste each year, said Jamie Choi, a toxics campaigner with Greenpeace China in Beijing. That adds up to roughly 5 million television sets, 4 million fridges, 5 million washing machines, 10 million mobile phones and 5 million personal computers, according to Choi. "Most e-waste in China comes from overseas, but the amount of domestic e-waste is on the rise," he said.

In October 2005, I was visiting Shanghai and came across a piece in the *China Daily* that caught my eye. It was a column proposing that the Chinese consider eating with their hands and abandon chopsticks.

Why? Because, the columnist Zou Hanru wrote, "we no longer have abundant forest cover, our land is no longer that green, our water tables are depleting and our numbers are expanding faster than ever . . . China itself uses 45 billion pairs of disposable chopsticks a year, or 1.66 million cubic meters of timber"—millions of full-grown trees. The more affluent the Chinese become, he added, "the more the demand for bigger homes and a wide range of furniture. Newspapers get thicker in their bid to grab a bigger share of the advertising market." In the face of rising environmental pressures, he said, China must abandon disposable wooden chopsticks and move to reusable steel, aluminum, or fiber ones, "or, better still, we can use our hands."

When flat meets crowded, it shows up everywhere. And the message to me from Zou's column was that China will not be able to be China if it continues to just copy American-style consumption.

America, of course, won't be America either.

On July 24, 1959, then vice president Richard Nixon and Soviet premier Nikita Khrushchev held a public discussion at an exhibition set up at the United States Embassy in Moscow. The exhibition included what was supposedly a typical American house, full of typical American consumer goods, affordable to a typical American family. This triggered the famous "Kitchen Debate" between Nixon and Khrushchev over whose citizens had a better quality of life, which is worth recalling for a moment:

> NIXON: There are some instances where you may be ahead of us, for example in the development of the thrust of your rockets for the investigation of outer space; there may be some instances in which we are ahead of you—in color television, for instance.
> KHRUSHCHEV: No, we are up with you on this, too. We have bested you in one technique and also in the other.

NIXON: You see, you never concede anything.
KHRUSHCHEV: I do not give up.
NIXON: Wait till you see the picture. Let's have far more communication and exchange in this very area that we speak of. We
should hear you more on our televisions. You should hear us
more on yours.

Then, a few minutes later:

NIXON: The way you dominate the conversation you would make
a good lawyer yourself. If you were in the United States Senate
you would be accused of filibustering. [Halting Khrushchev at
model kitchen in model house]: You had a very nice house in
your exhibition in New York. My wife and I saw and enjoyed it
very much. I want to show you this kitchen. It is like those of our
houses in California.
KHRUSHCHEV: [after Nixon called attention to a built-in panel-
controlled washing machine]: We have such things.
NIXON: This is the newest model. This is the kind which is built
in thousands of units for direct installation in the houses.

The message from Nixon to Khrushchev was very simple: Our
kitchens are better than your kitchens, our washers are better than your
washers, our televisions are better than your televisions, so that proves
our system is better than your system. The "American way" stood for free
markets and free elections but also for a certain way of life. Given that
outlook, it is not surprising that my generation—I am a baby boomer—
was raised on the notion that if everyone in the world could live like us,
that would be a good thing. We wanted everyone to be converted to the
American way of life, although we never really thought about the implications. Well, now we know. We know that in the Energy-Climate Era, if
all the world's people start to live like us—as growing numbers of Rus-
sians and Chinese and Indians and Brazilians and Egyptians are now
starting to do—it would herald a climate and biodiversity disaster.

Does that mean we don't want people to live like us anymore? No. It
means that we have to take the lead in redesigning and reinventing what
living like us means—what constitutes the "American way" in energy
and resource consumption terms. Because if the spread of freedom and

free markets is not accompanied by a new, more sustainable approach to how we produce energy and treat the environment—Code Green—then Mother Nature and planet earth will impose their own constraints on our way of life. That is why it is essential going forward that a Code Green strategy for sustainable growth be included in America's gift bag to the world today, right along with the Bill of Rights, the Declaration of Independence, and the Constitution. Because without it, we are not going to be free much longer—and neither will anybody else. There will be too many Americans—old-style Americans. And the earth can't handle that many of *that kind* of Americans.

——

SIX

Fill 'Er Up with Dictators

PETROPOLITICS

Russia has started a diplomatic effort to curtail the activities of the most influential election observers in the former Soviet Union, submitting proposals to the Organization for Security and Cooperation in Europe that would sharply cut the size of observation missions and prohibit the publication of their reports immediately after an election. The proposals . . . also call for forbidding observers from making any public statements about a government's electoral conduct in the days after citizens cast their votes.

—The International Herald Tribune, October 25, 2007, front page

Oil reached a record $90.07 a barrel in New York on Friday.

—Bloomberg News story in the same paper, same day, page 20

A [planned] $10bn university on the Red Sea is central to the Arab kingdom's plans for educational reform . . . The university plans to guarantee academic freedom, bypassing any religious pressure from conservative elements . . . "It's a given that academic freedom will be protected," says Nadhmi al-Nasr, an Aramco executive who is [the proposed new Saudi university's] interim president.

—Financial Times, October 25, 2007, page 6

Saudi Arabia has banned the latest issue of the Arabic-language edition of Forbes *magazine for an article about the wealth of [King Abdullah] and other Arab leaders, its managing editor said yesterday . . . "Instead of ripping out the pages of the report, the authorities decided to ban the magazine altogether," said one government official . . . Saudi authorities have twice this year ordered columns by Khalid al-Dakhil, a prominent Saudi analyst and university lecturer, to be ripped out of* Forbes Arabia.

—Same paper, same day, same page

A month after the U.S.-led coalition invaded Afghanistan in 2001, I visited the frontier town of Peshawar, a hotbed of Islamic radicalism near the Afghan border. You needed only to spend an afternoon walking through the Storytellers' Bazaar in Peshawar to understand that this was not Mr. Rogers's neighborhood. What made the visitor feel that way? Maybe it was the street vendor who asked me exactly what color Osama bin Laden T-shirt I wanted—the yellow one with his picture on it, or the white one simply extolling him as the hero of the Muslim nation and vowing "Jihad Is Our Mission"? (He was doing a brisk business among the locals.) Or maybe it was the wall poster that my Pakistani traveling companion translated as saying, "Call this phone number if you want to join the 'Jihad against America.'" Or maybe it was the cold stares and steely eyes that greeted the obvious foreigner. Those eyes did not say, "American Express accepted here." They said, "Get lost."

Welcome to Peshawar. Oh, and did I mention that Peshawar is in Pakistan? These guys were on our side.

On the way into Peshawar, I had gone with my Pakistani friend to visit the Darul Uloom Haqqania, the biggest madrasah, or Islamic school, in Pakistan, with 2,800 live-in students—all studying the Koran and the teachings of the Prophet Muhammad with the hope of becoming spiritual leaders or just more devout Muslims. I was allowed to sit in on a class of elementary-school-age boys who sat on the floor, learning the Koran by rote from texts perched on wooden holders. This was the core of their studies. Most of them will never be exposed to critical thinking or modern subjects. It was at once impressive and disquieting. It was impressive because the madrasah provided room, board, education, and clothing for hundreds of Pakistani boys who would otherwise have been left out on the streets because of the erosion of Pakistan's secular state education system. (In 1978, there were roughly 3,000 madrasahs in Pakistan; today there are over 30,000, large and small.) It was disquieting because their religious curriculum was largely designed by the Mogul emperor Aurangzeb Alamgir, who died in 1707. There was one shelf of science books in the library—mostly from the 1920s.

The air in the Koran class was so thick and stale you could have cut it into blocks and sold it like cakes. The teacher asked an eight-year-old boy to chant a Koranic verse for us, which he did with the beauty and elegance of an experienced muezzin. What did it mean? It was a famous verse, he said through a translator: "The faithful shall enter paradise and the unbelievers shall be condemned to eternal hellfire."

It was disquieting because when I asked one of the students, an Afghan refugee, Rahim Kunduz, age twelve, what his reaction was to the September 11 attacks, he said: "Most likely the attack came from Americans inside America. I am pleased that America has had to face pain, because the rest of the world has tasted its pain." And his view of Americans generally? "They are unbelievers and do not like to befriend Muslims, and they want to dominate the world with their power."

The Darul Uloom Haqqania madrasah is notorious because the Taliban leader Mullah Muhammad Omar once attended classes there, as did many other top Taliban figures. Mullah Omar never graduated, our host explained, "but we gave him an honorary degree anyway, because he left to do jihad and to create a pristine Islamic government." What I remember most about my visit, though, was a sign that was hanging high on the wall in that Koran classroom where those boys were studying. It was in English, and it said that this classroom was "a gift of the Kingdom of Saudi Arabia."

I am sure it was.

And why not? In 2006, members of the OPEC oil cartel earned $506 billion from oil exports. In 2007, OPEC income rose to roughly $535 billion, according to the London-based Centre for Global Energy Studies. In 1998, OPEC earned $110 billion for selling roughly the same quantity of oil at much lower prices. Saudi Arabia's oil income is expected to climb from $165 billion in 2006, and about $170 billion in 2007, to around $200 billion in 2008.

In my view, the mass murder on September 11, 2001, of nearly 3,000 people—perpetrated by nineteen men, fifteen of whom were Saudis—was one of those big events that illuminate a whole set of underlying trends that had been building for a long time. What it illuminated was that our oil addiction is not just changing the climate system; it is also changing the international system in four fundamental ways. First, and most important, through our energy purchases we are helping to strengthen the most intolerant, antimodern, anti-Western, anti–women's rights, and antipluralistic strain of Islam—the strain propagated by Saudi Arabia.

Second, our oil addiction is helping to finance a reversal of the democratic trends in Russia, Latin America, and elsewhere that were set in motion by the fall of the Berlin Wall and the end of Communism. As I'll explain later in this chapter, I call this phenomenon "the First Law of

Petropolitics": As the price of oil goes up, the pace of freedom goes down; and as the price of oil goes down, the pace of freedom goes up.

Third, our growing dependence on oil is fueling an ugly global energy scramble that brings out the worst in nations, whether it is Washington biting its tongue about the repression of women and the lack of religious freedom inside Saudi Arabia, or China going into partnership with a murderous African dictatorship in oil-rich Sudan.

Finally, through our energy purchases we are funding both sides of the war on terror. That is not an exaggeration. To the extent that our energy purchases enrich conservative, Islamic governments in the Persian Gulf and to the extent that these governments share their windfalls with charities, mosques, religious schools, and individuals in Saudi Arabia, the United Arab Emirates, Qatar, Dubai, Kuwait, and around the Muslim world, and to the extent that these charities, mosques, and individuals donate some of this wealth to anti-American terrorist groups, suicide bombers, and preachers, we are financing our enemies' armies as well as our own. We are financing the U.S. Army, Navy, Air Force, and Marine Corps with our tax dollars, and we are indirectly financing, with our energy purchases, al-Qaeda, Hamas, Hezbollah, and Islamic Jihad.

American energy policy today, says Peter Schwartz, chairman of Global Business Network, a strategic consulting firm, can be summed up as "Maximize demand, minimize supply, and make up the difference by buying as much as we can from the people who hate us the most."

I cannot think of anything more stupid.

The American public has certainly become aware of all these connections. You can see it in bumper stickers that have come out since 9/11: "How Many Soldiers per Gallon Does Your SUV Get?" or "Osama Loves Your SUV" or "Nothin' Dumber Than a Hummer" or "Draft the SUV Drivers First" or "America Needs an Oil Change." You can see it in the political discourse, as when President Bush (in his 2006 State of the Union address) declared that Americans were "addicted to oil."

But bumper stickers and slogans aside, the truth is that America has done precious little since 9/11 to end our addiction to oil.

We have to do better, because ending our oil addiction is not simply an environmental necessity anymore. It's a strategic imperative. We will only breathe freely—in every sense of that phrase—if we can reduce global demand for oil and gas. Our own oil dependence is behind more bad trends domestically and around the world than any other single factor I can think of. Our addiction to oil makes global warming warmer, petrodictators stronger, clean air dirtier, poor people poorer, democratic countries weaker, and radical terrorists richer. *Have I left anything out?*

Oil and Islam

Islam has always been practiced in a variety of forms. In the modern era, some are more embracing of modernity, reinterpretation of the Koran, and tolerance of other faiths—like Sufi Islam or the urban-centered, populist Islam still found in Cairo, Istanbul, Casablanca, Baghdad, and Damascus. Some strands, like the Salafiyyah movement in Islam—followed by the Wahhabi ruling family of Saudi Arabia and by al-Qaeda—believe Islam should be returned to its purest roots, an austere "desert Islam" supposedly practiced in the time of the Prophet Muhammad. It is a version of Islam that never fully embraced modernity because its roots were premodern and it never aspired to evolve. The term "As-Salaf us-Salih," or "the Salaf" for short, refers to the Prophet Muhammad's immediate companions and the two generations that followed them, who supposedly set the best example for how Islam is to be practiced. Today's followers of this fundamentalist path are called Salafis.

Before the twentieth century, the fundamentalist Salafi version of Islam had little appeal outside the Arabian Desert. Not anymore. Salafi proselytizers, funded by petrodollars from Saudi Arabia, have made a big impact on the way many mainstream Muslims interpret their faith today, as well as how they relate to the faiths of others and to both less orthodox Muslims and non-Sunni Muslims, particularly Shiites. In the hands of Muslim extremists, this oil-funded Salafism has served as the ideological justification for violent jihadism, which aims at restoring the seventh-century Islamic caliphate, and it has energized groups such as the Taliban, al-Qaeda, Hamas, and the Sunni suicide bomb squads of Iraq, Palestine, and Pakistan.

The Saudi drive to export Salafi Islam went into high gear after radical fundamentalists challenged the Muslim credentials of the Saudi ruling family by taking over the Grand Mosque of Mecca in 1979—a year that, by coincidence, coincided with the Iranian revolution and a huge spike in oil prices. As Lawrence Wright notes in his definitive history of al-Qaeda, *The Looming Tower*:

The attack on the Grand Mosque . . . awakened the royal family to the lively prospect of revolution. The lesson the family drew from that gory standoff was that it could protect itself against religious extremists only by empowering them . . . Consequently, the muttawa, government subsidized religious vigilantes, became an overwhelming presence in the Kingdom, roaming through the shopping malls and restaurants, chasing men into mosques at prayer time and ensuring that women were properly cloaked.

Not content to cleanse its own country of the least degree of religious freedom, the Saudi Government set out to evangelize the Islamic world, using the billions of riyals at its disposal through the religious tax—zakat—to construct hundreds of mosques and colleges and thousands of religious schools around the globe, staffed with Wahhabi Imams and teachers. Eventually, Saudi Arabia, which constitutes only 1 percent of the world Muslim population, would support 90 percent of the expenses of the entire faith, overriding other traditions of Islam. Music disappeared in the Kingdom. Censorship smothered art and literature, and intellectual life, which had scarcely had the chance to blossom in the young country, withered. Paranoia and fanaticism naturally occupy minds that are closed and fearful.

There are roughly 1.5 billion Muslims in the world, living in every major city. Because Saudi Arabia has enormous oil resources and is the keeper of Islam's two holiest mosques, in Mecca and Medina, it has both a unique legitimacy in the Muslim world and a unique level of resources to advance its ultraconservative brand of Islam. Never has so much wealth been given to such an extreme minority of one of the world's biggest religions, with so many long-term consequences.

Fifty years from now, when we look back at this onset of the Energy-Climate Era, we may conclude that the most important geopolitical trend to come out of it was this shift in the center of gravity of Islam—away from a Cairo-Istanbul-Casablanca-Damascus urban/Mediterranean center of gravity in the nineteenth and twentieth centuries, which tended to be softer-edged, more open to the world and other faiths, and toward a Salafi Saudi/desert-centered Islam, which was much more puritanical, restrictive toward women, and hostile to other faiths.

The rise of this more fundamentalist strain of Islam in the past two decades is by no means entirely attributable to Saudi money. A broader backlash against globalization and Westernization is also at work in the Muslim world, as well as a rejection of all the previous failed ideologies—Arab nationalism, Arab socialism, and Communism—by a new generation of Muslim youth. But Saudi money has certainly helped to fuel and consolidate this upsurge in rigidly orthodox Islam, which comes at a time when, as the *Financial Times* reported (June 4, 2008), nearly two-thirds of the Middle East's population is under the age of twenty-five and more than one in four are unemployed. Many of these frustrated, unemployed youth are finding succor in faith.

The writer William G. Ridgeway, who penned a thoughtful and provocative series of "Letters from Arabia" for the iconoclastic British research institute the Social Affairs Unit, argued in an essay (August 22, 2005) that this shift is in some ways a modern version of a long-running struggle between a puritanical desert Islam, represented by sects like the Saudi Wahhabis, and a much more cosmopolitan, woman-friendly, and open-to-ideas "urban Islam."

"Encroaching modernity has resulted in an increase in the place and power of Desert Islam in everyday society," wrote Ridgeway.

Contrary to widespread Western beliefs about the trajectory of the Middle East as a hesitant but inevitable climb to liberal democracy, the region is actually going the other way—fast. Academics call this "Islamicisation," the spread of radical Shi'a and Wahhabi beliefs and practices throughout the region. Because of this trend, the Middle East one sees nowadays is nothing like it was, say, fifty years ago. Around the 1950s, about the time oil was being discovered in the Gulf, many Muslim nations were relatively liberal by today's standards. Alcohol flowed freely, women went uncovered and there was lively public debate about "Ataturk's way," the separation of Islam and state, modernization, and dialogue with the West. The Middle East seemed to be going in the right direction.

The explosion of oil wealth in Saudi Arabia served to change all that. "Oil meant that the Saudis now had the means to change the world to more resemble them," said Ridgeway. "The mountain would come to Mohammed . . . In true puritanical style, Desert Islam has taken the spice and color out of Arab life, and it looks like doing so for a long time yet. The joys of flirtation or provocative self-expression through dress, or lack of it, are gone—all replaced by black." Ridgeway argues that the now oil-funded Saudi Wahhabi version of Islam represents "an attack on liberal urban Islam by a desert sect that was peripheral in the golden age of Arab culture or, indeed, filmmaking. Perhaps the best symbol of all that has been lost is the coquettish, slightly tipsy Arab woman so beloved of old Arab comedies. Then she was laughed at. Now she would be stoned to death."

In addition to Saudi Arabia, other conservative Gulf states—Kuwait, Qatar, and the United Arab Emirates—have also enjoyed a massive influx of oil funds, which have also found their way to more conservative charities and religious institutions, at home and abroad.

Here is what a professor friend of mine, an Egyptian who teaches in a Persian Gulf state, told me over breakfast in the Gulf in August 2007. For personal security reasons, he could not let his name be used. Saudi Arabia, he said, has had a huge impact on Islamic life all across the Muslim world. "Look at the relations between men and women. Men and women in the same family used to sit with each other in the same room. Now they are separate. Today in [the Persian Gulf] the relationship between the two sexes is sensitive. You don't know if you should shake a woman's hand or not . . . This Saudi Islamization of the region has left a very bad impact and it will take decades to fix it. If you go to university in [a Persian Gulf state] there is no mixing in education. When I was a student in Egypt, I used to sit next to a girl in class. Now both sexes exist in the same classroom, but they tend to divide [on their own]. This is not Egyptian Islam. It is the Saudi way. The worst thing is that the Saudis had the money, but Egypt was the body that practiced their ideas . . . We imported the Saudi way of life into Egypt, the dress, the books sold at the doors of mosques—these carry the same Wahhabi interpretation of Islam. Unfortunately, Egypt did not have the resources to fight back."

And it still doesn't. A story from Cairo by *Newsweek's* Middle East correspondent, Rod Nordland (June 9, 2008), made this clear:

Abir Sabri, celebrated for her alabaster skin, ebony hair, pouting lips and full figure, used to star in racy Egyptian TV shows and movies. Then, at the peak of her career a few years ago, she disappeared—at least her face did. She began performing on Saudi-owned religious TV channels, with her face covered, chanting verses from the Qur'an. Conservative Saudi Arabian financiers promised her plenty of work, she says, as long as she cleaned up her act. "It's the Wahhabi investors," she says, referring to the strict form of Sunni Islam prevalent in Saudi Arabia. "Before, they invested in terrorism—and now they put their money in culture and the arts."

Egyptians deplore what they call the Saudization of their culture. Egypt has long dominated the performing arts from Morocco to Iraq, but now petrodollar-flush Saudi investors are buying up the contracts of singers and actors, reshaping the TV and film industries and setting a media agenda rooted more in strict Saudi values than in those of freewheeling Egypt. "As far as I'm concerned, this is the biggest problem in the Middle East right now," says mobile-phone billionaire Naguib Sawiris. "Egypt was always very liberal, very secular and very modern. Now . . ." He gestures from the window of his 26th-floor Cairo office: "I'm looking at my country, and it's not my country any longer. I feel like an alien here."

At the Grand Hyatt Cairo, a mile upstream along the Nile, the five-star hotel's Saudi owner banned alcohol as of May 1 [2008] and ostentatiously ordered its $1.4 million inventory of booze flushed down the drains. "A hotel in Egypt without alcohol is like a beach without a sea," says Aly Mourad, chairman of Studio Masr, the country's oldest film outfit. He says Saudis—who don't even have movie theaters in their own country—now finance 95 percent of the films made in Egypt. "They say, here, you can have our money, but there are just a few little conditions." More than a few, actually; the 35 Rules, as moviemakers call them, go far beyond predictable bans against on-screen hugging, kissing or drinking. Even to show an empty bed is forbidden, lest it hint that someone might do something on it. Saudi-owned satellite channels are buying up Egyptian film libraries, heavily censoring some old movies while keeping others off the air entirely.

Some Egyptians say the new prudishness isn't entirely the Saudis' fault. "Films are becoming more conservative because the whole society is becoming more conservative," says filmmaker Marianne Khoury, who says Saudi cash has been a lifeline to the 80-year-old industry. From a peak of more than 100 films yearly in the 1960s and '70s, Egyptian studios' output plunged to only a half dozen a year in the '90s. Thanks to Saudi investors, it's now about 40. "If they stopped, there would be no Egyptian films," says Khoury.

At least a few Egyptians say Saudi Arabia is the country that's ultimately going to change. "Egypt will be back to what it used to be," predicts the single-named Dina, one of Egypt's few remaining native-born belly dancers. And it was a Saudi production company that financed a 2006 drama that frankly discusses homosexuality, "The Yacoubian Building." Sawiris has launched a popular satellite-TV channel of his own, showing uncensored American movies. He's determined to win—but he's only one billionaire, and Saudi Arabia is swarming with them.

An America addicted to oil has never figured out how to deal with this phenomenon. During the Cold War, notes the former CIA director Jim Woolsey, Americans got used to dealing with Soviet totalitarians, whose secular, economic-based ideology, inspired by a long-dead nineteenth-century thinker, could be contained. There weren't too many Marxists, said Woolsey, who really wanted to commit suicide for the idea "from each according to his ability and to each according to his needs." The ideology that our energy purchases are indirectly fueling today is much more malevolent and openly embracing of suicide. Wahhabi teachings, as articulated in the fatwas of their imams, are extremely hostile "with respect to Shiites, Jews, homosexuals and apostates, and horribly repressive with respect to everyone else, especially women," notes Woolsey. "They are essentially the same basic beliefs as those expressed by al-Qaeda." In other words, in purely ideological terms there is very little difference between the reigning religious tenets in Saudi Arabia (a key U.S. ally) and those of al-Qaeda (a key U.S. enemy). It's their means that differ. "Indeed," said Woolsey, "the fundamental argument between the Wahhabis and al-Qaeda is not about underlying beliefs. It is rather a struggle, a bit like that between the Stalinists and Trotskyites of the twenties and thirties, over which of them should be in charge. The hate-filled underlying views of both, however, point in the same overall direction. Many Wahhabi-funded madrasahs, worldwide, echo and perpetrate this hatred and thus promote its consequences."

No one has chronicled the impact that Saudi oil money has had in Muslim communities beyond the Middle East better than Greg Mortenson and David Oliver Relin in their classic book *Three Cups of Tea: One*

Man's Mission to Promote Peace . . . One School at a Time. The book details how this American mountain-climber-turned-educator built the Central Asia Institute, and constructed more than fifty progressive schools across rural Pakistan and Afghanistan, to fight Islamic extremism by trying to alleviate poverty and improve access to education, especially for girls. (The number of schools is now up to seventy-eight, and counting.)

"'I'd known that the Saudi *Wahhabi* sect was building mosques along the Afghan border for years,'" Mortenson says in the book.

> "I was amazed by all their new construction right here in the heart of Shiite Baltistan, [Pakistan]. For the first time I understood the scale of what they were trying to do and it scared me." . . .
>
> In December 2000, the Saudi publication *Ain-Al-Yaqeen* reported that one of the four major *Wahhabi* proselytizing organizations, the Al Haramain Foundation, had built "1,100 mosques, schools, and Islamic centers," in Pakistan and other Muslim countries, and employed three thousand paid proselytizers in the previous year.
>
> The most active of the four groups, *Ain-Al-Yaqeen* reported, the International Islamic Relief Organization, which the 9/11 Commission would later accuse of directly supporting the Taliban and Al Qaeda, completed the construction of thirty-eight hundred mosques, spent $45 million on "Islamic Education," and employed six thousand teachers, many of them in Pakistan, throughout the same period.

Mortenson said the resources he had to build his little network of progressive schools across Pakistan and along the Afghan border

> "were peanuts compared to the *Wahhabi*. Every time I visited to check on one of our projects, it seemed ten *Wahhabi madrassas* had popped up nearby overnight."
>
> Pakistan's dysfunctional educational system made advancing *Wahhabi* doctrine a simple matter of economics. A tiny percentage of the country's wealthy children attended elite private schools . . . [but] vast swaths of the country were barely served by Pakistan's struggling, inadequately funded public schools. The *madrassa* system targeted the impoverished students the public system failed. By offering free room and board and building

schools in areas where none existed, *madrassas* provided millions
of Pakistan's parents with their only opportunity to educate their
children. "I don't want to give the impression that all *Wahhabi* are
bad," Mortenson says. "Many of their schools and mosques are doing good work to help Pakistan's poor. But some of them seem to
exist only to teach militant *jihad*."

Mortenson was very clear-eyed about the extent that this phenomenon was being subsidized by our energy purchases.

"This wasn't just a few Arab sheikhs getting off Gulf Air flights
with bags of cash. They were bringing the brightest *madrassa* students back to Saudi Arabia and Kuwait for a decade of indoctrina-
tion, then encouraging them to take four wives when they came
home and breed like rabbits . . . They're churning out generation
after generation of brainwashed students and thinking twenty,
forty, even sixty years ahead to a time when their armies of extremism will have the numbers to swarm over Pakistan and the rest of
the Islamic world."

If desert Islam overwhelms urban Islam, thanks in part to our energy purchases, it will have a profound impact on the geopolitics of the
Energy-Climate Era. According to the Egyptian scholar Mamoun
Fandy, the author of *(Un)Civil War of Words: Media and Politics in the
Arab World* and senior fellow for Gulf security in the Middle East program at the International Institute of Strategic Studies in London, it will
push Islam toward the Red Sea and the Persian Gulf.

I like to say that there is the "Islam of the Mediterranean" and the
"Islam of the Red Sea." As Islam's center of gravity moves toward
the Mediterranean, which is a universe of shipping and trade and
interaction, the world of Beirut, Istanbul, Alexandria or Andalu-
sia, the religion and its community becomes more cosmopolitan,
outward-looking and engaging. As Islam moves toward the Red
Sea, close to the harsh, isolated desert and the sources of crude
oil, it becomes more frightened, inward-looking and xenophobic.

Lately, there is good news and bad news from Saudi Arabia. The good
news is that the ruling al-Saud family has begun taking real steps to try to

rein in their most virulent jihadist preachers, religious scholars, and youth, and to crack down on Saudis who either join domestic terrorist organizations or volunteer for suicide missions abroad. The bad news is that the Salafist-Wahhabi ideology is so deeply embedded in the Saudi religious/education system that trying to dial it down is no easy task. The Saudi ruling family never worried that much about the violent jihadists as long as their militancy was directed abroad. But in recent years, as the jihadists have launched attacks against Saudi institutions at home, the regime has taken the threat much more seriously.

On March 20, 2008, the BBC quoted the Saudi-owned newspaper *Asharq Alawsat* as saying that the kingdom "is to retrain its 40,000 prayer leaders—also known as imams—in an effort to counter militant Islam." That is the equivalent of a remedial course for the country's entire top clerical leadership. It also gives you some idea how deep the problem had become when you read that these same Saudi prayer leaders have been expressly called upon to stop cursing Christians and Jews. In the government-directed newspaper *Al-Riyadh* (February 1, 2008), the columnist Dr. Sa'd Al-Quway'i wrote, "The call to destroy all Christians and all Jews contravenes divine law." He added that curses "should not be directed at the infidels as a collective, but only at those who hurt the Muslims and fight them."

Are petrodollars fueling more positive trends? One does have to note that this massive influx of wealth is also stimulating some powerful forces of modernization in every oil-rich state. More women are getting educated, and not only in religious schools. Many more men and women are able to study abroad. New universities are being opened. More media are being started in the Arab-Muslim world, including some new, reasonably independent and progressive television channels and newspapers. Arab Gulf states are rapidly globalizing, hosting international conferences and inviting American and European universities to open branches in their countries. Have these American academic seedlings taken root? Not yet. But the whole trend needs to be watched.

Particularly in Saudi Arabia. Having reported from Saudi Arabia, I can say without hesitation that there are moderate and even emphatically pro-Western Saudis, who have studied in America, visit regularly, and still root for their favorite American football teams. I've met with them. I've argued with them. I enjoy their company. They deeply love their faith and are embarrassed by the excesses of Salafi-Wahhabi extremists, who have given Saudi Arabia a black eye in the world—most grotesquely in 2002, when fifteen Saudi schoolgirls died after the Muttawa would not let them out of their burning school building, or allow firemen in, because the girls' faces and bodies weren't covered according to Saudi tradition. I am ready to believe that many Saudis would prefer to see a more open Islamic nation. But they are not the ones setting religious policy and it is not their progressive outlook that is being exported to the madrasahs of Pakistan, London, Mosul, and Jakarta.

More is at stake here than how many women have to wear veils. In Iraq, young Sunni Muslims from Saudi Arabia, North Africa, and across the Arab world, who were inspired by Saudi Wahhabi imams or their ideology, have become the heart of the suicide bombing corps that has done more to hold the U.S.-led forces to a stalemate in the war in Iraq, and to poison relations between Sunnis and Shiites there, than any other factor.

"If I could somehow snap my fingers and cut off the funding from one country, it would be Saudi Arabia," Stuart Levey, the Bush administration's undersecretary of the treasury, told ABC News (September 12, 2007).

Two months later (November 22, 2007), *The New York Times* reported that data taken from a cache of documents and computers found during a raid on a tent camp in the desert near Sinjar, Iraq, near the Syrian border, had revealed that

> Saudi Arabia and Libya, both considered allies by the United States in its fight against terrorism, were the source of about 60 percent of the foreign fighters who came to Iraq in the past year to serve as suicide bombers or to facilitate other attacks . . . The raid's target was an insurgent cell believed to be responsible for smuggling the vast majority of foreign fighters into Iraq. Saudis accounted for the largest number of fighters listed on the records by far— 305, or 41 percent—American intelligence officers found as they combed through documents and computers in the weeks after the raid. The data show that despite increased efforts by Saudi Arabia to clamp down on would-be terrorists since Sept. 11, 2001 . . . some Saudi fighters are still getting through.

The article quoted senior American military officials as saying that they also believed that Saudi citizens provided the majority of financing for al-Qaeda in Mesopotamia, in order to prevent Shiites from dominating the Baghdad government. The article noted that the Sinjar documents "indicate that each foreigner brought about $1,000 with him, used mostly to finance operations of the smuggling cell. Saudis brought more money per person than fighters from other nations, the American officials said."

On a visit I made to Kurdistan in August 2007, a senior Kurdish security official remarked to me: "The Saudis are exporting their terrorists. It works two ways for them: One, they get rid of their terrorists, and two, in Iraq, [the terrorists] are killing people [the Saudis] hate, like Shiites." All that the Sunni al-Qaeda types in Iraq have to do, he added, is make "one trip to Qatar or the UAE or Saudi Arabia and they come back with bags of money."

Petropolitics helps to lubricate this whole process. The Institute for the Analysis of Global Security, a Washington-based think tank that tracks the impact of oil on geopolitics, explained how in a paper entitled "Fueling Terror," authored by IAGS's codirectors, Gal Luft and Anne Korin:

> Take Saudi Arabia, for example . . . Many of [its] charities are truly dedicated to good causes, but others merely serve as money laundering and terrorist financing apparatuses. While many Saudis contribute to those charities in good faith, believing their money goes toward good causes, others know full well the terrorist purposes to which their money will be funneled. What makes penetration and control of money transactions in the Arab world especially difficult is the Hawala system — the unofficial method of transferring money and one of the key elements in the financing of global terrorism. The system has been going for generations and is deeply embedded in the Arab culture. Hawala transactions are based on trust; they are carried out verbally, leaving no paper trail. The Saudi regime has been complicit in its people's actions and has turned a blind eye to the phenomenon of wealthy citizens sending money to charities that in turn route it to terror organizations.

"If not for the West's oil money, most Gulf states would not have had the wealth that allowed them to invest so much in arms procurement and sponsor terrorist organizations," argued the IAGS, noting that Saudi Arabia's oil revenues make up 90–95 percent of total Saudi export earnings and 70–80 percent of state revenues. "Most wealthy Saudis who sponsor charities and educational foundations that preach religious intolerance and hate toward the Western values have made their money from the petroleum industry or its subsidiaries. Osama bin Laden's wealth comes from the family's construction company, which made its fortune from government contracts financed by oil money." When I visited Pakistan and Afghanistan in the summer of 2009, U.S. military officials made it quite clear that one reason that the Taliban was still able to successfully recruit in both countries was in part thanks to drug money and in part thanks to donations coming from Saudi Arabia and elsewhere in the Gulf.

While Saudi Arabia provides the financial fuel for the global spread of Salafi fundamentalist Islam, Iran, since the toppling of the shah in 1979, has done the same for its brand of revolutionary Shiite Islam. Indeed, the two states see themselves as rivals for the role of authentic leader and model state for the Muslim world. In other words, the year 1979 gave birth to the first modern global religious arms race between an oil-rich Saudi Salafi state (Saudi Arabia is OPEC's largest oil producer) and an oil-rich Shiite revolutionary Islamic republic (Iran is OPEC's second-largest oil producer) over who would most influence the direction of the Muslim world.

Immediately after Hezbollah launched a reckless war against Israel from Lebanon in the summer of 2006, Hezbollah's leader, Hassan Nasrallah, declared that Hezbollah would begin paying out cash to the thousands of Lebanese families whose homes were destroyed by Israeli retaliations. "We will pay compensation, a certain amount of money for every family to rent for one year, plus buy furniture for those whose homes were totally destroyed," said Nasrallah. "These number 15,000." Nasrallah also vowed that his organization would help rebuild damaged houses and businesses, promising those affected that they will "not need to ask anyone for money or wait in queues" to get relief funds. To paraphrase the Allstate commercial, "You're in good hands with Hezbollah."

But wait—where would Hezbollah get the $3 billion–plus needed to rebuild Lebanon? The organization doesn't manufacture anything. It doesn't tax its followers. The answer, of course, is that Iran would dip into its oil income and ship cash to Nasrallah, so that he would not have to face the wrath of the Lebanese for starting a war that reaped nothing but destruction. Yes, thanks to then $70-a-barrel oil, Hezbollah could have Katyusha rockets and butter at the same time. When oil money is so prevalent, why not? Hezbollah and Iran were like a couple of rich college students who rented Lebanon for the summer, as if it were a beach house. "C'mon, let's smash up the place," they said to themselves. "Who cares? Dad will pay!" The only thing Nasrallah didn't say to the Lebanese was "Hey, keep the change."

For all these reasons, George W. Bush's refusal to do anything significant after 9/11 to reduce our gasoline consumption really amounted to a policy of "No Mullah Left Behind." The former CIA director Jim Woolsey put it more bluntly: "We are funding the rope for the hanging of ourselves."

Oil and Freedom

This massive transfer of wealth for oil is tilting not just the Muslim world, but also global politics at large. Wherever governments can raise most of their revenues by simply drilling a hole in the ground rather than tapping their people's energy, creativity, and entrepreneurship, freedom tends to be curtailed, education underfunded, and human development retarded. That is because of what I call the First Law of Petropolitics.

I started mulling the First Law of Petropolitics after 9/11, reading the daily headlines and listening to the news. When I heard Venezuela's president, Hugo Chávez, telling British prime minister Tony Blair to "go to hell" and telling his supporters that the U.S.-sponsored Free Trade Area of the Americas coalition "can go to hell" too, I couldn't help saying to myself: "I wonder if the president of Venezuela would be saying all these things if the price of oil today were $20 a barrel rather than $60 or $70 a barrel and his country had to make a living by empowering its own entrepreneurs, not just drilling holes in the ground!"

As I followed events in the Persian Gulf during the past few years, I also noticed that the first Gulf state to hold a free and fair parliamentary election, in which women could run and vote, was Bahrain, the tiny island state off the east coast of Saudi Arabia. Bahrain was also the first Gulf state to hire McKinsey & Company to design an overhaul of its labor laws to make its people more productive, more employable, and less dependent on imported labor, and the first Gulf state to sign a free-trade agreement with the United States. Bahrain's king and his advisers minced no words about the objectives: to break the culture of dependency on the oil welfare state that had dominated their economy since independence in 1971, to link wage increases to increases in productivity, and to put an end to the practice of starting a manufacturing business by importing five hundred low-wage workers from India or Bangladesh—which meant that a Bahraini factory was supporting the owner's family very well, along with the families of five hundred workers from South Asia, but not supporting any Bahraini workers or their families. Bahrain, which is a constitutional monarchy with a king and an elected parliament, also overhauled its education system, creating a program to retrain all its teachers and establishing a new system of polytechnics to impart vocational skills to young Bahrainis who might not want to go to college. Bahrain also opened itself more than ever to foreign direct investment from abroad and privatization of state-supported industries at home in order to stimulate real competition between firms within Bahrain—and to differentiate its economy from the forms of economic "competition" elsewhere in the Gulf, which usually consists of two government-financed companies supposedly competing with each other.

Now why was all this happening in Bahrain in the middle of the 2007 oil boom? Because Bahrain was not only the first Persian Gulf country to discover oil, in 1932; it was, more important, *the first Gulf oil state to start running out of oil*, around 1998. Not surprisingly, Bahrain's first public debate about corruption was in 1998, when crude oil prices fell to below $15 a barrel.

Unlike all its oil-rich neighbors, Bahrain in the 1990s could practically mark the day on the calendar when it would have no more oil revenue to rely upon, so it had no choice but to nurture and exploit the talents of its people instead. I couldn't help asking myself: "Could that just be a coincidence? The first Gulf state that runs out of oil is also the first to explore all these political and economic reforms?" I don't think it was a coincidence at all. Also, when I looked across the Arab world, and saw a popular democracy movement in Lebanon evicting Syria's occupying army, I couldn't help saying to myself: "Is it an accident that the Arab world's first and only real democracy—Lebanon—also happens to be one of the few Arab states that never had a drop of oil?"

The more I pondered these questions, the more it seemed obvious to me that there must be a correlation—a literal correlation that could be measured and graphed—between the price of oil and the pace, scope, and sustainability of political freedoms and economic reforms in certain countries. One afternoon over lunch with Moisés Naím, the editor of *Foreign Policy* magazine, I laid out my napkin and drew a graph showing how there seemed to be a rough correlation between the price of oil, between 1975 and 2005, and the pace of freedom in oil-producing states during those same years. When one went down, the other went up.

Think about it, I told Moisés: In 2001, when oil was $25–$30 a barrel, George W. Bush looked into Russian president Vladimir Putin's soul and saw a friend of America there. "I looked the man in the eye. I found him to be very straightforward and trustworthy . . . I was able to get a sense of his soul." But you look into Putin's soul with oil topping $100 a barrel and you'll see the Gazprom and Lukos oil companies, the *Izvestia* and *Pravda* newspapers, the parliament, and every other democratic institution in Russia that Putin has swallowed courtesy of $100-a-barrel oil. Or as one world leader, who asked not to be named, remarked to me during an interview, "When oil was $20 a barrel, Putin had 20 percent of the Russian vote; when it was $100 a barrel he had 100 percent of the Russian vote!" When oil dipped below $20 a barrel in 1997, Iran elected the reformer Mohammed Khatami as president, and he called for a "dialogue of civilizations." In 2005, with oil selling around $60–$70 a barrel, Iran elected Mohammed Ahmadinejad, who said the Holocaust is a myth.

"I guarantee you," I told Moisés, "at $20 a barrel, the Holocaust won't be a myth anymore." Moisés took the napkin, went back to his office, and showed it to his staff. An hour later he called me and asked that I turn my napkin into an article for *Foreign Policy*, which I did (May–June 2006).

On one axis, I plotted the average global price of crude oil going back to 1979, and along the other axis I plotted the pace of expanding or contracting freedoms, both economic and political—as measured by the Freedom House "Freedom in the World" report and the Fraser Institute's "Economic Freedom of the World Report"—for Russia, Venezuela, Iran, and Nigeria. This included free and fair elections held, newspapers opened or closed, arbitrary arrests made, reformers elected to parliaments, economic reform projects started or stopped, companies privatized and companies nationalized, and so on. (I would be the first to point out that this is not a scientific lab experiment, because the rise and fall of economic and political freedom in a society can never be perfectly quantifiable or interchangeable.) Here's the way the graph came out:

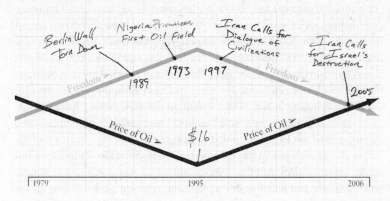

While the correlations were rough, they were also unmistakable enough for me to offer the First Law of Petropolitics, which posits the following: In oil-rich petrolist states, the price of oil and the pace of freedom tend to move in opposite directions. That is, the higher the average global crude oil price rises, the more that free speech, free press, free and fair elections, freedom of assembly, government transparency, judicial independence, rule of law, and the formation of independent political parties and nongovernmental organizations are eroded. All these negative trends are also reinforced by the fact that the higher the price goes, the less petrolist leaders care about what the world thinks or says about them. They have more disposable income to build up domestic security forces, bribe opponents, buy votes or public support, and resist international norms.

Conversely, according to the First Law of Petropolitics, the lower the price of oil goes, the swifter the pace of freedom: Petrolist countries are forced to move toward a politics and a society that is more transparent, more sensitive to opposition voices, more open to a broad set of interactions with the outside world, and more focused on building the legal and educational structures that will maximize the ability of their citizens (men and women) to compete, start new companies, and attract investments from abroad. And, naturally, the lower the price of crude oil falls, the more petrolist leaders are sensitive to what outsiders think of them.

I define petrolist states as authoritarian states (or ones with weak state institutions) that are highly dependent on oil production for the bulk of their exports and government income. In virtually every case, these states accumulated their oil wealth before they established sound and transparent institutions of governance. High on my list of petrolist states would be Angola, Gabon, Nigeria, Iran, Russia, Egypt, Kazakhstan, Kuwait, Uzbekistan, Azerbaijan, Indonesia, Venezuela, Qatar, United Arab Emirates, Syria, Equatorial Guinea, Sudan, Burma, and Saudi Arabia. Countries that have a lot of crude oil but were well-established states, with solid democratic institutions and diversified economies, before their oil was discovered—Norway, the United States, Denmark, Great Britain—are not subject to the First Law of Petropolitics.

As the accompanying graphs of four petrolist states indicate, as oil prices went down in the early 1990s, competition, transparency, political participation, and accountability of those in office all tended to go up in these countries—as measured by free elections held, newspapers opened, reformers elected, economic reform projects started, and companies privatized. But as oil prices started to soar after 2000, free speech, free press, fair elections, and the freedom to form political parties and NGOs tended to erode in these countries.

In a country like Bahrain, where the leadership used the fact that it was gradually running out of oil as a "burning platform" to drive its reform agenda, the steep run-up in oil prices from 2006 to 2008 was actually something of a problem. It forced the Bahraini reformers to reframe their argument, Sheikh Mohammed bin Essa Al-Khalifa, the CEO of the state-appointed Bahrain Economic Development Board, told me. "We had to change our argument about why we needed to reform from a 'need' to an 'aspiration.'" It was a much harder sell. One-hundred-dollar-a-barrel oil has not stopped Bahrain's reform process, said Al-Khalifa, "but it slows you down." The parliament is just a little slower in approving laws that require more open competition and less government intervention.

To be sure, professional economists have long pointed out that an abundance of natural resources can be bad for a country's economy and politics. This phenomenon has been variously diagnosed as "Dutch disease" or the "resource curse." Dutch disease refers to the process of deindustrialization that can come about as a result of a natural resource windfall. The term was coined in the Netherlands in the early 1960s, after the Dutch discovered huge deposits of natural gas in the North Sea. What happens in a country with Dutch disease is this: First the value of

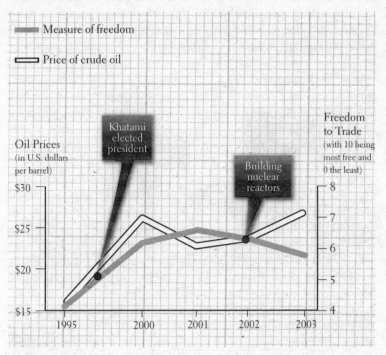

IRAN: Freedom to Trade Internationally vs. Crude Oil Prices

Sources: BP *Statistical Review of World Energy 2005* and IEA; and Fraser Institute "Economic Freedom of the World Report."

the currency rises, thanks to the sudden influx of cash from oil, gold, gas, diamonds, or some other natural resource discovery. The strong currency in effect raises the price of the nation's goods to foreign buyers, making the country's manufactured exports very noncompetitive and imports very cheap for its citizens. The citizens, flush with cash, start buying cheaper imported goods without restraint; the domestic manufacturing sector gets wiped out; and, presto, you have deindustrialization.

The "resource curse" can refer to the same economic phenomenon, as well as to the way a dependence on natural resources can skew a country's political, investment, and education priorities, so that everything revolves around who controls those resources and who gets how much money from them. Very often in petrolist states, the public develops a distorted notion of what development is all about. The people conclude

RUSSIA: Freedom House "Nations in Transit" Rankings
vs. Crude Oil Prices

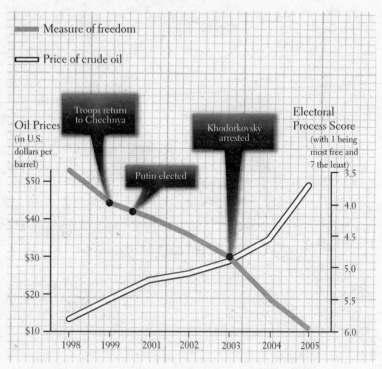

Sources: BP *Statistical Review of World Energy 2005* and IEA; and Freedom House "Nations in Transit."

that their country is poor and the leaders, or some other group, are rich—
not because the country has failed to promote education, innovation,
rule of law, and entrepreneurship, but only because someone is stealing
the oil money and depriving them of their due. Often, they are right.
Someone is stealing. But people start to think that in order to become
prosperous all they have to do is stop those who are stealing—not build a
society, brick by brick, on the foundations of better education, rule of
law, innovation, and entrepreneurship.

"If Nigeria had no oil, then the entire political equation would be different," Clement Nwankwo, one of Nigeria's leading human rights cam-
paigners, told me during a visit to Washington in March 2006. "The

VENEZUELA: Freedom House "Freedom in the World" Rankings vs. Crude Oil Prices

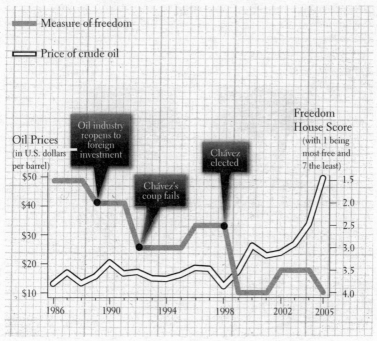

Sources: BP *Statistical Review of World Energy 2005* and IEA; and Freedom House "Freedom in the World 2005."

income would not be coming from oil, and therefore the diversification of the economy would become an issue and private enterprise would matter more and people would have to expand their own creativity." Nwankwo's remarks reminded me what a Westernized Iranian woman reporter in Tehran once said to me as we were walking down the street: "If only we didn't have oil, we could be just like Japan."

The First Law of Petropolitics tries to build on such arguments but also takes the correlation between oil and politics one step further — proposing that not only does the presence of excessive oil revenues in petrolist states tend to have broad negative effects on democratization, but so does the actual *price*. The actual *price* of oil and the actual pace of, or retreat from, democratization are roughly correlated.

NIGERIA: LEGAL SYSTEM AND PROPERTY RIGHTS VS. CRUDE OIL PRICES

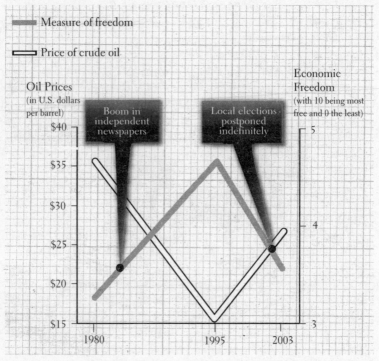

Sources: BP *Statistical Review of World Energy 2005* and IEA; and Fraser Institute "Economic Freedom of the World Report."

One of the most incisive analyses that I have come across as to why this correlation exists was a study, "Does Oil Hinder Democracy?," by the UCLA political scientist Michael L. Ross (*World Politics*, April 2001), in which he provides a detailed explanation of how and why massive oil exports and democracy usually do not mix. Using a statistical analysis from 113 states between 1971 and 1997, Ross concluded that "a state's reliance on either oil or mineral exports tends to make it less democratic; that this effect is not caused by other types of primary exports; that it is not limited to the Arabian Peninsula, to the Middle East, or to sub-Saharan Africa; and . . . it is not limited to small states."

What I find particularly useful about Ross's work is his list of the precise mechanisms by which excessive oil wealth impedes the growth of democracy. First, he argues, there is the "taxation effect." Oil-rich governments tend to use their revenues "to relieve social pressures that might otherwise lead to demands for greater accountability . . . from— and representation in—their government."

The way I like to put it is: The motto of the American Revolution was "No taxation without representation." The motto of the petrolist authoritarian state is "No taxation, so no representation, either." Oil-backed regimes that do not have to tax their people for revenue—because they can just drill an oil well and sell the oil abroad—also do not have to listen to their people or represent their wishes.

The second mechanism through which oil dampens democratization, argues Ross, is the "spending effect." Oil wealth leads to greater patronage spending, which in turn dampens pressures for democratization. The third mechanism he cites is the "group formation effect." When oil revenues provide an already nondemocratic or weak state with a cash windfall, "the government will use its largesse to prevent the formation of social groups that are independent from the state," Ross writes. In addition, he argues, an overabundance of oil revenues can create a "repression effect," because it allows governments to spend excessively on police, internal security, and intelligence forces that can be used to choke democratic movements. Finally, he argues, there might also be an antimodernization effect at work. This refers to the fact that massive oil wealth in a society tends to diminish pressures for occupational specialization, urbanization, and the securing of higher levels of education— trends that normally accompany broad-based economic development and also produce a public that is more articulate, free to organize, and endowed with multiple autonomous economic power centers of its own.

In a later study, based on data from 169 countries, Ross demonstrated why women in Middle Eastern countries continue to be undereducated, underrepresented in the workforce, and politically disempowered: oil.

"In the Middle East," Ross wrote in his essay "Oil, Islam, and Women" (*American Political Science Review*, February 2008),

> fewer women work outside the home, and fewer hold positions in government, than in any other region of the world. According to most observers, this troubling anomaly is due to the region's Islamic traditions . . . Some even argue that the "clash of civilizations" between the Islamic world and the West has been caused,

in part, by the poor treatment of Muslim women . . . This paper
suggests that women in the Middle East are underrepresented in
the workforce and in government because of oil—not Islam . . .
The failure of women to join the nonagricultural labor force has
profound social consequences: it leads to higher fertility rates, less
education for girls, and less female influence within the family. It
also has far-reaching political consequences: when fewer women
work outside the home, they are less likely to exchange information and overcome collective action problems; less likely to mobilize politically and to lobby for expanded rights; and less likely to
gain representation in government. This leaves oil-producing
states with atypically strong patriarchal cultures and political institutions.

In other words, Ross is arguing, the same high oil prices that lead to
overvalued currencies, drive massive imports, and kill domestic manufacturers—aka Dutch disease—keep women subordinate in society. In
particular, he notes, jobs in the textile and garment industries—the sort
of entry-level work that represents the first rung of the economic ladder
for poor and less educated women—disappear, as do export industries in
general, when citizens spend oil money on cheap imports. Meanwhile,
oil booms tend to lead to more construction and construction jobs, and
therefore more employment and more power, for men. Ross's study offers data indicating that when a nation's oil income goes up, the number
of women in the workforce and the number of women who gain political office both go down—other factors being equal. "These results are
consistent with the claim that oil production reduces female political influence by reducing the number of women who work outside the home,"
he writes.

Some ask why low oil prices, or no oil incomes at all, in the 1960s
didn't lead to more democratization in the Arab world back then. (Actually, countries like Egypt, Syria, Lebanon, and Iraq were much more politically liberal in the 1940s and early 1950s, before oil, than they are
today.) Answer: Between 1950 and 1989, the Cold War often worked
against democratic trends everywhere, since America was much more interested in whether a country was pro-American or pro-Soviet outside
than democratic or nondemocratic inside. Moreover, the dominant ideology and political culture in the Arab world at the time was not liberal-

ism but Arab nationalism and Arab socialism, and women's empowerment was weak to nonexistent. Also, many of the Arab military cliques
that seized power in the post–World War II Middle East *were* propped up
by an outside resource, like oil: "foreign aid" during the Cold War from
either the Soviet Union or the United States.

All that started to change in the 1980s, with population bulges, large
numbers of unemployed youth, a global information revolution, and a
real global democracy movement after the collapse of Communism.
That was when high oil prices made it much easier for regimes to buy off
their people, and low oil prices made it much more difficult.

It is hard for me to imagine that the military regimes in Egypt and
Syria could have held on as long as they have were it not for the combination of "diplomatic oil"—foreign aid from Moscow and Washington in
the Cold War—followed by aid and real estate investments from oil-rich
Gulf states and finally their own oil and gas discoveries in the 1980s and
1990s. That surplus cash has surely helped to sustain President Hosni
Mubarak in office for over twenty-five years of economic and political
stagnation in Egypt. This fact triggered a joke about Mubarak that made
the rounds in Cairo, but could have been told in many oil capitals. It was
reported by my *New York Times* colleague Michael Slackman and went
like this: "President Hosni Mubarak is on his deathbed when an aide
comes to his side and says, 'Mr. President, aren't you going to give a
farewell speech to the people?' The President opens his eyes and replies,
'Really? Why? Where are the people going?'"

When money can be extracted from the ground, people simply don't
develop the DNA of innovation and entrepreneurship. *The Jerusalem Report* (February 4, 2008) quoted an essay from the Kuwaiti daily *Al-Siyasa*
by Dr. Ahmed al-Baghdadi, a rare outspoken government critic: "What
do we actually produce?" Dr. al-Baghdadi asked his fellow Kuwaitis.
"Our oil is produced and marketed by expats. The vegetables we produce in greenhouses are cultivated and looked after by expats. The
Kuwaiti owners of these greenhouses get huge amounts of subsidies from
the government for products, which, if we imported, would cost one-
tenth of the price produced locally . . . We produce nothing, we import
everything, and we consume a lot."

That is surely one reason that there is not a single world-class university or scientific research center in the entire Arab world or Iran today. A
leading Arab businessman I know, someone who has built a services

company that actually does compete globally, once remarked to me that because of the perversions of oil money, and the way that enables governments to dominate every Arab economy, "there are many Arab entrepreneurs today, but there is no entrepreneurship in the Arab world . . . Entrepreneurs in this part of the world live off [income] coming from oil or fighting terrorism . . . There is no nurturing of talent. We imported cheap labor and exported our people. We exported white collar and imported blue collar. How do you create new wealth here? It is all still made in real estate and on government contracts. The whole process of privatization only hit when the price of oil hit $10 a barrel."

This isn't all that complicated. If you are living in a society where the easiest way to make a dollar is to steal it, or to stick a pipe in the ground, or to sit on top of a government-granted monopoly, or to get ahold of the biggest government contracts through cronyism, your smartest and most talented people will get drawn to precisely those endeavors. In short, if you make a lot of nonproductive, quasi-corrupt activities the lifeblood of your economy, you will suck the life out of it. That is precisely what we can see happening in so many petrolist states, and why so much talent there goes to waste or just picks up and goes away.

It is true in the Middle East and it is true in Russia, which, despite its huge population, has only two universities rated among the world's top five hundred. "When oil prices became higher, the reforms became slower," Vladimir Ryzhkov, a liberal Russian Duma member from Altay (and one of the few in the Duma still willing to speak out), told me on a visit to Moscow in February 2007. "Russia became a more closed country with a more state-oriented economy. Last year we saw record oil prices and not one reform. [That is the] reason Freedom House last year proclaimed Russia a 'nonfree' country. The question for you Americans is: 'When will prices go down?' It is the only hope for us Russian democrats."

Oil and Geopolitics

We thought the fall of the Berlin Wall was going to set loose an unstoppable tide of free markets and free people, and for about a decade it did just that. The proliferation of free elections around the world in the decade after 1989 made that tide very concrete. But those years coincided with oil priced in the range of $10 to $40 a barrel. As the price of oil surged into the $50–$120 range in the early 2000s, it triggered a countertide—a tide of petroauthoritarianism—from Russia to Venezuela to Iran to Sudan to Angola all the way over to Turkmenistan. The elected or self-appointed elites running these states used their oil windfalls to ensconce themselves in power, buy off opponents, and counter the post–Berlin Wall freedoms.

It is a key reason why the world is facing a "democratic recession" today, says Larry Diamond, the Stanford University democracy specialist and author of *The Spirit of Democracy*. According to Diamond, of the twenty-three nations in the world that derive a clear majority of their export income from oil and gas, not a single one is a democracy. Record high oil prices only feed that trend.

When she was Secretary of State, Condoleezza Rice would never admit that the Bush team was in any way responsible for strengthening the petroauthoritarian trends, but she was candid about how much petropolitics affected her job. As she testified to the Senate Foreign Relations Committee (April 5, 2006), "I can tell you that nothing has really taken me aback more as secretary of state than the way that the politics of energy is—I will use the word warping—diplomacy around the world. It has given extraordinary power to some states that are using that power in not very good ways for the international system, states that would otherwise have very little power.

The "warping" of geopolitics would certainly include China's embrace, in order to secure access to oil and gas, of the authoritarian government in Sudan, which has been involved in a murderous policy of repression in Darfur. It would include America's reluctance to talk frankly with Saudi Arabia about the role of its mosques and preachers in supporting suicide bombers in Iraq. Addicts never tell the truth to their pushers, I like to say. It would include Russia's attempts to plant its flag in oil-rich areas underneath the Arctic. It would certainly include the decision by the British government (December 14, 2006) to drop its Serious Fraud Office investigation into whether bribery was involved in BAE Systems' massive arms deal with Saudi Arabia. BAE is the world's fourth-largest weapons manufacturer. Under the deal, BAE sold fighter jets worth $80 billion to the Saudi air force. In the process, though, it was alleged that BAE paid almost $2 billion—yes, $2 billion—in bribes to Saudi officials, reportedly including Prince Bandar bin Sultan, the former Saudi ambassador to the United States, to help secure the huge arms contract. Then prime minister Tony Blair justified the decision to shut down the corruption investigation on "national security" grounds, explaining: "I have no doubt at all that had we allowed [this investigation] to go forward we would have done immense damage to the true interests of this country, leaving aside the fact that we would have lost thousands of highly-skilled jobs and very, very important business for British industry." This seemed to be a diplomatic way of Blair's government saying: "The Saudis told us if this investigation exposing which Saudis got which bribes went ahead, they would never buy another bullet from BAE systems. So we shut it down." It may have been the biggest, baldest oil-driven perversion of justice in a Western democracy of all time.

It is worth noting that the Saudis were not threatening to cut off oil to Britain. They were threatening to turn off the money tap—threatening not to invest in the U.K. or to bank there. And the higher oil prices are, the more money comes out of that tap. Which is why, at a minimum, perpetually high oil prices will result in a shift in the balance of economic power from the West toward the oil- and gas-producing countries—be it Russia, Venezuela, Iran, or the Persian Gulf states. Up to now, Persian Gulf–based sovereign wealth funds have played a relatively helpful role in stabilizing the Great Recession, by buying substantial stakes in some of the biggest, but most troubled, Western financial instutitions—like Citigroup—and industrial companies—like Porsche. But it is hard to imagine over time that their economic clout will not get translated politically. After all, that's what America and Britain did when they had financial clout: They used their money to advance their national interests abroad.

Post-Iraq

So what I am saying? That we need to bankrupt all these oil producers? No, I don't want to bankrupt Saudi Arabia or Kuwait or Egypt or Syria or Russia or Indonesia. That would only cause a different kind of destabilization, born of impoverishment. Besides, the price of oil is not going to drop to zero any time soon, even if we all drive plug-in hybrids. We will need petroleum-based products—from plastics to fertilizers—for as far into the future as anyone can see. But the world will be a better place politically if we can invent plentiful renewable energy sources that eventually reduce global demand for oil to the point where even oil-rich states will have to diversify their economies and put their people to work in more innovative ways.

Up until 9/11, America treated the Arab world basically as a collection of big gas stations—the Saudi station, the Libyan station, the Kuwaiti station. "Guys," we told them—it was only guys we talked to—"here's the deal: Keep your pumps open, keep your prices low, and don't bother the Jews too much, and you can do whatever you want out back. You can treat your women badly. You can deprive your people of whatever civil rights you like. You can print whatever crazy conspiracy theories about us you like. You can educate your children to be intolerant of other faiths as much as you like. You can preach from your mosques any venom that you care to . . . Just keep your pumps open, your prices low, don't hassle the Israelis too much—and do whatever you want out back."

Well, on 9/11 the United States got hit with the distilled essence of all the pathologies going on out back. That is what al-Qaeda and Osama bin Laden personify. Alas, in trying to bring democracy to Iraq, an effort I supported, the Bush administration was actually trying to collaborate with Iraqis to change what was going on out back.

Unfortunately, Mr. Bush did virtually nothing to reduce our dependence on oil, or reduce the price of oil, as part of a strategy to weaken those forces of tyranny out back and beneath the surface. He bet everything on the quick success of the Iraq invasion. No one knows how the Iraq saga is going to end. But there are two things I know for sure: One is that the need to drive reform in the Arab-Muslim world is as vital as ever—educational reform, empowerment of women, religious modernization, and more consensual politics. The other is that no matter what happens in Iraq, we, the United States, are not going to invade another Arab-Muslim country in the name of reform any time soon. We need to find another way to partner with people there to change the context out back.

I believe that the best post-Iraq strategy for driving reform in the Persian Gulf is to bring down the global price of oil and keep it down—by developing clean power alternatives—and then to count on the forces of globalization from outside, and economic pressures inside, to push the leaders of these countries to change. That's the combination of forces that stoked the reform process in Bahrain. If the price of oil were half of what it is today, these regimes would not be able to resist political and religious modernization so easily. As the Johns Hopkins University foreign policy expert Michael Mandelbaum observes: "People don't change when we tell them they should. They change when they tell themselves they must." Falling oil prices would make them tell themselves they must.

We know from history that this can work. Consider the Soviet Union.

In February 2007, I went to Moscow to give a lecture at the U.S. embassy on the subject of globalization and energy politics. Afterward, I was chatting with Vladimir Mau, the director of Russia's Academy of National Economy. I asked him if he thought that I was correct in arguing that it was $10-a-barrel oil, not Ronald Reagan, that brought down the Soviet regime. (Actually, the oil price on Christmas Day 1991, when the Soviet Union collapsed, was $17.)

Professor Mau did not hesitate. He shook his head. No, he told me, I was wrong. It was $70-a-barrel oil *followed* by $10-a-barrel oil that killed the Soviet Union. It was, he explained, the sharp rise in oil prices in the 1970s, due to the Arab oil embargo and the Iranian revolution, that deluded the Kremlin into propping up inefficient industries by overextending economic subsidies at home, into postponing real economic reforms, and into invading Afghanistan abroad—and then it was the collapse of prices in the 1980s and early 1990s that brought down the overextended, petrified empire.

Here's the exact story: The inefficient Soviet economy survived in its early decades, Professor Mau explained, thanks to cheap agriculture, grown by peasants forced into collective farms, and cheap prison labor, used to erect state industries. Beginning in the 1960s, however, even these cheap inputs weren't enough, and the Kremlin had to start importing, rather than exporting, grain. Things could have come unstuck then for the Communists. But the 1973–74 Arab oil embargo and the sharp upsurge in oil prices—Russia was the world's second-largest producer after Saudi Arabia—gave the Soviet Union a fifteen-year lease on life from a third source of cheap resources: "oil and gas," Professor Mau said. The oil windfall gave the Brezhnev government "money to buy the support of different interest groups, like the agrarians, import some goods, and buy off the military-industrial complex," said Professor Mau. "The share of oil in total exports went from 10 to 15 percent to 40 percent." This made the Soviet Union only more sclerotic. "The more oil you have, the less policy you need," he noted.

In the 1970s, Russia exported oil and gas and "used this money to import food, consumer goods, and machines for extracting oil and gas," Professor Mau said. The Soviet state extended itself and its subsidies into more and more areas, based almost entirely on oil revenues, not real manufacturing or agricultural productivity gains or tax revenues. By the early 1980s, though, global oil prices had started to sink—thanks in part to conservation efforts by the U.S. "One alternative for the Soviets was to decrease consumption [of other goods], but the Kremlin couldn't do that—it had been buying off all these constituencies," Professor Mau explained. So the Kremlin "started borrowing from abroad, using the money mostly for consumption and subsidies, to maintain popularity and stability." Oil prices and production kept falling as the Soviet premier Mikhail Gorbachev tried reforming Communism, but by then it was too late.

Yegor Gaidar, currently director of the Institute for Economies in Transition in Moscow, saw this change firsthand. Between 1991 and 1994, he was acting prime minister of Russia, minister of economy, and first deputy prime minister. In a November 13, 2006, speech to the American Enterprise Institute entitled "The Collapse of an Empire: Lessons for Modern Russia," Gaidar noted that "the timeline of the collapse of the Soviet Union can be traced to September 13, 1985. On this date, Sheikh Ahmed Zaki Yamani, the minister of oil of Saudi Arabia, declared that the monarchy had decided to alter its oil policy radically. The Saudis stopped protecting oil prices, and Saudi Arabia quickly regained its share in the world market. During the next six months, oil production in Saudi Arabia increased fourfold, while oil prices collapsed by approximately the same amount in real terms. As a result, the Soviet Union lost approximately $20 billion per year, money without which the country simply could not survive."

There is an obvious parallel between the Soviet Union at the height of its oil folly and today's Iran, argues Professor Mau. After the OPEC-led oil shock of 1973–74, the shah used Iran's oil windfall to push major modernization onto a still-traditional Iranian society. The social backlash against forced modernization produced the Islamic revolution and the ayatollahs of 1979. The ayatollahs used Iran's oil revenues to lock themselves into power by extending the state and state subsidies into all areas of life.

All of Iran's oil wealth, though, couldn't keep pace with the country's population explosion—there were about thirty million Iranians in 1979 when the Islamic revolution toppled the shah and there are over seventy million today—thanks largely to the economic mismanagement of the regime. President Ahmadinejad so mangled the Iranian economy, passing out subsidies and failing to invest in innovation and export industries, that unemployment in Iran spiraled toward 20 percent—even when global oil prices were over $140 a barrel. Because of insufficient refining capacity, Iran also found itself having to import gasoline.

From 2008 to 2009, Iran went from exporting about 2.4 million barrels of oil a day at close to $140 a barrel to exporting 2.4 million barrels a day at around $60 to $70 a barrel, and the huge drop in revenue had to have crimped the Iranian regime's spending power. According to a Dow Jones Newswire report (September 9, 2008), the International Monetary Fund has concluded that Iran needs to earn about $90 a barrel for the government to pay its bills. "Iran's break-even price is $90 a barrel," Mohsin Khan, Middle East and central Asia director at the IMF, told the Dow Jones reporter. "If prices dip below $90 a barrel . . . they would have to tighten their public expenditure policy, and probably cut subsidies, which would be an issue for the government there—the public would not be content," he added, speaking about nine months before Iran's explosive June 2009 election. (Iran is not alone with this problem. Khan forecasted a break-even price of $56 per barrel for Algeria, while the figure stood at $49 for Saudi Arabia, $33 for Qatar, and $23 for the United Arab Emirates.)

No, it was no accident that the popular "green revolution" in Iran against the country's incompetent clerical leaders—after the Ahmadinejad government stole the June 2009 election—coincided with this prolonged dip in crude oil prices as a result of the Great Recession. It was not the only reason for that post-election uprising, but it was surely a factor. Unfortunately, the same oil wealth had enabled the Islamic regime and its Revolutionary Guards to build up a very powerful domestic security apparatus and a broad network of state-owned corporations and economic collaborators, which together managed to smother the popular revolution, at least enough for Ahmadinejad and his cronies to stay in power. Yes, the revolutionaries were empowered with new technologies to organize, inform, and mobilize—Twitter, blogs, and Facebook—but the regime had the guns, and, as of the publication of this book in the fall of 2009, "bang-bang" had beaten "tweet-tweet."

I am convinced, though, that if we were able, over time, to bring the price of oil down sharply, and keep it there, the ayatollahs would face the same impossible choices that the Soviet leadership faced and that led to the collapse of Communism.

Iran's hard-line Islamists would either have to start taking subsidies away from more and more of their supporters and opponents, which would only make the ruling ayatollahs more unpopular, or have to empower Iran's human talent—men and women—and give them free access to the learning, science, trade, and collaboration with the rest of the world that would enable this once great Persian civilization to thrive without oil. Such a fundamental shift would almost certainly give birth to an "Ayatollah Gorbachev" and undermine the regime and its ideology from within. We know how that ends. "Just look at the history of the Soviet Union," Professor Mau said.

So let's be serious: Iranian democrats and reformers don't need our praise. They need the one thing we could do, without firing a shot, that would truly weaken the ruling theocrats and force them to unshackle their people: End our addiction to the oil that funds Iran's Islamic dictatorship. Yes, it would take time. It takes a lot to influence global oil prices. But America consumes roughly 25 percent of global output, so what we do really matters.

That is why launching a real green revolution in America would, over time, be the best way to support the "green revolution" in Iran. An American green revolution to end our oil addiction—to parallel Iran's green revolution to end its theocracy—helps us, helps them, and raises the odds that whoever wins the contest for power there will have to be a reformer.

And that is also why going green is no longer simply a hobby for high-minded environmentalists or some "personal virtue," as Dick Cheney once sneered. It is now a national security imperative. Any American strategy for promoting democracy in an oil-rich region that does not include a plan for developing renewable energy alternatives that can eventually bring down the price of oil is doomed to fail.

Today, you cannot be either an effective foreign policy realist or an effective democracy-promoting idealist without also being an effective energy-saving environmentalist. That's the Second Law of Petropolitics . . .

SEVEN

Global Weirding

CLIMATE CHANGE

WASHINGTON, DC— *Fall, the long-running series of shorter days and cooler nights, was canceled earlier this week after nearly 3 billion seasons on Earth, sources reported Tuesday.*

The classic period of the year, which once occupied a coveted slot between summer and winter, will be replaced by new, stifling humidity levels, near-constant sunshine, and almost no precipitation for months.

"As much as we'd like to see it stay, fall will not be returning for another season," National Weather Service president John Hayes announced during a muggy press conference Nov. 6. "Fall had a great run, but sadly, times have changed."

Said Hayes: "Frankly, we're amazed it lasted as long as it did."

Though it came as a surprise to many, the cancellation was not without its share of warning signs. In recent years, fall had been reduced from three months to a meager two-week stint, and its scheduled start time had been pushed back later and later each year . . .

Though disappointed by the cancellation, a number of Americans have admitted that the last few seasons of fall were "completely underwhelming" and often lacked the trademark mood and temperatures of earlier years.

—"Fall Canceled After 3 Billion Seasons," front-page story in the satirical newspaper *The Onion,* November 7, 2007

There have been many warning signs telling us that we have entered a new era in climate terms. Scientists point to new data— changes in global average temperature, rising sea levels, and quickening glacial melt. For me, the most telling sign was that I started asking new questions. Two in particular: "Who's making it hot?" and "Doesn't Al Gore owe us all a big apology?"

I began asking the first question shortly after Hurricane Katrina in August 2005. Like many people, I found Katrina more than just upsetting. I was upset at the number of people devastated by this unusually powerful hurricane, upset at the disproportionate way that it hit the poor and the racial disparities it uncovered, upset at the pathetic response of the Bush administration. But I also found Katrina unnerving—I found it raising as many philosophical questions as meteorological ones.

It is well known that hurricanes draw strength from heat in ocean surface waters, and at the time Katrina gathered force on its way to New Orleans the surface waters in the Gulf of Mexico were about 2 degrees Fahrenheit warmer than the historical average for that time of year. Katrina, in particular, scientists say, gained strength when it passed over the "loop current," an oceanic conveyor belt of stored solar heat that snakes through the Gulf. Many climatologists believe that Katrina's unusual ferocity was fed by the warmer waters in the Gulf of Mexico, which, they believe, are partly attributable to global warming. And that's the really troubling part.

In early 2007, I was having lunch with my friend Nate Lewis, an energy chemist at the California Institute of Technology. We were eating at the faculty club on the palm-tree-lined Caltech campus in Pasadena, and I could not resist asking Nate: "Why was Katrina so unnerving?" Nate rolled this over in his mind for a moment, sipped his strawberry lemonade, a specialty of the house, and finally answered my question with questions of his own: "Did we do that? Or did God do that?"

At first I didn't understand—and then it clicked. When hurricanes and other natural disasters hit, insurance companies and the general media often call them "acts of God." What Nate was asking was this: Have we introduced so much CO_2 into nature's operating system that we no longer know where nature stops and we start in shaping today's weather? We no longer know, he said, "what is an act of God and what is an act of man," or, to put it another way: Did we make it hot, or did He make it hot? Did we make those Gulf waters extra warm, revving up Katrina, or did God acting through nature make them extra warm? That is the big philosophical question raised by Katrina, said Lewis: "Whether soon, if not already, what we used to call acts of God will be really acts of man—or at least partially acts of man."

And if that is the case, if we are contributing to shaping the weather, said Lewis, what do we say going forward? How do we explain huge typhoons or hurricanes or unusual droughts? "Do we say: 'We made it hot. We flooded Bangladesh. We made it rain.' Is that what we will have to start to say? And who is 'we'?" America has poured more CO_2 into the atmosphere than any country. Do we say, "America made it hot"? But what if China continues building a new coal-fired power plant every other week? Do we say, "China made it hot"?

Heidi Cullen, the former climate expert for the Weather Channel, has a compelling way of framing this philosophical issue. "It used to be that an unseasonably warm day in the middle of winter felt like a gift," she once told me. "But now it feels like we're paying for it."

Now, when my pals call me to play golf a few days before Christmas in Washington, D.C., because it is 60 degrees and there's not a flake of snow on the ground, I will still take advantage of it—but I no longer think of it as something I got for free. There is an almost eerie realization now, said Cullen, that you can't tinker with nature's operating system without eventually paying for it, sometime, somewhere.

"Nature is like a big, complex symphony," said Cullen, "and the sun is like the bass drum. Its beat drives everything—from when we had ice ages to when we had warming periods. But now the influence of humans has penetrated so deeply into this symphony that we, us humans, are affecting everyday weather. It's like we are now playing a really loud lead electric guitar in nature's symphony."

This change is ironic, when you consider for how long, and how intently, the great philosophers struggled to understand nature as a system that acted according to its own laws, without human—or divine—intervention. The ancient Greeks, noted the Israeli political theorist Yaron Ezrahi, "were always worried that the gods were acting through nature. Natural disasters were seen as divine retribution and thunder was interpreted as the threatening voice of Zeus." These beliefs set in motion a philosophical movement that aimed to prove that, on the contrary, science and nature were not wars played out by gods against humans, but, in fact, autonomous natural phenomena.

"This is the origin of the modern Western notion that nature is a realm of necessary rules and laws outside of human control," said Ezrahi. "The [later] Greeks insisted on proving that nature was an independent system so that humans would not feel a double anxiety—that natural events were not something they caused. So they created the concept of nature as a system independent of human agency and indifferent to human agency." The Greeks disconnected human morality or immorality from anything that happened in nature, and one effect of this was to basically relieve human anxiety and reassure people that they did not cause the flood, the storm, or the drought by their actions.

Now human anxiety about nature is back—only instead of us asking, "Did Zeus create that hurricane because of something we did?" we are asking, "Did we create that hurricane because of something we did?" "Instead of us asking, 'Can we control the gods and thus control the weather?'" Ezrahi said, "we're now asking, 'Can we control ourselves and [thus] control the weather?'"

We are not just the objects of nature anymore; to some degree, we are now, with our global industrial activities, also subjects. We have made ourselves part of the symphony—although some people still refuse to accept that they're part of the orchestra.

And that brings me to why Al Gore owes us all an apology.

In January 2008 I moderated a discussion between the former vice president and Bono at the World Economic Forum in Davos, Switzerland. It was a great treat. After listening to Gore's compelling argument, I humbly suggested that he write an op-ed piece that would begin like this: "I'm sorry. I am truly sorry. I want to apologize. I completely *underestimated* global warming. I beg your forgiveness."

That would get your attention, wouldn't it?

Of course, I was being tongue in cheek. Al Gore doesn't owe anyone an apology. We all owe him a huge debt of gratitude for his singular, Nobel Peace Prize–worthy effort to alert the world to the disruptive potential of climate change through his documentary An Inconvenient Truth, at a time when many, many people wanted to just ignore it—and they still do. Never has one man done more to wake up the world to a serious problem than Al Gore has. The point I was trying to make when I jokingly suggested that he apologize was about how we can best reverse the damage done to the climate debate by the climate-change deniers, delayers, and skeptics—who have tried to transform our uncertainty about some things into uncertainty about everything.

The climate-change deniers come in three basic varieties: those paid by fossil fuel companies to deny that global warming is a serious human-caused problem; those scientists, a small minority, who have looked at the data and concluded for different reasons that the rapid and extensive increase in greenhouse gas emissions since the Industrial Revolution is not a major threat to the planet's livability; and, finally, those conservatives who simply refuse to accept the reality of climate change because they hate the solution—more government regulation and intervention.

The net effect of all their writings, though, has been to muddy the question of whether there is any certainty that humans are causing dangerous climate change and to leave the impression that any assertion that human actions are changing the climate is merely a political opinion, not a scientific fact. Because Al Gore, a liberal politician, had become the most prominent voice for the threat of climate change, it was easy for the climate-change deniers and skeptics to insinuate that this was not a debate between science and politics, but between politics and politics.

How Al Gore, a politician, became the global figure to popularize— in the best sense of that word—the threat of climate change is itself a revealing tale. The physicist Joseph Romm, who was an acting assistant secretary in the Department of Energy in the Clinton administration and is the author of several books on climate change, including *Hell and High Water*, argues that Gore's prominence is due to the convergence of several factors. To begin with, said Romm, scientists in America are reluctant to become popularizers, which is why the average American could more likely name the three judges on *American Idol* than a single top American scientist. "In the science world," said Romm, "if you are a popularizer, you are not seen as a serious scientist, and if you are a serious scientist, you don't talk to the public." At the same time, some normally attentive environmentalists were slow to take up the climate-change issue, in terms of its full potential global and human impact. Finally, argues Romm, who also edits the global warming blog Climateprogress.org, the American media largely adopted the view of the climate-change deniers—the view "that climate change was a political issue, not a scientific reality, and therefore it had two sides"—that, in effect, nothing about it was certain.

But this is not politics. That the climate changes naturally over time is settled science. That the climate is now changing in ways unusual against the backdrop of long-term natural variation is accepted by nearly everybody. Finally, there's a very strong understanding among knowledgeable scientists that human activities are responsible through industrial activities for most of what's unusual about the current pattern of climate changes. Yet many in the media, said Romm, have treated climate change as if every one of these points were still in doubt and the expert community were divided down the middle on them. "The media is so used to seeing its job as being the honest broker that it tends to view the middle ground as always right," Romm argued. Or as George Monbiot, a British environmental activist and writer, noted (*The New York Times*, April 24, 2009), the climate deniers took full advantage of the media's instinct to give "balanced" coverage to any controversial issue and used it to put doubts in many people's minds. "They didn't have to win the argument to succeed," Monbiot said of the climate deniers, "only to cause as much confusion as possible."

So Al Gore stepped into this vortex, using his celebrity and political authority to draw global attention to the catastrophic potential of climate change. Because Gore, not a celebrity scientist, was the messenger, and because he presented his facts in an intentionally alarming way to get maximum attention, enormous time and energy have gone into debating about Al Gore rather than what is certain about changes in our climate system. That debate has diverted way too much public discussion from the current reality—which is that not only is the climate changing because of human activities, but there is now also mounting evidence that it is *changing considerably faster* than even the most worried climatologists were predicting just three or four years ago, and the change may unfold in an even more unmanageable and disruptive manner than they expected. This updated paperback easily could have been called "Hotter, Flatter, and More Crowded."

Consider just one of the assessments that came out in 2009—a study released by MIT's Joint Program on the Science and Policy of Global Change. It quietly updated its Integrated Global System Model, which tracks and predicts climate change from 1861 to 2100. "In our more recent global model simulations," the study explained, "the ocean heat-uptake is slower than previously estimated, the ocean uptake of carbon is weaker, feedbacks from the land system as temperature rises are stronger, cumulative emissions of greenhouse gases over the century are higher, and offsetting cooling from aerosol emissions is lower. No one of

these effects is very strong on its own, and even adding each separately together would not fully explain the higher temperatures. [But] rather than
interacting additively, these different effects appear to interact multi-
plicatively, with feedbacks among the contributing factors, leading to the
surprisingly large increase in the chance of much higher temperatures."

There, wrapped in the sober language of a policy study, is an alarming fact: the climate is changing even more rapidly than the experts
thought. Alarming, but not surprising. After all, almost every day now
there is a story in the newspaper that tells us something unusual is
happening—something outside the normal variability of the climate.
"The heat wave in Europe in July–August 2003—when it was consistently
over 100 degrees Fahrenheit—killed 35,000 people," concluded John
Holdren, the Harvard University climate expert who is now serving as
President Obama's science adviser. "That heat wave was estimated as a
one-in-a-hundred-year event. Before we started fiddling with the climate,
it was considered a one-in-250-year event. What the models now show is
that by 2050 it will be a one-in-two-year event and by 2070 it will be an
unusually cool summer in Europe."

A decade ago, people were thinking that at worst, the Arctic summer
sea ice would be entirely gone by 2070, said Holdren. A few radical pes-
simists said 2040. And now people say it could all be gone in just a few
years. No wonder: In the summer of 2007, warm temperatures melted so
much Arctic sea ice that stretches of the Arctic Ocean that had never
been fully navigable by ship were made so. The Northwest Passage was
ice-free for the first time in recorded history, enabling ships to pass
through. The Associated Press (December 11, 2007) published the following story apropos of this unprecedented and unexpected event:

> An already relentless melting of the Arctic greatly accelerated this
> summer, a warning sign that some scientists worry could mean
> global warming has passed an ominous tipping point. One even
> speculated that summer sea ice would be gone in five years.
> Greenland's ice sheet melted nearly 19 billion tons more than the
> previous high mark, and the volume of Arctic sea ice at summer's
> end was half what it was just four years earlier, according to new
> NASA satellite data obtained by the Associated Press. "The Arctic
> is screaming," said Mark Serreze, senior scientist at the govern-
> ment's snow and ice data center in Boulder, Colo. Just last year,

two top scientists surprised their colleagues by projecting that the Arctic sea ice was melting so rapidly that it could disappear entirely by the summer of 2040. This week, after reviewing his own new data, NASA climate scientist Jay Zwally said: "At this rate, the Arctic Ocean could be nearly ice-free at the end of summer by 2012, much faster than previous predictions." So scientists in recent days have been asking themselves these questions: Was the record melt seen all over the Arctic in 2007 a blip amid relentless and steady warming? Or has everything sped up to a new climate cycle that goes beyond the worst-case scenarios presented by computer models? "The Arctic is often cited as the canary in the coal mine for climate warming," said Zwally, who as a teenager hauled coal. "Now as a sign of climate warming, the canary has died. It is time to start getting out of the coal mines."

These are the news stories and headlines that we should be talking about! Hence, my tongue-in-cheek suggestion that the best way to draw attention to them and others would be to have Al Gore simply apologize—for *underestimating* climate change! That might actually wake people up to what is really happening. "Yes," he could say, "I got it wrong. It's going to be so much worse, so much sooner, than I thought."

While Vice President Gore declined to write that op-ed piece, he understood exactly what I was trying to get at. For the last thirty years, Gore explained to me, scientists have spoken about dangers to the climate by using "a range of projections"—the best case, the medium case, and the worst case, along with what damage will be done, including how high average temperatures will rise and how much ice will melt. In recent years, though, every time they have made these projections and the year passes and the evidence of what actually happened becomes available, the results tend to be at or above worst-case projections. We are at a point now where business as usual is expected to produce as much as an 11-degree Fahrenheit increase in average global temperatures by 2100. "That is so unthinkable it would bring civilization to a screeching halt and tear apart the fabric of life," said Gore.

But the climate-change deniers want us to believe that our business as usual could still lead to business as usual. They want us to believe that we are playing with dice that can come up only somewhere between two and twelve—with two being no climate change and twelve being the wild, crazy, outside possibility that something Al Gore says might come true. Sorry, boys, but these are Mother Nature's dice. They are like those polyhedral dice in the game Dungeons & Dragons. They are twenty-sided, thirty-sided, even sixty-sided dice. Don't think that they can only come up twelve. They might come up sixty—and there are increasing indications that we could be heading toward sixty, some wild outside range. As Romm put it, the only important holes left in the science of climate change are whether climate change will be "serious or catastrophic" and whether we will reach that point sooner rather than later.

"You remember how when you were a kid, your mom would ask you what you wanted to do when you grew up and you would say, 'I want to change the world'?" Nate Lewis said to me one day. "Well, guess what, Mom: We did."

"But Somebody Told Me . . . I Read That . . . I'm Sorry, but I Just Don't Believe It."

When I am out somewhere and the subject of climate change comes up, often someone declares: "I don't believe any of this climate change stuff. Somebody told me . . . Somebody told me that last year was a record cold season . . . How come the climate changed a thousand years ago even though there were no cars emitting CO_2 back then? I read somewhere that this is all about sunspots . . . I just don't believe any of this. Somebody told me . . ."

I hear that a lot. So how do I answer those questions? For starters, I try to explain the difference between "climate variability" and "climate change."

According to the World Meteorological Organization Web site, "climate" is usually defined as the "average weather" in any region. That is, the mean over a certain period of time of surface variables like temperature, precipitation, and wind. "Climate variability" refers to the deviations from the means for temperature, winds, or precipitation. Because the climate is so complex (and involves so many interactions and feedbacks between physics, biology, and chemistry), we don't always understand what drives climate variability—why you get a cold year in the middle of a broad warming period, why you get a rainy year in the middle of a long-term drought. And because the climate can be variable, one should never focus on any single year or weather event. "Year to year, we may observe in some parts of the world colder or warmer episodes than in other parts, leading to record low or high temperatures. This regional climate variability does not disprove long-term climate change," observed Michel Jarraud, secretary general of the World Meteorological Organization, in a letter published in the *Washington Post* (March 21, 2009). "While 2008 was slightly cooler than 2007, partially due to a La Niña event, it was nonetheless the 10th-warmest year on record."

So what then is "climate change"? As the WMO defines it, "climate change refers to a statistically significant variation in either the mean state of the climate or in its variability, persisting for an extended period (typically decades or longer)."

The important thing to keep in mind here is that the climate changes because it is forced to change. And it is forced to change either by natural forces or by forces introduced by mankind. In other words, the climate *varies* naturally because of its own complex internal dynamics, but it *changes* because something forces it to change.

The most important natural forces inducing climate change are changes in the earth's orbit—which change the intensity of the sun's radiation hitting different parts of the earth, which changes the thermal energy balance of the lower atmosphere, which can change the climate. Climate change, scientists know, can also be triggered by large volcanic eruptions, which can release so many dust particles into the air that they act as an umbrella and shield the earth from some of the sun's radiation, leading to a cooling period. The climate can be forced to change by natural, massive releases of greenhouses gases from beneath the earth's surface—gases, like methane, that absorb much more heat than carbon dioxide and lead to a sudden warming period.

What is new about this moment in the earth's history is that the force driving climate change is not a change in the earth's orbit, not a volcanic eruption, not a sudden natural release of greenhouse gases—but the burning of fossil fuels, the cultivation of rice and livestock, and the burning and clearing of forests by mankind, which together are pumping carbon dioxide, methane, and other heat-trapping gases into the atmosphere a hundred times faster than nature normally does.

How do scientists know that? I got a firsthand tutorial on climate variability and climate change in August 2008 by visiting an ice core research station above the Arctic Circle on the Greenland ice sheet—at latitude 77 degrees, 45 minutes north, longitude 51 degrees, 6 minutes west. I traveled there with a group of experts led by Denmark's minister of climate and energy, Connie Hedegaard, and including Rajendra Pachauri, the chair of the UN Intergovernmental Panel on Climate Change, which shared the Nobel Peace Prize with Al Gore. We flew in on a U.S. Air Force National Guard C-130, which landed on skis—not wheels—since the landing strip was just a plowed strip through a field of ice and snow. You have not lived until you have touched down in a plane with skis for landing gear. And you certainly have not lived until you have taken off in one. It took us three tries to get up enough speed to lift off, and the pilots were just about to use the booster rockets—that's right: small rockets affixed to the wings—to make sure we got up.

This middle-of-nowhere dot on the Greenland Ice Sheet was surely one of the most remarkable and isolated research stations in the world. Everywhere I looked, I saw a perfectly flat expanse of snow and ice stretching to the horizon. In fact, I could see so far in every direction that it felt as though I could see the curvature of the earth. The camp consisted of a heated geodesic dome where the scientists ate, a dozen barely heated tents where they (and guests) slept in insulated sleeping bags, and an underground research laboratory, carved out of the ice, where they had installed their drill and ice lab equipment. Over three "summers," their plan was to unearth ice core samples all the way down to Greenland's bedrock—roughly 1.5 miles, or the equivalent of 150,000 years of accumulated ice layers. Greenland is one of the best places to observe the effects of climate change. Because the world's biggest island has just 57,000 people and virtually no industry, the condition of its huge ice sheet—as well as its temperature, precipitation, and winds—is influenced by the global atmospheric and ocean currents that converge here, rather than by local factors. Whatever happens in China or Brazil eventually gets felt in Greenland.

I had never been exposed to ice research before, and I was stunned to discover how much you can learn from these tiny core samples of ice dating back tens of thousands of years. My education began when one of our hosts, the Danish researcher Jorgen Peder Steffensen, made me an offer I couldn't refuse: "If you come to Copenhagen, I will show you a Christmas snow—a real Christmas snow, the snow that fell between 1 B.C. and 1 A.D . . . I can also show you a sample of the very last snow that fell right at the end of the last ice age, which was 11,700 years ago." Or, he asked me, "how would you like to see the air samples that contain the sulfuric traces of the Mount Vesuvius volcanic eruption" that buried Pompeii in A.D. 79?

Those are not offers you get every day. But Steffensen actually has un-
earthed the ice from all those years. He is an ice specialist and curator of
the world's most comprehensive collection of ice core samples, a kind of
atmospheric DNA drilled out of the glaciers of Greenland and now preserved in refrigerated vaults in the Danish capital. The more and deeper
scientists can drill the ice, the better the picture they can give of the climate in previous eras—and therefore the better we can understand climate change. Each layer of ice contains water and air bubbles that were
trapped in the snow, which, when analyzed by expert scientists, reveal in
great detail the temperature, the amount of greenhouse gases in the atmosphere, the amount and origins of volcanic dust, and even the
amount of sea salt in the air and therefore how close the glacier was to
the ocean.

Imagine for a moment a freezer filled with such revealing ice cubes.
Each ice cube represents one year's atmospheric data, beginning
150,000 years ago, which is how far back the current Greenland ice cap
dates. Well, Steffensen, his wife, Dorthe Dahl-Jensen, both of the Centre for Ice and Climate at the Niels Bohr Institute of the University of
Copenhagen, and a team of international experts are assembling precisely that kind of freezer-museum from ice cores drilled in the far north
of Greenland above the Arctic Circle. Their objective is to do something
that has never been done before: project a complete picture of the
Greenland climate, from the ice age that lasted from 200,000 to 130,000
years ago, through the warming period known as the Eemian that lasted
from 130,000 to 115,000 years ago, through the last ice age from 115,000
to 11,703 years ago, right up to the present warming period we've been
in since. (Remember: the earth is usually an ice ball; the warm interglacial periods are the exceptions.)

Their last drilling project in Greenland, which was completed in
2004, focused on the layers 14,700 to 11,500 years ago. It offers a great
lesson in natural climate change. In an article published in 2008 in the
journal *Science Express*, Dahl-Jensen's team wrote about how it had discovered from the ice cores that the atmospheric circulation in the Northern Hemisphere over Greenland "changed abruptly" just as the last ice
age ended around 11,700 years ago. It seems to have been driven by a
sudden change in monsoons in the tropics. Something happened in nature there, possibly volcanic eruptions, that forced the climate to change.
The change was so abrupt that it warmed the Northern Hemisphere over
Greenland by 10 degrees Celsius in just fifty years—a dramatic increase.

"It shows that our climate system has the ability to make very abrupt changes all by itself" when forced by something, said Dahl-Jensen. Is that a reason to doubt that mankind can also be one of those forcers? I asked her. Not at all, she answered. What it means is that when the climate is quite capable of changing on its own, due to natural forcings, why would mankind want to add its collective foot to the pedal by pumping more man-made climate-changing greenhouse gases into the atmosphere at unprecedented levels and speed? Because while we don't always know why the climate changes, we do know the laws of physics: We know that greenhouse gases trap heat, we know that adding more greenhouse gases to the atmosphere and thereby thickening the greenhouse blanket around the earth will trap more heat, and we know that once greenhouse gases are lodged in the atmosphere and trapping more heat, those gases do not dissipate for several thousand years. Therefore their effects on the planet's average temperatures and climate will be cumulative and, therefore, more greenhouse gases in the atmosphere will lead to higher average temperatures on earth, over and above whatever naturally driven variations or changes are happening in the climate at that time. It will make a cooling period less cool and a warming period warmer.

Climate deniers often use the uncertainties around climate variability and climate change to suggest that, since we don't know everything, we don't know anything. If we're uncertain about anything, they argue, we must be uncertain about everything. And because so many people want so badly not to have to worry about temperatures rising when their retirement funds are falling, they will cite any uncertainties as reason not to act. But beware. We delay at our peril. Climate-change deniers are like the person who goes to the doctor for a diagnosis, and when the doctor tells him, "If you don't stop smoking, there is a 90 percent chance you will die of lung cancer," the patient replies: "Oh, Doctor, you mean you are not 100 percent sure? Then I will keep on smoking."

We cannot make the mistake of thinking that just because scientists tend to focus on the 10 percent they don't know, the 90 percent they do know isn't already a call to action. Sure, we don't know exactly how high and fast global average temperatures will rise, given the thickening of the greenhouse gas blanket; we don't know therefore precisely how much ice will melt and how fast, and therefore we don't know precisely how high sea levels will rise and how soon. And we cannot say for certain when and to what degree all this will make the climate system go haywire, over and above its natural variability. But what we do know is that more man-made CO_2 in the atmosphere will be a forcing function. It will mean, over time, steadily rising average temperatures, less ice, and higher seas—and this process cannot be reversed, only slowed.

"The most important conclusions about global climatic disruption—that it's real, that it's accelerating, that it's already doing significant harm, that human activities are responsible for most of it, that tipping points into really catastrophic disruption likely lurk along the 'business as usual' trajectory, and that there is much that could be done to reduce the danger at affordable cost if only we would get started—have not been concocted by the Sierra Club or the enemies of capitalism," noted Harvard University's Holdren. "They are based on an immense edifice of painstaking studies published in the world's leading peer-reviewed scientific journals. They have been vetted and documented in excruciating detail by the largest, longest, costliest, most international, most interdisciplinary, and most thorough formal review of a scientific topic ever conducted."

It is often said, Holdren continued, that there are three stages of skepticism in relation to issues like climate change—that is, great challenges that emerge at the science-society interface: "One, they tell you you're wrong and they can prove it: 'Climate isn't changing in unusual ways or, if it is, human activities are not the cause.' Two, they tell you you're right, but it doesn't matter: 'OK, it's changing and humans are playing a role, but it won't do much harm.' Three, they tell you it matters but it's too late to do anything about it: 'Yes, climate disruption is going to do some real damage, but it's too late, too difficult, or too costly to avoid that, so we'll just have to hunker down and suffer.' All of these positions are populated by subsets of the climate-change skeptics who infest talk shows, Internet blogs, letters to the editor, op-ed pieces in undiscriminating or 'balance'-fixated newspapers, and cocktail-party conversations. Individual skeptics often move over time from category 1 to 2 and from 2 to 3, as the parts of the evidence that have come to their notice become harder to ignore or refute. The very few skeptics with any credentials in climate-change science have virtually all shifted in the past few years from category 1 to 2. And jumps from 2 to 3—and from 1 straight to 3—are becoming more frequent. All three positions are deeply wrong."

Holdren, who has spent much of his life studying different aspects of the climate-change issue, has what he wryly calls "Holdren's First Principle" when it comes to climate change. It goes like this: "The more aspects of the problem you know something about, the more pessimistic you are. Someone who studies atmospheric science is pessimistic. Someone who knows atmospheric science and oceans is more pessimistic, and someone who knows atmospheric science, oceans, and ice is even more pessimistic, and someone who knows about the atmosphere, oceans, ice, and biology is still more pessimistic, and someone who knows about all those things, as well as engineering, economics, and politics, is the most pessimistic of all—because then you know how long it takes to change all the systems that are driving the problem.

"The way I like to put it," Holdren added, "is that we're driving in a car with bad brakes in a fog and heading for a cliff. We know for sure now that the cliff is out there, we just don't know exactly where it is. Prudence would suggest that we should start putting on the brakes."

Or as my colleague Andrew C. Revkin, the *New York Times* environment reporter, likes to say: "Uncertainty is the reason to act. If I know that I have built my house on the edge of forest and that there is an ever-increasing likelihood of droughts and forest fires," noted Revkin, "I am going to buy more home insurance and I am also going to invest in fire-proof shingles, cutting the risk and hedging against the worst-case outcome. I am not going to sit around and say: 'Gosh, no one can predict with any certainty when lightning is going to hit that forest, how many trees will go up in flames, how far the fires will burn, or if my home will be engulfed, so why buy fire insurance?'"

Our planetary version of fire insurance would be to do all that we can to take our collective foot off the pedal that is forcing more CO_2 into the atmosphere. We cannot stop global warming, because too much CO_2 is already baked into our future from what we have already pumped up there, but we can reduce the rate of global warming and therefore reduce the odds that our house will be hit by the climate equivalent of a forest fire.

The Really Scary Stuff We Already Know

So with all that in mind, what exactly do we already know about what we as a species have done to force climate change? To the extent that there is a consensus scientific answer to that question, it is represented by the conclusions of the UN Intergovernmental Panel on Climate Change, which issued its most recent assessment in 2007.

These are the core facts: Before the Industrial Revolution, in the mid-eighteenth century, and for the previous 10,000 years or so, planet earth had roughly 280 parts per million by volume of CO_2 in its atmosphere. That means that if we could have cut out a block of a million molecules of air from the atmosphere in 1750, it would have contained 280 molecules of CO_2. Today, that same block would contain roughly 384 molecules of CO_2. The only explanation for that large a differential in such a short period of time is the emission of carbon from the industrial use of fossil fuels by humans and from deforestation since the onset of the Industrial Revolution.

Yes, as climate-change deniers often note, other factors besides human-injected CO_2 affect the cooling and warming of the planet. The climate system has its own heartbeat, and the earth's orbit around the sun is indeed the pacemaker—it drives that heartbeat and determines broadly how much heat there is on our planet. One reason average temperatures vary throughout history is the fact that the earth's orbit is not circular; it is a stretched-out circle—an ellipse. So the earth's distance from the sun changes ever so slightly as its orbit changes, and this affects how much radiation we get from the sun. Those changes go in cycles of roughly 100,000 years. Another factor is the tilt of the earth's axis. The fact that the earth is tilted on its axis is what gives us seasons; if there were no tilt, New York would have the same season all year round, because its latitude would always get the same amount of sun radiation. Because the earth is tilted, we get more solar radiation in summer and less in winter at different latitudes. But what happens over periods of roughly 40,000 years is that the tilt of the earth gradually changes by a degree or two and that, in turn, increases or decreases the amount of sun radiation that hits different places. A third factor has to do with subtle changes in the plane of the earth's orbit relative to the sun. These changes, which happen in 21,000-year cycles, also lead to slight increases and decreases in the solar radiation that hits the earth. These three periodic processes are called the Milankovitch cycles. They are happening constantly and the sum total of all of them makes up the distribution of solar radiation on the earth at any given time.

"We know these periods exist, and we can calculate how much more or less sun radiation different parts of the earth get when we get a little closer or farther from the sun and when the seasons are a bit shorter or longer in time," said Nate Lewis, the Caltech energy chemist. "And we can measure from ice core data going back 670,000 years the average temperature year by year of our planet, as well as the average CO_2 concentrations. From that we know that the average temperature has varied by around 6 degrees centigrade. So when it is warm—in the interglacial periods, like we are in now—we have a climate like we have now. And when we are in glacial periods—when the average temperature falls by 6 degrees centigrade—you have glaciers from the North Pole down to Indiana."

Many climate-change deniers argue that the variability of the earth's orbit and the different solar radiation impacts that this has on the planet— and only those factors—are what account for the big temperature fluctuations. They claim that human activities have no real effect. There is just one problem with that argument, says Lewis: The 6-degree-Celsius change in global average temperature that distinguishes warm periods from glacial periods is too big to be accounted for simply by the changes in sunlight. The large observed temperature differences cannot be explained solely by the small differences in the amount of the sun's radiation hitting the earth as a result of the small variations in the earth's orbit.

"What we know happens is that as we get closer to or farther from the sun, it warms or cools the oceans, and the oceans respond by releasing or absorbing CO_2," explained Lewis. "When the oceans are warmed up, they release CO_2, just like you would if you heated up an open bottle of Sprite. It bubbles out the carbon dioxide gas. That is what the oceans do. They bubble out the CO_2 and that warms the atmosphere, and then that warms the oceans more and they release more CO_2. In addition, when it gets warmer, the ice melts, which [means the ice] reflects less sunlight, which in turn causes more sunlight to be absorbed, [which] causes even more warming."

Even when the earth went from glacial to interglacial periods, we know that the total change in concentrations of CO_2—from high to low—was no more than 120 parts per million, said Lewis. It would go from 180 ppm to 300 ppm and then back again to 180 ppm—and those 6-degree-Celsius temperature changes would go along with it. For the last 10,000 years, though, it has been stable at around 280 ppm of CO_2, and our climate has been pretty stable as well.

That suddenly changed, beginning in 1750 or so. After the onset of the Industrial Revolution, and particularly in the last fifty years, the amount of CO_2 in the earth's atmosphere shot up from 280 ppm to 384 ppm, where it has probably never been for twenty million years—and at a speed of increase that took the sun thousands of years in each cycle to produce. And we are on a track now to add 100 or more ppm of CO_2 to the atmosphere in the next fifty years. This extra CO_2 is not coming from the oceans. It is coming from humans burning fossil fuels and from deforestation. We know this because carbon can be dated, and the carbon in the carbon dioxide that is produced from burning fossil fuels is of a different age than the CO_2 that is contained in the oceans. And measurements definitively show that the carbon dioxide increase in the atmosphere in the last fifty years has come from carbon released in fossil fuel combustion.

We also know that in the last hundred years the earth's relationship to the sun has not changed significantly, but the net quantity of CO_2 in the atmosphere has gone up dramatically. "Just because in the past the initial trigger for CO_2 increase was the sun doesn't mean that something else cannot be amplifying the release of CO_2, or even causing its release now, and leading to the observed warming we are feeling—and that something else is us," said Lewis. "The sun pulled the trigger on a shotgun and it fired out CO_2. But humans are pulling the trigger on a cannon, and it's now firing out even more. And we know that this increase of CO_2 is going to give us a different climate than the one we have now, because in 670,000 straight years, whenever CO_2 has gone up, temperatures have gone up, and whenever CO_2 in the atmosphere has gone down, temperatures have gone down. So to say that the additional CO_2 added by humans is not a problem is to bet against 670,000 straight years of data, and to hope that we are going to get lucky this time."

As the latest IPCC report (January 2007) concluded: Global warming is "unequivocal" and is "very likely" the cause of most of the temperature increases since 1950. The report said with 90 percent confidence that carbon dioxide and other greenhouse gases from industry and agriculture have been the main culprits.

Based on current science, the IPCC concluded that if the total human influence on the atmosphere reaches the equivalent of 550 ppm of CO_2, which is exactly where we're heading, by mid-century that will probably lead in time (there is a time lag, because it takes a while to heat up the oceans) to an approximately 3-degree-Celsius rise in global average temperature. If, through mitigation efforts, we manage to cap the changes in the atmosphere to the equivalent of 450 ppm of CO_2, that would probably result in an approximately 2-degree-Celsius rise in global average temperature.

"In our judgment," said the climate scientists who put together the Sigma Xi/UN Foundation report on global warming, increases of 2 to 2.5 degrees Celsius above 1750 levels "will entail sharply rising risks of crossing a climate 'tipping point' that could lead to intolerable impacts on human well-being, in spite of all feasible attempts at adaptation." This is why the European Union has called for a cap at 2 degrees. And that is why we need to do both mitigation—trying to slow down climate change by emitting less CO_2—and adaptation. But if we don't do mitigation now, the changes may well be too great to adapt to in any meaningful way.

"For a long time," said Harvard's John Holdren, who participated in the Sigma Xi study, "people tended to argue that stopping at 550 ppm and 3 degrees Celsius has to be the target—not because it won't cause harm but because it was hard to see how we would do better. What has happened since the mid-1990s is that almost all the scientific evidence has caused increased concern that 3 degrees will not be tolerable."

Why? Many reasons: Scientists realized that they were underestimating the effects on agriculture (in a hotter world, for example, many pests that harm crops would not be killed by winter freezes); they realized that the Greenland and West Antarctic ice sheets were melting or slipping faster than anticipated; and, finally, they saw that the acidification of the oceans was imperiling coral reefs and seashell-forming organisms— critical to the undersea food chain—much faster than originally believed. (Here is how acidification happens: Add more CO_2 to H_2O and you get more H_2CO_3—also known as carbonic acid, a weak acid that affects the pH level of the ocean and dissolves the calcium carbonates needed for corals and seashell-forming organisms to make their hard exteriors.)

There are other reasons that we may be underestimating global warming. To begin with, scientists—the good ones—are congenitally afraid of overstating anything. They are punished for overstating and not punished for understating, and this produces caution generally. "A charlatan can tell a lie in one sentence that a scientist needs three paragraphs to rebut," said Holdren. Also, the raw data that went into the IPCC model and other models has a real time lag. To make climate models, scientists take little pieces of information of what we know happened in the past, check how it corresponds to what actually happened, and then try to project into the future from the earlier trend lines. But most of the data in the IPCC model related to China's economic activities, for instance, says Bill Collins, senior scientist in the Earth Sciences Division of Lawrence Berkeley National Laboratory, predates the last five years, when China greatly intensified its already booming efforts in heavy manufacturing, cement making, and construction and ramped up the coal-fired power plants needed to sustain it.

"Nobody captured in their energy economy models the acceleration of emissions from China in the last five years," said Collins. "That is what is so scary. A lot of the IPCC math was developed when emissions from China were going down in the 1990s, and the Soviet Union was collapsing. What is happening now is worse than the worst-case projections that went into the IPCC model."

The Even Scarier Stuff We Don't Know

What leaves climate experts lying awake at night is the scary stuff that they know could happen but that is impossible to predict. For instance, we know very little about how different, highly disruptive, nonlinear changes in climate might interact with and amplify one another. These are called positive and negative feedback loops. What will happen to the planet if we get a drying of the Amazon interacting with a rising sea level, and those two developments start interacting with a melting of the Greenland Ice Sheet? If we get a concert of feedback loops all playing at once, there isn't a supercomputer in the world that can tell you with any assurance what might happen as a result.

How might different forms of climate change interact with one another? Jim Woolsey, a former CIA director and an energy expert, likes to point to the stretches of tundra in the Arctic, in Western Siberia, and in a smaller area of Alaska, in which approximately 500 billion tons of carbon—about one-third of all the carbon in the world's soils—is trapped in frozen peat bogs. If the permafrost in those bogs were to thaw, much of this carbon would be quickly converted to methane, another greenhouse gas. Because methane is more potent than CO_2, explained Woolsey, a massive release of it could provide a substantial short-term kick to climate change—the equivalent of billions of tons of CO_2. This in turn could lead to higher average temperatures, more ice melt, and more catastrophic and unpredictable amplifications.

It is difficult to persuade government decision-makers to take account of and prepare for this sort of nonlinear change. This may be because most people have what the inventor and futurist "Ray Kurzweil calls an 'intuitive linear' view of phenomena rather than an 'historical exponential' view," argues Woolsey. "In *The Singularity Is Near*, Kurzweil suggests that most of us have great difficulty grasping exponential change. He compares us to an individual who has a small lake on his property and who regularly cleans out lily pad growth every few days. Then, with the pads covering only 1 percent of the lake, the property owner decides to go on vacation, but when he returns a few weeks later he is surprised to find the lake covered with lily pads and the fish dead. The property owner forgot that the lily pads didn't know that they were not supposed to expand exponentially just because the human mind tends to think linearly." Our generation and future ones need to understand, added Woolsey, that "nature is not always going to behave in a linear fashion because our minds think that way."

And therefore, in the Energy-Climate Era, we need to think exponentially. "Some human behaviors that seemed acceptable or at least insignificant in the past might now be most unwise, because they increase the chance of, essentially, metastasis in the system," Woolsey concluded. We have no idea when a little change can make a big difference.

To be sure, there can also be feedback loops that might help keep the atmosphere in balance between warming and cooling. For example, global warming might create more low clouds and some of these might drift up and create high clouds, which would actually help to cool the earth. "There are positive and negative cloud feedbacks," explained Lewis, "and a lot of the differences in climate models depend on how they treat clouds and when and how they treat the positive and negative feedbacks of clouds." As we sit here today, though, we can identify a lot more worrying feedback loops than reassuring ones.

All the models that tell us what's ahead are just extrapolations of what the average temperature will be at different levels of CO_2 and how the new levels will affect the overall climate, our biosphere, and civilization. The different climate models are all averages of many different factors, and they can give you an average projection for where we're heading. But don't be lulled into thinking that that average is where we will come out.

"The earth is not on an average path," adds Lewis. "It's on one path — we just don't know yet which one it is. But there is more and more evidence that this path could be at the high end of climate-change models in speed and scope, especially if some of the nonlinear runaway feedback effects start to kick in . . . Would 450 ppm be safe? Would 550 ppm turn out to be safe? We don't know. The only level of CO_2 that we know is safe is the one that we have been at for the last 10,000 years—280 ppm—and we have left that behind. Would you feel good about leaving your kids a 550 ppm world? I wouldn't. It may be fine—but it is a world no humans have ever lived in."

Let Us Pray

And more people are getting an inkling that climate change is real, even if they can't articulate why, because climate change has started to jump out of the science books and into their lives. I see this in my own travels, and have lately started asking myself: "I began in journalism thirty years ago listening to the BBC World Service. Am I going to end my career glued to the Weather Channel?" When I was growing up, the local news featured segments of "news, weather, and sports." But my gut tells me that in 2030 the evening news is going to feature "weather, other news, and sports." Weather and climate are starting to become so acute in so many places, they have become the news. They have become politics too. In fact, in two cases in 2007 alone, I encountered politicians calling on their people—in earnest—to pray for rain.

I visited Australia in May 2007, and found myself in the middle of what Aussies were calling the "Big Dry," a roughly seven-year drought that had become so severe that on April 19, 2007, then prime minister John Howard actually asked his countrymen to put their hands together and beseech the Good Lord for a gully-washing downpour. Because if it didn't start to pour, said Howard, he was going to have to ban water allocations for irrigation purposes in the Murray-Darling river basin, which produces 40 percent of Australia's agriculture. That would be like an Egyptian pharaoh banning irrigation from the Nile or a U.S. president from the Mississippi.

Australians were shocked. But Howard wasn't kidding. He said to me during an interview in his office in Sydney, "I told people you have to pray for rain. I said it without a hint of irony." And here's what's really funny: It actually started to rain a little! Howard remarked to me that one parliament member from his own Liberal Party, who lived in Mallee, in northern Victoria Province, one of the areas worst affected by drought, called him to say that when some rains finally came his young children delighted in cavorting in the downpour, because they were all under six years old and could not remember playing in rain before. The Big Dry had been around their whole lives.

But praying for rain was not enough. The election held in Australia later that year was the first election in history in which climate change— specifically the Howard government's failure to respond to it with poli- cies rather than prayers—was among the top three voting issues, right along with union rules and mortgage rates. Exit polls showed that Howard's insistence on keeping Australia out of the Kyoto Protocol process a few years earlier was a key reason he was defeated by the Labor Party. Immediately after the election, in December 2007, Mr. Howard's victorious opponent, Kevin Rudd, personally handed the United Nations a set of ratification papers for the Kyoto Protocol at the Bali climate- change conference. It was his first global diplomatic initiative.

A few months after visiting Australia, I was back in the States and planning a trip to Atlanta when I noticed a story on the Internet that Georgia's governor, Sonny Perdue, had led a public prayer vigil on the steps of his state capitol, seeking relief from the epic drought that had af- flicted Georgia and the whole Southeast.

"We have come together for one reason only—to very reverently and respectfully pray up a storm," said Governor Perdue, joined by a hundred other rain-worshippers. "O Father, we acknowledge our wastefulness," Perdue added. That was at least honest. The next week's *Time* magazine (November 19, 2007) rightly tweaked Perdue and his state for relying too much on the Good Lord and not enough on common sense. "It wasn't God who allowed an outdoor theme park to build a million-gallon mountain of artificial snow while the Southeast was running dry; it was Governor Perdue and his elected officials," the *Time* piece put it. "They also allowed the wasteful irrigation of Georgia's cotton farms and the rampant overbuilding and overslurping of metropolitan Atlanta."

Georgia's water-wasting was threatening to become news in more ways than one. As the drought lingered and broke records, North Florida, whose huge oyster-bed industry depends on water flowing down from Georgia, was practically threatening a civil war within the South. It hadn't quite reached the level of drought-parched Somalis and Sudanese fighting murderous civil wars over water, but it was definitely in the same spirit.

On December 14, 2007, Diane Roberts, author of *Dream State*, a book about Florida, wrote an op-ed essay in the *St. Petersburg Times* about neighboring Georgia and Governor Perdue. "Atlanta sprawls like your sorry drunk cousin after Thanksgiving dinner, bloated and out of control," Roberts complained.

> Spread out over 28 counties, the population has swollen by a million in the past seven years: a vast kudzu-tangle of malls, golf courses, gated "communities," McMansions and apartment complexes. Nobody thought to see if there was enough water . . . Perdue's solution to the water crisis so far has been: 1. Pray for rain; 2. Blame the Endangered Species Act. I'm all for prayer. I'm for rain dances, Santeria chicken sacrifice, Wiccan weather spells or any other magic that might coax H_2O from heaven. But Perdue, pointing an accusing finger at the marine creatures who depend on a flow of fresh water down the Chattahoochee-Flint-Apalachicola system, wants to frame the problem as man versus mussel. He told a television interviewer that no mollusk "deserves more water than the humans and children and babies of Atlanta . . ." "People like to define this as babies versus oysters," says David Guest, an attorney with the environmental law firm Earthjustice. "But the real principle is: why does Atlanta think it should get more water than it used to?" Lake Lanier was created 50 years ago to keep barge traffic afloat on the Chattahoochee. It was not supposed to be a primary drinking water reservoir. But since there's been no adult supervision of the area's growth, Lanier has become metro Atlanta's holy well . . . Guest questions Georgia's demand that the U.S. Army Corps of Engineers keep back more water for its use: "Is there a basis in right beyond 'I want it'?" Never mind the downstream destruction: "Allowing Atlanta to take still more water is like lending your ATM card to a crack addict on the promise that he'll only use it once."

And that's also why one should not assume that the effects of climate change will only be felt through a big natural disaster like Hurricane Katrina. Not necessarily, says Minik Thorleif Rosing, a top geologist at the National History Museum of Denmark and one of my traveling companions to Greenland. "Most people will actually feel climate change delivered to them by the postman," he explained to me. It will come in the form of higher water bills, because of fiercer droughts in some areas; higher energy bills, as the true cost of the use of fossil fuels becomes prohibitive; and higher insurance and mortgage rates, because of much more violently unpredictable weather.

Hunters, farmers, and fishermen are generally a conservative lot, not the kind of people you'd find at an Al Gore movie. But they know their rivers, their fields, their hunting grounds, and their mountain valleys. And they have figured out lately that they don't need to see *An Inconvenient Truth*, because they are starring in it. It's now their home video. Just a quick trip to Montana will tell you that.

It was early January 2007 when I ventured up there, and I will confess that there was no evidence of global warming happening in Montana that day. I had come up to Colstrip, Montana, to see what a strip coal mine actually looks like, and I had the best tour guide imaginable— Montana's Democratic governor, Brian Schweitzer, and his dog Jake, who, the governor was quick to point out, had a higher popularity rating than he did.

The governor, a bulldozer of a man with a quick smile and a quicker wit, met me in Billings in his little twin-engine propeller plane. We flew to Colstrip through a winter gale that tossed us around like salad pieces, and then we set down on a makeshift runway in the heart of coal country. (On the way back, after flying through another howling storm that caused me to dig my nails so deeply into the armrests I left my fingerprints in the leather, I thanked the pilots profusely. The governor simply bellowed, "I'm glad we had our best interns flying today!" Very funny . . .)

Along the way, between pointing out different landmarks from the air, Governor Schweitzer mused about how he and his fellow Montanans' views on climate change have changed—and fast.

"Here in Montana we make our living outside," said the governor, an agronomist who got his start building farms in Saudi Arabia, "and when you do that, you know the climate is changing . . . So when Exxon Mobil hires someone who calls himself a 'scientist' to claim this is not true, you don't have to get *The New York Times* to know the guy is blowing smoke."

Schweitzer later ticked off for me in detail the reasons why the hunters, farmers, and fishermen in his state have become climate-change believers. Every year the state checks the temperature of its trout rivers in July. Trout like the rivers chilled by the summerlong runoff from mountain glaciers. Unfortunately, over the past decade or so, the snowcap on some mountains has all melted by July, so the rivers are not getting the steady cold runoff, and the trout are getting stressed. The temperature in Montana's famed Flathead River, which flows right out of Glacier National Park, was 11.3 degrees Celsius in July 1979, he said. By July 2006, it was 15.95 degrees Celsius in the same month, and rivers that were rushing with almost 100 percent snowmelt twenty years earlier were now 50 percent rainwater and springs. Montana's trout have become so stressed that the state is having to close down some rivers to fishing.

"Trout fishing is important for the soul," said Schweitzer. "When people can't fish their favorite rivers, they get upset." And then there are the forest fires. In northwest Montana, the mountains are covered with fir and larch forests up to the tree line. Due to warmer average winter temperatures, however, the trees have become much more vulnerable to insects and other pests, whose larvae used to be killed by the –20 to –30 degree Fahrenheit temperatures that could be counted on each winter in January and February. That has not been the case in recent years.

"We now have acres and acres of dead and dying trees in the Rockies," said Schweitzer. "Nature has her way of dealing with that—lightning strikes. A healthy forest will burn a little and then a little rain will come and it will all stay in balance. Now, with so many dead and dying trees, you get a lightning strike and boom—500,000 acres of trees are gone. It is changing the whole composition of the forest."

This is, in turn, affecting Montana's hunters. The big-game hunting season in Montana, mostly for elk, always began on the third Sunday in October. "Half of Montana goes hunting then," said Schweitzer. "Montana women count on their husbands going away then and giving them a little break—and the boys count on being out in the forests for a few days without having to shower and shave." By October, Montanans always knew that heavy mountain snows, above 6,000 to 8,000 feet, would force the mountain elk down to lower elevations, where they would bunch up and feed in the valleys. There, hunters could track and kill them. To keep a balance in nature, the herds need to be culled. But with the snows now coming later, the elk come down the mountains later, and the elk season had to be pushed back into November. It is not a disaster—it just tells you that your environment is changing and that your way of life could change as a result.

"Changing the date for the start of the elk hunting season is not being driven by scientists," said Schweitzer. "It's just driven by guys who want to hunt and are telling me, 'I have not shot an elk in three years.' These are just regular people, and they may not have the climate data, but they know what they know, and they know something is different."

Some problems can't be fixed by changing dates on the calendar, though. Roughly 70 percent of the water that flows into the Missouri River drainage system, which is the largest in America, comes from the snows of Montana, as does 50 percent of the water in the Columbia River basin. When Montana gets less snow, not only do those rivers get less water, but the many dams on those rivers produce less clean hydroelectric power, and the shortfall has to be made up through the burning of coal. When there is less snowmelt and runoff, farmers then need to install bigger and bigger electric pumps to get water up to the surface for irrigation, and that means greater demand for electricity.

"Montana is the headwater state," said Schweitzer. "Our snowmelt flows to the Atlantic, to the Pacific, and to the Arctic. We refresh this country every year and the snowmelt used to last all year long. Now it stops melting in the middle of July—the mountain freezer is empty by then—and the snows start later in the fall."

In February 2008, an analysis by the Scripps Institution of Oceanography at the University of California, San Diego, published in the journal *Science*, concluded from data collected since 1950 that the water content of the Western mountain snowpack as of April 1 each year has steadily declined in eight of the nine mountain regions studied. The researchers said there was no question that climate change was the cause and that, given the importance of this snowmelt for everything from irrigation to drinking water to powering dams in the West, "modifications to the water infrastructure of the Western U.S. [is] a virtual necessity."

No wonder climate-change deniers don't get much of a hearing these days in Montana.

"I have seen a few polls in the course of the last year that showed more than 60 percent of Montanans would agree to change their lifestyle and pay higher taxes if it would lead to a decrease in climate change," said Schweitzer. "Old-timers, just regular old-timers who have never had a tie on their whole life and don't plan to, will tell you, 'Oh boy, things are changing.' All they have to do is look up at the mountains in August and see that they are not snowcapped. You know what it was supposed to look like, and it doesn't anymore. And they know that [the] spring that ran when their grandpa homesteaded at the turn of the century is drying up in summer. They don't know the causal agent—but they know something is going on and it is something they don't like."

Daffodils in January

As more people encounter climate change, more of them are also coming to understand that it is not just some cuddly-sounding phenomenon called "global warming." "Oh, well, things will just get a little warmer, how bad can that be—especially if you're from Minnesota, like me?" It is, instead, going to be "global weirding."

"Global weirding" is a term used by Hunter Lovins, cofounder of the Rocky Mountain Institute, to explain to people that the rise in global average temperature (global warming) is actually going to trigger all sorts of unusual weather events—from hotter heat spells and droughts in some places to heavier snows in others, to more violent storms, more intense flooding, downpours, forest fires, and species loss in still others. The weather is going to get weird. It already has. When the daffodils near our driveway in Bethesda, Maryland, which usually come up in March, came up this year in early January, I found it weird—like something out of an old *Twilight Zone* episode. I half expected to look out the window and see Rod Serling, the show's host, mowing our front lawn.

Get used to it. The weather may feel like science fiction, but the science underlying it is very real and mundane. It takes only a small increase in global average temperatures to have a big effect on weather, because what drives the winds and their circulation patterns on the surface of the earth are differences in temperature. So when you start to change the average surface temperature of the earth, you change the wind patterns—and then before you know it, you change the monsoons. When the earth gets warmer, you also change rates of evaporation—which is a key reason we will get more intense rainstorms in some places and hotter dry spells and longer droughts in others.

How can we have both wetter and drier extremes at the same time?

As we get rising global average temperatures and the earth gets warmer, it will trigger more evaporation from the soil. So regions that are already naturally dry will tend to get drier. At the same time, higher rates of evaporation, because of global warming, will put more water vapor into the atmosphere, and so areas that are either near large bodies of water or in places where atmospheric dynamics already favor higher rates of precipitation will tend to get wetter. We know one thing about the hydrologic cycle: What moisture goes up must come down, and where more moisture goes up, more will come down. Total global precipitation will probably increase, and the amount that will come down in any one storm is expected to increase as well—which will increase flooding and gully washers. That's why this rather gentle term "global warming" doesn't capture the disruptive potential of what lies ahead.

"The popular term 'global warming' is a misnomer," says John Holdren. "It implies something uniform, gradual, mainly about temperature, and quite possibly benign. What is happening to global climate is none of those. It is uneven geographically. It is rapid compared to ordinary historic rates of climatic change, as well as rapid compared to the adjustment times of ecosystems and human society. It is affecting a wide array of critically important climatic phenomena besides temperature, including precipitation, humidity, soil moisture, atmospheric circulation patterns, storms, snow and ice cover, and ocean currents and upwellings. And its effects on human well-being are and undoubtedly will remain far more negative than positive. A more accurate, albeit more cumbersome, label than 'global warming' is 'global climatic disruption.'"

CNN.com reported (August 7, 2007) about a study that had just been released by the UN's World Meteorological Organization of unprecedented weather extremes that had happened so far that year. It could have just been called "Global Weirding 2007":

Four monsoon depressions, double the normal number, caused heavy flooding in India, Pakistan and Bangladesh . . . England and Wales have experienced their wettest May-to-July period since record-keeping started in 1766. In late July, swollen rivers threatened to burst their banks . . . Late last month in Sudan, floods and heavy rain caused 23,000 mud brick homes to collapse, killing at least 62 people. The rainfall was abnormally heavy and early for this time of the year . . . In May, swell waves up to 15 feet high swept into 68 islands in the Maldives, causing severe flooding and damage . . . Also in May, a heat wave swept across Russia . . . Southeastern Europe did not escape the unusual weather. The area suffered record-breaking heat in June and July . . . An unusual cold southern winter brought wind, blizzards and rare snowfall to various parts of South America, with temperatures reaching as low as 7 degrees below zero Fahrenheit (−22 degrees Celsius) in Argentina and 0 degrees Fahrenheit (−18 degrees Celsius) in Chile in July. In June, South Africa had its first significant snowfall since 1981, as almost 10 inches (25 centimeters) of the white stuff fell in some parts of the country . . .

This trend of more extreme extremes continued right into the summer of 2008, when unprecedentedly heavy rains in Iowa caused the Cedar River to flood and overwhelm downtown Cedar Rapids, rising well above thirty feet over sea level—far, far above what anyone had ever seen or expected. A quote in the *New York Times* report (June 13, 2008) captured perfectly the sense of global weirding that Iowans felt: "'Usually if you break a record, you only do it by an inch or two,' said Jeff Zogg, a hydrologist for the Weather Service in Davenport, Iowa. 'But breaking it by six feet? That's pretty amazing.'"

We're Not in Kansas Anymore

So where are we, then, as we enter the Energy-Climate Era? Where we are is that many people think the weather has gotten strange, but not enough think it has gotten so dangerous that we need to do what is necessary to manage the unavoidable and avoid the unmanageable. We need to stretch our imaginations. We need to understand that boundaries of change are far wider than the average of projections.

One of the things Heidi Cullen, formerly the Weather Channel's climatologist, has argued—in order to stimulate people's understanding and imagination regarding climate change—is that local TV meteorologists should give climate-change science some mention in their daily weather reports. "We owe it to viewers to connect climate to weather when there is a meaningful connection in terms of broad trends," said Cullen, who holds a Ph.D. in climatology and ocean-atmosphere dynamics from the

Lamont-Doherty Earth Observatory of Columbia University. "It would be a disservice if your local meteorologist wasn't able to tell you, 'If we continue along this emissions trajectory, we are going to have ten more red-alert smog days each month and we are going to see ozone levels and heat indexes skyrocket.' Local meteorologists are the interface between the general public and the scientific community. People look to them and trust them, so it is critical that they make these connections, based on the science. This is an environmental literacy opportunity."

The Weather Channel regularly tracks the number of record highs versus record lows. "You can pull up just about any month now, and the number of record highs outpaces the number of record lows. For example, during the third week of March [March 15 to 21, 2008], 185 record highs were either tied or set, while twenty-eight record lows were either tied or set. When you start seeing these numbers, week in and week out, it begs some pretty big questions," said Cullen. "Why don't meteorologists talk about that? People sense the weather is weird, but it's incredibly rare to hear the phrase 'global warming' spoken by your local TV meteorologist. This is an opportunity to teach people about climate, just like we did with weather. The terms 'low pressure' and 'high pressure' have become part of our vernacular, but that didn't happen overnight. Hurricane Katrina wasn't so much an example of global warming as it was an example of the long-term infrastructure decisions society needs to make in order to survive. The weather is so much more than 'Do I need an umbrella?' It's also 'Should I buy a condo on the coast?' and 'Did we build these levees high enough?'"

Cullen's proposal kicked up a revealing backlash, beginning in December 2006, when she posted a blog entry on Weather.com—entitled "Junk Controversy Not Junk Science"—about how reticent some broadcast meteorologists were to report on climate change. For some reason meteorologists—as a group—tend to be climate skeptics even though most are certified by the American Meteorological Society, which has issued a very clear statement that global warming is largely due to the burning of fossil fuels.

In late 2007, I went to Atlanta and visited the eye of the hurricane she set off: the Weather Channel's headquarters itself, located in a nondescript office block. Cullen's desk was crammed into the Weather Channel's newsroom—where she was the sole climatologist amid a hundred meteorologists. She shared with me the blog she posted that kicked off the storm. It read:

Capitalweather.com, a website for hard-core weather junkies in the DC area, recently published an interview with a local meteorologist that highlights the unfortunate divide that exists right now between the climate and weather communities. Yup, that divide is global warming. When asked about the science of global warming, the meteorologist responded: "The subject of global warming definitely makes headlines in the media and is a topic of much debate. I try to read up on the subject to have a better understanding, but it is complex. Often, it is so politicized and those on both sides don't always appear to have their facts straight. History has taught us that weather patterns are cyclical and although we have noticed a warming pattern in recent time, I don't know what generalizations can be made from this with the lack of long-term scientific data. That's all I will say about this."

Cullen went on to note that the American Meteorological Society has issued a statement on climate change that reads: "There is convincing evidence that since the industrial revolution, human activities, resulting in increasing concentrations of greenhouse gases and other trace constituents in the atmosphere, have become a major agent of climate change." So, Cullen wrote:

If a meteorologist has an AMS Seal of Approval, which is used to confer legitimacy to TV meteorologists, then meteorologists have a responsibility to truly educate themselves on the science of global warming. Meteorologists are among the few people trained in the sciences who are permitted regular access to our living rooms. And in that sense, they owe it to their audience to distinguish between solid, peer-reviewed science and junk political controversy. If a meteorologist can't speak to the fundamental science of climate change, then maybe the AMS shouldn't give them a Seal of Approval. Clearly, the AMS doesn't agree that global warming can be blamed on cyclical weather patterns. It's like allowing a meteorologist to go on-air and say that hurricanes rotate clockwise and tsunamis are caused by the weather. It's not a political statement . . . it's just an incorrect statement.

Within twenty-four hours of her blog posting, Cullen found herself being denounced on the Web sites of those famous scientists and climate experts Senator James Inhofe, Republican of Oklahoma and protector of his state's oil and gas industry, and Rush Limbaugh. The Weather Channel's own Web site was hit with some 4,000 e-mails in one day, mostly angry ones, telling Cullen, as she put it, "to just be a good weather bimbo and stick to pointing out high pressure systems—and shut up about climate change." Cullen's reaction: "A lot of viewers wrote in and said, 'Stop talking about politics. I didn't come to the Weather Channel to hear about politics.' That is how they saw climate. To talk about climate was to talk about politics. All scientists are afraid of being advocates, but advocates are not afraid of being scientists. By virtue of the fact that I talked about climate change, some people saw me as an advocate. But the only thing I'm an advocate for is science. The science is what matters."

One thing people always loved about the Weather Channel was that the weather "was nobody's fault," mused Cullen, who got her training working as a researcher at the National Center for Atmospheric Research in Boulder, Colorado. "We didn't point fingers. Our news was not political. And then Katrina came along and suddenly the weather wasn't the weather anymore. It was something else." Before, the weather was always seen as an act of Mother Nature, "and then suddenly the weather was potentially our fault."

I can understand why a senator who is just fronting for the oil industry would stick his head in the sand. But I absolutely do not understand why Rush Limbaugh and other conservatives would make climate-change denial a conservative Republican plank. I would have thought that conservatives, of all people, would be most insistent on being conservative—being prudent, and siding in the debate with those who say that even if there is just a 10 percent chance of a major disruption as a result of climate change, we should make sure to conserve the world we have. What could be more crazy-radical—more Trotskyite and more reckless—than standing in the face of an overwhelming consensus among climate experts and saying, "I am throwing my lot in with the minority. I am going to bet the farm, my future, and my kids' future that the tiny minority is right—all other consequences be damned"?

California governor Arnold Schwarzenegger, who has tried to keep the Republican Party from making climate skepticism a plank in the GOP platform, put it to me this way: "If ninety-eight doctors say my son is ill and needs medication and two say, 'No, he doesn't, he is fine,' I will go with the ninety-eight. It's common sense—the same with global warming. We go with the majority, the large majority."

I am with the ninety-eight. I am convinced that climate change is real. But we need people not only to accept that it is real, but also to accept just how real it could be—that the dice may come up sixty if we don't act now to begin mitigating and adapting. We need, as EcoTech's Rob Watson said, to "use the one faculty that distinguishes us as human beings—the ability to imagine. We need to fully grasp the nonlinear, unmanageable climate events that could unfold in our lifetime. Because if we hit the wall, there will be no seat belts or air bags, and we will end up being a bad biological experiment on the planet."

Mother Nature "is just chemistry, biology, and physics," Watson likes to say. "Everything she does is just the sum of those three things. She's completely amoral. She doesn't care about poetry or art or whether you go to church. You can't negotiate with her, and you can't spin her and you can't evade her rules. All you can do is fit in as a species. And when a species doesn't learn to fit in with Mother Nature, it gets kicked out." It's that simple, said Watson, and that's why "every day you look in the mirror now, you're seeing an endangered species."

EIGHT

The Age of Noah

BIODIVERSITY

Nature is the art of God.
—Thomas Browne, *Religio Medici,* 1635

"Development" is like Shakespeare's virtue, "which grown into a pleurisy, dies of its own too-much."
—Aldo Leopold, "A Plea for Wilderness Hunting Grounds," 1925

One day in December 2007 I picked up the newspaper and wondered if I was reading the Bible. There was a story on the front page by my colleague Jim Yardley of *The New York Times* (December 5, 2007), who was reporting from China that the world's last known female Yangtze giant soft-shell turtle was living in a decrepit Chinese zoo in Changsha, while the planet's only known male giant soft-shell turtle was living in another zoo in Suzhou—and together this aging pair were "the last hope of saving a species believed to be the largest freshwater turtles in the world."

Describing the female, Yardley wrote: "She is fed a special diet of raw meat. Her small pool has been encased with bulletproof glass. A surveillance camera monitors her movements. A guard is posted at night. The agenda is simple: The turtle must not die . . . She is about 80 years old and weighs almost 90 pounds." As for her unlikely would-be lover, "he is 100 years old and weighs about 200 pounds." In 2008 the two were housed together in the Suzhou zoo in the hope that they would produce offspring. They did mate, but all the embryos died in early development. Scientists are hoping for better luck in future mating seasons. There is still only one female, but two more males have been discovered in Vietnam.

"For many Chinese, turtles symbolize health and longevity," Yardley noted, "but the saga of the last two Yangtze giant soft-shells is more symbolic of the threatened state of wildlife and biodiversity in China," where pollution, unbridled hunting, and runaway economic development are destroying habitats and wiping out plant and animal populations with stunning speed.

With more and more species threatened with extinction by the flood that is today's global economy, we may be the first generation in human history that literally has to act like Noah—to save the last pairs of a wide range of species. Or as God commanded Noah in Genesis: "And of every living thing of all flesh, you shall bring two of every sort into the ark, to keep them alive with you; they shall be male and female."

Unlike Noah, though, we—our generation and our civilization—are responsible for the flood, and we have the responsibility to build the ark. We are causing the flood, as more and more coral reefs, forests, fisheries, rivers, and fertile soils are spoiled or overwhelmed by commercial development; and only we can build the ark that is needed to preserve them.

The beginning of wisdom is to understand that it is our challenge and our responsibility to act like Noah—to create arks, not floods. The Energy-Climate Era is about more than just addressing soaring energy demand, drastic climate change, and proliferating petrodictatorships. It is also about dealing with another effect of a world that is hot, flat, and crowded—the threat to the earth's biodiversity, as more and more plant and animal species are endangered or go extinct.

In the past decade, I have traveled throughout the world with Conservation International, which specializes in biodiversity preservation. My wife, Ann, is a member of the CI board, and I frequently call on CI scientists for insight when writing about biodiversity, as I do in this chapter. Species are constantly being discovered and others are going extinct, either due to biological circumstances or to economic development, hunting, or other human activities. But Conservation International currently estimates that one species is now going extinct every twenty minutes, which is a thousand times faster than the norm during most of the earth's history. It is understandably hard to imagine what it means that we humans are causing something in the natural realm to happen a thousand times faster than normal. That is a big number.

"Imagine what would happen to us or to our lives and livelihoods and our planet were any other natural rate to be a thousand times higher today than normal," asked Thomas Brooks, a senior director with Conservation International's Center for Applied Biodiversity Science. "What if rainfall were a thousand times more than normal? We would be flooded. What if snowfall were a thousand times more than normal? We would never dig out. What if rates of disease transmission for malaria or HIV/AIDS were a thousand times higher than they are now? Millions would perish. But that is what is happening to plant and animal biodiversity today."

This is not just a problem for zoos. We have no idea how many natural cures, how many industrial materials, how many biological insights, how much sheer natural beauty, and how many parts and pieces of a complex web of life we barely understand are being lost.

"The biodiversity of the planet is a unique and uniquely valuable library that we have been steadily burning down—one wing at a time—before we have even cataloged all the books, let alone read them all," said John Holdren, the Harvard and Woods Hole environmental scientist.

Imagine if the trend toward rapid and widespread extinction continues and accelerates. Imagine a world with little or no biodiversity—a stainless-steel-and-cement world stripped bare of every plant and animal, every tree and hillside. Not only would such a world be barely livable, from a biological point of view—it would be a world we would barely want to live in.

From what landscapes or flower beds would future painters draw their inspiration? What would move poets to write their sonnets, composers to craft their symphonies, and religious leaders and philosophers to contemplate the meaning of God by examining his handiwork up close and in miniature? To go through life without being able to smell a flower, swim a river, pluck the apple off a tree, or behold a mountain valley in spring is to be less than fully alive. Yes, one supposes, we would find substitutes, but nothing that could compare with the pristine bounty, beauty, colors, and complexity of nature, without which we are literally less human. Is it any wonder that studies show that hospital patients who have a view of natural scenery from their rooms recover more quickly?

"Destroying a tropical rain forest and other species-rich ecosystems for profit is like burning all the paintings of the Louvre to cook dinner," explained the famed entomologist Edward O. Wilson when I visited him in his lab at Harvard, where the walls are lined with drawers and drawers full of the thousands of different ant species that he and his colleagues have collected from across the world: "That is what we're doing. 'We need this money from our oil palm plantations—sorry about the great forest of Borneo and the orangutans.'"

But for those not persuaded by the aesthetic, elegiac, religious, or spiritual values of biodiversity, there are some often overlooked practical benefits to keep in mind. These are known to environmentalists by the rather dry and undescriptive term "ecosystem services." Natural ecosystems provide a wide range of benefits and "services" to people who do not have or cannot afford a local supermarket or plumbing: They supply fresh water, they filter pollutants from streams, they provide breeding grounds for fisheries, they control erosion, they buffer human communities against storms and natural disasters, they harbor insects that pollinate crops or attack crop pests, they naturally take CO_2 out of the atmosphere. These "services" are particularly crucial to poor people in the developing world who depend directly on ecosystems for their livelihoods.

"Critics of environmentalism . . . usually wave aside the small and the unfamiliar, which they tend to classify into two categories, bugs and weeds," Wilson wrote in *The Creation*.

> It is easy for them to overlook the fact that these creatures make up most of the organisms and species on Earth. They forget, if they ever knew, how the voracious caterpillars of an obscure moth from the American tropics saved Australia's pastureland from the overgrowth of cactus; how a Madagascar "weed," the rosy periwinkle, provided the alkaloids that cure most cases of Hodgkin's disease and acute childhood leukemia; how another substance from an obscure Norwegian fungus made possible the organ transplant industry; how a chemical from the saliva of leeches yielded a solvent that prevents blood clots during and after surgery; and so on through the pharmacopoeia that has stretched from the herbal medicines of Stone Age shamans to the magic-bullet cures of present-day biomedical science . . . Wild species [also] enrich the soil, cleanse the water, pollinate most of the flowering plants. They create the very air we breathe. Without these amenities, the remainder of human history would be nasty and brief.

If we destabilize nature by degrading it, Wilson continued, "the organisms most affected are likely to be the largest and most complex, including human beings."

Biodiversity doesn't only help us to live—it helps us to adapt. There is nothing more practical than the role that biodiversity plays in easing adaptation to change for all living things—including us humans. Mark Erdmann, a marine biologist with Conservation International in Indonesia, gave me a mini-lecture about this in March 2008, as we sat on a beachfront overlooking the Lombok Strait, on the island of Nusa Penida in Indonesia. I had gone there to learn about CI's work to save the diversity of marine life in the Indonesian archipelago.

"Change is the one constant in life, and without diversity—of species, cultures, crops—adaptation to this change becomes much more difficult," Erdmann explained. "Talk to the farmer who grows just one crop and a disease wipes out his whole farm. Talk to the financial adviser who puts all his money into a single stock . . . In a nutshell, diversity bequeaths resilience—and we're gonna need all the resilience we can muster to deal with the global changes rapidly descending upon us." Who knows what catastrophic diseases lie in wait in our future? If we have plowed up our tropical rain forests for palm oil and sugarcane ethanol, it will be like emptying our tool kit of natural medicines. "We need diversity precisely because change is constant, and diversity provides the raw material we need to adapt to change," added Erdmann.

In a world that is hot, flat, and crowded, where all kinds of things are going to be moving and shifting much faster than in ages past, the last thing we want to lose is the tools we need to adapt to change.

When we speak about preserving biodiversity, what exactly does that include? I like the definition offered by the dictionary Biologyreference.com, which defines biodiversity as "the sum total of life on Earth; the entire global complement of terrestrial, marine, and freshwater biomes and ecosystems, and the species—plants, animals, fungi, and microorganisms—that live in them, including their behaviors, interactions, and ecological processes. Biodiversity is [also] linked directly to the nonliving components of the planet—atmosphere, oceans, freshwater systems, geological formations, and soils—forming one great, interdependent system, the biosphere."

In this whole biosphere, scientists today have discovered and described between 1.7 and 1.8 million species of plants, animals, and microorganisms, says Russell A. Mittermeier, president of Conservation International, but some estimates suggest that the total number of species ranges between 5 and 30 million, and some scientists believe there may be as many as another 100 million species that we just have not identified, because they are hidden beneath the earth or seas or in remote locales. Some eighty to ninety new species of primates have been identified in just the last decade and a half, noted Mittermeier, "which means that 15 to 20 percent of all primates have been described by science in just the last fifteen years."

That's why Code Green has to involve both a strategy for the *generation* of clean energy—in order to mitigate climate change and its effects on weather, temperatures, rainfall, sea levels, and droughts—and a strategy for the *preservation* of the earth's biodiversity, so we don't also destroy the very plant and animal species that sustain life. Remember: Climate change is a critical issue, but biodiversity loss could also destabilize the systemic and vital carrying capacity of our planet—as much as climate change. In all the very welcome attention to climate change in recent years, the issue of biodiversity loss has gotten lost. That's why Code Green focuses on both *generation* of a new kind of energy and *preservation* of the natural world.

"Global warming and pollution are just a couple of things that happen when we overtax our natural resources," said Glenn Prickett, senior vice president of Conservation International and an expert on economics and the environment. "What also happens is that oceans get overfished, forests and coral reefs are destroyed, and this has a real impact, not only on the plants and animals who live in these ecosystems, but also on the people who live off them."

We have to consider this problem comprehensively. If the whole world just thinks about halting the emissions of CO_2 into the atmosphere and ignores what is happening within our ecosystems, "much of the world's biodiversity could be wiped out while we're looking the other way," added Prickett. "And don't think for minute that you can have a healthy climate, or a healthy civilization, on a dead planet. Our climate is directly impacted by the health of our tropical forests and other natural systems."

Over the past decade, I have traveled with Glenn to some of the world's biodiversity hot spots and other endangered regions where CI is working—from the Pantanal wetlands in southwestern Brazil to the Atlantic rain forest on Brazil's coast, from the Guyana Shield forest wilderness in southern Venezuela to the Rio Tambopata macaw research station in the heart of the Peruvian jungle, from the exotic-sounding highland of Shangri-La in Chinese-controlled Tibet to the tropical forests of Sumatra and the coral-ringed islands off Bali, in Indonesia. For me, these trips have been master classes in biodiversity, as were my own travels to the Masai Mara in Kenya and the Ngorongoro Crater in Tanzania and the vast Empty Quarter of the Saudi Arabian Desert and—before I had kids—a rappelling trip inside the salt domes of the Dead Sea.

In many ways, though, the first trip Glenn and I ever took taught me everything I needed to know about the biodiversity challenge we are facing. In 1998 we went to Brazil, and the trip began with the most unusual interview—locationwise—that I have ever conducted. It was with Nilson de Barros, then superintendent for the environment for the Brazilian state Mato Grosso do Sul, who insisted that we conduct our talk in the middle of the Rio Negro.

Mato Grosso do Sul is at the heart of the Pantanal region, along the border between Brazil, Bolivia, and Paraguay. The Pantanal is the largest freshwater wetland in the world (the size of Wisconsin), and is home to jaguars and a host of endangered species. Glenn and I flew in on a tiny prop plane, which landed in the front yard of the Fazenda Rio Negro, a ranch and nature lodge on the Rio Negro. We then boarded motorized launches and set off for the meeting point at a shallow bend in the river.

The Pantanal nature reserve is Jurassic Park without the dinosaurs. Moving downriver, we passed scores of caimans lounging on the bank, giant river otters bobbing up and down, with egrets, hyacinth macaws, toucans, ibises, marsh deer, spoonbills, jabiru storks, foxes, ocelots, and rheas (relatives of ostriches) all poking their heads through the forest curtain at different points along our route. It was, quite simply, the most stunning cornucopia of biodiversity—plants and animals—that I have ever encountered at one time. De Barros and his team were waiting for us, standing waist-deep in the middle of the Rio Negro.

"First a beer, then a bath, then we talk," he said, cracking open a can of Skol as the river flowed by.

And I thought I had the best job in the world.

The broad threat to biodiversity and ecosystems worldwide today comes from two directions, de Barros explained. The first is from regions where the poorest of the poor are trying to scrape out a living from the natural ecosystems around them. When too many people try to do that, you lose whatever forests, reefs, and species are within reach. That is a huge problem around the Amazon wetlands and rain forest, but not in the Pantanal. The Pantanal, he explained, is not threatened by poor residents who chop down trees and sell them to timber companies to escape from poverty. The culture in the Pantanal is a rare example of man and nature thriving in harmony—through a mixed economy of ranching, fishing, and, lately, ecotourism.

No, the main biodiversity challenge to the Pantanal came from the outside: from globalization. A global triple threat was converging on the Pantanal: Soy farmers on the plateau above the Pantanal basin, eager to feed a rapidly expanding world soybean market, were widening their fields, and pesticides and silt runoff from their farms were fouling the rivers and wildlife. At the same time, the governments of Brazil, Argentina, Uruguay, Paraguay, and Bolivia had formed a trading bloc in the hope of making their economies more globally competitive. To better get the Pantanal's soy products to market, these governments wanted to dredge and straighten the rivers in the area in ways that could greatly alter the ecosystem. Finally, a consortium of international energy companies was building a pipeline across the Pantanal, from natural-gas-rich Bolivia to the vast, energy-guzzling Brazilian city of São Paulo.

The Pantanal, in fact, is a laboratory of globalization's economic upsides and biodiversity downsides. The biggest upside is that globalization is bringing more people out of poverty faster than ever before in the history of the world. The biggest downside is that in raising standards of living, globalization is making possible much higher levels of production and consumption by many more people. That's flat meeting crowded. And that, in turn, is fueling urban sprawl around the world, an increase in highways and motorized traffic, and bigger homes with more energy-guzzling devices for more people. To feed this ravenous global economy, more and more companies are tempted to take over vast native forests in places like Indonesia and Brazil and convert them to oil palm plantations, soybean farms, and other large-scale commercial enterprises at a speed and scope the world has also never seen before.

Over the years, Glenn Prickett explains, NGOs like Conservation International, The Nature Conservancy, and the World Wildlife Fund have developed tools and large-scale education campaigns that can help the rural poor live more sustainably and preserve the very natural systems on which they depend. "But we have not yet developed the tools and scale of operation to meet the globalization threat to biodiversity, which is becoming overwhelming," he explained.

To be sure, in recent years we've seen many collaborations between conservation groups and global companies like Walmart, Starbucks, and McDonald's, which aim to show these companies how to reduce the impact their supply chains and manufacturing processes have on the natural world. But all their efforts are just fingers in the dike. Global growth is driving up commodity prices, prompting companies to put more land under agricultural cultivation for food, fiber, and biofuels, and stimulating demand for more tropical forests to be stripped of timber, more coral reefs to be lost to destructive fishing practices, and more mines to be dug for minerals.

Without governments that are highly attentive to where and how lands are developed, and able to restrain the pressures from the global marketplace, the growth pressures from a world getting flat and crowded at the same time could simply overwhelm the world's last remaining biodiversity-rich forests and reefs, which will only make the world hotter, because deforestation accounts for some 20 percent of all CO_2 emissions.

In the same twenty minutes that will see some unique species vanish forever, Conservation International notes, 1,200 acres of forests will be burned and cleared for development. The CO_2 emissions from deforestation are greater than the emissions from the world's entire transportation sector—all the cars, trucks, planes, trains, and ships combined. Less forest cover means fewer acres of habitat for species, so they must move or adapt. Those that can, survive; those that cannot, go extinct. It's that simple—only it is now happening faster than ever in more places than ever.

This is why we need a strong ethic of conservation. There have to be limits to how much and where we encroach on the natural world. Without such limits, we will see the living and nesting areas of more and more species paved over, rivers fouled, corals bleached, and forests plowed under for industrial agriculture. We will continue to lurch from single-issue response to single-issue response—without ever developing a systematic approach that can marry global growth and biodiversity protection.

It starts with connecting the dots. To help cut emissions and boost energy security, the entire European Union has set the target of producing 20 percent of its energy from renewable sources by 2020, including increased use of biofuels—transportation fuels derived either from crops like corn, oil palm, soybeans, algae, or sugarcane or from plant waste, wood chips, or wild grasses, like switchgrass. The EU has declared that the "bio" ingredients of biofuels sold in Europe—palm oil and corn, for example—must not come from tropical forests, nature reserves, wetlands, or grasslands with high biodiversity. But fuels are fungible in a world market and are not always easy to monitor. It is hard to believe the EU mandate about renewable fuels will not accelerate the conversion of rain forests in Southeast Asia to oil palm plantations; some say it already has. Palm oil is the most efficient base for biodiesel fuel, although it is also used for cosmetics and in cooking. The cruel irony is that deforestation will result in more greenhouse gases being released into the atmosphere than the use of biofuels will eliminate. I have flown over an oil palm plantation in north Sumatra, in Indonesia. It looked like someone laid down twenty-five footfall fields in the middle of a tropical forest—just one rectangular block after another.

Michael Grunwald wrote a piece for *Time* (March 27, 2008) in which he described flying over a similar plantation in Brazil with an eco-activist.

> From his Cessna a mile above the southern Amazon, John Carter looks down on the destruction of the world's greatest ecological jewel. He watches men converting rain forest into cattle pastures and soybean fields with bulldozers and chains. He sees fires wiping out such gigantic swaths of jungle that scientists now debate the "savannization" of the Amazon. Brazil just announced that deforestation is on track to double this year; Carter, a Texas cowboy with all the subtlety of a chainsaw, says it's going to get worse fast. "It gives me goose bumps," says Carter, who founded a nonprofit to promote sustainable ranching on the Amazon frontier. "It's like witnessing a rape." Carter adds, "You can't protect it. There's too much money to be made tearing it down," he says. "Out here on the frontier, you really see the market at work."

The numbers tell the story. Our planet is four billion years old and life has existed on earth for a little more than two billion years. Over those two billion years there has been a very, very slow "normal" pace of extinctions. On average, a species might live for one million years, then go extinct. That very gentle, very slow, background rate of extinctions has been punctuated over the centuries by five massive, catastrophic extinction events that have lead to the loss of an extremely high proportion of our planet's life at different periods. The most recent mass extinction, said Thomas Brooks, the Conservation International biodiversity expert, was about sixty-five million years ago—the mass extinction of the dinosaurs, apparently due to an asteroid smashing into the Yucatán Peninsula, in what is now Mexico. That asteroid is believed to have expelled a thick dust cloud into the atmosphere, which apparently triggered global cooling and ended up starving a large proportion of the earth's plants and animals.

When one looks at more recent history—the last tens of thousands of years that humans have been on earth—one finds localized wide-scale extinctions as human groups moved from place to place: from the Polynesians in Hawaii, to Indonesian seafarers on Madagascar, to our Pleistocene predecessors, who walked across the land bridge that existed in what is now the Bering Strait at least 12,000 years ago and wiped out many of the large mammals of North America, including the woolly mammoths and saber-toothed tigers.

As we enter the modern age, though, the impact of globalization is metastasizing to cause what is already being called the earth's sixth great mass extinction. This is not a local extinction event anymore. It "is unfolding at a scale equal to the asteroid, or the impacts of the rest of our planet's five mass extinctions, as best we can measure from the fossil record," Brooks said.

We are the flood. We are the asteroid. We had better learn how to be the ark. For more than forty years now, the International Union for the Conservation of Nature has tracked the status of the world's biodiversity and assessed the probability of extinction of every known plant and animal species. Its Red List of Threatened Species monitors current extinctions, and gives us a picture of what is happening right now.

What we learn from the IUCN Red List is that when mass human-driven extinctions happened in places like the Hawaiian islands, after the arrival of the Polynesians around A.D. 400, "they were 'closed system extinctions'—terrible in themselves, but confined to those regions," said Brooks. But due to globalization, we are now seeing extinctions that used to be isolated to one island or region happening all over the world at the same time.

We know that we can restore natural habitats, said Brooks. We know that we can restore populations in order to bring back species whose survival is threatened, like the buffalo. We know that we can clean up pollution, even a river as polluted as the Thames. "It is even within our grasp to reverse climate change," he added. "But extinctions are irreversible. Jurassic Park is a fiction: Once a species is gone, it is lost forever—we have lost that million years of our planetary heritage forever."

Later Is Over

As many beautiful things as there are to behold in the rain forest, I actually prefer the sounds to the sights. In June 2006, Glenn, my family, and I went by riverboat up Peru's Rio Tambopata to visit a CI-sponsored research station that specializes in rescuing scarlet macaws. I liked to lie awake inside a mosquito net and listen to the rain forest symphony outside. It sounded like one of those dissonant pieces of modern music: a cacophony of birds, red howler monkeys, wild pigs, frogs, and insects making bizarre clicks, snorts, croaks, chirps, wails, and whistles that sound like car alarms, strange doorbell chimes, and an orchestral wind section that had lost its music but was playing on anyway. Occasionally, this symphony would get punctuated by the shrill, desperate scream of a member of the human species in our lodge who had just encountered a spider in the toilet.

The stretch of Amazon rain forest we were visiting, in southern Peru, is a largely uninhabited (by humans) wilderness that is home to some of the planet's most endangered wildlife and one of the world's largest macaw clay licks—a cliff of red clay, where blue, red, and gold macaws flock for a dirt breakfast every morning. Look down in the rain forest and you might see a hunting wasp stinging a caterpillar and depositing its eggs inside. Look up in the verdant canopy and you will see the hanging nest of oropendula weaver birds. You will notice, though, that the oropendulas have located their nest on a branch right next to a large white wasp's nest. Why? So if any predators try to attack the birds, they will also rile the wasps—an ingenious natural security system.

Look around, though, and you will see trouble looming.

Going up the Rio Tambopata on our riverboat, we saw gold miners using big motorized barges and mercury to dredge and sift—and destroy—riverbanks in search of gold. With global gold prices soaring, the incentives to dredge the Tambopata are enormous. Some of the miners clear forests for camps and hunt rare animals for food. And access is getting easier by the week. The Interoceanic Highway, running from the Atlantic coast of Brazil to the Pacific coast of Peru, is nearing completion. More roads lead to more agriculture, more logging, more mining, and more oil and gas extraction, which converts more forests to cropland, which releases more climate-changing greenhouse gases as millions of trees are cut down.

That whole scene reminds me of the climatologist Heidi Cullen's remark that we humans are now playing lead electric guitar in Mother Nature's symphony orchestra. In doing so, we forget a fundamental truth: We are the only species in this vast web of life that no animal or plant in nature depends on for its survival—yet we depend on this whole web of life for our survival. We evolved within it. As we adapted to it, it shaped us into what we are. We humans need that web to survive—it doesn't need us. But we sure need it—and it thrives only if the whole system works in harmony.

That is why, at the end of the day, this biodiversity issue is not just about saving nature—it is equally about saving humanity, as Edward O. Wilson has said. It is about understanding who we are as a species and deciding how we intend to continue living on this planet and relating to its natural environment.

"Without the biosphere that made us what we are, in which we evolved, we are not fully human," Wilson explained as we sat in his laboratory at Harvard. The more we change the climate and the natural world by our actions, he added, the more we eliminate the plants and animals, forests, rivers, oceans, and glaciers that regulate life on the planet to the great benefit of human beings for free—the more we humans are going to have to try to regulate everything ourselves. And anyone watching the political debates about climate change should be very, very wary about our ability to manage things as well as Mother Nature has done.

"The more we destroy the natural world," said Wilson, "the more we have to take over and employ our own ingenuity to maintain it moment by moment all by ourselves . . . So unless we plan to change earth literally into a spaceship in which our hands are on the controls, moment by moment, of all the necessities of human life—where we manage the atmosphere, moment by moment—then we better make sure we return the maintenance of the biosphere back to where it started and belongs and where these millions of species support us, cheerfully, scot-free."

Mindlessly degrading the natural world the way we have been is no different than a bird degrading its own nest, a fox degrading its own den, a beaver degrading its own dam. We can't keep doing that and assume that it is just happening "over there." The scale of biodiversity loss happening today is having global impacts. As the team at Conservation International likes to say: "Lost there, felt here." And we can't keep doing that and assume that we will repair it later.

Later is over. That is the psychological biodiversity redline we have passed as we entered the Energy-Climate Era. "Later" was a luxury for previous generations, eras, civilizations, and epochs. It meant that you could paint the same landscape, see the same animals, eat the same fruit, climb the same trees, fish the same rivers, enjoy the same weather, or rescue the same endangered species that you did when you were a kid—but just do it later, whenever you got around to it. Nature's bounty seemed infinite and all the threats to it either limited or reversible. In the Energy-Climate Era, given the accelerating rates of extinction and development, "later" is going to be removed from the dictionary. Later is no longer when you get to do all those things in nature you did as a kid—on your time schedule. Later is when they're gone—when you won't get to do any of them ever again. Later is too late, so whatever we are going to save, we'd better start saving now.

As Denis Hayes, the cofounder of Earth Day, once observed: If environmentalism turns out to be just a fad, "it's going to be our last fad."

NINE

Energy Poverty

How will we know when Africa as a continent stands a chance to climb sustainably out of poverty? My metric is very simple: It's when I see Angelina Jolie posing next to a vast field of solar panels in Ghana or a wind farm crowded with turbines in Zimbabwe. In recent years, Jolie and other celebrities have done a great service by drawing attention to Africa's travails. In highlighting the issues of poverty and disease, they have brought some much-needed global aid and debt relief. But there is one problem in Africa that almost never gets the spotlight, and that is Africa's shortage of light. If you look at satellite pictures of the earth at night, it is quite stunning. Little lights flicker across Europe, the Americas, and Asia, while vast swaths of Africa are simply pitch-black.

AIDS relief has its champions, as do water purification, forest preservation, malaria treatment, and the alleviation of poverty. But the problem of "energy poverty" has no champion. It's not sexy; it has no international constituency, no buzz, no wristband, no human face. No one wants to embrace power plants, which are either dirty politically or just plain dirty. Worse, they take years to finance and build, and you can't see the results of your investment for a long time.

Energy, in fact, is Africa's oldest orphan. But how, one wonders, will the tides of poverty, HIV/AIDS, unsafe drinking water, and malaria be turned back in Africa for good without enough energy to turn on the lights? According to the World Bank, the Netherlands today produces as much electrical power annually as all of sub-Saharan Africa, excluding South Africa: 20 gigawatts. Every two weeks or so China adds as much power—1 gigawatt of electricity—as the forty-seven countries of sub-Saharan Africa, excluding South Africa, add every *year*.

But despite this staggering power gap, the problem of energy poverty rarely gets discussed. Universal access to electricity was not even one of the eight Millennium Development Goals that were set out by the UN and the world's leading development institutions in 2000. Those goals range from halving extreme poverty to providing universal primary education, all by 2015. How are we going to eradicate poverty without eradicating energy poverty?

I first heard the term "energy poverty" from Robert Freling, executive director of the Solar Electric Light Fund (SELF.org), which delivers solar power and wireless communications to rural and remote villages throughout the developing world. The right of every person to have access to energy is as fundamental as the right to access to air and water, Freling argues, "but it is often overlooked by very smart people, who are dedicated to solving the problems of development."

It is hard to believe in this day and age, but the World Bank estimates that roughly 1.6 billion people—one out of every four people on the planet—don't have regular access to an electricity grid. Every night is a blackout for 1.6 billion people. In sub-Saharan Africa, excluding South Africa, according to the World Bank, 75 percent of households, or 550 million people, have no access to network electricity. In South Asia— places like India, Pakistan, and Bangladesh—700 million people, 50 percent of the overall population and 90 percent of the rural population, are not on the grid. And under business-as-usual scenarios, the International Energy Agency projects that 1.4 billion people will still lack access to electricity in 2030.

Meanwhile, indoor air pollution caused by the smoke emitted from cooking over open fires with inefficient stoves and pots—the most common alternative to grid electricity—is responsible for 1.6 million deaths per year, mostly of young children and mothers. That means that this biomass cooking as a cause of death ranks just behind malnutrition, unsafe sex, and lack of clean water and sanitation, according to the World Health Organization.

Why is there still so much energy poverty in the world? It has different causes in different regions. In some places, surging economic growth and population explosions have combined to overwhelm supply. In others, high oil and natural gas prices have forced poor countries to ration. In still others, prolonged droughts have crippled hydroelectric power.

But if there is one common denominator that cuts across all energy-poor countries, it's the simple fact that they don't have functioning utilities that are able to raise financing on the scale needed to build and properly operate power plants and transmission lines. And the reason is that these countries are plagued by either persistent misgovernance or persistent civil war—or both. The two are usually interrelated, particularly in Africa. If a country doesn't have a functioning government or a state of relative domestic peace that would enable it to enter into the long-term planning, designing, financing, building, and operating of expensive power plants and transmission grids—and they are all long-term projects— the lights will never come on or stay on for very long or for very many people. And even in places where the government works and the society is stable, power projects often run aground because that government doesn't allow the utility to operate as an independent commercial entity and charge the prices it requires to keep investing, or because it turns the utility into a honeypot of patronage or booty for political leaders. Much of the debt relief offered to Africa today is actually about forgiving loans made for power projects that were built but failed because of corruption or misrule.

Lawrence Musaba, the manager of the Southern African Power Pool, a twelve-nation consortium of electricity utilities at the continent's tip, told *The New York Times* (July 29, 2007): "We've had no significant capital injection into generation and transmission, from either the private or public sectors, for 15, maybe 20 years." My colleague Michael Wines, who wrote that story, also noted that in Nigeria, Africa's most populous nation, the government reported in April 2007 that "only 19 of 79 power plants work . . . Daily electricity output has plunged 60 percent from its peak, and blackouts cost the economy $1 billion a year, the Council for Renewable Energy in Nigeria says."

Energy is like any other economic good. It needs decent governance, functioning institutions, and effective markets to get electrons from the producer to the consumer on a sustained basis. Without reliable energy, virtually every aspect of life is negatively affected. After all, energy, at its most basic, is the capacity to do work.

"At the village level," Freling explained, "energy poverty means you can't pump clean water regularly, there's no communications, no way to have adult literacy classes, and certainly no way to run computers at school or have access to connectivity." This perpetuates social inequality. "It is mostly the women in rural villages that bear the greatest burden of energy poverty, [because] it is they who must walk for miles every day to fetch water for drinking and bathing, or to collect firewood. Young girls are often taken out of primary school to assist in the daily struggle for energy subsistence."

In addition, said Freling, because women in African villages are generally responsible for cooking family meals, they are the ones most seriously affected by indoor air pollution, which is caused by kerosene lamps and open fires in poorly ventilated kitchens. Teenage girls in many African countries will not go to school when they are menstruating if the school has no clean water, which usually requires some form of electric power to produce.

Energy use and gross national product are very closely correlated. Factories that don't have grid power have to rely on backup generators, which are usually much more expensive to run and more polluting. According to the World Bank, African manufacturing enterprises report an average of fifty-six days of power outages per year, causing firms to lose 5 to 6 percent of sales revenues—and for the informal/underground economy, such losses could be up to 20 percent of revenues each year. In Bangladesh, a World Bank study recently found that having access to electricity has a cumulative impact on increasing rural household incomes by as much as 20 percent—resulting in a corresponding drop in the poverty rate of about 15 percent. Another World Bank study quotes surveys in Bangladesh as finding that study time for schoolchildren is up to 33 percent higher for those whose homes have electricity.

To put it another way: Every problem of the developing world is also an energy problem. The problem of education is about a teacher shortage—and an energy shortage. The problem of health care in sub-Saharan Africa is about a shortage of doctors and medicines—and a shortage of energy to run medical equipment and refrigerate drugs. Unemployment in rural India is about a skills shortage, an investment shortage—and a shortage of the energy needed to keep factories running. Agricultural weakness in Bangladesh is about shortages of seeds, fertilizer, and land—and a shortage of energy to pump water or power equipment.

"Energy poverty," concluded Freling, "creeps into every single aspect of existence and wipes out any hope of climbing out of [economic] poverty into the twenty-first century."

To be sure, the rural and urban poor have long survived with limited energy—wood and dung to burn, animals to pull plows, water to carry boats. And for a hundred years or so after electricity became widespread in the industrialized world, they carried on using their traditional forms of energy, augmenting it when possible with petrol or some battery-powered devices or a jerry-rigged line to an electricity pole.

But being energy-poor is not what it used to be—not in a world that is hot, flat, and crowded. It is so much more punishing and destabilizing. When the world is hot and you don't have access to electricity, your ability to adapt to climate change is dangerously limited. When the world is flat and you don't have access to electricity, you have no ability to use computers, cell phones, or the Internet—all the tools that are now central to global commerce, education, collaboration, and innovation. When the world is crowded and you don't have access to electricity, your ability to thrive in your village is limited and you are much more likely to have to move to an already overcrowded slum in a megacity like Mumbai, Shanghai, or Lagos.

Today more than ever, economic growth comes with an on/off switch. Energy today unlocks so much more knowledge, unleashes so much more potential, provides so much more protection, and, as a result, creates so much more stability than it used to. Therefore, energy poverty not only holds back the world's most vulnerable people—it deprives the rest of us of their potential contributions. Let's look closer to see why.

Energy Poverty and the Hot World

In a world that is hot—a world that is more and more affected by global warming—guess who is going to suffer the most? It will be the people who caused it the least—the poorest people in the world, who have no electricity, no cars, no power plants, and virtually no factories to emit CO_2 into the atmosphere. Many of the 2.4 billion people who live on $2 a day or less reside in rural areas and depend directly on soil, forests, and plants in their immediate vicinity for subsistence.

Climate-change experts broadly agree that increases in global average temperature, wind, evaporation rates, and precipitation are going to increasingly produce more meteorological extremes: heavier and more violent rains in some regions and more intense and prolonged droughts in others. All this will be a nightmare for the energy-poor in the countryside: Heavier and more intense rains mean that less water soaks into the ground and more runs off to the sea, so soils can become thinner and more vulnerable to higher evaporation rates between rainfalls. This drying out of the land also increases the possibility of wildfires.

Without electricity, adaptation to these extremes is only going to be that much more difficult. Many areas populated by the rural poor already have overstressed water supplies, due to overexploitation, deforestation, population explosions, and poor water quality maintenance. If climate change increases droughts in these areas, as it has already started to do in parts of Africa and southern Europe, the energy-poor will not be able to resort to running a fan longer, refrigerating more food or medicine, or desalinating water, as people with electricity could do. And the deeper the water tables sink, the more the poor will need electricity or fuel to pump water up from deeper wells.

Those of the world's poor living in low-lying coastal areas, like Bangladesh, will also be forced to migrate inland by any significant rise in sea levels. Meanwhile, those living at higher elevations will be more exposed to insect-borne diseases, because the higher elevations of Africa and Latin America are warming faster than the lowlands—so mosquitoes can now carry malaria to higher slopes. If temperatures continue to rise, this will expose millions more people in both continents, and the energy-poor cannot escape by closing the windows and turning on an air conditioner.

Take just one country, Rwanda: In most of its countryside, there is no grid, and generators that run on gasoline or diesel are becoming more expensive by the day to operate. How are the Rwandans going to maintain vaccines, provide clean water, run fans, or operate a clinic to improve health care over the long run, or simply adapt to climate change, without reliable energy—clean or dirty, cheap or expensive?

(While the energy-poor wait to get connected, they need all the help we can extend for protecting and restoring the forests, coral reefs, and other natural habits in and around which they live—because these natural systems can help buffer poor people against climate disruptions before they get connected to the grid. For example, coastal mangrove forests protect low-lying communities against floods and rising sea levels. In the 2004 Asian tsunami, communities that had protected their coral reefs and mangrove forests suffered less damage than those that had converted them to beachfront hotels and shrimp farms. Also, upland forests help to provide more reliable water supplies as droughts become more prevalent and glaciers recede, leaving less water available. There is even a connection to malaria. Recent research has shown that areas that have been deforested are more prone to malaria because the muddy pools left behind by loggers provide more breeding habitats for mosquitoes. Adaptation to climate change is not just about electrons and sea walls. It's about conservation.)

Even some of those with a connection to the grid are seeing their power diminished because of climate change. In June 2006, I visited Peru, where, in the Sacred Valley of the Incas, I met José Ignacio Lambarri, who owned a sixty-acre farm. He did not describe what was happening to him as "global weirding," but he certainly described the symptoms. Lambarri told me that for most of his life he had been growing giant white corn, with kernels that used to be as big as quarters. This giant corn, which was exported to Spain and Japan, grew in his valley because of a unique combination of water, temperature, soil, and sun. But recently, Lambarri said, he started to notice something: "The water level is going down, and the temperature is going up." As a result, the giant corn kernels weren't growing quite as large as they used to, new pests had started appearing, and there was no longer enough water to plant the valley terraces that date from Incan times. He also noticed that the snow line he had grown up looking at for forty-four years was starting to recede. "I tell my wife," he said to me, "the day that mountain loses its snow, we will have to move out of the valley."

Like Lambarri, farmers all over the world have come to depend on glaciers to feed their rivers and drive their hydroelectric dams. But with temperatures rising, and winters shortened, the glaciers are not providing the snowmelt they once did. This is already sparking conflict. Lambarri told me that every year he and his fellow farmers decide by committee how to divide up the water. Now, "every year the meetings get more heated, because there is less water to distribute and the same amount of land that needs it," he said.

When I shared this story with the physicist and climate specialist Joseph Romm, he recalled that "the word 'rival' actually comes from people who share the same river—look it up." I did. The Random House Webster's Unabridged Dictionary says the word derives from "rivalis[,] orig., one who uses a stream in common with another."

If global warming plays out anywhere near the projections, the world is going to have a lot more rivals.

Energy Poverty and the Flat World

Fifty years ago, if you were a poor person living in the developing world and didn't have electricity, you were certainly at a disadvantage. But though the gap between you and someone in the developed world was large, it was not unbridgeable. You could still write a letter with pen and paper, you could still walk to the local post office to drop off that letter, and you could still find a library in your capital and read a book printed on paper, even if you had to walk fifty miles to get there. Fifty years ago, poor or middle-class people in America might also have to walk to the library or post office, or hop on a bicycle, but it was just a mile or two away. Still, once they arrived, they too found books and letters printed on paper.

In other words, there was a gap, it was big, but it was not unbridgeable. Fast-forward to today. If you don't have access to electricity, you don't have access to *all the world's libraries, all the world's post office boxes, and almost all the world's stores and manufacturers*. Because without electricity you don't have access to a computer, a browser, the Internet, the World Wide Web, Google, Hotmail, or any form of e-mail or e-commerce. Therefore, you can't search those libraries online, you can't shop for the lowest prices, you can't send or receive an e-mail from anyone to anywhere, and you can't write a letter or a book or a business plan on a screen that allows you to cut and paste with the click of a mouse. That means that you can't use any of the basic tools that people in the flat world are using to compete, connect, and collaborate. That's why, in a flat world, the gap between those who have electricity and those who don't grows exponentially, not arithmetically.

Experts have probably known this for a long time. I discovered it quite by accident on a tour to a remote collection of villages in India in October 2007. (The tour was organized by the charitable foundation Byrraju, which was set up by B. Ramalinga Raju, the founder and then chairman of Satyam, one of India's premier technology firms. I actually got to know Raju not through Satyam but when he contacted me about his charitable work. Sadly, Raju and his brother Ramu were indicted in 2008, after the first edition of this book came out, for massively embezzling funds from Satyam. The case is still pending. What made it so surprising to many Indians, though, was that while Raju may have been engaged in fraud at Satyam, his charitable work, which focused on alleviating rural poverty and establishing India's first 911 emergency call number, was very real and widely appreciated.) Byrraju was working on a range of antipoverty projects in a cluster of Indian villages in northeast Andhra Pradesh, about 350 miles from Hyderabad. Those villages were a tiny peephole, but they introduced me to the whole universe of energy poverty.

In Podagatlapalli, I was greeted with a traditional shower of yellow flower petals, and had a red dot smudged on my forehead. After a quick lunch, I was taken to see one of the village's crown jewels, a new health clinic, funded by Byrraju. As I entered a small room, I was startled to find a very elderly man, with dark brown skin and shocks of white hair covering his chest and arms, stripped down to his underwear and laid out on a table, where he was connected to an electrocardiogram machine. Standing between him and a television set was a nurse-technician in a white uniform, who was operating the EKG monitor. On the television screen was a heart specialist sitting in a hospital in Bangalore, some five hundred miles to the south. He was observing the EKG via satellite hookup and preparing to read the results and dispense a diagnosis.

"How wonderful," I thought to myself. "This kind of telemedicine is the information technology revolution at its best. The world really is flat!"

But then I looked over into the right-hand corner of the room, and what I saw certainly sobered me up. The whole process—the EKG and the TV—was being powered by sixteen car batteries, connected to the electronic gear by a spaghetti-like tangle of wires. Why? Because in India many, many villages—where 70 percent of the population resides—are not connected to an electricity grid. This was the energy technology revolution at its worst.

When I wrote *The World Is Flat*, I included a chapter called "The Unflat World." I was aware that the technological forces that were leveling the global economic playing field had not completed their work. Many people still were unable to plug into the flat world platform. It was equally clear to me that every day this was becoming less true—that more and more people who made just $2 a day were able to buy cell phones with Internet capability or get access to $100 laptops. In India today, roughly seven million new cell phone subscribers are signed up each month, bringing the total by early 2008 to 200 million subscribers in a country of 1.1 billion people. And tomorrow, the cost of these tools of connectivity will fall further—hence my view that the "flattening" of the world is continuing apace.

That is still true, but I have since come to appreciate that no matter how cheap these tools of connectivity become, the people at the bottom of the pyramid will only truly be connected when the world is both flat and green—when they have universal connectivity powered by abundant, clean, reliable, and cheap electrons. Why flat and green? Because it is critical that the developing world leapfrog the developed world in energy the same way it did with telephony. Many developing countries went from no phones to cell phones—and never stopped for landlines and telephone poles. We have to hope that many of the 1.6 billion people without electricity will go from no electric grid to clean distributed energy—like solar or wind—without stopping for centrally generated coal-fired power.

Yes, a certain amount of centrally generated coal-fired power is necessary for Africa or South Asia in the immediate future. Green alternatives are not yet scalable. But if all 1.6 billion people without electricity today were to connect to a power grid based on coal or natural gas or oil, the climate and pollution implications could be devastating. When you think how much climate change we have already triggered with just three-quarters of the world using fossil-fuel-based electricity, imagine if we added another quarter? This is why we desperately need abundant, clean, reliable, cheap electrons—fast. The more we can bring down the price of solar, wind, or even nuclear energy, and safely get these technologies into the hands of the world's poor, the more we can alleviate one problem (energy poverty) and prevent another (climate change and air pollution).

During a winter break from college in January 2008, my daughter Natalie worked for several weeks as an intern in a community center in Bulawayo, Zimbabwe, for children who had lost parents to HIV/AIDS or were themselves afflicted. She could barely communicate with us while she was there, though, because repeated power outages had rendered the computers at her day care center and many phones useless. Zimbabwe depends on South Africa for some of its electricity and the grid there is under constant stress. "The power outages have called into question the government's ability to meet its target of 6 percent [annual] growth," CNN.com reported from South Africa (January 29, 2008). "They also have imperiled efforts to combat a 25 percent unemployment rate." That is hardly surprising: A computer that can't be booted up or a cell phone that can't be recharged is nothing more than a paperweight—less useful than a pen, paper, or a carrier pigeon.

Just as you miss more when you don't have reliable electricity in a flat world, you also gain much more when you do have it, and so, potentially, does the whole global system. I caught a glimpse of that too, through another peephole, also in the village of Podagatlapalli, at a small elementary school supported by Byrraju. The school was a bare-bones cement structure, but the classroom I visited was packed with Indian kids, who were taking turns working on four colorful "kidproof" learning stations manufactured by Little Tikes and IBM that come loaded with interactive educational software. Each of these KidSmart Early Learning Program terminals was made of blue plastic and had a computer touch screen in the middle. They are specifically designed to promote learning in remote areas, where qualified reading and writing teachers are always in short supply.

But what I remember most is the image of two Indian kids, a boy in little blue shorts and a tiny girl in a white dress, who were sitting scrunched together on a single square stool at a KidSmart terminal, interacting with the touch screen and listening to instructions through headphones. The headphones were adult size, and they dwarfed the heads of these two little kids, like giant helmets. But sitting there, intensely operating that KidSmart terminal, those two kids looked so curious, so hungry to learn.

I thought about them the whole way home, and the thought that kept coming back to me was that one of these kids could very well be the next Thomas Edison or Marie Curie; one of them the next Sally Ride or A.P.J. Abdul Kalam, India's former president and premier rocket scientist. But that won't happen unless they get reliable access to energy technology to go with their now reliable access to information technology.

"The implications of bringing computers into rural classrooms, and wirelessly linking those classrooms to the rest of the world, are profound," said Robert Freling. "Students and teachers become excited as new programs in distance learning are introduced. Electronic friendships are established with people from faraway lands. Music and dance are shared. Cultural diversity is strengthened, even as the world becomes smaller."

Wireless connectivity that doesn't need landlines and telephone poles and distributed energy that doesn't need electricity lines and electricity poles would do more to cure rural poverty in the developing world than any other innovations. In 2000, the Solar Electric Light Fund spearheaded an initiative to create the first solar-powered high school in South Africa, two hours from Durban, in the Valley of a Thousand Hills. Myeka High School was equipped with a solar electric system that powered a computer lab as well as an Internet-connected satellite dish. Later, SELF encouraged the students to participate in an essay contest (sponsored by the International Solar Energy Society) about the impact of solar power. The winner was eleventh grader Samantha Dlomo, who wrote:

> I am sixteen years old and have lived in the rural area for the past fourteen years. In all these past years I used a candle stick to study and do my homework. The chalkboard has been the mainstay teaching aid at school. When a few solar panels were installed at school, I did not have even a faintest notion of how it was going to work. A few months later we received an overhead projector. That was the beginning of a new school experience. The following equipment was later received: 20 computers, 2 television sets and a video machine. Recently we have been connected to the Learning Channel Campus and the Internet through the satellite. Learning is now going to be research orientated. That is, we shall use worksheets and we shall use the Internet as the main source of information. In the past we spent much of our time copying notes from the chalkboard. The school has set itself a new vision for the new millennium. By the year 2005 it wants to produce learners who will follow careers in the fields of Science, Technology, Engineering, Medicine and others. This was a far-fetched dream a few years ago.

Imagine—*imagine*—if we could tap into the creativity and innovative capacity of the world's poorest people. Imagine if we could empower them with the tools and the energy they need to really compete, connect, and collaborate. It would lead to an explosion of innovation—from science and technology to art and literature—the likes of which the world has never seen. Abundant, clean, reliable, cheap power would "create the world's first truly level playing field," notes Curt Carlson, CEO of SRI International, a scientific research think tank in Silicon Valley. In doing so, it would "unlock the innovative power of the very people who will help us solve the last remaining big problems we have [around health, education, and energy]. These solutions need to come from both the bottom up and the top down."

Jeff Wacker, the futurist for Electronic Data Systems, likes to say that innovators are those people who know the 99 percent that everybody knows and therefore are able to create the 1 percent that nobody knows. If you don't know the 99 percent, or cannot get access to it, you will not have the foundation to create the new 1 percent. More likely, you will just re-create part of the 99 percent that everyone already knows. If we can make the unflat world flatter by extending electricity to the 1.6 billion people who don't have it, we can connect all those brains to the 99 percent that everybody knows, and have so many more people working on the 1 percent that nobody knows. "That is when you will have innovation everywhere," says Wacker.

The Economist has dubbed it "the age of mass innovation." As their writer Vijay Vaitheeswaran put it (October 11, 2007):

The history of innovation is filled with elites and centralized processes. But look closer and you find that ordinary people have always silently played a role. In his *A Culture of Improvement: Technology and the Western Millennium*, Robert Friedel shows how countless small efforts by individuals, from all rungs on society's ladder, contributed to the astonishing advances that we enjoy in today's post-modern, post-industrial societies. Imagine how much better firms and countries could innovate if they could harness the distributed creative potential of all these innovators in waiting . . . In an age of mass innovation, the world may even find profitable ways to deliver solutions to the 21st century's greatest needs, including sustainable clean energy, affordable and universal health care for aging populations and quite possibly entirely new industries. The one natural resource that the world has left in infinite quantity is human ingenuity.

Energy Poverty and the Crowded World

Energy can not only make a hotter world more tolerable and a flatter world more equitable; it can also make a crowded world more comfortable. I saw that through one more illuminating peephole in Andhra

Pradesh. It was in the village of Ethakota. There, Satyam, whose main business is running the back office and outsourced operations for large global companies, had set up a remote data center. Beginning in 2006, Satyam dispatched some of the simpler outsourcing work that the company had been doing from its Hyderabad headquarters to be performed by villagers in Ethakota. Amid the banana and palm groves, 120 college-educated Indian villagers, trained by Satyam and connected to the world by wireless networks, were processing data for a British magazine publisher and selling services for an Indian phone company. The data center operates in two eight-hour shifts, but it could run three—if only the electricity didn't go off for six hours a day!

As I interviewed workers at the Ethakota data center, I discovered something I did not expect. Several of them were city slickers. They had been born in the area, had migrated to India's megacities for work, and then had chosen to come back to Ethakota to live, because, although the pay was lower, the life was richer and more tranquil. Thanks to the Satyam facilities, they could live locally and act globally—as long as they had the electricity to do so. Suresh Varma, age thirty, one of the data managers, was working for a U.S. oil company in Hyderabad, but decided to move back to this lush village where his parents came from. It was like moving from a Silicon Valley to a real valley, he explained: "I have a much higher quality of life here than in an urban area anywhere in India . . . The city is concrete. You spend most of your time in traffic, just getting from one place to another. Here you walk to work . . . Here I am in touch with what is happening in the cities, but at the same time I don't miss out on my professional aspirations."

Unlike in the city, where there is now a high turnover rate at outsourcing centers that operate overnight, "in the village, nobody gives up these jobs," said Verghese Jacob, who heads Byrraju, which plans to gradually hand over ownership of the data-processing centers to the villagers. "They are very innovative and positive, and because some of them had never worked on a computer before, their respect for the opportunity is so much more than for a city child who takes it for granted."

This phenomenon, if it could be implemented on a large scale, could provide relief for India's strained megacities, like Mumbai (nineteen million people) and Calcutta (fifteen million), which simply cannot keep growing. The social and environmental implications of packing more and more people into such relatively small areas are already becoming unbearable for those on the bottom rung.

The only solution is to strengthen villages. Jacob estimates that just one of his rural outsourcing centers creates the same amount of employment and income as four hundred acres of rural Indian farmland. India, in other words, could in effect mint more farmland in its countryside by creating these knowledge-service centers with a couple hundred jobs each. This could make its villages much more viable places than cities for young people to build their futures. But they need both abundant, clean, reliable, and cheap electrons and connectivity—Internet and telephones. With connectivity, villagers can get up-to-date knowledge of farming techniques and market prices that will help them to obtain higher value for their produce. Internet access enables village artisans to upload digital pictures of locally made arts and crafts, and to make their goods directly available to a world market.

People in India and China leave their villages and cram themselves and their families into megacities not because they actually like living that way, but, in many cases, simply because that is where the jobs and opportunities are. That is always going to be true to some extent, but we can make it less true if we can bring to villages what Satyam did—an ecosystem of energy plus education plus connectivity plus investment. That is what makes a sustainable village. And we need to make a lot of sustainable villages. Every time you make a village work, not only do you help the poor, most of whom still live in villages, but you also create a better balance in the world. To make villages work, though, you have to empower people to live locally and act globally; you have to give them opportunity and access. But to empower takes power—electric power.

"For the first time in the history of the world we have the opportunity to achieve a balance between localization and globalization" at scale, says K. R. Sridhar, the Indian-born cofounder and CEO of Bloom Energy. If the rural poor on every continent no longer feel they have to move to cities and take manufacturing jobs or drive taxis or work as maids, because they have the tools and skills to connect globally and the abundant, clean energy to support their connectivity, "they will be able to get the best out of both localization and globalization," said Sridhar.

They will be able to remain in the countryside, enjoy its benefits, maintain their traditions, food, dress, and family ties, but also be able to generate the income they need to thrive. Also, the more that rural populations have their standards of living raised, the fewer children mothers will have—another way to reduce crowding.

"And when you can get localization and globalization into balance, what you end up with is humanization—an age of humanization," argues Sridhar. "When you have roots—local—and wings—global—you can be both grounded and aspiring." You can realize your full human potential. But that can happen only if IT and ET, information technology and energy technology, flat and green, are working together, because only then can everyone and everything be both distributed and connected. If we can get that, said Sridhar, "the world will have a new operating system."

TEN

Green Is the New Red, White, and Blue

We have exactly enough time—starting now.
—the late Dana Meadows, Dartmouth College environmentalist

I n 2006, I was invited by a student energy/environment group at Stanford to give a talk on campus about green innovation. As I was pacing around backstage, the school's president, John Hennessy, went through the standard introduction, but then offered his own framing of the issues, saying that confronting today's energy-climate challenge is the epitome of what John Gardner, the founder of Common Cause, once described as "a series of great opportunities disguised as insoluble problems."

I love that description—*a series of great opportunities disguised as insoluble problems*. In a few words it captures perfectly how we should approach the future.

In the first half of this book, I have tried to describe the seemingly insoluble problems that have emerged in the Energy-Climate Era—energy supply and demand imbalances, petrodictatorship, climate change, energy poverty, and biodiversity loss—and that are going to shape our lives and our planet in the coming years. In the second half, I will try to show that solving these problems is, indeed, a great opportunity for any country that rises to the challenge.

Why an opportunity? Several reasons. To begin with, the human race can no longer continue to power its growth with the fossil-fuel-based system that we have employed since the Industrial Revolution. If we do, the earth's climate, forests, rivers, oceans, and ecosystems are going to be ravaged and poisoned beyond repair. We need a new Clean Energy System that can drive our economies forward—sustainably—and bring more people out of poverty, without despoiling our planet.

It is my conviction that adopting a Clean Energy System will not be an option for much longer. For years, we have spoken as if particular countries could go green or not go green—depending on their politics or level of development. No more. I am convinced that in a world that is hot, flat, and crowded—where energy, water, land, natural resources, and energy resources are all being stressed at once—everybody, in time, is going to be forced to pay the true cost of the energy they are using, the true cost of the climate change they are causing, the true cost of the biodiversity loss they are triggering, the true cost of the petrodictatorship they are funding, and the true cost of the energy poverty they are sustaining. Mother Nature, the global community, your own community, your own customers, your own neighbors, your own kids, and your own employees are going to demand that you, your company, or your country pay "the total cost of ownership" for whatever you, or they, produce or consume, argues Andrew Shapiro, founder and president of GreenOrder, a strategy firm that helps companies profit from environmental innovation. That total cost of ownership will include "the costs that are near-term and long-term, direct and indirect, seen and hidden, financial, social, geopolitical, and environmental."

We'll all have to pay the true cost because there are no cushions left. There's nowhere to hide. There are no more green fields left to dump your garbage into, no more oceans to overfish, no more endless forests to cut down. We have reached a stage where the effects of our way of life on the earth's climate and biodiversity can no longer be externalized, socialized, ignored, or confined. Our environmental savings account is empty. It is not pay now or pay later. It is pay now, or there will be no later.

Moreover, none of these costs of what we are doing to the planet can be hidden any longer. The true costs of all these things are becoming visible, measurable, assessable, and inescapable. In a flat world, everyone can see what everyone else is doing, and everyone is coming to know the harm it is causing. There will be no avoiding accountability for the total cost of ownership of what you produce and consume.

It's a grim picture, I know. We *need* to change. Say no more. But from this necessity comes the opportunity. Whichever companies, communities, or countries can come up with the most sources of abundant, cheap, clean (non-CO_2-emitting) electrons will actually have the answer to all five of the big problems plaguing the world in the early twenty-first century. With abundant, cheap, clean, reliable electrons, we will be able to dramatically ease energy and natural resource supply and demand constraints, undermine petrodictatorship, mitigate climate change, sharply reduce biodiversity loss, and eliminate energy poverty. How exciting is that? All five of the world's biggest problems have the same solution!

What does that tell you? What it tells me is that the search for abundant, cheap, clean, reliable electrons will be the next great global industry. It has to be. I call that industry ET—energy technology. ET is the new IT. Given the size of the future demand for clean power technologies, it has to be. And therefore the country that dominates ET will have, I believe, the most national security, the most economic security, and the most energy security; it will have the most innovative companies (you can't make a product greener without making it smarter, with smarter materials, design, or software) and the most healthy environment; it will enjoy the most global respect and global trust. That country will also be seen as the most inspiring country because it will be solving more problems that affect more people than any other country.

In other words, clean energy is power. CE = P. But it is much more than just electric power. It is economic, political, innovative, and reputational power. The ability to design, build, and export green technologies for producing clean electrons, clean water, clean air, and healthy and abundant food is going to be the currency of power in the Energy-Climate Era—not the only one, but right up there with the capability to design and produce computers, microchips, information technologies, and planes and tanks.

"The green economy is poised to be the mother of all markets, the economic investment opportunity of a lifetime, because it has become so fundamental," observed Lois Quam, formerly managing director of alternative investments at Piper Jaffray, an investment company. "The challenge of global warming presents us all with the greatest opportunity for return on investment and growth that any of us will ever see. To find any equivalent economic transformation, you have to go back to the Industrial Revolution. And in the Industrial Revolution there was a very clear before and after. 'After,' everything was different: Industries had come and gone, civic society changed, new social institutions were born, and every aspect of work and daily life had been altered. With that came the emergence of new global powers. This [clean technology transformation] will be an equivalent moment in history."

Put it all together and what it means is that in the Energy-Climate Era, "green" is no longer a fad, green is no longer a boutique statement, green is no longer something you do to be a good citizen in the hope that somehow it will pay off in ten years. No: Green is the way you grow, build, design, manufacture, work, and live, "because it is just better," said Andrew Shapiro of GreenOrder. Green becomes the smartest, most efficient, lowest-cost way—when all the true costs are included—to live, build, work, and play. That is the huge transition we are just beginning to see. Green is going from boutique to better, from a choice to a necessity, from a fad to a strategy to win, from a source of electric power to a source of national power, from an insoluble problem to a great opportunity—economic and geopolitical.

Some see that now. Others will see it soon. Eventually it will be obvious to all. I hope every country gets there sooner rather than later, but as an American I want to make sure that my country is in the lead.

Redefining Green

If there has been a method to my own madness on this issue, it has been to try to get policymakers to redefine green. I say to them: This is not your grandfather's green movement anymore. This is Code Green. It's about something much broader than just electricity. Anything any country can do to go green today will make it stronger, healthier, more secure, more innovative, more competitive, and more respected. Redefining green is important.

I am big believer in the notion that to name something is to own it. If you can name an issue you can own the issue. The problem with "green" for so long was that, in America at least, it was named by its opponents. They named it "liberal," "tree-hugging," "sissy," "girly-man," "unpatriotic," and "vaguely European."

Well, I am here to say that when you consider the problems we face, and the opportunities and riches that will go to the countries and companies that take the lead in solving them, green is none of those things. No, green is "geopolitical," "geostrategic," "capitalistic," "patriotic." Green is the new red, white, and blue.

In short, Code Green is a strategy that can help to ease global warming, biodiversity loss, energy poverty, petrodictatorship, and energy supply shortages—and make America stronger at the same time. We solve our own problems by helping the world solve its problems. We help the world solve its problems by solving our own problems.

Depending on which audience you are speaking with, you can stress one or the other, but these truths are mutually reinforcing. To environmentalists I say: "Let's make America the greenest country in the world, the leader in mitigating climate change, innovating clean power, and protecting biodiversity—and the by-product will be a stronger America." To conservatives I say: "Let's make America the strongest country in the Energy-Climate Era, by adopting a Clean Energy System—and the by-product is that we will help the world mitigate all that stuff Al Gore is talking about."

But that's also why when I hear voices in America saying, "How can we afford to transform our whole economy in order to prevent climate change, when climate change could turn out to be a hoax or a fad and we could misallocate all that capital?," my answer is always the same: If climate change is a hoax, it is the most wonderful hoax ever perpetrated on the United States of America. Because transforming our economy to clean power and energy efficiency to mitigate global warming and the other challenges of the Energy-Climate Era is the equivalent of training for the Olympic triathlon: If you make it to the Olympics, you have a much better chance of winning, because you've developed every muscle. If you don't make it to the Olympics, you're still healthier, stronger, fitter, and more likely to live longer and win every other race in life. And as with the triathlon, you don't just improve one muscle or skill, but many, which become mutually reinforcing and improve the health of your whole system.

On top of it all, mounting a real revolution—going Code Green—is a "quintessentially American opportunity," added Lois Quam. It plays to all our strengths. It requires enormous amounts of experimentation—the kind you find in our great research universities and national laboratories; it requires lots of start-up companies that are not afraid to try, risk, fail, and try again, and plenty of venture capitalists ready to make big bets for big returns; it requires lots of teamwork and collaboration among business, government, and academe; it requires thousands of people working in their garages, trying thousands of things. And, most important, it is one of those national projects that is about big profits and big purposes; not just about making America richer, but about making the world better.

If those of us who have become concerned about climate change turn out to be wrong—but we refocus America anyway on producing clean electrons and the most energy-efficient vehicles, appliances, and buildings in the world, and we make America the global leader in aiding the protection of tropical forests and natural habitats, what is the worst that will happen? Our country will have cleaner air and water, more efficient products, more workers educated in the next great global industry, higher energy prices but lower bills, greater productivity, healthier people, and an export industry in clean power products that people across the world will want to buy—not to mention the respect and gratitude of more people around the world than ever. And we'll have to fight fewer wars over natural resources—because if the human race cannot create greater abundance, we will fight over everything that is in shortage, which is going to be a lot of things in a world that is hot, flat, and crowded.

And what if the climate skeptics and deniers who say climate change is a hoax turn out to be wrong—but we listen to them and do nothing? What will happen? We will have a future full of droughts, floods, melting glaciers, rising sea levels, resource conflicts, massive disruptions along coastal areas all over the world, and, as Rob Watson put it, "the human race as a bad biological experiment on the planet."

That, in a nutshell, is why I believe we need to both redefine green and refocus America around a Code Green agenda. It would make America stronger, and, by giving us more options, would also make us more free in the era we're heading into.

But those are not the only reasons. We also have a moral responsibility—because we consume the greatest portion per capita of the world's resources, because we have more resources for innovation than any other country, because we have the standing to affect more people on the planet than any other country, and because giving more people around the world the clean power tools they need is totally consistent with America's mission to expand the frontiers of freedom for everyone.

America's capitalist system and research universities are, in combination, still the most powerful innovation engine ever created. For precisely that reason, the world cannot effectively address the big problems of the Energy-Climate Era—quickly and at scale—without America, its president, its government, its industry, its markets, and its people either leading the revolution or aspiring to do so. California has already proven how great an impact just one state can have on the other forty-nine by dramatically reducing its per capita energy consumption through innovation and regulations. To be sure, as a state, California has woefully mismanaged its budget because of a long-time tax revolt. But in the realm of energy-efficiency policy it has been a real trendsettter—the same sort of trendsetter America should be for the world. We need to make the big early-stage investments in the new clean power technologies—as we did with PCs, DVDs, and iPods—and then leverage the low-cost service economy of India and the manufacturing platform of China to quickly get those new technologies down to the "Chindia price," the price at which they can really get adopted in China and India. If America doesn't seize this opportunity, others eventually will.

Follow Me

If America becomes the world leader in building clean energy technologies and promoting conservation, it will tip the whole world decisively in that direction. That probably sounds a little old-fashioned or jingoistic. I do not mean it that way. It is just that I continue to hold the view that many large-scale bad things happen in the world without American leadership, but few large-scale good things happen without American leadership—whether it is defeating Nazism and Fascism or confronting Communist totalitarianism or rebuilding Europe after World War II.

And the world is waiting for America to lead on this energy-climate issue. I am not against global climate treaties, such as the Kyoto Protocol and the Copenhagen process, but I think the chances of their having the impact that their advocates predict are slim. Getting all the signatory countries to comply would be an endless challenge—as hard as getting them to agree to a treaty in the first place.

I would much prefer to put America's energy into developing a green business model in America, one so compelling that other countries would want to follow it on their own. I am convinced that if America becomes the example of a country that takes the lead in developing clean power, energy efficiency, and conservation systems, and grows more productive, healthy, respected, prosperous, competitive, innovative, and secure as a result, many more countries and many more people around the world will emulate us voluntarily than will ever go green through the compulsion of some global treaty. A truly green America would be more valuable than fifty Kyoto Protocols. Emulation is always more effective than compulsion.

To paraphrase Archimedes: Give me a green America and I shall green the earth.

It is easy for Americans to forget (especially in recent years, when so many people around the world seem to be criticizing us) how much America is still the model to be followed—and it is easy for us to forget that when America either stops setting trends or sets bad ones, the whole world feels the effects.

Remember: America has long been an innovator in the conservation of natural resources, and we can promote this value globally as well. A century ago, we invented the national park system, and this idea has been emulated around the world. For the past thirty years, our foreign aid programs have helped developing nations from Brazil to Indonesia conserve their forests, grasslands, coral reefs, and endangered species. Those programs not only help other nations to grow sensibly—they also bring out the best in America and present our best face to the world.

As the British environmentalist Tom Burke noted, it was the Environmental Protection Act, signed into law during the Nixon administration, that led to the whole concept of an "environmental impact statement" to precede large-scale, environment-threatening projects. "Every country in Europe copied that," said Burke. "It's been copied by the whole world now."

Listen to French president Nicolas Sarkozy. He made his first official visit to Washington in November 2007. I got to ask him one question at a journalists' breakfast, and I made it this: "What would be the impact if America became the world leader on combating climate change rather than the world's laggard?" Sarkozy began by talking about his love for American culture: "I grew up listening to Elvis Presley . . . I grew up watching American films . . . America is a story of unprecedented economic success, unprecedented democratic success . . . I will always love America. So when I see the U.S. hated by everyone, it really pains me." And when America is not taking the lead on such an important global issue as climate change, added the French president, "I am asking, 'Where

is the American dream? What happened? Where has it gone?' You are
whistled at at global conferences like the G8. That is what has happened.
You are bounded by two oceans. You will be the first to be affected by rising sea levels. You should be setting the example. You should be spear-
heading the battle for the environment . . . You cannot be the first
champion of human rights and the last when it comes to obligations and
responsibilities on environment."

I got a similar message from Germany. Europe's own leadership in
this area has been hugely important, but Europe just doesn't have a grip
on the world's imagination the way America does—when America is at
its best. "America is the most dynamic country in the world and the
biggest economy in the world," Sigmar Gabriel, Germany's federal environment minister, remarked to me in an interview. "We need the power
of its markets, the power of its innovators. We need American capitalism
applied to this problem. If the Americans are going green, the whole rest
of the world is going green."

When do we Americans feel best about ourselves? *It's when we are
doing things for others with others*. Leading the green technology
revolution would enable us to do just that. Again, it's one of the ways we
can get our groove back, our moral authority. A country cannot go green,
really green, without being committed to the idea that there is something
bigger than itself, its own community, and its own borders—that the state
of the world really matters too. Jacqueline Novogratz, who founded the
Acumen Fund, a social entrepreneurship organization that operates in
the developing world, remarked to me once: "When I was working as a
young woman in rural Kenya, there was an old wives' tale that if there
was a sick woman in the village, the healer would come in and the first
thing he would do would be to ask the sick woman to cook for the whole
village. The idea was that sickness was often about sickness of the heart,
and when you gave of yourself you would also heal yourself."

George W. Bush offered a lot of moral clarity after 9/11—but along
the way, in the war on terrorism, America and Mr. Bush lost a lot of their
moral authority. Setting an example on clean energy, energy efficiency,
and conservation would be one of the best ways to restore some of that
lost authority, because Code Green is a sign of humility. It says to the
world: Even though we are a superpower, even though we are the rich-

est nation on the planet, we do not think we are entitled to a bigger slice of the world's resources than anyone else.

Believing this doesn't mean we should give up acting in our own self-interest—never. But it is precisely in our self-interest, at times, to behave more selflessly—to let people know that there are some problems we will approach as Americans and others that we can only address together as a species, and that we want to do both.

As Governor Arnold Schwarzenegger put it: Moving America from laggard to leader on climate change would "create a very powerful side product." Those who dislike America because of the war in Iraq, he explained, would at least be able to say, " 'Well, I don't like them for the war, but I do like them because they show such unbelievable leadership—not just with their blue jeans and hamburgers but with the environment.' People will love us for that. That's not existing right now."

In his history of nineteenth-century America, *What Hath God Wrought*, Daniel Walker Howe quotes Ralph Waldo Emerson as telling a meeting of the Mercantile Library Association in 1844 that "America is the country of the Future. It is a country of beginnings, of projects, of vast designs and expectations."

That is as true today as it was in 1844. And what is equally true is that it is time for another new beginning, another vast project, with grand designs and unlimited expectations. The only way America will remain a big power and a big player in the global system is if it is big in big things. And there will be no bigger undertaking in the world we are heading into than the production of clean power, energy efficiency, and protection of our forest, plant, and animal heritage.

Plan A: Code Green

But let's have no illusions: Code Green is a big project. *We need a whole new system for powering our economy.* This is a systems problem, and the only answer is a new system.

Since the Industrial Revolution and the rise of modern capitalism, the global economy has been driven by what I would call the Dirty Fuels System. The Dirty Fuels System was based on three key elements: fossil fuels that were dirty, cheap, and abundant; wasteful use of those fuels for many years as if they could never run out; and unbridled exploitation of our other natural resources—air, water, land, rivers, forests, and ocean fisheries—as if they too were infinite. (I truly mean to cast no aspersions on the people who mined all the coal or pumped all the oil and gas that produced much of the energy the world used to grow over the last two centuries. They were just doing what they were asked to do, and their work provided the fuel that was used to raise living standards all over the world. I also know that today's coal can be burned much more cleanly than in the past, and natural gas, now widely in use, is much cleaner than coal. I am using the word "dirty" only to describe the impact that these fuels have had on our environment and climate.)

No one designed this Dirty Fuels System, exactly. It just evolved from the eighteenth century until today, first powering the growth of the industrial West and more recently the soaring, trying-to-catch-up-as-fast-as-we-can growth of developing giants, like India, China, South Africa, Poland, and Egypt.

As systems go, it works quite efficiently. Coal, oil, and gas are extracted all over the world, tankers and trains and pipelines deliver these fossil fuels to power plants or refineries across the globe, and gasoline stations and power grids deliver their energy directly to consumers, who never think for a moment whether the lights will go on or a gas station will appear around the corner in the next few miles. The same is true for timber, water, and fish—it's all you can eat, all the time, until nothing is left. It is a system, and it is deeply embedded.

But we cannot continue on with this Dirty Fuels System. If we do, the energy implications, the climate implications, the biodiversity implications, the geopolitical implications, and the energy poverty implications will undermine the quality of life for every person on this planet and eventually imperil life on earth itself.

Unfortunately, up to now we have been trying to solve the problems caused by the Dirty Fuels System piecemeal, one at a time, instead of trying to create a new system to replace it. The result has been that as we try to fix one problem, we end up creating or exacerbating another.

Think about it: People working on preserving biodiversity go out and establish protected areas for endangered plants and animals—which are vitally important—but then climate change shifts habitat temperatures and rainfall patterns, making some protected areas uninhabitable for the very creatures they were created to protect. As long as we are trying to protect biodiversity—within a Dirty Fuels System that is changing the climate in a runaway fashion—we are never going to be successful.

Think about it: America invaded Iraq partly in the name of promoting democracy in the Middle East—which is vitally important—while maintaining a transportation system based on tens of millions of gasoline-powered cars that run on oil from the Middle East, which means that our way of life is indirectly funding the very forces in that region that are working to undermine America's democracy efforts. As long as we are trying to promote Middle East democracy within a Dirty Fuels System that also funds democracy's most powerful foes, we are never going to be successful.

Think about it: We are trying to ease world poverty—a vitally important effort—while maintaining a Dirty Fuels System that gives massive subsidies to American farmers and agribusinesses to encourage them to grow corn for ethanol, a process that is driving up food prices for the poor all over the world. As long as we try to combat poverty within a system that is encouraging people to use food to power their cars rather than to drive less, to use more mass transit, or to demand vehicles that get dramatically better gas mileage, we are never going to be successful.

All of these are attempts to solve a set of very big, interconnected problems—systemic problems—without going about it in a systemic way. The results are not impressive. We need to create a new system. So let's stop for a moment and consider the two most important features of a system—one that you can grasp by observing nature and the other that you can grasp by driving a Toyota Prius hybrid.

The first rule of systems is that everything is interconnected, and no one teaches us that better than Mother Nature. What John Muir, the founder of the Sierra Club, wrote about nature in 1911 is still true today: "When we try to pick out anything by itself, we find it hitched to everything else in the Universe."

One of my favorite examples of this truth is a story that appeared in *The New York Times* (August 5, 2007) about the mysterious disappearance—and sudden reappearance—of aspen trees in the western United States, most notably from the Lamar Valley of Yellowstone National Park. The author, Chris Conway, explained that their disappearance was no mystery: The elk were eating the young aspen shoots before they had a chance to grow. But over the last few years, the aspens had suddenly started flourishing again, Conway reported, and the reason, researchers discovered, was surprising: "Scientists credit the wolves that were reintroduced to Yellowstone in 1995 after an absence of nearly 70 years."

Wolves are good for aspen trees?

"Wolves eat elk, of course, at an average of one elk per wolf per month in winter, according to park statistics," wrote Conway.

But the return of aspens to the Lamar Valley is not simply the product of the old ecological formula, predator eats prey. It may also have something to do with fear, according to a new study by scientists at Oregon State University. Despite the presence of wolves—more than fifty, in at least six packs—at least 6,500 elk roamed the study area, more than enough to continue the plunder of the aspens. But the study found that an "ecology of fear" has helped to restore balance to the valley, protecting young aspen shoots from browsing elk for the first time in decades.

William J. Ripple, a professor in the university's College of Forestry and an author of the study, said aspens were recovering in areas where it would be difficult for elk to escape a wolf attack. "We think these elk need to balance the risk of being killed versus eating in their favorite places. So it's a trade-off between food and risk in an ecology of fear," he said. Another of the authors, Robert L. Beschta, an emeritus professor at the university, likened the situation to doing research in grizzly bear country, something he has done. "When I'm in bear country, I change what I do," he said. "I become more careful when I enter blind areas, places I can't see. We think elk are doing something similar. In tight situations where it's difficult for an elk to see or escape a wolf, we're seeing increases in the vegetation growth. It's like they're afraid to go there."

Who'd have thunk it? More wolves leads to more aspen trees in Yellowstone Park because more elk are afraid to eat more aspen shoots in blind alleys. As it is in nature, so it is with energy, climate, poverty, biodiversity, and petropolitics: To influence them in the most efficient and effective manner possible, you need to think and act in a systemic way. We need to mimic nature—the ultimate complex adaptive system.

Jonathan F. P. Rose, a national real estate developer specializing in green buildings and communities, a board member of the Natural Resources Defense Council, and an amateur systems theorist, once put it to me this way: "The systemic nature of the planet earth is persistent and robust. Nature is a system and always responds systematically. It is intrinsic. It does not wax or wane. It always operates that way, and it does so in a robust manner."

The only thing that ever varies is our ability to see and act in tune with nature's systemic ways, added Rose. "But to see and think holistically requires you to expand your mind and really think in an interconnected manner. The intrinsic interdependent quality of the natural universe is just like gravity. As a builder, I don't get to decide which part of my building responds to the laws of gravity and which one does not. You don't negotiate with gravity. It is just there. And interdependence is as much an intrinsic quality of nature as gravity is."

Modern men and women living in urban settings have become so disconnected from nature's interdependence that we actually have to relearn this systemic truth. And the only way to really relearn it is by immersing yourself in nature. In the summer of 2009, I had a chance to do that by going on safari in the Okavango Delta, in northwestern Botswana—where there are no paved roads, no televisions, no Internet connectivity, and no cell-phone towers. But there are daily newspapers—sort of. True, these are not your normal newspapers. They are published on the roads. The wetlands where we were staying on the Jao Flats were bisected by hippo trails and narrow roads made from pure white Kalahari Desert sand. And every morning, when you set out to investigate the wilderness there, it is normal for your guide to lean out of his jeep, study the animal and insect tracks, and pronounce that he's "reading the morning news." We were lucky to be accompanied by Map Ives—the fifty-four-year-old director of sustainability for Wilderness Safaris, which supports ecotourism in Botswana. Thinking systemically about nature was second nature to him—and it was fascinating to watch him read Mother Nature's hieroglyphics. The day's "news," Ives explained, studying a stretch of road as we set out into the wilderness, was that some lions had run very quickly through here, which he could tell by the abnormal depth of and distance between their paw prints. They were in stride. The "weather" was windy coming out of the east, he added, pointing to the side of the paw prints that had been lightly dusted away. Flood waters remained high this morning, because the nearby hyena tracks were followed by little indentations—splashes of water that had come off their paws. Today's "sports"? Well, over here, the hyenas were dragging a "kill," probably a small antelope or steenbok, which is very obvious from the smooth foot-wide path in the sand that ran some fifty yards into the bushes. Every mile you can read a different paper.

It is a challenge to keep up mentally with someone like Ives, who was raised on the edge of the Okavango Delta. He points out the connections, and all the free services nature provides, every two seconds: Plants clean the air; the papyrus and reeds filter the water. Palm trees are growing on a mound originally built by termites. Yes, thank God for termites. All of the raised islands of green in the delta were started by them. The termites keep their mounds warm. This attracts animals whose dung brings seeds and fertilizer that sprout trees, making bigger islands. Ives will be talking to you about zebras and suddenly a bird will zip by— "greater blue-eyed starling," he'll blurt out in midsentence, and then go back to zebras.

"If you spend enough time in nature and allow yourself to slow down sufficiently to let your senses work, then through exposure and practice, you will start to sense the meanings in the sand, the grasses, the bushes, the trees, the movement of the breezes, the thickness of the air, the sounds of the creatures, and the habits of the animals with which you are sharing that space," said Ives. Humans were actually wired to do this a long time ago.

Unfortunately, he added, "the speed at which humans have improved technology since the Industrial Revolution has attracted so many people to towns and cities and provided them with 'processed' natural resources" that our innate ability to make all these connections "may be disappearing as fast as biodiversity."

That is the problem. We're trying to deal with a whole array of integrated problems—climate change, energy, biodiversity loss, poverty alleviation, and the need to grow enough food to feed the planet—separately. The poverty fighters resent the climate-change folks; climate folks hold summits without reference to biodiversity; the food advocates resist the biodiversity protectors.

They all need to go on safari together.

"We need to stop thinking about these issues in isolation—each with its own champion, constituency, and agenda—and deal with them in an integrated way, the way they actually occur on the ground," argues Glenn Prickett, from Conservation International. "We tend to think about climate change as just an energy issue, but it's also about land use: One-third of greenhouse gas emissions come from tropical deforestation and agriculture. So we need to preserve forests and other ecosystems to solve climate change, not only to save species."

But we also need to double food production to feed a growing population. "So we'll need to do that without clearing more forests and draining more wetlands, which means farmers will need new technologies and practices to grow more food on the same land they use today—with less water," he added. "Healthy forests, wetlands, and grasslands not only preserve biodiversity and store carbon, they also help buffer the impacts of climate change. So our success in tackling climate change, poverty, food security, and biodiversity loss will depend on finding integrated solutions from the land."

In short—and as any reader of the Okavango daily papers will tell you—we need to make sure that our policy solutions are as integrated as nature itself. And the only way to do that is to reimmerse ourselves in systemic thinking. You don't really need to go on safari in Africa to do that. All you need to do is take a walk in the park or along a river—without your iPod, without your cell phone, without your BlackBerry, just with your eyes and ears paying attention to every sight, sound, and smell around you.

But if the first rule of systems is that everything is connected to everything else, the second rule is: You can optimize individual pieces only up to a point. If you don't scrap the old system and put a new system in place, ultimately everything you do will be constrained. But if you put together a new system, and you do it right, *everything* starts to get better. The new system ends up benefiting many individual pieces, as well as the whole. As Rose puts it: "Optimizing individual components can only lead to incremental change; optimizing the system can lead to a transformational ecology."

The Toyota Prius hybrid car is a perfect example of a new system replacing an old one and creating a whole new function that is greater than the sum of its parts. The Prius is not a better car. It is a better system! The Prius has brakes. All cars have brakes. The Prius has a battery. All cars have batteries. The Prius has an engine. All cars have engines. What is new about the Prius is that its designers looked at it as a system that could perform more than one function—not as just a collection of car parts whose primary function was to turn the wheels. They said to themselves, "Why not use the energy from braking to generate electrons that we could then store in the battery and then use that for driving as many miles as possible, instead of using the gasoline in the tank? And when this Prius is going downhill, let's use that kinetic energy created by the spinning of the wheels and store that in the battery too, to power the car when it wants to go uphill."

By taking a systems approach, in other words, Toyota was able to move from an incremental change in miles per gallon to a quantum leap—*a car that could generate some of its own energy*. Toyota went from a problem fix (how to make a car get better gas mileage) to a transformational innovation (how to make a car that produces energy as well as consuming less of it). It created a system whose product was so much greater than the sum of its parts that ordinary people, just average drivers like you and me, could do extraordinary things—like drive fifty miles on a gallon of gasoline in a Prius. And once you start working systemically, the benefits are endless—as are the opportunities.

Our challenge today, as individual nations and as a civilization, is to develop a Clean Energy System that can do exactly that—*enable ordinary people to do extraordinary things* when it comes to generating and consuming clean energy, and in the process alleviate energy supply and demand issues, petrodictatorship, climate change, biodiversity loss, and energy poverty.

If you don't have a system, though, you don't have a solution. If you hear a politician calling for "renewable energy," walk away. If you hear a politician calling for a "renewable energy system," listen up.

In my view this Clean Energy System would consist of five interlocking and mutually reinforcing parts: innovating clean electrons, intensifying energy efficiency, diffusing family planning services across the planet, embracing an ethic of conservation, and preparing to adapt to the climate change that is already locked into our future. Let's look at each and how we can tie them together.

Clean Electrons

I start from the bedrock principle that we as a global society need more and more growth, because without growth there is no human development and those in poverty will never escape it. But it can't be growth based on CO_2-emitting dirty fuels from hell. We have to have growth based as much as possible on clean fuels from heaven. So, for starters, we need a system that will stimulate massive amounts of innovation and deployment of abundant, clean, reliable, and cheap electrons.

"The great transformation of the century is when we move from molecules to electrons, and from silos and smokestacks to networks," said Michael Totten, senior director on climate and water for Conservation International. It is precisely that move from molecules to electrons that will enable the systemic connections and efficiencies that will result in a clean power network—stretching from power plants to businesses to homes to electric cars and back. And that network—which I'll describe in detail in chapter 12—will enable ordinary people to do extraordinary things when it comes to creating, using, and saving energy.

No single solution would defuse more of the Energy-Climate Era's problems at once than the invention of a source of abundant, clean, reliable, and cheap electrons. Give me abundant, clean, reliable, and cheap electrons, and I will give you a world that can continue to grow without triggering unmanageable climate change. Give me abundant, clean, reliable, and cheap electrons, and I will give you water in the desert from a deep generator-powered well. Give me abundant, clean, reliable, and cheap electrons, and I will put every petrodictator out of business. Give me abundant, clean, reliable, and cheap electrons, and I will end deforestation from communities desperate for fuel and I will eliminate any reason to drill in Mother Nature's environmental cathedrals. Give me abundant, clean, reliable, and cheap electrons, and I will enable millions of the world's poor to get connected, to refrigerate their medicines, to educate their women, and to light up their nights. Give me abundant, clean, reliable, and cheap electrons, and I will create networks where people all over the world will start contributing their energy innovations, like programmers creating shareware on the World Wide Web.

The ability to generate clean electrons is not a solution to every problem, but it is the enabler of solutions to more problems than any other single factor I can think of. And that is why job number one of the Clean Energy System is to stimulate *innovation*. Because no one has yet come up with a source of electrons that meets all four criteria: abundant, clean, reliable, and cheap.

But there are two ways to stimulate innovation—one is short-term and the other is long-term—and we need to be doing much more of both.

First, there is innovation that happens naturally by the massive deployment of technologies we already have—that we know can provide clean power—and by moving them more quickly along the manufacturing learning curve. The history of technology is one story after another of how inventions get improved—become smaller, smarter, cheaper, more productive, more abundant, and more reliable—as they achieve volume and we learn how to make them better and better. Think of your first cell phone and the one you own today; think of your first laptop and the one you own today; think of your first air conditioner and the one you own to-day. They all got better and cheaper, thanks to innovation, but it was the innovation that comes from mass production and learning how to make little improvements with each new generation. This form of innovation is often underestimated, but it is precisely the kind of innovation we need to be, and can be, stimulating right now to overcome the technological barriers that prevent existing wind and solar systems from becoming cheap, abundant, and reliable—today. The way you stimulate this kind of innovation—which comes from learning more about what you already know and doing it better and cheaper—is by generous tax incentives, regulatory incentives, renewable energy mandates, and other market-shaping mechanisms that create durable demand for these existing clean power technologies.

And second, there is innovation that happens by way of eureka break-throughs from someone's lab due to research and experimentation. The way you stimulate that is by increasing government-funded research and also by, again, shaping the market to demand more clean power innovations. We need many more people, companies, and universities trying many more things and a market that will quickly scale up the most promising new ideas. This second kind of innovation—breakthrough innovation—is always hard to predict, and the case of energy will be no different. "You are not going to see it coming," Bill Gates said to me in an interview. "The breakthrough will probably come out of somewhere you least expect, and we'll only know how it happened looking backward."

While we desperately need to be doing both kinds of innovation at a massive scale, when it comes to energy, *we tend to focus only on the latter*. We tend to focus largely on searching for eureka breakthroughs, when steady breakthroughs are hiding in plain sight. "Myriad [wind and solar] technologies are already cost-effective today," says Joseph Romm, the energy physicist and former Clinton Department of Energy official. Simply breaking down the market barriers to their deployment, he added, would have a much bigger impact now than betting on a new "breakthrough TILT—Terrific Imaginary Low-carbon Technology."

Romm notes that a critical historical fact was explained by Royal Dutch Shell, in its 2001 scenarios for how energy use is likely to evolve over the next five decades: "Typically it has taken 25 years after commercial introduction for a primary energy form to obtain a 1 percent share of the global market." Pay attention, adds Romm, "this tiny toehold comes 25 years after commercial introduction. The first transition from scientific breakthrough to commercial introduction may itself take decades. We still haven't seen commercial introduction of a hydrogen fuel cell car and have barely seen any commercial fuel cells—over 160 years after they were first invented. This tells you two important things. First, new breakthrough energy technologies don't enter the market fast enough to have a big impact in the time frame we care about. We are trying to get 5 percent to 10 percent shares—or more—of the global market for [clean] energy, which means massive deployment by 2050 (if not sooner). Second, if you are in the kind of hurry we are all in, then you are going to have to take unusual measures to deploy technologies far more aggressively than has ever occurred historically."

That is why we need to be constantly trying to invent new forms of abundant, clean, reliable, and cheap electrons and constantly trying to make the technologies that already exist today for producing clean electrons—solar photovoltaic, wind, solar thermal, and geothermal—more abundant, reliable, and cheap. The first will come from discovering something we don't know and the second will come from learning more about what we do know—by quickly deploying these existing technologies in larger quantities so they take advantage of the manufacturing learning curve. (I will talk about how we stimulate both these forms of innovation in chapters 13 and 14.)

Solar photovoltaic energy, which uses sunlight to make electricity from materials such as silicon, is clean and getting steadily cheaper. But it will not be abundant until we invent a battery that can store massive amounts of solar-generated electricity, so that those electrons will be available when the sun is not shining. Solar thermal electricity, which is made by using mirrors to concentrate the sun's rays to heat a fluid that drives an electric generator, is enormously promising, because it doesn't need a battery for storage. (In my view it is the most promising base-load clean power technology of all.) It produces electricity from steam the same way a coal plant does, only with no emissions. But solar thermal, though clean and reliable and already being deployed, particularly in Spain, is still expensive to build. It needs to be deployed in many more places to become abundant and competitive with coal. Wind power is clean and cheap, but is abundant only when and where the wind blows; it will also require better storage batteries to scale.

The power from distributed diesel generators is cheap and abundant, but it is not clean (think of what it smells like when you are driving behind a tractor trailer) and is not always reliable at scale: Generators break. Geothermal power drawn from steam generated by nature and volcanic rocks is clean and reliable, but not that abundant and not yet cheap. Burning coal and capturing and sequestering the CO_2 could give us clean, abundant electrons, but they would not be cheap (the more emitted CO_2 you sequester, the lower the overall power yield), and no one knows how reliable the sequestration process would be: Some CO_2 could leak. Nuclear power is reliable and clean, but is certainly not cheap or abundant, and there is the problem of storing the nuclear waste, which always has the potential to leak or can be processed into bomb-making material.*

This litany of pluses and minuses explains why Royal Dutch Shell's scenario planning team reports that wind energy in 2007 made up only about 0.1 percent of total world primary energy production and solar power hadn't yet risen to that level. Given the present trends of innovation and technology diffusion, Shell predicts that if we do everything right, by 2050 renewable energy sources would make up 30 percent of total world primary energy and fossil fuels still 55 percent. That is not a new system—not even close. We need to do better, and in order to do better we need much more innovation.

In many ways, innovation is the only way out for the Re-Generation. How else are they going to pay off the massive debts that the Grasshopper Generation has left behind? To support the world's growing population, they will need to generate more wealth with fewer resources, and the only way to do that is with massive amounts of innovation.

---

*What about biofuels—fuels made from food crops, agricultural waste, wood chips, or special grasses? I am wary of biofuels: They cannot be a large-scale solution to our energy problem, and we should not try to make them one. Only electrons can provide power at the scale we need. As we move from gasoline-powered vehicles to electric-powered vehicles, though, biofuels can be a bridging solution—on four conditions. First, the biofuel has to have a significant positive energy balance when you consider all the inputs—water, fertilizer, gasoline, and transport—that go into growing, harvesting, processing, and delivering the fuel. Biofuels made from sugarcane have a roughly eight to one positive energy balance. Biofuels made from corn have at best just over one to one. Second, the biofuels cannot be grown by taking large carbon loans from nature. If you are chopping down a tropical forest to create oil palm plantations for biofuels, the amount of carbon you are emitting from soil and trees would take fifty to eighty years' worth of biofuels to compensate for. Third, your biofuel production cannot destroy areas rich in biodiversity; you need to plan very carefully where you intend to plant. Fourth, you cannot be trading fuel for food at scale; otherwise you will be solving one problem by starting another. For a country like Brazil, with a tremendous amount of arable land and abundant sugarcane, biofuels can be a transport solution. The same may be true for other countries in the tropics, from Africa to the Caribbean. But beyond that, biofuels—as the technology exists today—are not the answer and trying to scale them will produce a backlash. Maybe innovation can change that, and we should be investing in ways to make biofuels from nonfood plants and waste. But today, what makes sense in Brazil does not make sense in the United States. Our future is with clean electrons.

Jeff Wacker, the EDS futurist, likes to put it this way: If you were a copper miner one hundred years ago, you might pick up a shovelful of earth and find that about 20 percent of it was copper ore and 80 percent of it was rock. Today, in a typical copper mine, it would not be unusual for you to pick up a shovelful and find that it is 1 percent copper and 99 percent rock. "To separate the copper from the rock takes energy, and when you have to process that much more rock to get that much less copper, it takes even more energy," said Wacker. "That is true of so many resources—the abundant, easily processed resources that we exploited to grow in the past" are gone or in short supply. And in the flat world, more and more people are competing for those resources. That means that the Re-Generation, at least in America, has to create wealth on a different model. Our parents built wealth on readily available resources that were inexpensive to extract and process; the Re-Generation has to build wealth from resources that are fought over and difficult and expensive to extract.

In this kind of a world, if we want to keep raising our standards of living, "We can either work twice as hard, like the Chinese, or innovate twice as fast," said Wacker. That is why innovation around clean energy—and every other field of endeavor—is America's future. We have gone from the agricultural economy to the industrial economy to the information economy and now to the innovation economy. We have to extract wealth and energy from minds, not from mines, from wellsprings of innovation, not wells of oil.

"In terms of how we generate wealth, the next twenty years are going to be dramatically different from the previous two hundred," said Wacker. Thriving in the agricultural economy was all about having more land, thriving in the industrial economy was all about having more raw materials, and thriving in the information economy was all about gathering and applying information more quickly than your competitor. Today, innovation—creating more productivity, comfort, housing, mobility, power, and entertainment with fewer inputs—is how you both grow your economy and keep it sustainable. Innovation is how we get more growth without harming the planet. Recycling will have to be a big part of it, because if we cannot dig for more and more copper we will need to innovate ways to recycle what we have. When your neighborhood consists of green homes that are energy positive—which actually generate more energy than they consume—and are made entirely with recycled building materials, and when your neighbors are all driving solar-powered cars made of recycled plastics, you'll know that we have reached a form of sustainable globalization.

Energy Efficiency and Resource Productivity

Here's a scary statistic (*Time*, January 12, 2009): "Only 4 percent of the energy used to run a typical incandescent light bulb produces light; the rest is frittered away as heat at the plant, over transmission lines or in the bulb itself, which is why you burn your fingers when you touch it." We have to learn to do better things with the energy we have. And that brings me to the second element of any Clean Energy System: efficiency—the ability to perform the same function with less energy thanks to the use of better technology. You can find energy efficiency in some of the most surprising places when you start applying technology. As the U.S. Department of Energy notes on its official Web site, "Using recycled aluminum scrap to make new aluminum cans, for example, uses 95 percent less energy than making aluminum cans from bauxite ore, the raw material used to make aluminum . . . In the case of paper, recycling saves trees and water. Making a ton of paper from recycled stock saves up to 17 trees and uses 50 percent less water."

While our top priority must be to promote innovation of clean electrons, we cannot bet the future on such a breakthrough, so we must dramatically improve our energy efficiency and natural resource productivity now. "We can't just focus on innovation on the energy supply side," says Diana Farrell, director of the McKinsey Global Institute. "We also have to focus on the demand side"—innovating better ways to drive growth with fewer and fewer electrons and less and less "input" from forests, water, and land. That is what energy and resource productivity means—more growth from less stuff. A breakthrough in the creation of abundant, clean, reliable, and cheap electrons may be many years off, but improving our energy and resource productivity offers us the chance to significantly lower our energy use and CO_2 emissions today. The more energy and resource productivity we bring about today, the fewer clean electrons we will need to generate, and the fewer natural resources we will need to exploit.

A study by the McKinsey Global Institute (February 2008) concluded that the world could cut projected global energy demand growth between now and 2020 "by at least half by capturing opportunities to increase energy productivity—the level of output we achieve from the energy we consume." So much of this involves just being smarter about how we design buildings, packages, vehicles, refrigerators, air conditioners, and lighting systems and constantly insisting on higher and higher standards of efficiency from each of them—so we get the same comfort, mobility, and illumination from fewer resources.

So, before the combination of hot, flat, and crowded forces us to shrink our economic growth, bake a smaller pie, and divide up the smaller pieces, we need to take our very best shot at building a bigger, more sustainable pie pan through innovation around clean electrons and energy efficiency. Before we resign ourselves to a world of scarcity and imposed limitations—which is the world our children will inherit if we just stay with business as usual—we need to do everything we can, as Jim Rogers, the president and CEO of Duke Energy argues, "to expand the world of possibilities" by driving all forms of innovation.

"I don't want to be the first generation telling my kids you can't have a life as good as I did," said K. R. Sridhar, the Indian-American fuel cell inventor and founder of Bloom Energy. "Let someone else say that. I am going to die trying to invent our way out of this."

Family Planning

While I am a huge believer in the power of innovation and efficiency, there are limits to the carrying capacity of our earth, when more and more people can and are living a high-energy-usage, high-consumption American lifestyle. The spreading of that high-energy lifestyle is a real problem. But when you combine it with a rising global population, it is a prescription for disaster. It is hard to believe that the earth can sustain this many "Americans" without more family planning, by more people, everywhere.

Thanks to family planning efforts in both the developed and developing world, there has been some progress in slowing the rate of population growth. But as Paul and Anne Ehrlich, the Stanford University authors of the 1968 classic *The Population Bomb*, put it in a 2009 essay (Powells.com): "The depressing fact is that even with good news on the population *growth-rate* front, humanity may still add some 2.5 billion people to the population before growth stops and (we hope) a slow decline begins. Those additional people will have disproportionate negative impacts on our life-support systems. Our ancestors naturally farmed the richest land and used the most accessible resources first. Now people are increasingly forced to turn to marginal land to grow more food; and instead of extracting rich ores on or near the surface, deeper and much poorer deposits must be mined and refined, at ever greater environmental cost. Water and petroleum must come from lower-quality sources or deeper wells and be transported over longer distances. The environmental consequences of past and future population growth will haunt humanity for a long time, and the effects will be determined by how the present population and the future additions behave toward our common environment."

Slowing the rate of population growth makes every other part of this system easier to function. You need to innovate fewer clean electrons for fewer people; you need to implement less energy efficiency across fewer buildings; you have fewer mouths to feed from the same amount of land, so conservation becomes less of an economic burden.

People have run the numbers. My colleague Andrew Revkin reported in *The New York Times* (September 15, 2009) that "a study by researchers at the London School of Economics and commissioned by the Optimum Population Trust came to the following conclusion: '*Contraception Is "Greenest" Technology* . . . UN data suggest that meeting unmet need for family planning would reduce unintended births by 72 per cent, reducing projected world population in 2050 by half a billion to 8.64 billion. Between 2010 and 2050 12 billion fewer "people-years" would be lived—326 billion against 338 billion under current projections. The 34 gigatons of CO_2 saved in this way would cost $220 billion—roughly $7 a ton [metric tons]. However, the same CO_2 saving would cost over $1 trillion if low-carbon technologies were used.' "

"We actually know what works," said Gretchen Daily, a Stanford University ecologist, who then ticked off the list for me: First, there is a huge unmet need for contraception devices and family planning education and methods. Second, educating young women and girls has a profound impact on fertility, because the better educated women become, the more they are able to work outside the home, earn incomes that can sustain them and the children they do have, and, more broadly, have more control over their own bodies and sexual choices. All these things lead them to bear fewer children. But we should not forget men, either, Daily added. Involving men in family-planning programs, enabling them to improve their education, and working with them to change social attitudes over family size generally can also pay important dividends. Third, improved health care generally is extremely important, said Daily, "because when you lower child mortality, people don't feel the need to have eight kids in order to just have two sons that will survive and sustain the parents in old age, so you lower birth rates." Fourth, microcredit systems can have a big impact, explained Daily, particularly in agrarian economies where "having a home-grown child labor force is very useful if you don't have the money to hire migrant labor." So can drilling water wells or electrifying villages; the more that happens, the more you don't need children to collect water for drinking or dung and wood for cooking. "If you can lower the immediate economic benefit of kids," said Daily, "and provide the resources for people to invest more in fewer offspring, those things have a huge impact on fertility." Put it all together and the conclusion is inescapable: to sustain higher living standards, and preserve our natural world and a livable climate, world population size must stabilize, and soon.

To be sure, we can never lose sight of the fact that determining the size of one's own family is a personal matter. I, for one, would not be comfortable telling anyone how many children they can or cannot have. But I do believe it should be our goal as a country and as a global community to make sure that every couple in the world has a basic education in reproductive health issues and the family planning services available, so they can choose the best size for their own family.

The truth is that we are not doing all we could or need to do in that regard. As a result, the world could actually get even more crowded than we anticipate by 2050. According to Geoff Dabelko, director of the Environmental Change and Security Program at the Woodrow Wilson Center for Scholars, by 2050 the world will have 9.2 billion people. "But this figure assumes a substantial increase in use of contraception in the world's poorest countries. If fertility rates remain constant, the world's population could reach the staggering total of 11.9 billion . . . Ten years ago, the UN's 1998 population revision projected that Niger's fertility rate would decline from 7.4 to 6.3 children per woman by 2005. Instead, Niger now has the highest fertility rate, 7.4 children per woman, in the world. In the most recent UN forecast, the country's projected total population in 2050 has soared from 32 to 58 million people—and this assumes that fertility begins a steady decline in the next decade, dropping below four children per woman at mid-century." The potentially huge impact of a stall in family planning efforts in even a few countries could throw a lot of our projections for global population by 2050 out of whack.

"Currently, women's unmet need for family planning is estimated at more than 200 million women—and this demand is projected to grow 40 percent by 2050," said Dabelko. "To achieve the lower—rather than the higher—population estimates will require great political attention and financial resources."

An Ethic of Conservation

While family planning, innovation, and greater energy efficiency might all work together to both enlarge our energy pie and reduce emissions, the fact is, we also need to learn to consume less stuff and make what we do consume last longer—either by building it to last or making it easily recyclable. No Clean Energy System will work without infusing citizens with an ethic of conservation and the values of sustainability. No matter what we invent, with this many people aspiring to rising standards of living, using fewer things for a longer time is vital, especially for those of us who already use a disproportionate share. "The consumption levels of the developed world are just as unsustainable as the fertility levels of the developing world," said Gretchen Daily. That is why an "ethic of conservation" is essential today and is going to be even more so tomorrow—especially if we do invent a source of abundant, clean, reliable, cheap electrons. Because one thing we absolutely know from the Dirty Fuels System is that when resources are free or cheap—air, water, land, forests, fisheries, gasoline, electrons—people abuse and overuse them. Without an ethic of conservation—a deeply ingrained habit of trying to minimize our impact on the natural world—the availability of abundant, clean, reliable, cheap electrons would turn into a license to rape our natural world. If energy is abundant, clean, reliable, and cheap, then why not buy a Hummer and drive it through the rain forest?

To put it another way: Since we have already seen how much people are willing to overconsume using dirty fuels, imagine if they had the license of clean fuels? I like the way that Paul and Anne Ehrlich put it in their Powells.com essay: "In recent years the connection between overconsumption and environmental deterioration has become increasingly clear, and many environmental scientists, including us, believe that overconsumption will prove much more difficult to cure than over-population. So far there are no consumption condoms or buying-spree morning-after pills."

What constitutes an ethic of conservation? We can start to answer that question by saying what ethics are not. Ethics are not laws. They are not imposed by the state. Rather, they are norms, values, beliefs, habits, and attitudes that are embraced voluntarily—that we as a society impose on ourselves. Laws regulate behavior from the outside in. Ethics regulate behavior from the inside out. Ethics are something you carry with you wherever you go to guide whatever you do.

An ethic of conservation, explained Michael J. Sandel, a political philosopher at Harvard, would embrace several norms, beginning with "a sense of responsibility, a sense of stewardship, for the natural world." An ethic of conservation, said Sandel, "is an ethic of restraint that says we have a responsibility to preserve the earth's resources and natural wonders in and of themselves," because they constitute the very web of life on which all living creatures on this planet depend.

But, in addition to a sense of stewardship toward the natural world, an ethic of conservation also has to include a spirit of trusteeship, argued Sandel. "Stewardship involves responsibility for the natural world. It is born of wonder and awe for the diversity of life and the majesty of nature. Trusteeship involves responsibility for future generations, for those who will inhabit this place after our time. It is a form of solidarity with our children and grandchildren," said Sandel. "An ethic of conservation requires both stewardship and trusteeship—habits of restraint that express respect for the earth that we inhabit, and respect for future generations."

To become good stewards and good trustees, added Sandel, "we will need to rein in our tendency to regard the earth and its natural resources as wholly at our disposal for present needs, wants, and desires. We have to develop new habits and attitudes toward consumption."

Otherwise, whatever technologies we devise will simply be used to extend our current habits of profligate consumption to the huge, burgeoning middle classes of a hot, flat, and crowded world. Does this mean that America, or the world economy, should stop growing? Does it mean that we, as individuals, have to edit our lifestyles down to a bare minimum, or get by with much less than the average American upper- or middle-class family consumes today? There is an anticapitalist, anticonsumerist, back-to-nature wing of the environmental movement that believes we should and almost delights in advocating that. By the way, that may be right, and should not be dismissed. My point is that we don't know yet, because we have not tried even the obvious stuff that we do know would have real effects and would not involve fundamental changes in our lifestyle.

Telling every individual on the planet who wants or can afford a car that they cannot have one would be changing our lifestyle. But banning cars over a certain weight or engine size, or bringing maximum speed limits back down to 55 miles per hour, or banning taxis that are not hybrids—such efforts do not strike me as fundamentally cramping anyone's lifestyle. Telling people that henceforth we are going to ration electricity (you can have only so much per month) would certainly involve changing our lifestyle. But making it illegal for office buildings in America to leave their lights on after hours, as tens of thousands of companies mindlessly seem to do, as you can see by driving through any major city after midnight, does not strike me as fundamentally cramping anyone's lifestyle. Telling people that they cannot have an iPod or laptop would certainly involve changing our lifestyle. But requiring all iPods and laptops to be made with easily recyclable materials doesn't strike me as fundamentally cramping anyone's lifestyle. Telling people they cannot live in anything more than a five-thousand-square-foot space would certainly involve changing our lifestyle (in the developed world, at least). But telling anyone who wants to live in a more than five-thousand-square-foot home that they can do so only if the home is energy net zero—only if it generates through solar, wind, or geothermal power as much clean energy as it uses—doesn't strike me as fundamentally cramping anyone's lifestyle. Banning urban sprawl to suburbia and requiring instead that cities grow upward, not outward, would certainly involve changing our lifestyle—but probably for the better. Imagine how nice it would be not to have to commute in traffic for an hour back and forth to work and instead being able to walk your child to school and then turn around and be at your office. Forcing everyone to ride a bike to work would involve changing our lifestyle. But requiring municipalities to set aside bike lanes running from suburbs to inner cities doesn't strike me as cramping anyone's lifestyle (and might make our whole society healthier). Implementing congestion pricing in every major downtown in America, as London and Singapore have done, could involve some lifestyle changes, but if it were accompanied by big new investments in mass transit, not only might we not be worse off, we might actually be better off. In the last year, I have started to take the Washington-area subway to work more regularly, instead of driving myself. I get there just as fast or even faster, I breeze through two newspapers along the way, and I arrive at work feeling less stressed. A lot of people in a lot of countries might actually enjoy giving up some personal mobility if their governments spent more money on mass transit and less on subsidizing gasoline.

In sum: We don't know how many millions of barrels of oil or kilowatts of energy we could save just by *thinking more about how we live* rather than *shrinking more of how we live*. We don't know how many millions of barrels of oil or kilowatts of energy we could save if, and when, people discover that green is better, not harsher, and offers more, not less. As I indicated, it may be that a radical change in lifestyle is all that can save us and the planet. I would not rule it out. But we don't know whether we'll need to opt for the drastic, because we haven't yet tried the obvious.

"Conservation is not the opposite of consumption," argues Glenn Prickett of Conservation International. "We need to consume to live and to grow our economies. But we can consume more and conserve more at the same time. We need to identify those places and resources that we need to preserve in their natural state—and grow around them." And we need to identify the practices that are just wasteful—out of habit or ignorance, not necessity or design—and eliminate them. There is still plenty of room for conservation and consumption, "if we are smart, properly plan, and are vigilant about protecting what we have set aside," said Prickett.

People on both sides of the energy-environment debate often confuse this issue: Too many environmentalists oppose *any* growth, a position that locks the poor into poverty. Too many critics of environmentalism characterize any conservation as some flaky anticapitalist ideological dalliance. They fail to recognize how important nature—clean water, clean air, healthy forests, healthy oceans, and species diversity—is to our daily life and our spiritual well-being, not to mention our economy, and how vulnerable it is to destruction.

"Not every acre of land or sea has to be protected," says Prickett, "but the ones that do [warrant protection] are the ones that provide the critical ecological life-support systems, because they harbor endangered species, because they protect watersheds, because they buffer streams and keep sediment and nutrients out of rivers, because they are breeding grounds for the fish we eat, because they keep CO_2 out of the atmosphere, because they maintain species diversity that makes larger landscapes more resilient to climate change, and ultimately because nature provides a spiritual richness to life that is an essential part of being human."

So, yes, let us do all we can to make available clean, cheap, reliable electrons as soon as possible to as many people as possible so more people can live better cleaner lives—but without illusions. "There are people who believe that unlimited cheap energy is a recipe for disaster in the long run," said Peter Gleick, the climate expert at the Pacific Institute. "But in the short run, our problem is not having enough clean energy. That is much more dangerous to us right now, because of the threat of climate change. But in the long run, we do have to think about the implications of cheap."

Adaptation

Unfortunately, any Clean Energy System will require one more element: a strategy for adaptation. No matter what we do starting tomorrow, the fact is that humans have already put enough additional greenhouse gases into the atmosphere to make some degree of climate change and the disruptions that will come with it—ice melt, flooding, sea level rise, and more frequent and more severe storms, droughts, and heat waves—an inevitable part of our future. Climate change is already baked in. Therefore, we cannot rely on mitigation alone. Certain regions, ecosystems, and socioeconomic groups are going to have to adapt to changes in their climates, which could be quite severe and emerge quite abruptly. The Intergovernmental Panel on Climate Change (2007) defines adaptation as the "adjustment in natural or human systems in response to actual or expected climatic stimuli or their effects, which moderates harm or exploits beneficial opportunities."

Not surprisingly, some climate-change deniers have tried to use adaptation as a means of halting mitigation efforts or as an excuse for not tackling the challenges of mitigation: "Forget about mitigation," they say, "just focus on adaptation." This, of course, is nonsense. Adaptation can never be a substitute for mitigation. Think of what it cost just to try to prepare one city, New Orleans, to "adapt" to the next Category 5 hurricane by rebuilding its major levees, and you will understand why mitigation is always going to be cheaper than adaptation.

Trying to prevent more climate change—mitigation—always has to be job number one. Because the very tools and strategies that we might invent to mitigate climate change would be enormously helpful in both adapting to the climate change that is inevitable *and* in reducing the scope of the climate change we will have to adapt to.

To be sure, adaptation to climate is as old as human history. Plants, animals, and humans have always had to adapt to climate fluctuations, whether by migrating to different habitats or planting different crops for different seasons. But in the past, we and the plants and animals around us have usually had the luxury of adapting gradually. As the Environmental Protection Agency notes on its Web site, "human-induced climate change represents a new challenge, and may require adaptation approaches to changes that are potentially larger and faster than past experiences with *recorded natural climatic variability* . . . All climate-sensitive systems of society and the natural environment, including agriculture, forestry, water resources, human health, coastal settlements, and natural ecosystems, will need to adapt to a changing climate or possibly face diminished productivity, functioning and health . . . For humans, adaptation is a risk-management strategy that has costs and is not foolproof. The effectiveness of any specific adaptation requires consideration of the expected value of the avoided damages against the costs of implementing the adaptation strategy."

According to a 2004 study by William Easterling, Brian Hurd, and Joel Smith, "Coping with Global Climate Change: The Role of Adaptation in the United States," "U.S. society can on the whole adapt with either net gains or some costs if warming occurs at the lower end of the projected range of magnitude, assuming no change in climate variability and generally making optimistic assumptions about adaptation. However, with a much larger magnitude of warming, even making relatively optimistic assumptions about adaptation, many sectors would experience net losses and higher costs."

With all those caveats in mind, the EPA offers a variety of examples of what an adaptation strategy might include. For instance, it might involve the U.S. government today mobilizing the Army Corps of Engineers to begin a broad-based plan for strengthening shore protection—dikes, bulkheads, beach nourishment—in order to "prevent sea level rise from inundating low-lying coastal property, eroding beaches, or worsen flooding." It also suggests urban tree planting to moderate temperature increases; developing county-scale maps depicting which areas will require shore protection and which areas will be allowed to adapt naturally; promoting shore protection techniques that do not destroy all habitats;

engaging state and local governments in defining responses to sea level rise; improving early warning systems and flood hazard mapping for storms; protecting water supplies from contamination by saltwater; breeding new plant species and crops that are more tolerant to changed climate condition; promoting fire suppression practices in the event of increased fire risk due to temperature increases; conserving soil moisture through mulching and other means; and diversifying power supply in the event of power plant failures due to excess demand created by extreme heat or by extreme weather events.

But, again, let's have no illusions about adaptation as a cure-all. As the EPA notes, "the ability of ecosystems to adapt to climate change is severely limited by the effects of urbanization, barriers to migration paths, and fragmentation of ecosystems, all of which have already critically stressed ecosystems independent of climate change itself . . . Although biological systems have an inherent capacity to adapt to changes in environmental conditions, given the rapid rate of projected climate change, adaptive capacity is likely to be exceeded for many species."

Bottom line: We need a Clean Energy System that is always trying to optimize these five elements: The more clean electrons we generate, the more growth we can have with fewer emissions. The greater the energy efficiency we bring about, the fewer clean electrons we need to get more growth. The more those who want to have smaller families can have them, the fewer mouths we have to feed and homes we have to build. The more conservation we promote, the fewer clean electrons and the less energy efficiency we need, and the fewer natural resources we con-

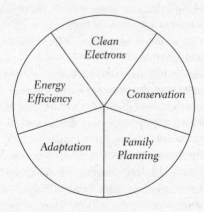

sume, as we grow. And the more we plan for adaptation, the more people will be cushioned from the worst effects of rising sea levels, heat waves, or violent storms.

Each part of the system works together to help us avoid the unmanageable and manage the unavoidable.

Senhor Verde

Let's fantasize for a moment and ask: What would an ideal farm in Brazil that was operating as part of such a Clean Energy System look like? Imagine Senhor Verde has a thousand-acre farm, with a river full of fish running through it that is adjacent to an expanse of natural forest loaded with a rich diversity of plants and animals. Here is how he would operate:

He would start his day using a smart tractor, the kind already made by John Deere. As he plows his field, the tractor takes real-time measurements of the moisture and nutrient content of each square meter and automatically inserts only the exact amount of fertilizer needed to produce the yield he seeks; that way there is no fertilizer left over to wash into his river and harm the aquatic life there and downstream. Less nitrogen fertilizer also means fewer emissions of nitrogen oxide—a potent greenhouse gas. Thanks to this technology, he is taking advantage all the time of the most productive parts of his land for farming, so he has less incentive to go into the rain forest or to denude the riverbanks of trees just to plant a few more acres of crops. In fact, he and his neighbors have worked with a local conservation NGO to zone their farms so that the most productive areas are farmed, and other areas are set aside and restored to their native vegetation, which protects the streams and allows wildlife to migrate across a much larger area of natural habitat. That smart tractor, by the way, is a plug-in electric hybrid, with a backup motor that runs on biofuel made from switchgrass planted in Brazil on degraded lands that were specifically set aside as part of a national plan to protect the Amazon from biofuel encroachment. All the information amassed about the amount of fertilizer that went into every square meter of his land, and the yield it ultimately produced, is captured on the onboard computer so he can make smarter decisions next year and increase his yield, even as he reduces his inputs. The sprinkler system is also a smart system and adds only the precise amount of water per square meter that is needed. The crop itself has been engineered to grow with the least amount of fertilizer and the least amount of water and fewest pesticides, so it is much stronger and produces a higher yield than non-bioengineered crops. It has also been engineered to be more nutritious, so people get healthier and healthier from less and less food.

In addition, because he is using fewer and cleaner fertilizers, the impact on the local river is tiny, so the water can be recycled with less energy and fewer chemicals. Also, by not cultivating the banks of the river and by maintaining the trees, he is preserving from erosion his most valuable asset—the arable land that produces his crops—and providing through the roots of trees and wetlands a natural water filter, which keeps sediment out of the river and prevents degradation of the wetlands downstream. Because the river is healthy, he can enjoy fishing it or swimming in it much more, but he can also license others to come and fish for peacock bass on it each summer, making another nice little side income. On the part of his land that abuts the tropical forest, he has built a small ecolodge, which draws all its electricity from a one-megawatt wind turbine and attracts hundreds of ecotourists each year.

By the way, Senhor Verde himself was one of eleven children. His parents, even as they loved him as one of their own, saw him as part of their social safety net and labor force. By contrast, he and his wife, who is a schoolteacher, practice family planning, which they were first exposed to through a government program in the nearby village, shortly after they got married. They have only three children, all of whom are in school.

Finally, the government allowed Senhor Verde to build the ecolodge on the condition that he protect the surrounding rain forest on his land and fund the protection of a nearby national park. It made sense to him to fund the park because he is protecting the habitat for bees that pollinate his crops and other insects that prey on his pests—enabling him to buy even fewer expensive chemical pesticides—and the virgin forest also provides a more reliable water supply for his farm by protecting the watershed (which becomes more important as climate change threatens more drought) and provides habitat for the wildlife that his ecotourists pay him to see. The net result is an ecosystem that is much healthier, more enjoyable, and more productive than the one we have now. All the parts reinforce one another, thereby producing more agricultural growth, protecting more biodiversity, and generating more clean power and efficiency savings with fewer, cleaner, smarter inputs. This is the ideal we need to be striving for.

Making the Transition

So how do we get there from here? How do we get from the Dirty Fuels System we have now to a clean-powered, energy-efficient, conservation-based system? We need to think strategically about how to build every part of the system. We need to start with a plan for the whole, instead of offering one-off projects without any strategic blueprint—the way we did with the massive subsidization of corn ethanol production in the United States.

Given the small net energy and CO_2 contribution made by corn ethanol, the whole craze reminded me of the late economist Ken Boulding's definition of suboptimal: doing the best possible job at something that should not be done at all.

What would a more systemic approach look like? Google gave us one example. In November 2007, the giant Web-search company announced that it would no longer just offer "power searching," but was itself going to be searching for power—clean power from non-fossil-fuel sources. Yes, Google said, it was going into the energy innovation and generation business, with the aim of producing one gigawatt of clean renewable power, enough to run all of San Francisco, as soon as possible. It is a daring effort, and Google should be commended for putting its capital and brains behind such an initiative.

I have only one tiny problem with it: Google summarized its revolutionary goal in a single, shorthand equation, "RE < C—renewable energy cheaper than coal," so that this clean energy can scale in China, India, and the rest of the developing world.

It is true that renewable energy that is cheaper than coal is necessary, but, as I have argued, it is not sufficient. We also need innovation to improve energy and resource productivity, we need family planning, we need an ethic of conservation, and we need strategies for adaptation—without which RE < C could wipe out massive amounts of biodiversity. Google's heart is in the right place—we need a bumper sticker that summarizes our objective in a focused manner. I would simply propose a longer bumper sticker. In fact, my bumper sticker might take up your whole bumper.

With tongue only slightly in cheek, I would argue that what we need is an REEFIGDCPEERPFPCA < TCOBCOG—a renewable energy ecosystem for innovating, generating, and deploying clean power, energy efficiency, resource productivity, family planning, conservation, and adaptation < the true cost of burning coal, oil, and gas. That is, we need clean energy that is cheaper than the *true cost* to society of fossil fuels, when you measure the climate change those fuels cause, the pollution they trigger, and the energy wars they engender.

In my view, moving to Code Green means putting in place *a system* of government policies, regulations, research funding, and tax increases and incentives that would stimulate *a system* for innovating, generating, and deploying clean electrons, energy efficiency, resource productivity, conservation, and adaptation. It takes a systemic approach to produce a systemic response. That has to be our strategy.

But there are no shortcuts. We need to replace the Dirty Fuels System with a Clean Energy System—an REEFIGDCPEERPFPCA < TCOBCOG. And in politics and economics, there is a simple term that describes the process of replacing one system with another: *revolution*.

Some people say that is what we're having right now—a green revolution. I beg to differ.

PART III

How We Move Forward

ELEVEN

205 Easy Ways to Save the Earth

"Oh God, here they come—act green."
  —A husband and wife speaking as another couple approaches them at a cocktail
    party. Cartoon in *The New Yorker*, August 20, 2007

*A recent study found the average American golfer walks about 900 miles a year. Another
study found American golfers drink, on average, 22 gallons of alcohol a year. That
means, on average, American golfers get about 41 miles to the gallon.*
  Kind of makes you proud.
  —from the Internet

What do you mean? We're not having a green revolution? But I
just picked up *Working Mother* magazine at the doctor's office and read the cover story: "205 Easy Ways to Save the
Earth" (November 2007). It so whetted my appetite for easy ways to save
the planet that I Googled for more books and magazine articles on this
topic—and boy, did I find more: "20 Easy Ways You Can Help the
Earth," "Easy Ways to Protect Our Planet," "Simple Ways to Save the
Earth," "10 Ways to Save the Earth," "20 Quick and Easy Ways to Save
the Planet," "Five Ways to Save the Earth," "The 10 Easiest Ways to
Green Your Home," "365 Ways to Save the Earth," "100 Ways You Can
Save the Earth," "1,001 Ways to Save the Earth," "101 Ways to Heal the
Earth," "10 Painless Ways to Save the Planet," "21 Ways to Save the
Earth and Make More Money," "14 Easy Ways to Be an Everyday Envi-
ronmentalist," "Easy Ways to Go Green," "40 Easy Ways to Save the

Planet," "10 Simple Ways to Save the Earth," "Help Save the Planet: Easy Ways to Make a Difference," "50 Ways to Save the Earth," "50 Simple Ways to Save the Earth and Get Rich Trying," "Top Ten Ways to Green Up Your Sex Life" (vegan condoms, solar vibrators—I'm not making this up), "Innovative Ways to Save Planet Earth," "101 Things Designers Can Do to Save the Earth," "Five Weird and Wacky Ways to Save the Earth," "Five Ways to Save the World," and for those with a messianic streak but who are short of both cash and time: "10 Ways to Save the Earth (& Money) in Under a Minute."

Who knew that saving the earth could be so easy—and in under a minute!

There is some good news in this trend. Thinking about how to live and work in a greener fashion—with cleaner electrons, greater energy and resource productivity, and an ethic of conservation—is being popularized and democratized. It is no longer an elite issue for those living on the West and East coasts or in the backwoods of Colorado or Vermont.

If you are in the technology business today and you have not been invited to a green-tech conference somewhere, you must not be breathing, or everybody has lost your e-mail address. To say that green is the color du jour is an understatement. "Green" was actually the single most trademarked term in 2007, according to the U.S. Patent and Trademark office. Environmental reporters in newsrooms, who used to sit in the corner farthest from the editor's desk, are suddenly cool. Universities are adding classes on environmentalism and looking to shrink their carbon footprints, as are more and more companies. No candidate can get elected today without uttering the trilogy: I will support cleaner fuels. I will liberate America from its oil dependence. I will combat climate change.

The politics of this issue have shifted so much that even al-Qaeda supporters, who always have their fingers on the global pulse, are getting in on the green branding thing. *Newsweek* (September 10, 2007) reported that in July 2007 "an umbrella group of Islamists that advocates a Sharia state in Indonesia—and whose leaders have publicly supported Osama bin Laden—hoisted placards bearing the name Friends of the Earth—Indonesia at a rally protesting a U.S. mining company and the Bush Administration . . . [The real] Friends of the Earth denounced the unauthorized use of their logo and denied any links. But don't be surprised if radical Islamists make more attempts to cloak their work in the garb of social activism."

Not to be outdone by the Muslims, the Jews are also getting in on the act. UPI reported (December 5, 2007): "A group of Israeli environmentalists has launched an Internet campaign encouraging Jews around the world to light at least one fewer candle this Hanukkah . . . The founders of the Green Hanukkia campaign say each candle burning all the way down produces 15 grams of carbon dioxide," and that many candles multiplied around Jewish households all over the world starts to add up to a kosher carbon footprint. "'The campaign calls for Jews around the world to save the last candle and save the planet, so we won't need another miracle,' Liad Ortar, a founder of the campaign, told *The Jerusalem Post*." (One blog I saw said in response: Why not ask everyone in the world to stop smoking cigarettes?)

You'll pardon me, though, if I've become a bit cynical about all of this. I have read or heard so many people saying, "We're having a green revolution." Of course, there is certainly a lot of green buzz out there. But whenever I hear that "we're having a green revolution" line I can't resist firing back: "Really? Really? A green revolution? Have you ever seen a revolution where no one got hurt? That's the green revolution we're having." In the green revolution we're having, everyone's a winner, nobody has to give up anything, and the adjective that most often modifies "green revolution" is "easy." That's not a revolution. That's a party. We're actually having a green party. And, I have to say, it's a lot of fun. I get invited to all the parties. But in America, at least, it is mostly a costume party. It's all about *looking* green—and everyone's a winner. There are no losers. The American farmers are winners. They're green. They get to grow ethanol and garner huge government subsidies for doing so, even though it makes no real sense as a CO_2-reduction strategy. Exxon Mobil says it's getting green and General Motors does too. GM put yellow gas caps on its cars that are flex-fuel, meaning they can run on a mix of gasoline and ethanol. For years, GM never bothered to highlight that its cars were flex-fuel, or use it as a selling point with customers, because the only reason GM made a certain number of cars flex-fuel was that, if it did so, the government would allow it to build even more gas-guzzling Hummers and pickup trucks and still remain under the CAFE standard mandated by Congress—but why quibble?

Coal companies are going green by renaming themselves "energy" companies and stressing how sequestration of CO_2, something none of them has ever done, will give us "clean coal." I am sure Dick Cheney is green. He has a home in Wyoming, where he goes hunting, and he favors liquefied coal. We're all green. "Yes, step right up, ladies and gentlemen, in the green revolution we're having in America today, everybody gets to play, everybody's a winner, nobody gets hurt, and nobody has to do anything hard."

As I said, that's not the definition of a revolution. That's the definition of a party.

Thankfully, more than a few people are on to this green party. A blogger at Greenasathistle.com, which tracks environmental issues, wryly observed:

> Raising awareness about global warming, enviro-friendly products and people doing green deeds is obviously a good thing—but does every single magazine on the rack have to come out with a green issue? I'm starting to believe that there actually can be too much publicity when it comes to climate change, especially when it reaches the fashion world. Seriously, if I read the word "eco-chic" one more time, I'll jab my eyes out with my biodegradable pen . . . I just fear that as soon as all the magazines get these green issues out of the way, they'll feel like it's out of their system, over and done with, like any other passing trend. By next month they'll probably declare . . . gas guzzling "in" and earnest recycling "out," with headlines like "Littering is the new black!"

The amount of time, energy, and verbiage being spent on making people "aware" of the energy-climate problem, and asking people to make symbolic gestures to call attention to it, is out of all proportion to the time, energy, and effort going into designing a systemic solution. We've had too many Live Earth concerts and Barneys "Have a Green Holiday" Christmas catalogs and too few focused lobbying efforts to enact transformational green legislation. In 2008, if the money and mobilization effort spent on Live Earth had gone into lobbying the U.S. Congress for more generous and longer-term production and investment tax credits for renewable energy, and for other green legislation, the impact would have been vastly more meaningful. Moving from the symbolic to the substantive is not easy. I live in Montgomery County, Maryland, which is chock-full of people who identify themselves as green and recycle and do all the other good things. But when I wanted to install two solar arrays in my side yard, I was told that it was against the law. Too unsightly. Zoning laws said they could go only in the backyard. Our backyard doesn't get enough sun. Our solar firm had to hire a lawyer and appeal to get the law changed, which we managed to do after almost a year.

Pentagon planners like to say: "A vision without resources is a hallucination." Right now we are having a green hallucination, not a green revolution. Because we are offering ourselves and our kids a green vision without the resources—without a systemic response shaped by an intelligent design and buttressed by market forces, higher efficiency standards, tougher regulations, and an ethic of conservation that might have a chance of turning that vision into reality. We have willed the ends, but not the means.

Sure, if you look at how far we have come in just the last five years, it can feel like we're having a green revolution. But if you look at where we have to go in the next ten years, we're having a party. No one has said it better than Michael Maniates, a professor of political science and environmental science at Allegheny College, who wrote in *The Washington Post* (November 22, 2007): "Never has so little been asked of so many at such a critical moment."

Several best-selling books "offer advice about what we must ask of ourselves and one another," Maniates noted.

> Their titles suggest that we needn't break much of a sweat: "It's Easy Being Green," "The Lazy Environmentalist," or even "The Green Book: The Everyday Guide to Saving the Planet One Simple Step at a Time."
>
> Although each offers familiar advice ("reuse scrap paper before recycling" or "take shorter showers"), it's what's left unsaid by these books that's intriguing. Three assertions permeate the pages: (1) We should look for easy, cost-effective things to do in our private lives as consumers, since that's where we have the most power and control; these are the best things to do because (2) if we all do them the cumulative effect of these individual choices will be a safe planet; which is fortunate indeed because (3) we, by nature, aren't terribly interested in doing anything that isn't private, individualistic, cost-effective and, above all, easy. This glorification of easy isn't limited to the newest environmental self-help books. The Web sites of the big U.S. environmental groups, the

Environmental Protection Agency and even the American Association for the Advancement of Science offer markedly similar lists of actions that tell us we can change the world through our consumer choices, choices that are economic, simple, even stylish.

Of course, we are not going to consume our way out of this problem. And there is no "easy" button we can press to make the world green. Maniates went on:

> The hard facts are these: If we sum up the easy, cost-effective, eco-efficiency measures we should all embrace, the best we get is a slowing of the growth of environmental damage . . . Obsessing over recycling and installing a few special light bulbs won't cut it. We need to be looking at fundamental change in our energy, transportation and agricultural systems rather than technological tweaking on the margins, and this means changes and costs that our current and would-be leaders seem afraid to discuss. Which is a pity, since Americans are at their best when they're struggling together, and sometimes with one another, toward difficult goals . . . Surely we must do the easy things: They slow the damage and themselves become enabling symbols of empathy for future generations. But we cannot permit our leaders to sell us short. To stop at "easy" is to say that the best we can do is accept an uninspired politics of guilt around a parade of uncoordinated individual action.

The problem is, the minute we leave the comforting realm of "the easy ways to go green," whatever facile consensus for action exists around this issue breaks down. The truth is, for all that we talk about going green, "we have not agreed as a society on what being 'green' actually means," remarked Peter Gleick, the climate expert from the Pacific Institute. That opens a door to everyone claiming to be green, without any benchmarks.

What I hope to do in the remainder of this book is lay out what a systemic green strategy would look like. But before we go there, we need to stop for just one moment at the weight scale.

You know how after you put on a few pounds, you stop weighing yourself—or at least I do—because you just don't want to know how many pounds you are going to have to shed? Well, the same has been true of the green issue. People tend to talk about it in the total abstract, without any connection to the actual scale of the challenge we have to meet in order to significantly reduce CO_2 emissions and become more energy and resource efficient. So before we take another step, we need to put this challenge on the scale, look down at the digital readout, and behold, without blinking, just how big a project this really is.

For starters, let's remember what we're trying to do: *We're trying to change the climate system—to avoid the unmanageable and manage the unavoidable!* We are trying to affect how much the rain falls, how strong the winds blow, how fast the ice melts. In addition to all that, *we're trying to preserve and restore the world's rapidly depleting ecosystems*—our forests, rivers, savannahs, oceans, and the cornucopia of plant and animal species they contain. Finally, we are trying to break a collective addiction to gasoline that is having not only profound climate effects, but also geopolitical ones. It doesn't get any bigger than this. This is not something you do as a hobby, and the adjective "easy" should never— ever, ever—accompany this task.

The truth is: Not only are there not 205 easy ways to *really go green*, there isn't *one easy way to really go green*! If we can pull this off, it will be the biggest single peaceable project humankind will have ever undertaken. Rare is the political leader anywhere in the world who will talk straight about the true size of this challenge.

As a result, the task often falls to oil, gas, and coal company executives. They are happy to tell us about the scale of the problem—but usually with secret delight, because they want us to believe that a real green revolution is impossible to pull off, so we have no choice but to remain addicted to oil, gas, and coal. They want to break our will to resist. Their hidden message is: "Surrender now, give in to your inner gas guzzler; the scale of what we need to do to really make a difference is too great. Surrender now, surrender now, surrender now . . ."

I am instinctively wary of their analysis—but I do make exceptions for companies that have actually made substantial bets in renewable energy and are actually looking to build real businesses there—if there is a market. Chevron, for instance, is the world's biggest private producer of electricity from clean geothermal sources (steam, heat, and hot water produced underground by volcanic material from the earth's core, which provides the force to spin turbine generators and produce electricity). Here's how Chevron's CEO, David O'Reilly, sees the scope and scale of our clean energy challenge:

"There is a problem with energy literacy," O'Reilly argued. "If you look at energy consumption in the world each day and convert it all into oil equivalent, we are consuming ten million barrels an hour—that is 420 million gallons per hour. Think about that. That means if we take all the hydro, coal, oil, and renewables—everything—and put them together, that is how much we are using. To really make a difference, there are three issues: There is the scale of the demand, the scale of the investment needed to produce alternatives at scale, and the scale of time it takes to produce alternatives. Many alternatives are just at the embryonic phase.

"Now let's look at the rising demand. I've heard people talk about 'the golden billion'—the billion people on the planet who [already] have the quality of life and standard of living we [Americans] are used to. But there are another two billion on the way up and three billion still in poverty. The two billion who are moving up want to get to where we are, and then the three billion want to move up—and from a global prosperity point of view, we want them to move up. Then there's another three billion coming along who have not even been born yet [but will be here by 2050]. This energy supply we have today is focused on meeting the demands of the one billion and the two billion—not the three billion who are still in poverty, let alone the three billion who have not been born yet. So this ten million barrels per hour [that we are consuming] is not static," said O'Reilly. "It is going to rise, because there is an inexorable connection between energy use and well-being."

Now, said O'Reilly, let's look at the challenge of creating new ways to produce and use energy. "People are overestimating the ability of the alternatives that are out there to get to scale," he explained. "Let's talk about efficiency: If you shut down the whole transportation system—I am talking about every car, truck, train, ship, and plane, anything that flies or is on wheels—and another vehicle never moved on planet earth, you would reduce carbon emission by 14 percent, globally. If you shut down all industrial activity, all commercial activity, all residential activity—shut everything off to every home—you would reduce carbon emissions by 68 percent . . . So efficiency can help, but let's not make false promises. We still need oil and natural gas. We need to make coal work, and we need to make energy efficiency work more."

As if that scenario doesn't already boggle the mind, O'Reilly argued that, absent some unexpected breakthrough, it will take decades for alternatives to be brought to scale. "I want my grandchildren to live in a world that has energy, environment, and economy in balance. But you cannot get there overnight," he insisted. "The system we have today is the product of over a hundred years of investments, and the next one will require a hundred years of investments. [So,] these quick promises that we hear in Washington and other places—be careful. My prediction [is that] global greenhouse gases will be higher ten years from now than they are today, but when my grandchildren are in my stage of life—their sixties— they could be substantially lower. We need leaders who will stand up and say this is hard, this is big, and it [requires] massive amounts of investment."

What about the $5 billion or so that I keep reading about that went into green venture capital investing in 2007? I asked O'Reilly. That would not even buy a sophisticated new oil refinery, he snapped. "If you want to really change the path we are on, you need a number that starts with a T in front of it"—T for *trillion*. "Otherwise we will stay on the path we are on."

But let's say you are an optimist. You believe that the renewable energy technologies available today, and opportunities for energy efficiency, are advanced enough to make a fundamental impact on both climate change and energy prices. What exactly would we have to do by way of deploying these existing clean power technologies and energy efficiency programs—starting today—to make that fundamental impact?

The answer to that question—and another way to look at the scale of the problem—is offered by Robert Socolow, an engineering professor at Princeton, and Stephen Pacala, an ecology professor there, who together lead the Carbon Mitigation Initiative, a consortium that has set out to design scalable solutions for the climate problem. Socolow and Pacala first argued in a now famous paper published by the journal *Science* (August 2004) that human beings can emit only so much carbon dioxide into the atmosphere before the buildup of CO_2 reaches a level unknown in recent geologic history, and the earth's climate system starts to go haywire. Like the Intergovernmental Panel on Climate Change, they argued that the risk of really weird global weirding grows rapidly as CO_2 levels approach a doubling of the concentration of CO_2 that was in the atmosphere before the Industrial Revolution, which was 280 parts per million (ppm).

"Think of the climate-change issue as a closet, and behind the door are lurking all kinds of monsters—and there's a long list of them," Pacala said. "All of our scientific work says the most damaging monsters start to come out from behind that door when you hit the doubling of CO_2 levels."

So, as a simple goal everyone can understand, the doubling of CO_2 is what we want to avoid. Here's the problem: If we basically do nothing, and global CO_2 emissions continue to grow at the current trajectory, we will easily pass the doubling level—an atmospheric concentration of carbon dioxide of 560 ppm—around mid-century, and we'll likely hit a tripling sometime around 2075, said Pacala. You don't want to live in a 560 ppm world, let alone an 800 ppm world. To avoid that—and still leave room for developed countries to grow, while using less carbon, and for developing countries like India and China to grow, emitting double or triple their current carbon levels, until they climb out of poverty and are able to become more energy efficient—will require a huge global industrial energy project.

To convey the scale involved, Socolow and Pacala created a pie chart with fifteen different wedges. Some wedges represent carbon-free or carbon-diminishing power-generating technologies; other wedges represent efficiency programs that could conserve large amounts of energy and prevent CO_2 emissions. Socolow and Pacala argue that beginning today—right now—the world needs to deploy any eight of these fifteen wedges on a grand scale, or sufficient amounts of all fifteen, in order to generate enough clean power, conservation, and energy efficiency to grow the world economy and still avoid the doubling of CO_2 in the atmosphere by mid-century.

Each of these wedges, when phased in over fifty years, would avoid the release of twenty-five billion tons of carbon, for a total of 200 billion tons of carbon avoided between now and mid-century, which is the amount that Pacala and Socolow believe would keep us below the doubling. To qualify as one of the fifteen wedges, though, the technology must exist today and must be capable of large-scale deployment, and the emissions reductions it offers have to be measurable.

So now we have a target: We want to avoid the doubling of CO_2 by mid-century, and to do it we need to avoid the emission of 200 billion tons of carbon as we grow between now and then. So let's get to the wedges. Choose your favorite "easy" eight:

- Double fuel efficiency of two billion cars from 30 miles per gallon to 60 mpg.
- Drive two billion cars only 5,000 miles per year rather than 10,000, at 30 miles per gallon.
- Raise efficiency at 1,600 large coal-fired plants from 40 to 60 percent.
- Replace 1,400 large coal-fired electric plants with natural-gas-powered facilities.
- Install carbon capture and sequestration capacity at eight hundred large coal-fired plants, so that the CO_2 can be separated and stored underground.
- Install carbon capture and sequestration at new coal plants that would produce hydrogen for 1.5 billion hydrogen-powered vehicles.
- Install carbon capture and sequestration at 180 coal gasification plants.
- Add twice today's current global nuclear capacity to replace coal-based electricity.
- Increase wind power fortyfold to displace all coal-fired power.
- Increase solar power seven-hundred-fold to displace all coal-fired power.
- Increase wind power eightyfold to make hydrogen for clean cars.
- Drive two billion cars on ethanol, using one-sixth of the world's cropland to grow the needed corn.
- Halt all cutting and burning of forests.
- Adopt conservation tillage, which emits much less CO_2 from the land, in all agricultural soils worldwide.
- Cut electricity use in homes, offices, and stores by 25 percent, and cut carbon emissions by the same amount.

If the world managed to take just one of those steps, it would be a miracle. Eight would be the miracle of miracles, but this is the scale of what will be required. "There has never been a deliberate industrial project in history as big as this," Pacala said. Through a combination of clean power technology and conservation, "we have to get rid of 200 billion tons of carbon over the next fifty years—and still keep growing. It is possible to accomplish this if we start today. But every year that we delay, the job becomes more difficult. Because every year you delay, you have to do that much more the next year—and if we delay a decade or two, avoiding the doubling or more will become impossible."

Nate Lewis, the California Institute of Technology chemist and energy expert, uses a somewhat different set of calculations than Socolow and Pacala, but his approach is also useful in conveying the challenge. Lewis put it this way: In the year 2000, the world's total average rate of energy usage was roughly 13 trillion watts (13 terawatts). That means that at any given moment, on average, the world was using about 13 trillion watts. That is what the world's electric meter would read. Even with aggressive conservation, that figure is expected to double by 2050 to around 26 trillion watts. But if we want to avoid the doubling of CO_2 in the atmosphere, and accommodate our own growth and that of India and China and other developing countries, we would actually have to cut global CO_2 emissions by 2050 by close to 80 percent, relative to current levels—starting today.

That means by 2050 we could use only about 2.6 trillion watts from carbon-emitting energy sources. But we know total demand is going to double by then, to about 26 terawatts. "That means, roughly speaking," said Lewis, "between now and 2050 we have to conserve almost as much energy as we are currently using, by becoming more energy efficient, and we also have to make almost as much clean energy as we currently use, by developing non-carbon-emitting energy sources."

An average nuclear power plant today produces about a billion watts—one gigawatt—of electricity at any given time. So if we tried to get all the new clean power we would need between now and 2050 (almost 13 trillion watts) just from nuclear power, we would have to build 13,000 new nuclear reactors, or roughly one new reactor every day for the next thirty-six years—starting today.

"It will take all of our investment capital and intellectual capital to meet this challenge," said Lewis. "Some people say it will ruin our economy and is a project which we can't afford to do. I'd say it is a project at which we simply can't afford to fail."

And make no mistake: We are failing right now. For all the talk of a green revolution, said Lewis, "things are not getting better. In fact, they are actually getting worse. From 1990 to 1999, global CO_2 emissions increased at a rate of 1.1 percent per year. Then everyone started talking about Kyoto, so we buckled up our belts, got serious, and we showed 'em what we could do: In the years 2000 to 2006, we *tripled* the rate of global CO_2 emission increases, to an average [increase] for that period of over 3 percent a year! That'll show 'em that we mean business! Hey, look what we can do when we're serious—we can emit even more carbon even faster."

This is where politics meets climate meets energy meets technology. Do we have the political energy—does anyone have the political energy—to undertake and deploy an industrial project of this scale?

Of course, being green at the rhetorical level we're at right now is not inconsistent with the broadly professed principles of either the Democratic or the Republican party. But implementing a green revolution at speed and scale is going to mean confronting some of the economic, regional, and corporate vested interests that live at the heart of both parties—from farmers in Iowa to coal lobbies in West Virginia. Therefore, without a real clash within the Republican and Democratic parties on this issue, there will be no real green revolution in America.

"When everyone—Democrats and Republicans, corporations and consumers—claims to embrace your cause, you should suspect that you have not really defined the problem, or framed it as a real political question," said the Harvard philosopher Michael J. Sandel. "Serious social, economic, and political change is controversial. It is bound to provoke argument and opposition. Unless you think there is a purely technological fix, meeting the energy challenge will require shared sacrifice, and political will. There is no real politics without disagreement and competing interests. Politics is about hard choices, not feel-good posturing. Only when a real debate breaks out—between or within the political parties—will we be on our way to a politically serious green agenda."

You can't call something a revolution when the maximum changes that are politically feasible still fall well short of the minimum needed to start making even a dent in the problem. The challenges posed by the Energy-Climate Era "can't be solved at the level of current political thinking," said Hal Harvey, an energy expert at the William and Flora Hewlett Foundation. "You cannot solve a problem from the same level of thinking that created it."

Rob Watson, the environmental consultant, said to me one day that meeting this challenge—for real—reminded him of an experience he had in the Boy Scouts. "I was overweight, and there were things I thought I could do in my head that I couldn't always do in real life," he explained. "Once my Boy Scout troop had a fifty-mile hike. And to prepare we had to do a series of training hikes. So I took hikes on my own. I thought I was going nine to twelve miles each time to prepare, but actually I was just going three or four. When I finally got out in the wilderness with my troop, I collapsed with heatstroke, because I was not really in shape. I endangered myself and everyone in my group, because I was not being real. I know the need to want to feel that you are doing well and doing right—but if we are not real about where we are, we are not going to do what we need to do to survive in this wilderness."

People don't seem to realize, he added, that it is not like we're on the *Titanic* and we have to avoid the iceberg. *We've already hit the iceberg.* The water is rushing in down below. But some people just don't want to leave the dance floor; others don't want to give up on the buffet. But if we don't make the hard choices, nature will make them for us. Right now, that acute awareness of the true scale and speed of this problem remains confined largely to the expert scientific community, but soon enough it will be blindingly obvious to everyone.

Don't get me wrong: I take succor from the number of young people being engaged by this issue. And as the Greenasathistle.com blogger rightly observed, "it's better to be hypocritical than apathetic when it comes to the environment"—as long as you know that's what you're doing, as long as you keep moving in the right direction, and as long as you don't prematurely declare victory. It's planting our flag prematurely that will get us in the most trouble. And that's what we've started doing lately—a green brand, some green buzz, a green concert, and we're on our way to solving the problem. Not a chance.

"It is as if we were climbing Mount Everest and we reached base camp six, the lowest rung on the mountain climb, and decided to look around, put down our gear, pat our Sherpas on the back, and open a celebratory brandy," said Jack Hidary, the energy entrepreneur. "But meanwhile, Mount Everest, all 29,000 feet of it, still looms before us."

What would it actually look like from the top of Mount Everest? That is, what would a truly disruptive and transformational clean power revolution look like? Let's try to see in the next chapter.

TWELVE

The Energy Internet: When IT Meets ET

Revolution is not a dinner party, not an essay, nor a painting, nor a piece of embroidery;
it cannot be advanced softly, gradually, carefully, considerately, respectfully, politely,
plainly and modestly.
—Mao Zedong

That view from Mount Everest would look like nothing you've ever seen. Actually, being a part of it would be like nothing you've ever experienced, either. It would feel like all the power systems in your home were communicating with all the information systems in your home and that they had all merged into one big seamless platform for using, storing, generating, and even buying and selling clean electrons. It would feel like the information technology revolution and the energy technology revolution, IT and ET, had merged into a single system. It would feel like you were living with an "Energy Internet."

I realize this may sound like science fiction or magic. But it's not. Many of the technologies that would make up an Energy Internet—a term used by *The Economist* to refer to the "smart grid"—already exist or are being perfected right now in garages and laboratories. What we need most now are the integrated government policies—laws and standards, taxes and credits, incentives and mandates, minimums and maximums—to guide and stimulate the marketplace to drive that innovation further, to commercialize these new ideas faster, and to bring this revolution to life sooner.

This chapter is the first of four that will describe what the key elements of a Clean Energy System might look like when implemented in the real world and how we might bring that about. This chapter will describe how an Energy Internet would enable you, me, and your next-door neighbor to do extraordinary things by way of saving energy and using clean power efficiently, and do them around the clock, all the time, whether or not you're thinking about it. The next two chapters will describe the integrated government policies we need to guide and stimulate our businesses and investors to commit the capital we'll need to erect such an Energy Internet and to invent the abundant, clean, reliable, and cheap electrons we would need to feed it. Those will be followed by a chapter on preservation: how we can also create the policies for the preservation of the natural world—the plants, animals, fish, oceans, rivers, and forests that sustain life.

While many of the pieces required to make this system a reality already exist in some form, it will not be easy to implement—no revolution is. But this definitely is not science fiction. So keep an open eye and an open mind, and remember what the late, great science fiction writer Arthur C. Clarke famously observed: "Any sufficiently advanced technology is indistinguishable from magic."

Before we lift the curtain on this magic show, I first need to do something really mundane. I need to explain how our current electricity system in America, primarily based on a network of publicly regulated utilities, actually works. Probably the last time you stopped and thought about utilities was when you landed on one in Monopoly and had to decide whether to shell out $150 to buy the Electric Company. That was certainly the case for me before I started researching this book. I knew how my car worked and where the closest gasoline station was. I knew where my local water tower and pumping stations were. But I knew absolutely nothing about this thing called an electric utility, which provided the electrons that powered my life every day. I knew we got an electric bill once a month and paid it, but that's about it. Well, our power utilities are more interesting than you think—and they are also more critical to getting the Code Green revolution right than people realize.

You may think you can skip this part. Don't. Love them or hate them, local and regional regulated electric utilities are going to remain at the heart of our nation's energy system for a long time. If we are going to build a clean energy platform, it will be largely through the actions implemented by and through America's electric utilities. They have the customer base, the ability to raise huge volumes of cheap capital, and the installed technology infrastructure that we need to drive the development of an Energy Internet. And the public trusts utilities. It is no accident that when people want to commit fraud, one of their favorite strategies is to knock on someone's door dressed as a service person from the local power company. Hey, come right in!

So how has this utility system worked up to now? The electric-utility-centric power system that exists today in the United States, and most other countries, was constructed according to one overarching principle: the obligation to serve load. This came about as the result of an arrangement in which local and state governments, and the regulatory boards they spawned, granted monopolies to power companies ("utilities") to provide electricity or natural gas to customers in a certain region. In return, those utilities were obligated to do three things: to provide *reasonably priced power*, provide *reliable power* (electricity that could be counted on 24/7/365), and provide *ubiquitous power* (power that would be available to every customer who wanted electricity in that utility's region of operation).

This was a system that Samuel Insull, the commercial protégé of Thomas Edison, crafted and sold to government agencies over one hundred years ago. It provided tangible benefits to utilities—which could raise funds cheaply and efficiently to make the big power plant and transmission investments, because they were guaranteed a customer base—and to customers, who for decades got cheap, reliable, and ubiquitous power. Most publicly regulated utilities lived up to this bargain very well, powering America's growth throughout the twentieth century.

(The utility regulators who set the rates are typically called public utilities commissions. The commissioners are usually appointed by the state governor or legislature, while regulation of interstate electronic commerce is handled from Washington by the Federal Energy Regulatory Commission.)

But there were downsides to this largely state-by-state system. To begin with, it is often said that the American electricity grid that evolved over the years, with all its power stations and transmission lines, is the biggest machine man has ever made. It may or may not be. But one thing I can tell you for sure about this grid—it is the dumbest big machine man ever made, and it isn't just dumb in one way.

I know I am being a bit unfair here. In terms of raw scope, the electrification of America's homes, towns, and factories, wherever they were, was truly one of the great engineering feats of the twentieth century. Our economy would not be where it is today without that achievement. But while this grid was indeed ubiquitous and reliable and provided cheap power, it was not built with any intelligent design. It just emerged, utility by utility, service territory by service territory, balance sheet by balance sheet, local market rules by local market rules. America, to this day, has no true national grid. It's actually a national patchwork that makes the Balkans look unified.

Today there are almost 3,200 electric utility companies in America, some of which have service territories spanning huge swaths of multiple states, while others serve just a single township or part of a county. Eventually these electric companies and their power lines coalesced into three regional grids in America: the Eastern Interconnection, which includes the eastern U.S. seaboard, the Plains states, and the eastern Canadian provinces; the Western Interconnection, which continues all the way to the Pacific, except in Texas, which has its own grid—ERCOT, the Electric Reliability Council of Texas. That's it. That's our electricity system.

There is surprisingly limited integration among these regional grids and even among the individual utilities within each region. Imagine trying to drive across America, from New York to Los Angeles, without our interstate highway system—taking just state and local highways—and using only county maps to figure out where you were going. That's what it would be like to try to send electrons from New York to Los Angeles. The fact is, you wouldn't really want to send electrons across the country, because too much electricity would be lost in transmission. But this patchwork is still a problem. It is very difficult just to move electrons around within regions. Imagine trying to drive even from Phoenix to Los Angeles only on local roads, and you have an idea of what it is like to try to move electrons generated at wind farms in northern Arizona to markets in southern California.

The system is also dumb in terms of pricing. Our utilities deliver electric power very reliably, but the electrons they sell are totally undifferentiated electrons. That is, in most cases you pay the same amount for electricity that comes into your home no matter how it is generated—coal, oil, nuclear, hydro, wind, solar, or natural gas—and no matter what time of day it is generated, whether at peak or off-peak demand periods. You cannot differentiate. You pay one price per kilowatt-hour and get one bill, whenever the electric company gets around to reading the meter on the back wall of your house. There's nothing in the electric power industry today that even remotely compares to the detail of a telephone bill.

Finally, the utility system is dumb in that, in most cases, there is no two-way communication between you and your utility. You as a consumer cannot demand, and the utility cannot provide, a specific kind of electricity generation for a specific price to a specific machine. And when the power to your house goes out, in most of the United States, you have to telephone the electric company and let them know. The utility has no other way of knowing.

But God bless the grid; while it is really dumb, the electricity it has provided was, for many years, cheap, and always ubiquitous and reliable—so reliable that most Americans have never even asked themselves where it came from, how it is made, or how it winds up being immediately available to flow out of the wall sockets on demand. We just expect it to be there, and when it isn't, even for fifteen minutes, there is hell to pay.

The state-appointed regulatory boards tell each utility operator how much it can charge for every kilowatt-hour of electricity. The regulator basically instructs the utility: "You will generate cheap, reliable, ubiquitous power, we will give you a monopoly to do so, and every few years we will determine the rate at which you can serve load in your area to ensure that your expenses are recovered and that you get a proper return on capital to run the business—provided you do your job right."

Specifically, the regulator and the utility operator work out a plan—sometimes called an integrated resource plan, other times just a plain-vanilla capital budget. In this plan, the utility operator tells the regulator, "Here is how I intend to serve my customers and meet my obligations to provide ubiquitous power as cheaply and reliably as I can—with this many power plants and power lines, costing this much money." And once that is approved, the operator says to the regulator, "I will need to recover this much money to cover all these costs."

And so the regulator takes the utility's statement of its monetary needs (called a revenue requirement), chops it down a bunch—because the initial request is usually bloated—and then divides it by the kilowatt-hours the utility is expected to sell. That becomes the price per kilowatt-hour, which the utility then charges the consumer for electricity. That price is calculated to cover the utility's fixed cost of operating its existing power plants and the cost of investing in new plants, as well as the variable costs of the fuel that goes into generating the electricity—that is, the coal, oil, natural gas, or uranium—plus the costs of labor, taxes, and insurance, and then a cherry on top: some after-tax profit for shareholders.

To put it at its most simple: Utilities made their money by building stuff—*more power plants and more power lines that enabled them to sell more and more electrons to more and more customers*—because they were rewarded by their regulators with increased rates on the basis of those capital expenditures. The more capital they deployed, the more they made. And since their new capital investments had to be justified by growth in demand, the utilities were motivated to encourage consumption, which in turn created the need for them to invest and build more, which in turn triggered the reward of increased income. The cycle became almost Pavlovian.

"Think about a utility," said Ralph Cavanagh, the legendary utilities expert at the Natural Resources Defense Council, which has spurred innovation around utilities in California. "Their business involves enormous sunk costs that must be recovered regardless of how much energy they sell. If they invest in a new natural gas power plant or a wind farm, it can cost hundreds of millions of dollars, even billions. And those costs do not vary if you, the customer, use more or less power. So the utility had a vital interest in boosting electricity and natural gas sales so it could be sure to recover its fixed costs."

In many ways, your local utility was "like a big all-you-can-eat-for-five-dollars energy buffet," explained Peter Corsell, the CEO of GridPoint, which makes an apparatus that can manage all the power systems in your home. "The old system was developed during a time when information was scarce, fuel was cheap, and pollution was free," he said. The utilities "were paid by the regulators to provide us reliable, cheap, all-you-can-eat power." And we came to that all-you-can-eat buffet every day, and we ate whatever we wanted. And it was always open. And it was always cheap. Life was good.

One reason it was cheap, though, was that the public and the regulators never asked the utilities to serve two additional things at this energy buffet. We didn't ask that the power they generated be free of CO_2 emissions. (We asked that traditional pollutants, particularly mercury, nitrogen oxides, and sulfur oxides emitted during the coal combustion process, be removed, which the utilities did very well, but not carbon dioxide.) And we didn't encourage them to offer energy efficiency or conservation programs—didn't encourage our utilities to reward consumers for saving energy or to enable consumers to respond to changes in supply or prices, so they could buy more electricity when it was cheaper to generate and use less when it was more expensive to generate.

The emphasis on cheap trumped efficiency and global warming considerations. It made sure that utilities relied as much as possible on coal-fired plants. And for many years, if utilities could deliver electricity at a nickel a kilowatt-hour, few people cared if those coal plants spewed out millions of tons of CO_2, and few people cared if you used those kilowatt-hours very inefficiently or in wasteful applications. In fairness, the regulators pressured the utilities to keep prices down and focus where possible on cheap sources like coal.

The mandates for "ubiquitous" and "reliable" also worked against efficiency. Why? Because they required utilities to overbuild their supply capacity so they always had an adequate "reserve margin"—at great cost, which was passed on to you—so they could always meet peak load demand on the very hottest days, which might occur only once or twice a summer. Adding supply was always the answer to every problem, never trying to manage demand.

But then one day a funny thing happened on the way to the all-you-could-eat electron buffet. A few people—like Al Gore—started to wander around out back into the kitchen, and what they saw there was not pretty. And then they came back to the front of the buffet line and told the rest of us: "Do you know what is going on out back? Do you know why this all-you-can-eat electron buffet costs only $5? It's because there are all sorts of costs being incurred that are not being passed on to us customers. They are being paid by someone else."

These costs were being paid by society at large or charged to our children's credit cards. In particular, the coal, natural gas, and oil that were generating all those cheap electrons for our all-you-can-eat buffets were causing global warming, childhood asthma, acid rain, deforestation, biodiversity loss, and petrodictatorship—and no one was factoring these costs into the price per kilowatt-hour you were paying. And since when something is free, or practically free, people usually demand more of it, more cheap electrons were demanded, and more destruction was occurring out back.

The people running these buffets are your neighbors and mine.

They're not out to harm society. They're part of it. But the Dirty Fuels System was set up to reliably deliver all-you-can-eat electrons at the cheapest price to every customer who wanted them (and low-cost gasoline to every driver who wanted it) even if that meant devastating our ecosystems and climate as side effects. We just didn't make all the connections until recently—and many people still haven't.

Now the public consensus is shifting. Now we are beginning to understand that we need a new system—a *Clean Energy System*. "Now," said Corsell, "we live in a world in which information is abundant and fuel is expensive and volatile, and we know that pollution is not free—it imposes huge societal costs." Yes, we still want energy to be cheap, reliable, and ubiquitous, but now we also want it to come as much as possible from non-CO_2-emitting sources and via a system that promotes energy efficiency and conservation, not just consumption and pollution. To be more specific, roughly 40 percent of America's total CO_2 emissions come from the production of electricity used in homes, offices, and factories. Another 30 percent of American emissions come from the transportation sector—primarily cars, trucks, boats, trains, and airplanes. So if we could electrify all of our transportation fleet, save for airplanes, and make all of them, and our buildings too, vastly more energy efficient at the same time—and then supply this whole 70 percent, buildings and transportation, with clean, abundant, cheap, reliable electrons through a smarter grid—that would be a revolution. It would be a giant step toward reducing America's consumption of fossil fuels and our carbon footprint.

That's the real green revolution we are seeking. But it is still too abstract for most people. So let's hop into a time machine and see what it would actually be like to live inside a real green revolution in the year 20 E.C.E.—Energy-Climate Era.

20 E.C.E.

Your alarm goes off at 6:37 a.m., playing the Beatles classic "Here Comes the Sun" just as you programmed it to the night before from 10,000 wake-up songs offered by your utility in collaboration with your phone company and iTunes. You have no alarm clock. The music was actually playing out of your home phone speaker, which itself is integrated into your home Smart Black Box—or SBB, as it is called. Everyone now has an SBB—your own personal energy dashboard. Just as when you sign up for cable television you get a set-top box or digital recorder with it, now, when you sign up for the Energy Internet with a progressive utility, you get an SBB.

It is a microwave-oven-size black box that sits in your basement and integrates the controls and assures the interoperability of all your energy, communications, and entertainment devices and services. That includes your temperature settings and other energy preferences in every room, your lighting, your home alarm system, your telephones and computers and Internet connections, all your appliances, all your entertainment devices, and your plug-in hybrid electric car and its storage battery. The SBB's digital touch screen can tell you exactly how much energy any of these devices is consuming at any moment.

Your car, by the way, is no longer called a "car." It is now called a RESU, or rolling energy storage unit, as in "I drive a Ford Mustang RESU." The term "car" is now considered so, gosh, twentieth century.

That is not the only thing considered old school. In the early years of the Energy-Climate Era, we progressed from an Internet that connected computers and a World Wide Web that connected content and Web sites to an Internet of Things: an Energy Internet in which every device—from light switches to air conditioners, to basement boilers, to car batteries and power lines and power stations—incorporated microchips that could inform your utility, either directly or through an SBB, of the energy level at which it was operating, take instructions from you or your utility as to when it should operate and at what level of power, and tell your utility when it wanted to purchase or sell electricity. You and your utility now have two-way communications. Suddenly you have a dashboard that allows you to see and control all your energy usage—and that allows you to respond as never before to changes in prices and environmental conditions.

Your heating and air-conditioning units, your lighting, and all your appliances—your dishwasher, dryer, refrigerator, and car battery—can now be programmed to run at lower levels when demand for electricity on the grid is highest and electrons are most expensive, and they can be instructed to run at fuller power during the night—or, in the case of your electric car, to charge and store energy at night, when electricity demand is lowest and power is cheapest.

Have no fear: Signing up for this kind of system is totally voluntary. There is no Big Brother who will force you to do so. If you don't want to have an SBB in your house, you don't have to have one. You can still get your electricity the old-fashioned dumb way. But have no illusions: If you opt out, you will be thrown into a general customer pool and your rates will go up, because the utility will not be able to optimize the energy usage to or from or inside your home—and other customers will not be willing to pay higher rates to subsidize your wasteful and environmentally irresponsible behavior.

After you read the newspaper and have your morning coffee, you call up the control panel of your SBB on your iPhone or your BlackBerry or your home computer. This colorful, easy-to-read screen will tell you how much power every device in your home is using and how much each kilowatt-hour costs at that time of day on your personal energy plan.

That's right: your own personal energy plan. Your utility now offers a number of different plans, the way the phone company does, so you can program your home's energy use—for lowest cost, cleanest energy, maximum efficiency, or time of day you are at home or work, among many other choices.

The most popular option is the "Bargain Power—Nights and Weekends" plan. This plan helps your utility to both balance and reduce overall energy demand by shifting electricity loads from peak hours of the day and evening when electrons are most expensive to off-peak hours at night when they are cheapest. Through your SBB, your utility adjusts your home thermostat up or down, very slightly, and instructs your water heater, refrigerator, and air conditioner to cycle off for short periods of time—so short that you don't even notice. It also allows the utility to run your dishwasher and dryer overnight, and even to turn off all your exterior lights for a few minutes at a time.

In return for letting the utility manage your energy use in this way, you get a 15 percent reduction in your monthly electric bill. It is a great deal for the utility, because it can now use its existing power plants with greater efficiency—as the load peaks are being flattened and the load valleys are being raised—so it doesn't have to build new ones just for peak hours.

Another popular plan is the one called "Day-Trading for Electrons." Under this plan, your appliances can, in effect, become your surrogate energy shoppers. You program into your SBB that you want certain of your appliances (your dryer, your dishwasher, your hot water heater, your air conditioner) to run only when electrons cost less than 5 cents a kilowatt-hour and that you want your home cooling or heating system (depending on the season) to cycle down if electricity exceeds 10 cents a kilowatt-hour.

(You will put on a sweater or open a window instead.) So you loaded the dishwasher before you went to bed, but it did not actually run until 3:36 a.m., when your SBB detected that the price of electrons had fallen to 4.9 cents a kilowatt-hour. And your air conditioner cooled the house all day, until about 6:00 p.m., when rates shot up to 12 cents a kilowatt-hour—then it automatically shut itself off. It came back on at 9 p.m., when the price of electrons fell to 9.9 cents a kilowatt-hour.

This is a far cry from Grandpa's day—pre-1 E.C.E.—when most utilities charged a flat rate per kilowatt-hour, regardless of actual demand and cost fluctuations. In this new era, all you do is choose the "Day-Trading" energy plan and your dishwasher and air conditioner, with their smart chips inside and working with your SBB, are day-trading electrons on your behalf, bidding into a real-time energy market every five minutes, to get the best price automatically.

Most consumers don't realize it, but the electricity market is an instantaneous, constantly shifting spot market, in which electricity costs bounce up and down as much as tenfold in the course of a day. Your very simple monthly bill with just one rate per kilowatt-hour masks this wild, gyrating electricity market going on every minute of every day, with prices changing depending on demand on your regional grid and available supplies from different coal or gas power plants, hydroelectric dams, wind farms, or nuclear facilities.

For instance, when demand on your regional grid outstrips the available supply of the cheapest electrons—those generated from coal—your utility has to call on its natural gas generators, which means that the cost of electrons to the utility immediately jumps to the cost of natural gas. When demand goes down, just the opposite happens, and the price might drop to the cost of cheap nuclear or hydro power. All of this was hidden in the Dirty Fuels System. But not anymore—not after you installed your SBB and smart appliances, and the utility installed much more intelligent technology on its grid, so your home could read the actual electricity costs from the utility and run discretionary appliances only when electricity hit your price points. Not only are you now using power when it is most cost-effective, but thanks to steadily rising efficiency standards, you are also using less power, period. Your appliances today use about one-third the electricity they needed to do the same tasks a decade ago.

With the smart grid, controlling your energy usage is as simple as turning the lights on and off. Under both these plans, you just press the "sleep" button on the SBB control panel when you walk out the door and all the *lights and every appliance in the house will shut down or go to its lowest necessary power setting until instructed otherwise. You can call up your SBB control panel on your cell phone and tell your house to "wake up" the minute you land at the airport after a long trip, so by the time you get home the hot water is available in the shower and the air conditioner has cooled down the house.*

Electricity is all about on/off, and the purpose of the smart grid is to make sure that whenever electricity is on, it is at its most productive. Why should all your appliances be on, sucking up what is called "vampire load," when you are not home? It is because your appliances are too dumb to know better. By turning appliances on and off at the right times, the smart grid can virtually eliminate the vampire loads that can consume up to 10 percent of all the power in a household. (Of course, when you do need to run your dryer or dishwasher at a particular time, you can just override the automatic controls, and the system will power the appliance using the cheapest power available at that moment.)

Your neighbor, who is a green fanatic, signed up for the "Fuels from Heaven/Fuels from Hell" plan. Under this plan, you pay a premium every month and the utility agrees to cover every kilowatt-hour you use with clean power from wind, solar, geothermal, or hydro—so that you are using no fuels from hell. This doesn't mean that your power is coming from clean sources for every second of every day. It means that every month the utility has procured an amount of clean power—tied to specific and actual generation sources—equivalent to the demand of all those customers on the "Fuels from Heaven/Fuels from Hell" plan. You can feel better about your electricity usage because you are driving the utility to constantly access more clean power sources and thereby make them more cost-competitive.

You and your neighbors also got together and signed up for the "How Slow Can My Meter Go" plan. It works like this: Where the four corners of your backyards meet, you installed four tracking solar arrays. Again, you leased them from your utility. The solar power feeds directly into each of your four homes and actually slows down your electric meters—reduces the amount of power you need to take from the grid—by providing you with your own distributed power. Known as RGSUs—regional generation and storage units—the panels are maintained by your utility. Just the other day, the Duke Energy truck was out replacing two of your solar panels damaged in a hailstorm. No one had to call the company. Each panel is connected by the smart grid to Duke's supercomputer, so it could send a message immediately when a panel went down. What a contrast from the stories Grandpa used to tell about the days when a bad storm would sweep through the neighborhood and his house would lose power, but the electric company wouldn't even know until he telephoned them! What a pain that must have been, Grandpa!

The utility was happy to install the solar panels, both because it is a way to earn income through new services and because you live in a densely populated area where the grid can often get stressed at peak times—so having some customers use distributed power takes some pressure off the grid. As long as you can seamlessly and safely generate your own wind or solar power to help run your lights or heat your water, the more customers who do it, the better.

Some of your relatives who live in Los Angeles have gotten even more adventurous. They got together with their utility and created their own plan: the "Green Friends and Family" plan. They leased three parking spaces behind the elementary school down the street. Then they leased from Southern California Edison a Bloom Energy reversible fuel cell machine and connected it to their homes. It is a big black box about the size of a passenger van, and it saves money, energy, and the environment in lots of ways. It can take electrical energy from the grid late at night, when power is cheapest, and, via a process of electrolysis, convert water into hydrogen and store it in a storage tank, and then convert it back to electricity for you and your neighbors to power homes or charge cars during peak hours, when electricity is twice as expensive. It can take hydrogen or solar power and convert it into electricity—and the only "waste" is clean water. You can even feed it agricultural waste, and it will use a little built-in furnace to convert that waste into hydrogen and then electricity. Classes at the elementary school—which shares the electricity with the neighbors— compete over who can feed the Bloom Energy box the most biomass and generate the most electrons.

Your utility is happy to be offering these services, because it's now making money from each one—rather than just selling cheap, dumb electrons at an all-you-can-eat buffet. The regulators are happy to see this, because they believe these services benefit customers, help the environment, and relieve stress on the grid, so that more costly power plants are not necessary.

What you don't see, but what is hugely important, is that this Energy Internet–smart grid enables your utility to use more renewable power. As noted earlier, in the old days utilities always built their generation systems *to ensure that they could handle all the air conditioners running on the four hottest days of the summer, when energy demand peaked. They did this, in part, by predicting demand and scheduling the supply a day or an hour ahead of time. They got very, very good at that. But just in case they miscalculated, or ran into an unexpectedly long and intense heat wave, they also overprovisioned their grids so that, ideally, no one would be denied electricity on the hottest days. They did that by building extra power plants. It sounds smart—but it was anything but efficient. Imagine that you owned a factory that made greeting cards. If you acted like the utilities did, you would build one $10 million factory that would run at capacity every day to handle your standard business. And then you would build another $10 million factory just to handle your excess business on the week before Christmas and the three days before Mother's Day, Father's Day, and Valentine's Day. The rest of the year, this second factory would produce nothing, but all the machines would be on standby low power, just in case there was a sudden run on birthday cards. That is a really inefficient way to use capital, but that's how we managed our utility grid for a long time.*

Now that the smart grid is in place, though, we can control demand. Because either the utility or the customer is able to optimize when power is used, so many more people automatically run things later at night when rates are cheapest and fewer things in the daytime when they are more expensive. The Energy Internet has become so smart about when you want to use power or when it would have to sell you power or when it could buy power off your car battery or home solar system that the load has become much more constant 365 days of the year. The "flatter" that any utility grid can make its load profile throughout the day for all its customers—so that its peaks are not very high or are eliminated altogether—the fewer backup power plants it needs to build or operate. It is, in effect, substituting energy efficiency for new power generation.

That is what the Energy Internet has made possible. But it didn't only increase energy efficiency. It has also made large-scale renewable energy practical for the first time ever. Why? Because the flatter your utility's load profile gets, the more it is able to go out and buy or generate renewable energy and sell it to you and your neighbors instead of energy powered by coal or gas. In 20 E.C.E., Southern California Edison now derives more than half of its power from two vast renewable energy sources—wind and solar—while using a mix of nuclear, natural gas, and carbon-sequestered coal for the rest. SoCalEd has built huge wind farms in Wyoming and Montana, and contracted with many smaller independents along the way. The Wyoming farm is so vast it is a tourist site, like the Hoover Dam, with turbines as far as the eye can see.

The smart grid made all this large-scale renewable energy practical. In the old days, the big drawback of wind and solar was that they were variable. The sun was there during the day, but not at night. The wind in most parts of the country tends to blow hardest at night and early in the morning—in other words, during off-peak hours. The energy produced by these clean renewable resources could not be cost-effectively stored using existing battery technologies. The most viable storage mechanism used by the power industry was pumped storage—using energy to pump water up a hill during the night and generating electricity via falling water during the day. The problem was that there were relatively few pumped hydro projects in this country, they were very expensive to construct, and you expended three units of energy moving water up the hill at night for every unit you got back the next day. Those facts made it very hard for any utility to depend on wind or solar for more than 20 percent of its power supply, because it had to be backed up with extra natural gas power plants for those days when the sun didn't shine or the wind didn't blow.

But now that we've moved to the Energy Internet—the smart grid— utilities can run your refrigerator or adjust your thermostat in line with when the wind is blowing or the sun is shining. It can match the supply with the demand. Therefore, it can use more of these renewable power sources at much lower cost. When clouds block out the sun or the wind dies down, the utility's smart grid lowers demand by raising prices (so your SBB decides not to do the laundry then) or by adjusting your home temperature settings. And when the sun is shining brightly and the wind is howling, the utility runs your dryer at the lowest price. So there is now a direct correlation between how smart your grid is, how much energy efficiency it can generate, and how much renewable power it can use.

*L*ike all revolutions, though, this one changed many things at once. When the smart grid extended into a smart home all the way to a smart car, it created a whole new energy market on the other side of your electric meter. In the old days, there was no market beyond the raw dumb electrons that came into your house. Everything stopped at the meter, and *you just paid the price calculated at the end of the month. But once your appliances became smart, and a Smart Black Box was introduced into your house, a market was also created beyond your meter and throughout your home, and, more broadly, inside every factory and business around the country.*

Some utilities have decided to step into that market and help you optimize your smart home to get the most cooling, heating, and other electricity services from the cleanest, fewest, cheapest electrons. Most utilities, though, have decided to serve as facilitators for this whole new industry—energy efficiency service companies, EESCs. These EESCs have emerged—just like Internet providers that crept up alongside the traditional phone companies—to help you optimize the smart grid for your home. The utility has created this market by telling you, the customer, that it will give you big discounts, even subsidies, for installing energy-efficient appliances or weatherizing your home to lower your consumption of electrons. This is because the government regulator has cut a new deal with the utility, whereby the utility is now being paid for how much energy it can help its customers save—rather than consume! (I will explain this in detail in chapter 14.) The EESCs then come in and help you do that job.

Just the other day, a salesman from General Electric's energy efficiency service company came to your door. Your home is twenty years old. The General Electric EESC man offered this deal: First, for free, they would give your whole house an efficiency checkup. They would bring in equipment to pressurize your entire home and show you where all the heat and air-conditioning was leaking from ducts that had not been connected properly and therefore were just warming or cooling the crawl spaces—much to the enjoyment of the mice. Then they would borrow the money to pay for sealing all the leaks in the ducts and fissures in your roof that had been silently draining energy from your house and raising your monthly bills by 30 percent. They would also install more energy efficient appliances. You don't need to put down any money up front. The EESC would share with you the money you saved on your monthly electric and gas bills and the money the EESC would earn from selling the carbon credits on the global market for reducing your carbon footprint. The General Electric EESC takes 75 percent of the savings, using 50 percent to pay off the loan, and keeps 25 percent as profit. And you get the other 25 percent savings. Your home is now more energy efficient and has a higher resale value. Meanwhile, the Sears EESC just dropped off a pamphlet offering you the same deal with a 60–40 split! Because the cash flow from all these efficiency deals is very predictable, the EESCs can sell them to investment banks, which turn them into green savings bonds.

A fter you showered and ate breakfast, you decided to head for the office for your first meeting. This involved taking a short walk—about twenty paces—down the hall to your home office, holding your Smart Card in your hand. Your Smart Card, which is sponsored by Visa and United Airlines Mileage Plus, looks just like a credit card, only slightly thicker. You start your workday by putting it into the docking bay of the Sun Ray terminal, made by Sun Microsystems, on your home office desk. That Sun Ray terminal uses only four watts, compared to fifty watts or more in your standard PC. The reason is that there is no hard drive sucking up energy. The Sun Ray terminal is just a screen with a slot beneath it, but as soon as you put the Smart Card into the slot, it connects you to the "network cloud," where all your software programs, e-mail, Internet applications, and personal files are located. The "cloud" is a data center, packed with servers, that is located close to a dam on the Columbia River, which is providing it with clean hydropower to run all your programs (and those of millions of other people) and to cool all those servers.

The smart lights in your office, triggered by motion sensors, went on as soon as you walked into the room, as did the air conditioner. No electricity is consumed in the room when you are not there. Every device, every new home, and every new building is now built with steadily rising efficiency standards from day one. In the 2007 energy bill, President George W. Bush effectively outlawed the Edison incandescent lightbulb, phasing it out by 2014, because it converts 90 percent of its energy into wasted heat—which we all noticed when we burned our fingers trying to remove a bulb before it cooled down. It has been replaced by a smart compact fluorescent. With one-fourth the electricity consumption, it not only reduces the energy required to produce light, but also reduces the energy required to cool your office, which was being warmed by the excess heat emanating from all your incandescent bulbs.

On your desk, next to the Sun Ray terminal, you have a six-watt desk lamp. That's right, only six watts—because this lamp uses a light-emitting diode and little mirrors to give you intense focused light, the equivalent of 100 watts, but at 6 percent of the energy use. The same is true for the appliances throughout your house. Your refrigerator is so efficient that it represents the electricity equivalent of a twenty-watt lightbulb. Your television, TiVo unit, and treadmill all shut down completely, no longer draining power when not in use.

Normally, your company encourages you to work from home as much as possible. But today, on the Sun Ray terminal, you found a message from your boss saying that a teleconference would be held downtown at 10:30 a.m., between your management team and your colleagues in Chennai, India, where your company is involved in a huge real estate development. At 9:45 a.m. you get in your Ford Mustang RESU. It is a plug-in hybrid electric that gets the equivalent of 100 miles per gallon. Plug-in hybrid electric vehicles are like regular hybrids but with larger batteries and the ability to recharge from a wall outlet. As a result, all your local travel is electric, but you always have a gas tank backup. The battery is charged every night, or whenever it needs juice, and, like your dryer and other appliances, automatically interacts with your electric utility to buy the lowest-cost electrons available during the depths of nighttime off-peak hours.

As you set out to the office, the GPS map in the car flashed a message that there was an accident on the highway that you normally use to get to the office and proposed an alternative route.

To enter into the downtown area, you had to pass through an electronic gateway, which automatically charged you $12 for entering the city between 10:00 a.m. and 2:00 p.m. (It costs $18 at rush hour.) This is another reason you work from home as often as you can, carpool, or take the bus to work. It's all part of the new congestion-pricing system that has dramatically reduced the number of cars coming into the city and thereby created more room for electric buses and other forms of mass transit, which can now take more people to more places faster than ever before. Your city's new mayor actually won the election with the motto "Price the road and clear the traffic." You don't need to be a rocket scientist, said the mayor: "If you want fewer CO_2 emitters, charge people money for emitting CO_2. If you want fewer cars on the roads during certain hours, charge people money for using them." It works everywhere it has been tried.

When you arrived at the office, you docked your car at a parking ramp where you can both charge your car battery and sell electricity into the grid. There is a universal two-way plug in every home and parking lot in America now. You decided to park at this ramp after it won a bidding contest against the parking ramp around the corner. These bidding con-

tests between parking ramp owners are now very common. Your ramp won by throwing in four free-parking days a month and a car wash every Friday.

Why does the ramp owner want you to park there so badly? Because you will be sharing with him the money you earn from selling extra electrons back to the grid. The entire roof of the parking ramp consists of solar panels that create clean electrons, which are then sold to the batteries of all the cars on the ramp. The owner calls it "e-gasoline." The parking lot's name is Bill's Artificial Oil Field. So the lot owner is both in the parking and the energy-generating business. At 2:32 p.m., when the temperature hit 87 degrees, your car, which still had most of its electrons from last night's charge, made a calculation that energy prices had moved up on the smart grid to a point where it was time to sell some electrons. Your smart car calculated how many electrons you would need to drive to your normal Wednesday after-work chores—to take the kids to soccer practice and stop at the grocery store—and saved 10 percent more just in case you altered your routine. Then it put a sell bid of 40 cents a kilowatt-hour out to the utility. SoCalEd bought 5 kilowatt-hours off your car battery through the universal plug. This helped the utility meet its peak load demand and keep its load profile flat, while you and the garage owner both made money. In this case, you made $2. The parking lot operator, who provided the solar panels and the plug connecting your car to the grid, also got a small cut of that. So far this month your car battery has earned you $24 selling and buffering electricity. At the same time, it cost you only $47 this month to charge your car with electricity, because you were usually charging at home at night at low off-peak rates and selling it during the day at peak rates. It means you are driving for the equivalent of about $1.50 per gallon. People still drive less and use more mass transit—because congestion pricing, which funds better mass transit, induces them to do so, rather than high oil prices that fund petrodictators.

While at the office, your boss gathered together the entire management team responsible for designing smart housing for a new suburb in Chennai. You met with your six Indian counterparts in Chennai for three hours to go over everything from financing to architectural problems. Once, such business would have had to be conducted face-to-face, with at least some of you flying over to Chennai, expending considerable time, money, and energy. Not anymore.

This three-hour meeting was held virtually through Cisco Systems'

TelePresence system, over the Cisco network, in which your team sat in a studio and the other team was vividly illustrated on a wall-size TV screen in 3-D. The Cisco TelePresence makes people look and sound just like they do in person, offering life-size images of each meeting participant, high-definition video, and spatial audio, which creates the dynamic of voices coming directly from the participants. It is so realistic you all felt as if you were at the same table in the same room, even though you were half a world apart. In fact, it was all so realistic, and the images so life-size, that when the meeting ended you got up and tried to shake hands with someone on the screen, eliciting laughter all around.

After the meeting, you returned home and docked your car back in the garage, around 4:00 p.m. As you were mowing the lawn with your all-electric mower, your kids came home on their hybrid electric school bus, just another big rolling energy storage unit that actually makes money for the school district by storing and selling clean electrons the way you do.

The neighborhood school is a dual-use education and commercial center—a DUECC. That is, the school kitchen, as soon as it is finished serving lunch, is taken over by Einstein Bros. Bagels. Instead of building their own new bakery, the bagel company uses the school's kitchens from 3:00 p.m. until 6:00 a.m. the next morning to bake bagels and deliver them to their outlets and grocery stores throughout the city. Dual-using has become a huge trend, saving enormous amounts of electricity, land, and new construction, and, by the way, earning the school extra cash to hire more teachers. Domino's Pizza also uses idle school kitchens during after-lunch hours for making and delivering pizzas throughout the city. Domino's has not leased or built a new commercial kitchen in years.

The school is also a net-zero building. It was designed and built so that all the parts—walls, windows, the lighting system, the water-handling system, the air-handling system—are both individually and collectively super-energy-efficient. At the same time, the external roof and walls of the school building are a mini-utility—a combination of solar panels, solar thermal generation, and smart windows. The school has a green roof, full of plants that the kids use for science experiments. The combination of that green roof and porous pavements in the playground and driveways ensures that there is no runoff from the school property—all rainwater is captured in a cistern and used for toilets and watering plants. The orientation of the building and its design optimize use of the sun, so you have no direct sunlight in the building in summer and a lot in the winter. The windows are made from dynamic electrochromic glass, which allows you to dial up and dial down the amount of light. In summer, the windows let in light but keep out solar heat, so less air-conditioning is required, and in winter they let in light and also solar heat so less heating is required. As a result of all these systems, during working hours, the school is a net energy producer, and it sells its excess electrons into the grid. At night, when Einstein is baking the next day's bagels in the kitchen, the school buys whatever electricity it needs from the grid at low, off-peak rates. At the end of each month, its utility bill reads "net zero." You cannot get a building permit in your city any longer unless your building is energy "net zero." Parents from all over the county are trying to get their kids into this school, which they believe is healthier for students and teachers, a living science experiment, and just, generally speaking, "cool."

Why are net-zero and dual-use buildings such a big deal? Well, here's a fun fact: The production of cement worldwide—the heat that has to be generated to roast the limestone and the CO_2 that is emitted in the process—releases almost as much CO_2 into the atmosphere as all the passenger cars in the world. So just throwing up dumb cement buildings is a huge energy drain and carbon dioxide generator. Once we realized how much of both we could save from smarter cars and smarter buildings, building standards became as important as mileage standards.

As the saying goes, "What gets measured gets managed." And when you put it all together, what the Energy Internet did was give people and their utilities the ability to measure and therefore to know and therefore to manage and therefore to reduce energy usage more than ever.

I am sure that what I have described above sounds far-fetched—like something out of a *Jetsons* cartoon or a science fiction novel. Well, it's not fetched from very far. A simple prototype of this Energy Internet was deployed in 2007 in Washington State's Olympic Peninsula, in an experiment organized by the Department of Energy's Pacific Northwest National Laboratory, in partnership with the Bonneville Power Administration and local utilities. On November 26, 2007, MSNBC ran a story about the preliminary results, headlined "Smart Appliances Learning to Save Power Grid." The story noted that "as part of the experiment, the researchers found that they could cut the peak electricity load among participating homes by half for three days in a row." It quoted Rob Pratt, the lab's program manager for a multiagency collaboration dubbed Grid-Wise, as saying:

> "That was astounding." . . . One homeowner, Jerry Brous of Se-quim, Wash., who signed up for the program as soon as he heard about it on a local radio station, said that his electricity load dropped by 15 percent, and he compiled his own Excel spread-sheet to determine the percentage of power flowing to his water heater, heat pump and dryer to pinpoint how he might save even more. He also received quarterly checks from the program reflect-ing his savings, including a recent one for $37. During several camping trips, Brous could tell his house to "go to sleep or wake up," simply by logging onto an Internet site and remotely turning his heat and hot water heater on or off.

The article explained that

> in the Brous household and others throughout Washington's Olympic Peninsula, smart water heaters and thermostats provided updated electric prices about every five minutes, depending on what was available and needed. Homeowners could adjust their settings to decrease power consumption and save money during peak demand or override the controls at any point, like when they were hosting dinner guests or a fussy relative . . . Richard Katzev, an expert on social and environmental behavior and president of Portland, Ore.,–based Public Policy Research, said merely provid-ing more information to consumers would be ineffective without also giving them incentives to act.

The article went on to say that

> researchers spent an average of $1,000 on appliances, equipment and monitoring capabilities for each of the roughly 200 homes participating in two related studies. But for more widespread and routine residential use, he expects the upfront costs to run about $400 to $500 and potentially less if computer chips can be built into the appliances before they leave the factory. "If this becomes cheap enough, even your coffeemaker can help the grid out,"

[Pratt] said. And if eventually adopted throughout the country, the energy-saving appliances could translate into savings of about $70 billion in new power plant construction and power distribution costs over 20 years.

Speaking of coffeemakers helping out the grid, Pratt and his colleagues Mike Davis and Carl Imhoff at the Pacific Northwest National Laboratory in Richland, Washington, gave me a demonstration when I visited them. They took me into a room that is set up like a home kitchen/laundry room, with a washer, dryer, water heater, refrigerator, and coffeemaker. Each device was outfitted with a special chip designed at PNNL. It is called a "Grid Friendly Appliance" controller, or GFA. This Grid Friendly controller is a 2-by-2.5-inch circuit board that can be installed in refrigerators, air conditioners, water heaters, and various other household appliances. It monitors the power grid and turns appliances off for a few seconds to a few minutes—without ruining the appliance—in response to power grid overload or commands. When power plants cannot generate enough power to meet customer needs, Grid Friendly Appliances reduce some of the load on the system to balance supply and demand.

So when I came into the mock kitchen, they had everything running, including the refrigerator with the door open. On a digital overhead display, they had a readout showing how many kilowatts all the appliances were using at full blast. It was very noisy. Then they dropped the electricity into the kitchen by 70 percent. What was amazing was that all the devices appeared to continue to run, making almost the same amount of noise, but they were using 70 percent less electricity. How? The Grid Friendly Appliances sensed the power dip and reacted by cutting off portions of their loads. For instance, the dryer turned off the heating element but kept the drum turning; the hot water heater's heating element went off, but there was enough hot water stored in the tank that if you were in the shower you never would have known. In the refrigerator, the defrost cycle was interrupted, but if you opened the door the light remained on and your food would easily have stayed cold for the two or three minutes in which the grid was under stress and the power got dialed down. These grid-friendly circuits cost only $25 per appliance, and the price would surely plummet with mass production.

The beauty of this technology, which is now being pilot tested in bigger communities, is severalfold. First, these sorts of power dips happen on your grid a few times a week. You just don't know it, and the reason you don't know it is because your utility protects against it by having a spare power plant or two spinning all the time, even when they are not producing electricity, so that its power can be drawn upon instantly whenever there is a dip. That is called "reserve requirement," and if the reserve plant is a coal plant, it is spitting out CO_2—just so you don't experience a dip.

If we could manage these dips by controlling demand, just dialing down appliances rather than always adding extra supply, we could save energy and money and cut back CO_2 emissions. "From the beginning of the grid, we have tried to solve every problem from the supply side with new technology—we've never been able to do it from the demand side with new technology," said Mike Davis, the associate director for PNNL's Energy Science and Technology Directorate. "Now we have the technology to do it. If someone wants to turn off the heating element in my coffeepot for a couple minutes every day—and do it with millions of other homes—so we don't have to have extra coal-fired power plants, I'm good with that."

The model that I envisaged above, and the model that Davis and his colleagues tested out, would involve a revolutionary change to the utilities industry. Utilities, instead of limiting their vision from the power plant to your home electricity meter, would be wholly transformed. Their universe would stretch from the generation of clean power on one end right into your home appliances, your car battery, and even the solar panels on your roof. Rather than just being a seller of dumb and dirty electrons, it would be an enabler of this whole smart grid–Energy Internet system. And it would make its money from optimizing this system.

Jim Rogers, the CEO of Duke Energy, based in Charlotte, North Carolina, likes to say that rather than spend $7 billion on building a new nuclear plant, he would rather the regulators let him spend that same amount of money building out a smart transmission grid and helping his customers to install solar panels on their roofs, Smart Black Boxes in their homes, smart batteries in their cars, and Grid Friendly chips in their appliances, and then have Duke Energy maintain and service every aspect of that network.

"For a hundred years we defined the boundaries of our market as being from the generator to the meter on the wall outside your house," said Rogers. Going forward, "I want that market to be from the generator to our customers' rooftops and to the energy applications and energy networks embedded in our customers' homes and offices and cars. That is where the real savings will come—from optimizing those energy networks and applications . . . I have to take my grid and make it smart and make everyone's home into a smart home and everyone's factory into a smart factory and then optimize them all so everyone gets the most service for the least money and least amount of CO_2."

That would be a very different job for utilities—from running an all-you-can-eat-for-five-dollars electron buffet to optimizing an Energy Internet. But that is the future.

And as Jeff Wacker, the EDS futurist, likes to say: "The future is with us, it's just not widely distributed yet." He is right in the sense that we can see today what the future could look like. We can see the technologies taking shape that could make it happen, but we still need a few key breakthroughs to get that future widely distributed.

The Energy Internet I've described, if we can get it built, has the potential to give us more growth with fewer power plants, better energy efficiency, and more renewable energy, like wind and solar, by smoothing out the peaks and valleys in energy demand. If we could just add another breakthrough on top of that—inventing a source of energy that would give us abundant, clean, reliable, and cheap electrons to power this Energy Internet and that would dramatically reduce our usage of coal, oil, and natural gas—the revolution would be complete. Then you would be feeding clean electrons into an energy-saving smart grid, into a smart home, and into a smart car.

That, when it happens, will be the great energy transformation. It will be like two giant rivers coming together—the IT revolution and the ET revolution. And when it happens—when it *really* happens—it will unlock more human potential, more innovation, more possibilities to lift people out of poverty in a sustainable way, than you can possibly imagine. I just want to live long enough to see that day dawn. The next chapters describe how we can make it happen.

THIRTEEN

The Stone Age Didn't End Because
We Ran Out of Stones

Recently reports have been current in certain newspapers that Mr. Thomas A. Edison, the inventor, has at last perfected the storage battery, and that within a few months electrically propelled vehicles, costing little to buy and next to nothing to maintain, will be on the market. The same story has appeared regularly for years and yet matters do not appear to have advanced much.

— International Herald Tribune, November 1, 1907

If I'd asked my customers what they wanted, they'd have said a faster horse.
— Henry Ford

The city of Tianjin, China, is home to many of China's big automakers, and in September 2007 I was invited to speak at the China "Green Car Congress" there. Yes, China, which has been steadily improving its own auto mileage and pollution standards, now holds a conference to talk about the latest in green-car technologies. Who knew? The venue was the Marriott in Tianjin and the audience was mostly Chinese auto industry executives—some pretty tough-looking car guys—who listened to my remarks, via translation, on headphones. I thought hard and long beforehand about what to say to this group that might stimulate their thinking and give them a perspective they hadn't heard before. In the end, I decided to go right for the jugular. The basic thrust of my talk was as follows:

"Every year I come to China and young Chinese tell me, 'Mr. Friedman, you Americans got to grow dirty for 150 years—you got to have your

Industrial Revolution based on coal and oil—now it is our turn.' Well, on behalf of all Americans, I am here today to tell you that you're right. It's your turn. Please, take your time, grow as dirty as you like for as long as you like. Take your time! Please! Because I think my country needs only five years to invent all the clean power and energy efficiency tools that you, China, will need to avoid choking on pollution, and then we are going to come over and sell them all to you. We will get at least a five-year jump on you in the next great global industry: clean power and energy efficiency. We will totally dominate you in those industries. So please, don't rush, grow as dirty as you like for as long as you want. If you want to do it for five more years, that's great. If you want to give us a ten-year lead on the next great global industry, that would be even better. Please, take your time."

At first, I could see a lot of these grizzled Chinese car guys adjusting their earpieces to make sure that they were hearing me right: *"What the hell did he just say? America is going to clean our clock in the next great global industry? What industry is that?"* But as I went on, I could also see some heads nodding and some wry smiles of recognition from those who got my point: Clean power *is* going to be the global standard over the next decade, and clean-power tools are going to be the next great global industry, and the countries who make more of them and sell more of them will have a competitive advantage. Those countries will have both the cleanest air and the fastest-growing businesses—not a bad combination.

That is the point I was trying to drive home in Tianjin, by making it into a competitive issue: The longer China focuses on getting its share from a world that no longer exists—a world in which people could use dirty fuels with impunity—and the longer it postpones imposing the policies, prices, and regulations on itself that will stimulate a clean power industry at scale, the happier I am as an American.

America wins! America wins! America wins!

If only . . .

If only our country understood this moment and was doing everything it could to put in place the winning formula—REEFIGD-CPEERPFPCA < TCOBCOG—a renewable energy ecosystem for innovating, generating, and deploying clean power, energy efficiency, resource productivity, family planning, conservation, and adaptation < the true cost of burning coal, oil, and gas. Then we really would be able to clean China's clock. But we don't understand this moment and we're not doing all we can, which is why China could still end up cleaning ours.

The Energy Internet I described in the previous chapter would be at the core of such a revolutionary new clean power system. That smart grid is vitally necessary to drive energy efficiency, to reduce demand, and to reduce emissions, but it alone is not sufficient. We also need abundant, clean, reliable, and cheap electrons to feed into that smart grid and create a complete Clean Energy *System*—from the power plant, to the transmission line to your home and business, to your car.

Unfortunately, as noted earlier, we have not found that magic bullet—that form of energy production that will give us abundant, clean, reliable, cheap electrons. All the advances we have made so far in wind, solar, geothermal, solar thermal, hydrogen, and cellulosic ethanol are incremental, and there has been no breakthrough in any other energy source. *Incremental breakthroughs are all we've had, but exponential is what we desperately need.*

That is why the green revolution is first and foremost an innovation challenge—not a regulation challenge. "Ultimately, this problem is going to have to be solved by the engineers," said Craig Mundie, Microsoft's chief research and strategy officer. But how could it be that, with all the green talk and all the green hype, we have not made such an exponential innovation/engineering breakthrough yet?

The answer is twofold. First, real energy innovation is hard. We are bumping up against the current limits of physics, chemistry, thermodynamics, nanotechnology, and biology, and we need to push out the frontiers in each of these disciplines.

But second, more important, and the subject of this chapter and the next: We haven't really tried. That's right, *we haven't really tried.*

We have not put in place the basic requirement for trying: a coordinated set of policies, tax incentives and disincentives, and regulations that would stimulate the marketplace to produce an Energy Internet, to move the clean power technologies we already have—like wind and solar—down the learning curve much faster, and to spur the massive, no-holds-barred-everybody-in-their-garage-or-laboratory innovation we need for new sources of clean electrons.

As Secretary of Energy Steven Chu once put it to me: We want to get away from a system dominated by lobbyists "who just want to preserve the way it was before" to a system that will be dominated by engineers who will "give us the way it will be in the future."

I cannot stress this point enough. If you take only one thing away from this book, please take this: We are not going to regulate our way out of the problems of the Energy-Climate Era. We can only innovate our way out, and the only way to do that is to mobilize the most effective and prolific system for transformational innovation and commercialization of new products ever created on the face of the earth—the U.S. marketplace. There is only one thing bigger than Mother Nature and that is Father Profit, and we have not even begun to enlist him in this struggle.

We don't need a Manhattan Project for clean energy; *we need a market for clean energy*. That's what we're missing. We don't need a secret government-led initiative involving a dozen scientists in a remote hideaway to come up with a single invention. We need 10,000 innovators, all collaborating with, and building upon, one another to produce all sorts of breakthroughs in abundant, clean, reliable, and cheap electrons and energy efficiency. And we need to create demand, huge demand—*crazy, wild, off-the-charts demand*—for existing clean power technologies, like wind and solar, in order to reduce the cost of these technologies and make them competitive with conventional fossil fuels—coal, oil, and natural gas. We could make these already existing clean power technologies so much cheaper and so much more effective today if we created the market pull that would demand their mass production all over the country. They would move quickly down the learning curve. We could do for solar and wind what China did for tennis shoes and toys.

But the only thing that can stimulate this much innovation in new technologies and the radical improvement of existing ones is the free market. Only the market can generate and allocate enough capital fast enough and efficiently enough to get 10,000 inventors working in 10,000 companies and 10,000 garages and 10,000 laboratories to drive transformational breakthroughs; only the market can then commercialize the best of them and improve on the existing ones at the scope, speed, and scale we need.

But markets are not just open fields to which you simply add water and then sit back in a lawn chair, watch whatever randomly sprouts, and assume that the best outcome will always result. No, markets are like gardens. You have to intelligently design and fertilize them—with the right taxes, regulations, incentives, and disincentives—so they yield the good, healthy crops necessary for you to thrive.

Up to now, we have not designed our energy garden to get the maximum amount of innovation in clean power—not at all. To the extent that we have designed it, we have designed it to produce energy from cheap, dirty fuels, primarily from oil, coal, and natural gas. And then we sat back and let all those in Congress and the private sector who bene-fited from the use of those fuels water and fertilize this garden like crazy with government supports—while paying scant attention to everything else. There has been only one rule in our energy garden: It is, to use a term coined by the British economist Paul Collier, "survival of the fattest"—those with the biggest lobbies and deepest pockets make policy.

Now our energy garden is overrun with a tangle of coal, oil, and nat-ural gas pipelines, refineries, and gas stations, and it is very hard for any-thing new to grow there without getting choked. Have no doubt: Our garden has been designed by the oil, coal, and natural gas interests to suit their needs—to keep these fuels cheap and abundant and difficult to supplant. And the global garden has been designed by the OPEC oil car-tel and the petrodictators to suit their interests too. There is no "free mar-ket" in energy, where everyone is competing on a level playing field. That is a complete fantasy.

In what free market would you find the U.S. government slapping a 54-cent-a-gallon tariff on sugarcane ethanol imported from Brazil, a democratic ally of the United States, while imposing only a 1.25-cent-a-gallon tariff on crude oil imported from Saudi Arabia, the home of most of the 9/11 hijackers? Only in a market where the American corn lobby has enough clout in Congress to prevent Brazilian sugar ethanol from competing with American corn ethanol—even though sugar ethanol packs seven or eight times more energy—and only in an America where at least some elements of the Big Oil lobby are so bent on keeping us dependent on gasoline for transportation fuels that they always want to make it difficult for any alternatives to undercut them on price. In what free market would we give billions in permanent or long-term tax incen-tives to the oil, coal, and gas industries, but stop and start every two or three years—for three decades—the puny tax breaks for wind and solar power, making long-term investing in these areas very precarious? Only in a market *designed* to keep fossil fuels cheap and renewables expensive and elusive. No wonder that, as my *New York Times* colleague Jad Mouawad wrote (November 9, 2007) when oil was approaching $100 a barrel, "even at today's highs, oil is cheaper than imported bottled water, which would cost $180 a barrel, or milk, at $150 a barrel."

You are not going to get energy innovation at scale when a barrel of oil is cheaper than a barrel of water or a barrel of milk.

If we want to see the innovation we need in clean electrons, smart grids, and energy efficiency, we need to intelligently redesign the garden—i.e., the market. When it comes to developing the next generation of clean power, "I don't believe in evolution—I only believe in intelligent design," says Amos Avidan, a principal vice president of Bechtel Corporation and an expert on building big power systems. "We need intelligently designed policies to give us the best chance possible to produce the breakthroughs we need."

People often ask me: "What's your favorite renewable energy? Are you a solar photovoltaic guy? A wind guy? A geothermal guy? A solar thermal guy?" My answer today is very simple: "My favorite renewable energy is an ecosystem for energy innovation. I'm an ecosystem for innovation guy." That's what we need above all else—an intelligently designed *system* of policies, tax incentives and disincentives, and regulations that will get every promising source of clean electrons and energy efficiency that we already have down the learning curve faster and will move every new idea for generating clean electrons out the lab door quicker. Only that kind of ecosystem for innovation can give birth to an Energy Internet–smart grid, fed by abundant, clean, reliable, and cheap electrons. It takes a system to make a system.

A single Manhattan Project wouldn't cut it now—not even close. "We need the government to be stimulating exponential innovation by reshaping the market," said Curt Carlson, the president and CEO of SRI, the Silicon Valley research firm, and coauthor of *Innovation: The Five Disciplines for Creating What Customers Want*. "If the government just did the reasonable things, the rest would come into place." Many other major industrial countries in the free world seem to understand this and have begun to take at least some intelligently designed steps to promote energy and environmental innovation and deployment. America has not kept pace. "The only thing we have an industrial policy in place for in this country is agriculture—a nineteenth-century industry," Carlson added. "We certainly don't have an intelligently designed national strategy for energy innovation and commercialization."

We don't want government to be picking the winners, added Carlson. (That is how we got too deep into corn ethanol.) We want government setting the right tax policies, regulatory policies, and education policies, and funding the basic research that pushes out the boundaries of materials science, chemistry, physics, biology, and nanotechnology—preparing all the soil, so the market and venture capitalists can pick off whichever sprouts look most likely to make the difficult transition from drawing board to marketplace. That's what intelligent design is all about. In the short term, a transformational breakthrough is unlikely, said Carlson, "but in the long term, if we do the right things, [clean energy] is a very solvable problem that will put the world in a better place . . . But it is not going to happen with an unintelligent design."

This chapter will look at the price signals that would have to be part of such an intelligently designed system.

Before I go into what sort of price signal we need, though, let me underscore for a moment just how feeble the American system has been during the last fifty years when it comes to stimulating clean energy innovation. Let's start with a statistic. The total investment in research and development by electric utilities in the United States in 2007 was about 0.15 percent of total revenues. In most competitive industries, the figure is 8 to 10 percent. If your total investment in R & D is 0.15 percent of revenues, that's not going to buy you much more than a few subscriptions to *Popular Mechanics* and *Scientific American*. In fact, the American pet food industry spends more each year on R & D than the American utilities industry does.

Another way to underscore this point is with a question: When was the last big breakthrough in clean energy production in the United States? Answer: 1957—with the opening of the world's first central station commercial nuclear reactor, located in Shippingport, Pennsylvania. That's right—we have not had a scale breakthrough in clean energy since the days of filterless cigarettes and segregation.

Still looking for more proof of how uninnovative we've been in the energy field? Ask Jeffrey Immelt, chairman and CEO of General Electric, one of the world's premier manufacturers of power systems. He told me the following story: He has worked for General Electric for twenty-six years. In those twenty-six years, he has seen "eight or nine" generations of innovation in medical technology in GE's health care business—in devices like X-ray equipment, MRIs, or CAT scans—because the government and the health care market created prices, incentives, and competition that drove a constant flow of invention. It was very profitable to innovate in this field and fairly easy to jump in. But in power? said Immelt. One—one generation of real innovation is all that he has seen.

"Today, on the power side," said the GE chairman, "we're still selling the same basic coal-fired power plants we had when I arrived. They're a little cleaner and more efficient now, but basically the same model." Nine generations of innovation in health care—one in power systems. What does that tell you? It tells you that you have a market that simply has not been shaped to produce clean energy innovation. "You can't look back at the last thirty years," concluded Immelt, "and say that the market in energy has worked."

Between regulated electricity and gas utilities that operate in a monopoly environment and oil companies who had a tacit monopoly over transportation fuels, the key players in the energy market had little incentive to innovate and the new start-ups had little room to emerge. "Energy fundamentally has been underinvested in from the technology standpoint," said Immelt.

Indeed, while the health care industry basically puts about 8 percent of revenue back into R & D every year, the entire energy industry—utilities, technology companies, plus the oil, gas, coal, and nuclear industries together—puts back less than 2 percent, and by some estimates less than 1 percent, into R & D every year. They certainly don't invest anywhere near 8 percent, noted Immelt.

Edward Goldberg, president of Annisa Group, business consultants, and adjunct professor at the Zicklin School of Business at Baruch College of the City University of New York, told the story in a succinct little essay he published in *The Baltimore Sun* (February 23, 2007). "Modern American capitalism," he noted,

> is the world's envy of growth. It successfully harnesses the human drive for competitiveness with the human need to create and innovate. Apple booms with the iPod, and Microsoft works day and night to create a better version. But when competition becomes muted and market innovation is deemed not essential, the cornucopia that we call today's capitalism stalls and society is harmed. This is exactly what has happened within our energy giants. The most efficient way of developing new energy resources should be through private enterprise. But our major energy companies have not been pressured by the forces of modern market capitalism to give anything but lip service to the development of new energy sources. While capitalism in America is constantly evolving, creating more efficiencies and innovations, the energy industry appears to be stuck in a mercantilistic mode . . . If this occurred in a

small industry, few people would really care. But when the market becomes complacent in its role of innovator in our most vital industry, the government as the guardian of our nation's independence must become the catalyst for innovation . . . In the energy industry, the need to compete for consumers—and thus to innovate—has not been an obligation for years. When was the last time anyone has seen an oil company advertising on TV that its products or services were better than the competition's? Although not monopolies, the energy companies are in effect large, privately owned utilities and delivery systems. Under the premise that energy is so important to the nation that it must be treated differently, these companies are supported unlike any other industry with massive American military investments to protect their supply lines and sourcing. Unlike modern high-tech companies, energy companies are free to ignore Harvard business professor Clayton Christensen's maxim of "disruptive technologies": that new technologies replace existing ones because they are cheaper and more consumer-friendly. Able to disregard this need to create "newness" in the marketplace, energy companies primarily invest in growing and maintaining their supply systems. Without market pressure to innovate to find alternative sources of energy, society receives a much-reduced benefit from the existence of these companies . . . If Toyota takes market share from Ford by manufacturing hybrids while Ford is still making SUVs, Ford is punished by the market. But because they derive most of their profits from sourcing, the energy companies do not need competitive innovation to survive. And because their profits have been extraordinary, they are not punished by the market for a lack of innovation; in fact, they are rewarded—while at the same time, they are at liberty to ignore the market-driven changes that have moved American capitalism forward. The energy majors know that if oil, year in and year out, remains cheaper than competitive energy products, there will be little pressure to invest in new forms of energy. And when the oil market falls . . . it reinforces this corporate stagnation . . . In a world of energy shortages, America no longer can afford the luxury of allowing old-fashioned, non-innovative capitalism to be at the heart of its industrial system, distorting and threatening the system as a whole.

The only way to change this situation and set off the forest fire of innovation in clean energy that we need is by reshaping the market in a way that will make it much easier for clean power technologies to compete and challenge the incumbent dirty fuels. And the only way to do that is with taxes and incentives that will stimulate more demand for the clean power technologies that already exist, like wind and solar, and pull them down the learning curve to the "Chindia price," with taxes and incentives that will stimulate more research and development by private companies and universities, and with taxes and incentives that will encourage more investors to quickly commercialize any breakthroughs that government or university or private sector labs might produce.

"No matter how much you tell the market what you want it to do, it is the price signal that markets respond to," said Dan Kammen, the University of California, Berkeley, expert on energy innovation. Therefore, "anyone who invokes markets and doesn't want to invoke a price signal failed Econ 101. We invoke the market in energy, but we don't use it. If you want a market to produce something and there is no price signal, you don't have a market. You have to have a price signal."

Prices and Innovation

The person who best expressed the critical importance that relative prices play in stimulating innovation in renewable energy was none other than the late great Saudi Arabian oil minister Sheikh Ahmed Zaki Yamani. Back in the 1970s, as OPEC was just starting to feel its oats, Yamani used to warn his colleagues not to raise oil prices too high, too fast, for fear of causing a government and market reaction in the West that would trigger massive innovation in wind, solar, and other forms of renewable energy.

The way Yamani put it to his OPEC colleagues reportedly went something like this: "Remember, boys, the Stone Age didn't end because we ran out of stones." It ended because people invented alternative tools made of bronze and then iron. Yamani knew that if the oil-consuming countries actually got their acts together to produce renewable energy at scale or to drive energy efficiency breakthroughs exponentially higher, the oil age would end with millions of barrels of oil still underground, just as the Stone Age ended with a lot of stones still on the ground. Yamani knew that the price signal—the price of oil versus the price of renewables—was everything, and OPEC needed to keep its crude prices exactly at the level where the cartel could earn the maximum returns without spurring the West to innovate any scale alternatives to oil.

Our goal needs to be to make Yamani's nightmare come true.

The way to do that is by creating our own price signal to trigger the market to launch those 10,000 innovations in clean energy in 10,000 garages and 10,000 laboratories. The market will give us what we want, but only if we give the market the signals it needs: a carbon tax, a gasoline tax increase, a renewable energy mandate, or a cap-and-trade system that indirectly taxes carbon emitters—or some combination of all these.

Nate Lewis, the Caltech energy chemist, employs a very useful analogy to explain why exactly taxing the dirty fuels is so critical in order to stimulate massive innovation in and deployment of clean power. It goes like this: Let's say I invented the first cell phone. And I came to you, dear reader, and said, "Have I got a deal for you! I have just invented a phone that you can carry in your pocket!"

You would probably say, "Wow, a phone that I can carry in my pocket? Really! That would change my life. I'll buy ten and pass them out to all my employees."

I'd say, "Ten it is! But I have to warn you: This is the first-generation model. They're going to cost you $1,000 each." You would no doubt say, "Sounds like a lot, but it'll be worth it—like I said, a phone that I could carry in my pocket would change my life."

So I sell you ten, and I sell the next reader ten, and the next reader ten . . . Six months later, guess what? I am back with a new version of my little cell phone. It's smaller, lighter, and costs only $850. I'm on my way down the learning curve.

Now I am on a roll. So I go back to my innovation lab and this time I invent a solar-powered light. I come back to you again, dear reader, and say, "Remember that cell phone I sold you? Worked out pretty well for you, right? Well, now I have another deal. See that light fixture above your head? I am going to power it with electrons created by the sun. But this is brand-new technology, and it's not cheap: It will cost you an extra $100 each month to power your light fixture that way."

And what would you say back to me, dear reader? You would probably say, "Tom, um, remember that cell phone you sold me? Now, that changed my life. I had never had anything like it. But in case you haven't noticed, there's already light coming from that fixture above my head. It works just fine, and, frankly, I really don't care where the electrons come from. Sorry, Tom, but I will pass."

There is only one way to change that outlook. The government needs to come in and tell you, dear reader, that from now on you are going to pay the full cost of all the CO_2 and pollution from your incandescent, coal-powered light fixture, and therefore it is going to cost you $125 more a month to turn on that light. Then my solar-powered light for only $100 more a month looks like a bargain, and you'll take ten and so will all the other readers of this book, and six months later, guess what? I will be back with the same solar lighting system for only $75 more a month. I will be down the cost-volume learning curve, and, innovation being what it is, I will eventually get that solar light cost below that of the coal-powered one. I will have taken my new innovation to scale.

Everyone says that building a renewable energy infrastructure is the moon shot of our generation. I wish.

"Building an emissions-free energy infrastructure is not like sending a man to the moon," explained Nate Lewis.

With the moon shot, money was no object—and all we had to do was get there. But today, we already have cheap energy from coal, gas, and oil. So getting people to pay more to shift to clean fuels is like trying to get funding for NASA to build a new spaceship to the moon—when Southwest Airlines already flies there and gives away free peanuts! I already have a cheap ride to the moon, and a ride is a ride. For most people, electricity is electricity, no matter how it is generated. Making [cleaner] energy doesn't provide them with something new. So you are asking them to pay for something they already have *that does the exact same thing*. Nobody would be buying iPods in the numbers they have if their cell phones could already download music.

The critical thing to remember is that clean energy gives you a new environment, but not a new function. "Electrons are electrons—not blue or green electrons," noted Lewis. "They all just make the lightbulb white. They don't search your e-mail, and they won't correct your spelling."

Therefore (I repeat) if we want to get both forms of innovation at a large scale—breakthroughs that lead to whole new ways of generating clean electrons and breakthroughs that come by getting the clean power technologies we already have down the learning curve faster—we need the government to level the playing field by taxing what we don't want (electricity from carbon-emitting sources) and subsidizing what we do want (clean power innovation). That's what will create the market demand we need at the scale we need.

If we can just stimulate the market with the right price signals to get these technologies down the price-volume learning curve faster, they could make a very big dent very quickly. Remember: oil, coal, and gas are all exhaustible resources. The more of them we use, the more their price goes up. Wind, solar, electric car batteries, solar thermal, and geothermal are all technologies. They benefit from learning curves. The more we use them, the more we move them down their cost-volume learning curves; they cost less, do more, and deliver more energy for less money.

In 2000, the International Energy Agency produced a report, "Experience Curves for Energy Technology Policy," that underscored how, if government increases demand by using price signals, it can move existing technologies quickly down the learning curve and get much bigger deployment at lower costs much sooner. "With historical annual growth rates of 15 percent, photovoltaic modules will reach break-even point around the year 2025," said the IEA study. "Doubling the rate of growth will move the break-even point 10 years ahead to 2015 . . . If we want cost-efficient, CO_2-mitigation technologies available during the first decades of the new century, these technologies must be given the opportunity to learn in the current marketplace."

To see that, all you have to do is watch how prices of solar panels and wind power are falling steadily around the country as the market demand for them expands. Manufacturers take advantage of economies of scale and learn new ways to produce solar panels or wind turbines more efficiently. But they still have a ways to go to be competitive with coal. That's why we want to expand the market for these existing renewables even more. And that is why I focus on the market, not on a Manhattan Project.

"The analogy of a massive government Apollo program or Manhattan Project is so flawed," argued Joseph Romm, the energy physicist. "Those programs were to create unique noncommercial products for a specialized customer with an unlimited budget. Throwing money at the problem was an obvious approach. To save a livable climate we need to create mass-market commercial products for lots of different customers who have limited budgets." Only a properly shaped market can do that, added Romm, and we should be creating that market "right now"— rather than just hoping and praying and betting the farm on some magic, totally new breakthrough for generating clean electrons. I love magic. We need a magic breakthrough. Close your eyes and pray that we will find one soon. But in the meantime, let's open our eyes and see all the clean electrons that can be generated from existing technologies hiding in plain sight—if we create the right price signals in the marketplace to get them to scale.

The price signal we use may not even have to be a tax. It could just be a floor price. When crude oil was $50 a barrel, the U.S. Congress wouldn't have dared to impose a $50-a-barrel tax and make it $100 a barrel. But if it ever gets over $100 again and this again starts stimulating large-scale investments in alternatives, the government could declare that it is imposing a floor price of $100 a barrel. If oil stays above that, fine. If it goes down to $90 a barrel, the government will add a $10 tax. It could fix a similar floor under gasoline at $4.50 a gallon.

This would remove a big source of uncertainty from the shoulders of energy investors. If inventors and venture capitalists believe that the price of their new clean energy invention can always be undercut by the dirty old alternative, we are not going to get new innovation at the scale we need. And we are not going to get existing clean power technologies down the learning curve at the scope we need. After the oil price spikes in the 1970s stimulated enormous innovation in solar and wind power, the OPEC price collapse a decade later wiped out all these investments and governments lost interest in supporting them. Companies and investors have just seen this play too many times. They are still wary that they will make a big bet on renewable energy and then the benchmark oil price will collapse, the market for alternatives will disappear, and their company will look very foolish to its shareholders.

Consider Toyota. When I started writing this book in 2007, gasoline was heading for $4.50 a gallon. When I went to buy a new Prius hybrid in Bethesda, Maryland, where I live, the waiting list at our local Toyota dealer was so long, they had stopped taking names. In other words, when gasoline is $4.50 a gallon, you cannot buy a Prius in Bethesda, Maryland.

As I worked on this paperback edition in the spring of 2009, with gasoline prices hovering around $2.25 a gallon, you could not *sell* a Prius in Bethesda, Maryland. That's an exaggeration, of course. You can sell one, but it is much harder at $2.25 a gallon than $4.50—and Toyota sells far fewer. In March 2009, Prius sales were down 55 percent compared to March 2008—down from 20,635 mid-size gas-electric Prius hybrids to 8,924.

Repeat after me: when it comes to energy innovation, "Price matters, price matters, price matters." If you want to bring about a mass movement toward more energy-efficient cars, windows, buildings, power-generation systems, lighting, and heating, the simplest way is to make sure that the true cost of using any and all hydrocarbon-based fuels is reflected in their price to consumers—the true climate costs, the true environmental costs, and the true geopolitical costs. "Put the true price on things in a durable and predictable way and capital formation, innovation, and entrepreneurship will all take place around making energy-efficient alternatives," said Marc Porat, chairman of Serious Materials, which makes super-energy-efficient windows for homes and offices. Consumers will also adjust and demand more energy-efficient homes, more energy-efficient offices and schools, and more energy-efficient transportation. And, as a result, the level of carbon emissions will go down. It is simple economics. It is not rocket science. The cheap plastic junk you buy at big-box stores is cheap only because the externalities of making it have not been priced in—the effects on air quality, the effects on water, the effects on climate. Price those into every product and the market will do the rest.

Well, why doesn't the market reflect the true cost of the things being sold? When it comes to energy, the reason, at least in America, is that the government has failed to shape the market with honest prices. It is not a "market failure." Market's don't price externalities when they don't have to. It is a leadership failure.

If the White House and Congress had instituted a Patriot Tax on gasoline after 9/11 or set floor prices for oil and gas, hybrid cars would be the norm in America today—plus, the U.S. Treasury, not the world's petrodictators, would have gotten the extra dollar or two paid for a gallon of gasoline. Bob Lutz, the vice chairman of General Motors, said it better than anyone I know: Here is the Congress and the administration ordering Detroit to make lighter, smaller, and more fuel-efficient vehicles, but when it comes to imposing a gasoline tax to shape the market so there will be lots of consumers demanding those cars, well, says Washington, "that's off the table." Lutz said that is like telling every shirt maker in America that it can only make size small, but never asking anyone in America to go on a diet. You are not going to sell a lot of size-small shirts. People will just go look for their size medium or large in used clothing stores. The same will happen with automobiles and trucks.

The lingering uncertainty about the long-term price of oil is also why some of our biggest energy companies have hesitated to make really big bets on green innovation. You've seen those poker games on TV when the guy from Las Vegas wearing sunglasses and his baseball cap backward takes his whole pile of chips and says, "All in," and everyone around the room gasps. That is what we want to see America's best industrial-innovation companies doing—pushing their piles of chips all in for innovation of clean electrons and energy efficiency systems. Yes, venture capitalism is important, but what is just as important are the bets that these giant companies make, because when they see a lasting, durable, and lucrative market for renewables, they can mobilize thousands of engineers, scientists, and researchers behind it, and with their global manufacturing and marketing abilities they can get products to scale farther, wider, and faster than anyone.

General Electric, DuPont, and Microsoft are America's premier engineering, chemical/biosciences, and software companies. And yet if you interview executives at all three, they will tell you that when it comes to renewable energy, or in the case of Microsoft, energy efficiency software, they have not been all in. Too bad. Microsoft's research budget alone is about $6 billion—which is more than all the venture capital money that went into clean energy technologies in 2007—and *triple* the federal government's combined investments in energy efficiency and renewable energy R & D.

All three of these companies are making bets on clean power and energy efficiency innovation, but those bets are still not as big as they could be. While they are all certainly intrigued and enticed to some degree by the ceiling price that crude oil has shot through—$140 a barrel in 2008—what will make them go all in would be a floor price on crude oil or carbon content that would tell them and their investors that the price of these fossil fuels will never again fall below a certain level. As Kenneth Oye, the MIT expert on innovation, likes to say: "Price fluctuations are not the same as high prices." The fact that the price of oil soared doesn't mean that one good recession, or one big discovery off the coast of Brazil, can't send the price tumbling again and wipe out investments in alternative energy—as we saw happen in 2009, when oil prices tumbled with the global economy. It's why companies like GE and DuPont focus not on the ceiling price of oil, but on the floor.

GE's Jeffrey Immelt put it best: The big energy players are not going to make "a multibillion-dollar, forty-year bet on a fifteen-minute market signal. That just doesn't work." Big industrial players like GE need some price certainty if they are going to make big long-term bets on clean power, and to those market dogmatists who say that the government should not be in the business of fixing floor prices or other incentives to stimulate clean power, Immelt says: Get real. "Don't worship false idols. The government has its hand in every industry. If we have to have them, I'd prefer they were productive rather than destructive."

Those governments that have figured this out have benefited enormously already. The one clean power area where GE is now into a third-generation innovation is wind turbines, "thanks to the European Union," Immelt said. Countries like Denmark, Spain, and Germany imposed portfolio standards for wind power on their utilities—requiring them to produce a certain amount each year—and offered long-term subsidies. This created a big market for wind-turbine manufacturers in Europe in the 1980s, when America abandoned wind because the price of oil fell. "We grew our wind business in Europe," said Immelt. It shows. According to Congressman Ed Markey, a senior member of the House Energy and Commerce Committee, in 2008, Portugal, Spain, and Denmark produced 9 percent, 12 percent, and 21 percent of their electricity from wind, respectively. America produced about 1 percent.

Right now about half the states in the United States have renewable energy mandates that require their utilities to acquire a certain amount of power from solar, wind, hydro, geothermal, or biofuels, but each state has a different standard! Congress has tried to pass a uniform national standard, but it failed. The Obama administration and the Democratic-led Congress are trying again in 2009. A serious renewable mandate would stimulate massive amounts of innovation, because it would take existing technologies, like wind and solar, and push them quickly down the learning curve by creating a huge national market that would be a sure thing for investors to dive into. The politician who actually proved that best was a guy named George W. Bush, when he was governor of

Texas. He pushed and signed the Texas Renewable Portfolio Mandate in 1999. The mandate stipulated that Texas power companies had to produce 2,000 new megawatts of electricity from renewables, mostly wind, by 2009. What happened? A dozen new companies jumped into the Texas market, including one from Ireland, and built wind turbines to meet the mandate—so many that the 2,000-megawatt goal was reached by 2005. So the Texas legislature upped the mandate to 5,000 megawatts by 2015, and everyone knows they will beat that too. Renewable energy mandates work.

"If you had a national renewable energy mandate that covered all fifty states, that would tell me that there is going to be so much demand for wind or solar or geothermal [so] you can really make a big bet," said Immelt.

When the minister of energy and environment in Europe said to me in 2000, there was going to be 10 percent renewables all across Europe, that is what got the wind industry going there. You have to build the certainty that demand is going to be there. We will take the technical risk, we will fund the technology breakthroughs, but I have to know that if I make it work there is a $20 billion market that I can step into. That is what has not existed in energy but has existed in health care and in aviation—you know you have a market . . . This has been a big problem holding back nuclear power. What scares us is making these big R & D bets and not knowing if we will ever get an order.

It doesn't much matter where the government sets a floor price for crude oil or gasoline—whether it is $80 a barrel or $4 a gallon, said Chad Holliday, the DuPont CEO. The important thing is that it be a credible floor.

Then my investors say, "I know that you are not wasting my money—the market is certain." If they set the market, all I have to do is to show the investor that the technology is real. That takes away half the problem. I am talking to investors all the time. [They] keep saying to me: "What if all this goes away?" We need some reasonable certainty . . . We used to own an oil company [Conoco] and we concluded that we could not be a great oil company and a great science company, so we decided to sell

[Conoco]. I paid the three best consulting companies in the world to tell me what the price of crude oil was going to be. They assured me that it could not go over $24 a barrel—or that the probability was very small. [Today,] the market is not sure where the oil price is going to go. Just like it [went way up there in 2008], no one can assure [how far] it will not go back down. That is why Jeff [Immelt] and I are arguing that there has to be a cost for carbon, no matter how you create it. There has to be a simple price signal.

In 2007, Holliday gave me a concrete example: "We have about a hundred scientists working on cellulosic ethanol," which is ethanol made from waste or switchgrass, not from food crops. "My guess," he added, "is that we could double the number and add another fifty to start working on how to commercialize it. It would probably cost us less than $100 million to scale up. But I am not ready to do that. I can guess what it will cost me to make it and what the price will be, but is the market going to be there? What are the regulations going to be? Is the ethanol subsidy going to be reduced? Will we put a tax on oil to keep ethanol competitive? If I know that, it gives me a price target to go after. Without that, I don't know what the market is, and my shareholders don't know how to value what I am doing . . . You need some certainty on the incentives side and on the market side, because we are talking about multiyear investments, billions of dollars, that will take a long time to take off, and we won't hit on everything."

Some will dismiss this as corporate whining. I don't. Energy innovation is hugely expensive and you are always competing against an existing cheap—dirty—alternative. Put in a floor for crude oil, natural gas, and gasoline in America, or a permanent tax on carbon to lift the price of coal, and you will see the ceiling that has existed on energy innovation blow right off. "Government is a huge player in health care, with huge subsidies," said Immelt. "Cancer will be cured in our lifetime because of that. Why not in [renewable] energy?" Other countries have certainly figured that out.

"We would like to go quickly to next-generation photovoltaics for solar," said Holliday. "The governments of Hong Kong and Singapore found out about it, and both are pursuing us heavily [with incentives] to build the plant in their cities. Why isn't the United States doing that? I'm out in Hong Kong, and the new governor of Hong Kong shows up at our meeting, uninvited ahead of time, just to tell us: 'This is really important. You have to be in Hong Kong. I know Singapore is talking to you, but you need to be here.' The U.S. bureaucracy is just not doing this kind of thing."

Bottom line: America needs an energy technology bubble just like the information technology bubble. In order to get that, though, the government needs to make it an absolute no-brainer to invest in renewable energy. Sure, we'll waste some money; yes, there will be plenty of people who go bust along the way; but in the end we will transform our economy and save ourselves from so many other problems in the process.

Right now, in America, we have a bubble in "stories" about clean energy, but we do not have a clean energy bubble. The amount of venture capital in clean energy in 2007 was less than $5 billion. The amount of venture capital that went into the dot-com boom at its height in 2000: $80 billion. If a few billion fell off the table in the dot-com bubble, nobody even bothered to pick it up.

I first learned about the value of bubbles from Bill Gates at the World Economic Forum in Davos, Switzerland, in 1999. I wrote about the impromptu tutorial he delivered there in my book *The Lexus and the Olive Tree*. Gates was giving his annual Davos press conference on the state of Microsoft and technology innovation. At the time, the Internet bubble was at its peak. All the reporters there kept asking him variations on the question, "Mr. Gates, these Internet stocks, they're a bubble, right? Surely, they're a bubble. They must be a bubble?" Finally, an exasperated Gates said to the assembled reporters: "Of course they're a bubble. But you're all missing the point. This bubble is going to attract so much new capital to this Internet industry that it is going to drive innovation faster and faster." Indeed, it was precisely the overexuberance of the dot-com bubble that led to the overinvestment of billions of dollars into fiber-optic cable from the late 1990s to the early 2000s, which accidentally wired — and flattened — the world, making Internet connectivity virtually free for everyone. That infrastructure was paid for largely by American and European investors. Many of them ended up losing their shirts in the dot-com bust, but the wired world they left behind made it possible for Indians, Chinese, Brazilians, and others from the developing world to compete, connect, and collaborate more cheaply and easily than ever before in history. The dot-com bubble funded so much innovation during the 1990s that in just a decade it spawned the Internet–World Wide Web–e-commerce ecosystem that became the IT revolution.

Economists have long known that bubbles, despite the money they waste and the grief they cause, can drive innovation at a fever pitch and finance the wires and plumbing that pave the way for the next big boom, bubble, and bust. The *Newsweek* economic writer Daniel Gross wrote a book about this phenomenon, called *Pop!: Why Bubbles Are Great for the Economy*, which underscores the economic logic of bubbles and makes the argument that they have actually been a key driver of "America's remarkable record of economic growth and innovation." Sure, he argues, most early investors went bust in the railroad or telegraph bubbles, but the infrastructure they left behind vaulted our economy forward. Gross, not surprisingly, also contends that the best way to trigger a real breakthrough in alternative energy would be to trigger a real energy bubble. It worked with IT. It can work with ET.

Prices as a Brake on Bad Behavior

But there is another reason, beyond the necessity of innovation, for a healthy society to want to reshape the energy market with taxes and regulations. It's called life and death, or stability and instability. This is becoming a survival issue. Quite simply: Continuing with the Dirty Fuels System, in a world that is hot, flat, and crowded, will drive all five trends shaping the Energy-Climate Era—energy supply and demand, climate change, petrodictatorship, biodiversity loss, and energy poverty—to unmanageable extremes. We need the market to send different signals. The legendary environmentalist Lester Brown, in his excellent book *Plan B 3.0*, quotes Oystein Dahle, former vice president of Exxon for Norway and the North Sea, as observing: "Socialism collapsed because it did not allow the market to tell the economic truth. Capitalism may collapse because it does not allow the market to tell the ecological truth."

What he meant, of course, is that the basic paradigm of modern, industrial-age capitalism, which flowered in the nineteenth and twentieth centuries, treated things like pollution, waste, and CO_2 emissions as essentially irrelevant "externalities" that could be ignored. As any economics textbook will tell you, an externality is any cost or benefit resulting from a commercial transaction that is borne by or received by parties not directly involved in the transaction. A factory that pours pollution and CO_2 into the atmosphere and toxic waste into the river is a classic example. Let's say that the factory makes toys. Those toys will be priced at the cost of labor and materials, plus a markup for profit. The two parties in the transaction are the manufacturer and the consumer. But there is an "externality" that is being paid for by some third parties—global society and planet earth—and that externality is the short- and long-term health consequences of polluting the air, poisoning the river, and intensifying global warming by making those toys with coal-fired power and toxic chemicals.

We have been fooling ourselves with fraudulent accounting by not pricing those externalities with surcharges that reflect the true risks and costs that they entail. As Lester Brown put it, we as a society "have been behaving just like Enron, the rogue energy giant, at the height of its folly." We rack up stunning profits and GDP numbers every year, and they look great on paper "because we've been hiding some of the costs off the books." Mother Nature has not been fooled. That is why we are having climate change. That which is not priced is not valued, and if our open lands, clean air, clean water, and healthy forests are not valued, the earth, when it is this flat and this crowded, will become a very hot, no-cost landfill very fast. When markets underprice goods and services by failing to price their externalities, and the impact of that underpricing has highly negative economic, health, and national security implications, it's the job of government to step in and shape the market to correct that failure.

"How can the invisible hand [of markets] be a rational allocator of resources if it is blind to the externalities?" asks Ray Anderson, founder and chairman of the eco-sensitive carpet manufacturers Interface Inc.

The government used a combination of taxes and education to get millions of people to stop smoking cigarettes and guzzling alcohol, and it needs to do the same thing to get the economy to stop smoking carbon and guzzling gasoline. Our economic, physical, and geopolitical health depends on it.

What Kind of Price Signal?

So if those are all the reasons to create a price signal, what are the strengths and weaknesses of each option? The options discussed most often are a carbon tax, a gasoline tax, "feebates," an indirect tax through a cap-and-trade system, and a renewable energy mandate. I would be happy to see us move in any of these directions, as long as the effective tax is high enough and long-term enough to really change behavior.

Under a cap-and-trade program, the government sets an overall cap on the level of CO_2 emissions the United States economy would put into the atmosphere by a certain date. This cap would define the absolute maximum amount of CO_2 that could be emitted in the United States. Over time this cap would be reduced, resulting in fewer CO_2 emissions and higher CO_2 emission costs. Each business would receive, either through issuance or auction, tradable allowances equal to their maximum permissible level of CO_2 emissions. Those firms that can reduce their emissions more cheaply and efficiently could sell their unused allowances to others who would otherwise have to pay more to comply. A cap-and-trade system was how the U.S. eventually controlled acid rain pollution—although there were far fewer players involved.

Eileen Claussen, president of the Pew Center on Global Climate Change, argues that cap-and-trade is preferable to a carbon tax on a number of grounds. To begin with, "while a tax provides for cost certainty, cap-and-trade provides for environmental certainty," she said. The cap is fixed by the government on the basis of what scientists tell us is the level of emissions we need to get to in order to protect the climate. The danger with a tax, Claussen argued, is that some people will just pay it, as they now pay higher gasoline prices, and still go out and buy a Hummer that pours more CO_2 into the atmosphere. And, as everyone knows, new taxes are also very difficult to get through Congress—especially a tax that might actually bite enough to make a difference on CO_2. Also, a cap-and-trade system does give the government a little more flexibility. It can, initially, adjust the allocations to utilities and businesses that are heavily dependent on coal—and therefore would get hit hardest—to ease their transition to a low-carbon economy. For a cap-and-trade system to work, though, you also have to have a serious price tag on spewing carbon—at least \$30 per ton of CO_2 emissions.

Advocates of a carbon tax see things differently. (I lean their way.) They argue that a tax is preferable to a cap-and-trade regime because it is simpler, more transparent, and easier to calculate, and that it would cut across the whole economy and could easily be adjusted to ease the burden on at least lower-income workers by lowering or eliminating their payroll taxes. Tax advocates argue that an economy-wide cap-and-trade system would be more complicated to implement and would invite all kinds of lobbying for special exemptions.

"Cap-and-trade is a Temple of Doom for life on our planet, worshipped by lawmakers who are afraid to confront fossil special interests," argued NASA climate specialist Jim Hansen, one of the most courageous and outspoken scientists warning about climate change, in an essay in *YaleGlobal Online* (May 14, 2009).

What is needed is a gradually rising fee on the carbon content of oil, gas and coal, with proceeds distributed fully to the public. This will spur innovation in efficiency and carbon-free energy, while providing the public the funds needed to transition toward the clean energy world of the future.

"Cap-and-trade" is supposed to answer climate change by setting targets for emission or capping it by issuing permits to emitting industries. To begin with, cap and trade is a misnomer. A "cap" increases the price of energy, as a tax does. It is wrong and disingenuous to try to hide the fact that a cap is a tax. [Another characteristic] of the "cap" approach is that because of unpredictable price volatility it makes millionaires on Wall Street and other trading floors but offers the public little. Offsets are usually allowed and often poorly substantiated and verified, creating more uncertainty. The case in point is the European experience: they spent $50 billion on carbon trading, their CO_2 emissions actually increased, and the largest payment went to a German coalburning utility! Cap-and-trade is fraught with opportunities for special interests, political trading, obfuscation from public scrutiny, accounting errors, and outright fraud.

As with any law, caps can and will be changed, many times, before 2050 . . .

The economic reality is that we will not move to an era beyond fossil fuel emissions until a substantially higher price is applied across-the-board to all carbon fuels, such that efficiency and carbon-free energies rapidly increase. In addition, I will contend, public acceptance of the needed rising carbon price demands complete transparency and fairness.

It is easy to speak of a planet in peril. It is quite another to level with the public about what is needed, even if the actions are in everybody's long-term interest. It seems they would not dream of being honest and admit that an increased price for fossil fuels is essential to drive us to the world beyond fossil fuels . . .

A higher carbon price is needed to transform consumer and lifestyle choices, to make zero-carbon energy and energy efficiency cheaper than fossil fuels, to spur business investment, innovation and associated economic activity, and to move the nation to the cleaner environment beyond the fossil fuel era. The carbon price will need to be significant, and the public and businesses must understand that it will increase in the future. It should be applied to all fossil fuels — oil, gas and coal — uniformly at the source (the first sale at the mine or port of entry).

I have to say, I agree with every word Hansen wrote, including "and" and "the." Beyond the complexity complaint, what bothers me about cap-and-trade is that it feels like a "hide-the-ball" strategy, which is precisely the kind of strategy that has gotten us into this problem. People need to know that we are in a new era that will require systemic change. But the whole point of a cap-and-trade regime is to disguise any pain and pretend that we aren't even imposing a tax. To my ear, it is like trying to desegregate the University of Mississippi, Ole Miss, in 1962 by letting James Meredith go to night school. That never would have worked. He needed to march right through the front door in broad daylight — and people needed to see him do it. Seeing him do it changed everything. So it is with the carbon tax. The price signal we need on carbon is not just about financial engineering to change economic behaviors. It is also meant to change the perception of the challenge we are facing as a country and a species. It can't be disguised. We have to go from "this is the best we can do" to "this is how we are going to do it best."

Some have argued that a carbon tax would handicap the American economy by making our exports more expensive and less competitive. I disagree. To begin with, there are many things that go into the price of exports, the most important being the value of your currency. Second, several European countries, such as Denmark and Norway, have long had CO_2 taxes. Denmark today is the world's leading exporter of wind turbines and has 4 percent unemployment — in part because the way it has taxed energy has helped to stimulate a whole new clean-tech industry there. Finally, if America were to establish a carbon tax and, say,

China didn't soon follow suit, it would not take long for Congress to impose a "carbon tariff" on Chinese exports made with dirty fuels.

As for gasoline, there are several sensible approaches. One is the price floor I suggested earlier. The energy economist Philip Verleger, Jr., long ago proposed a version of the "Cash for Clunkers" legislation that the U.S. Congress passed in 2009 that offered a subsidy—up to $4,500—for consumers to trade in older gas-guzzling vehicles for newer and better-mileage cars. "The best monument to 9/11 we could erect would be a mountain of crushed gas guzzlers," said Verleger.

Amory Lovins, the renowned environmentalist who cofounded the Rocky Mountain Institute, has proposed a system of "feebates" on automobiles to discourage people from buying gas guzzlers in the first place and to encourage them to always purchase fuel-efficient cars instead. "Within each size class, new-car owners pay a fee or get a rebate—which and how big depend on a car's efficiency—and the fees pay for the rebates," said Lovins. "The increased price spread encourages a buyer to buy an efficient model of the size he or she prefers. The buyer saves money; automakers make more profit; national security improves."

For now, though, the only price signal that seems to have any chance of passing the House and the Senate is cap-and-trade. Neither the president nor any other major politician appears ready to push for a carbon tax or gasoline tax, precisely because it is called a "tax." On June 26, 2009, the House passed the American Clean Energy and Security Act, spearheaded by Congressman Henry Waxman, Democrat of California, and Congressman Edward Markey, Democrat of Massachusetts. The bill would, for the first time, set domestic limits on the carbon emissions that cause global warming, establish a national renewable energy standard for state utilities, set many new energy efficiency regulations, particularly for buildings and appliances, and invest nearly $200 billion in the next fifteen years to make America a leader in ET. At the heart of the 1,300-page bill, though, is the creation of a national cap-and-trade mechanism to reduce greenhouse gas emissions from major emitting sources by 17 percent by 2020 and by 83 percent by 2050, relative to 2005 levels. The bill does that by empowering the government to issue emissions permits, called "allowances," which will each cover one ton of carbon dioxide or its equivalent. Under pressure from manufacturers, though, 85 percent of the allowances in the House bill will be distributed free of charge and only 15 percent will be auctioned in the first year. The idea is that over time, more and more allowances would be auctioned and thereby drive consumers, businesses, and communities to cleaner, but more expensive, energy sources.

Many environmentalists, myself included, were deeply unhappy with the final bill, feeling that it had compromised away so many things to win a majority that no molecule of CO_2 would ever be threatened by it. If it is all we can get, though, I would prefer it over nothing. The best that can be said for it is that the bill for the first time does establish a carbon price signal, albeit a weak and indirect one. That in itself, though, could have important long-term implications. My guess is that once the U.S. government puts a price on carbon emissions, even a weak one, it will usher in a new mind-set among consumers, investors, farmers, innovators, and entrepreneurs that in time will make a big difference—much like the first warnings that cigarettes could cause cancer. The morning after that warning, no one ever looked at smoking the same again. Ditto if this cap-and-trade bill ever becomes law. Henceforth, every person making investment decisions in America—about how homes are built, products are manufactured, or electricity is generated—would look for the least-cost low-carbon option. And weaving carbon emissions into every business decision would drive innovation and deployment of clean technologies to a whole new level and make energy efficiency much more affordable. As of fall 2009, the bill was being debated by the Senate and it was not clear when, if, or in what form it would pass.

I wish such a bill could be combined with an increase in the federal gasoline tax, still 18.4 cents a gallon. In most European countries, the gasoline tax is $4 to $5 a gallon. It is hard to imagine anything that would have a more positive impact on clean transportation than a gas tax hike. Gasoline taxes help reduce consumption, shift people to more fuel-efficient vehicles, shrink the amount of money we send to petrodictators, improve the air quality, strengthen the dollar and the balance of payments, help mitigate global warming, and give citizens a feeling they are contributing something to the war on terrorism.

"This is not just a win-win," said the Johns Hopkins foreign policy expert Michael Mandelbaum. "This is a win-win-win-win-win."

Finally, we built over a hundred nuclear power plants in the quarter century before 1979, when the accident at Three Mile Island brought a halt to all nuclear plant building in America. We need to do the same thing again, and we need to go on a crash program to extend the life of those nuclear plants we've already built. The threat of a nuclear leak, with today's new technology, is much less serious than the threat from climate change. But to build a new nuclear plant costs a minimum of $7 billion today, and would take probably eight years from conception to completion. Most CEOs have about eight years in office, and there are not a lot of utility CEOs who would bet $7 billion—which might be more than half their company's market cap—on one nuclear project. For many utilities in prior decades, the construction of nuclear plants became a "you bet your business" proposition, leading to the demise or economic crippling of utilities like the Long Island Lighting Company and the Public Service Company of Indiana. Therefore, because of the risks of lawsuits and delays, it is probably going to take at a minimum government loan guarantees to relaunch America's nuclear industry.

Read My Lips

The best way to fully appreciate the scope of the challenge we face in shifting to a Clean Energy System is to reread your Machiavelli. My favorite passage in *The Prince* goes like this: "It ought to be remembered that there is nothing more difficult to take in hand, more perilous to conduct, or more uncertain in its success, than to take the lead in introducing a new order of things, because the innovator has for enemies all those who have done well under the old conditions, and lukewarm defenders in those who may do well under the new. This coolness arises partly from fear of the opponents—who have the laws on their side—and partly from the incredulity of men, who do not readily believe in new things until they have had a long experience of them."

This is one more reason we need government to set a price signal to stimulate energy innovation. When you're moving from one system to another, the first step is always painful and more expensive than the status quo—and in a world that is hot, flat, and crowded, it is going to become more painful and more expensive every year that we wait. A price signal would spur the public and businesses to make the transition sooner rather than later. But our leaders have been afraid to lead. As a result, we have really moved only when external forces—like the 1970s Arab oil embargo—have caused enough pain (and long enough gas lines) that our leaders felt they had the political cover to do the right thing and order a doubling of fuel economy for American cars.

Who will tell the people? Yes, I know the experts say that asking the public to pay a tax without a short-term benefit is a political impossibility. Yet in the past, on the big issues like women's suffrage and civil rights, the public was out ahead of the politicians—and politicians can underestimate the public's willingness to do the right thing when it's clear what the right thing is and what the true costs and benefits of the alternatives really are.

It's all about framing. Let's imagine an election campaign in which one candidate favors a gasoline tax and the other opposes it. The anti-tax candidate would say what such candidates have been saying for decades: "There goes my liberal opponent again—demanding yet another tax. He's never seen a tax he didn't like. Now he wants to raise your gasoline taxes or impose some crazy tax on carbon dioxide. God bless our country, the American people have been taxed quite enough, thank you!"

But there is an answer to that, and a true green candidate would not shy away from the argument. He or she would say this: "The American people certainly have been taxed quite enough. I totally agree. Right now they are being taxed by Saudi Arabia, taxed by Venezuela, taxed by Russia, taxed by Iran. If you don't think that a global oil price that is controlled by the world's biggest cartel is not the equivalent of a tax, then you are not paying attention. So let's get one thing straight: My opponent and I are both for a tax. He's for the OPEC tax and I'm for a tax imposed by the U.S. government. Because I have this quaint, old-fashioned view that my taxes should go to the U.S. Treasury, not the Saudi Treasury, not the Iranian Treasury, not the Venezuelan Treasury, and not the Russian Treasury. It's just a little tic I have. I like my tax dollars to go to build my own country's roads, my own country's schools, my own country's hospitals, my own country's infrastructure, my own country's research. My opponent, on the other hand, doesn't care where his energy taxes go.

"Think about this: The price of gasoline on the morning of September 11, 2001, was between $1.60 and $1.80 a gallon in America. Had President Bush imposed a $1-a-gallon 'Patriot Tax' the next day, gasoline would have been close to $3 a gallon. The U.S. government would have gotten the revenue boost, demand for gasoline would have fallen, and demand for more fuel-efficient vehicles would have soared. It would not be out of bounds to speculate that even with the rising demand from China and India over the past seven years, gasoline at the pump in America today would be $3 to $4 a gallon, but we would already have been through the transition. Many more Americans would be driving much more fuel-efficient cars, like Europeans do, so their actual mileage per tank of gasoline would be dramatically better. And the U.S. Treasury rather than the Iranian Treasury would be getting the extra dollar in the gasoline price. But because we did not have the courage to make that transition on September 12, 2001, gasoline on September 12, 2008, was more than $4 a gallon, the fuel economy of American cars was still lousy, and the billions of dollars we've paid out due to the doubling of gasoline prices since 9/11 has all gone to the oil producers, including governments that have drawn a bull's-eye on our backs.

"We need to stop fooling ourselves that by rejecting a gasoline tax increase or a serious price on carbon we are actually saving our citizens money. It is a complete illusion—the epitome of short-sighted thinking. OPEC and the market are imposing their own taxes. America, you are paying a tax today. It is a tax every time you heat your home, power your small business, or drive your car. It is a burden on every transaction you make as a human being. I want to cut your taxes. Read my lips: I want to cut your taxes.

"Sure, I know what you are thinking. You are thinking: If the market is just going to push the price up anyway, wouldn't that be like a tax? Why wouldn't that stimulate innovation? Why add our own on top of that? Because there is a difference between a high price and a fixed, long-term tax on carbon. Sure, markets push the price of coal and oil and gasoline up, but they will also push it down, as we have seen many times. And therefore not enough investors want to make the long-term investment in alternatives, because they are never sure what the floor price of oil, coal, or gasoline will be and when their more expensive renewables will be undercut by these dirty fuels. And consumers worry that if they pay more for efficiency in their homes or cars, it will be money wasted, if the market brings energy prices down, as happened in the Great Recession. Therefore, when you just leave it to the market to set energy prices, you get the worst of all worlds—high prices and low investment in alternatives.

"So what I propose is that we stop leaving ourselves at the mercy of OPEC and the market. Let's offer people something different—a sustainable way of life. That means constructing buildings with the same level of comfort, but which consume much less energy. That means building cars that go just as fast and as far, but consume less energy. That means building factories that make more goods, but consume less power. If we can do that, it would be the equivalent of a gigantic tax cut, wouldn't it? Yes, unlike my opponent who wants to enslave us to OPEC and the fluctuations of the commodity markets, I want to give money back to the hard-working small-business people of America who have to pay a huge energy bill to keep their small stores lit and factories humming. And this would be a permanent tax cut. It is a gift that would keep on giving. Wouldn't that be a good thing? I think so.

"So how do we get there? We need to make that transition to a new energy economy, and that means shaping the market to give us different goods and services. Therefore, I propose that we fix a durable, long-term price on carbon-based fossil fuels. Once we do, every home builder, air-conditioning manufacturer, gasoline refiner, window-maker, and auto-maker will adjust by making more energy-efficient products, because consumers will demand that they do. Yes, the cost of energy per gallon of gasoline or per kilowatt-hour will rise in the short term. But in the long term, your actual bills and expenses will go down because your car, home appliances, and the factory next door will become steadily more energy efficient and give you more productivity, mobility, and comfort for less energy.

"I call that a 'Carbon Tax Cut.' You won't receive the dividend in the first week or month. There has to be a transition—a transition we keep trying to avoid. But once we make it, because the carbon price signal will force everyone to invest in greater efficiency, we will have, in effect, a permanent tax cut: homes that operate on less electricity, cars that operate on less gasoline, and factories that operate on less coal or natural gas. So pay no attention to what my opponent is saying. He is speaking utter nonsense. We have tried his way for thirty-five years now and all that has happened is that we have become more dependent for energy on some of the worst regimes in the world and have not seen a development of renewable energy resources or efficiency at the scale we need.

"Dear voters, every decade we look back and say, 'If only . . . If only we had done the right thing ten years ago.' Well, all we need to do to guarantee that we slowly become a second-rate country is to once again keep postponing doing the right things for another decade. We baby boomers grew up in an age when all we had to do to maintain our way of life was leverage and exploit the abundant natural resources we inherited. Going forward, if we want to maintain our way of life, we will have to leverage and exploit our intellectual resources through innovation and technology. And the only way to do that is to shape the market differently. I am convinced that most Americans will pay more for energy if they are convinced that we have a plan, that it will impose the burdens fairly across the whole country, and that when it is over our per gallon or per kilowatt costs may be higher but our overall energy bills will be lower. In addition, we will be stronger, healthier, more secure, and more innovative as a nation. Yes, there will have to be a transition where we will all have to pay more for a while. There is no avoiding that. But the sooner we make that transition, the sooner we will enjoy the tax cut. The longer we wait, the more we will be subject to the vagaries of the market and the more others will leap ahead of us in the next great global industry."

If you can't win an election in America with that argument, then we really are lost.

FOURTEEN

If It Isn't Boring, It Isn't Green

So here's a little news quiz:

Which city in Pennsylvania has a trade surplus with China, Mexico, and Brazil?
ANSWER: Erie.

How could an old-line, blue-collar manufacturing city like Erie have a trade surplus with China, Mexico, and Brazil?
ANSWER: One company, GE Transportation.

Well, what does GE Transportation make in Erie that is so exportable?
ANSWER: It makes big ol' locomotives—those huge industrial-size diesel engines that pull long trains!

So how did GE Transportation, located in the former heartland of American manufacturing, now the heartland of America's rust belt, become the most profitable maker of locomotives in the world?
ANSWER: A combination of great engineering by a traditional American company in a traditional American town, a global market looking for cleaner locomotives, and a U.S. government that demanded higher and higher standards. Those high standards helped to drive the innovation of a big train engine that spewed out less pollution, while also increasing fuel economy and thereby lowering CO_2 emissions in the bargain. And it is that interaction between government regulators and corporate man-

agers and engineers—that dull, gray, boring interaction about standards—that is essential on a grand scale if we are going to spur the innovation we need to have a real green revolution.

Sure, everyone wants to be an eco-star. Knowledgeable eco-stars like Al Gore are critical; they draw attention and passion to an issue. But they make a difference only if they are followed up by "revolutionary bureaucrats"—men and women who write emissions and efficiency standards, and who, with a flick of a pen, can change how much electricity fifty million air conditioners consume or how much diesel a thousand locomotives guzzle in one year. That's revolutionary.

When it comes to implementing a green revolution, the more boring the work, the more revolutionary its impact. If it isn't boring, it isn't green. I call this the "*Naked Gun 2½* rule," after the brilliant but wacky movie by that title, starring Leslie Nielsen. Nielsen plays Lieutenant Frank Drebin, a bumbling police detective who uncovers a plot to sabotage America's energy policy. The movie opens at a dinner being given by President George Herbert Walker Bush, and in attendance at the White House are the leaders of the American energy industry: the representatives of the Society of Petroleum Industry Leaders (SPIL), the Society for More Coal Energy (SMOKE), and the Key Atomic Benefits Office of Mankind nuclear group (KABOOM). The president has decided to base U.S. energy policy on whatever a top independent expert, Dr. Albert S. Meinheimer, recommends. Solar energy is also in the running and coming on strong. The oil, coal, and nuclear industries plot to kidnap Dr. Meinheimer and replace him with a stooge who will recommend oil, coal, and nuclear power—not solar power—for America's future. Nielsen exposes the plot and confronts the head of the oil industry, telling him: "You are part of a dying breed, like people who can name all fifty states." Dr. Meinheimer is saved, and in the end he recommends to President Bush a policy based on "energy efficiency and clean renewable energy sources." (The Natural Resources Defense Council was actually an adviser on the film!)

My favorite scene comes at the conclusion. It's a press conference at the National Press Club, and Dr. Meinheimer is onstage explaining the intricacies of the renewable energy policy he is recommending. He is pointing to various charts, graphs, and statistics to buttress his analysis—and the entire audience and all the waiters have fallen dead asleep and are snoring away.

If it isn't boring, it isn't green . . .

Regulations and standards matter—even if they do put you to sleep. While it is absolutely necessary that we impose price signals in order to move the clean power technologies we already have down their learning curves, and in order to stimulate the market to search for new ways to give us abundant, clean, reliable, and cheap electrons to feed an Energy Internet of smart grids, smart homes, and smart cars, price signals alone are not sufficient. And the next great clean power breakthroughs could take years to deploy.

That is why we also need breakthroughs in energy efficiency and the efficient use of natural resources, so we can get more growth, more mobility, more heat, more light, and more power from fewer energy and natural resource inputs right away. That will enable us to reduce CO_2 emissions *now*, even before we have abundant, clean, reliable, and cheap electrons. And that will enable us to use fewer clean electrons as they do become available.

That is why, in a nutshell, the right energy policy today really comes down to this: We need to nurture all the cost-effective energy efficiency we can get right now—because that is always cheaper than generating new electrons. And, at the same time, we need to nurture the cheapest emissions-free electrons to fill in the rest of our energy needs, so we can grow in the cleanest way possible.

As the last chapter focused on the role price signals can play in developing such a policy mix, this chapter will focus on how we can use these standards and regulations to stimulate deployment and innovation of clean electrons; to improve energy efficiency in the homes, appliances, buildings, vehicles, lights, and heating and cooling systems that would make up the smart grid; and to reshape how electric utilities relate to their customers, so utilities can become optimizers of the entire Energy Internet rather than just operators of cheap, all-you-can-eat electron buffets.

When it comes to the role of regulation in stimulating energy efficiency innovation, there is no better example than GE Transportation, which employs 5,100 people, many of them engineers, in its headquarters in Erie and in another plant in nearby Grove City. GE Transportation's president and CEO, John Dineen, describes his locomotive factory as a "technology campus," because "it looks like a hundred-year-old industrial site, but inside those hundred-year-old buildings are world-class engineers working on the next generation's technologies. People look at our big factory and they mistake it for a traditional manufacturing business, when what really drives this business is technology."

Hourly workers at GE Transportation make almost double the average wage in their respective cities—thanks largely to the export of the 240,000-plus-pound, $4 million Evolution Series diesel locomotive, or EVO for short. GE Transportation will have exported about three hundred of them to China by the end of 2009 and also sells them to railroad companies worldwide, including in Mexico, Brazil, Australia, and Kazakhstan. You'd think one thing that a railroad-based country like China would be making is its own locomotives, and you would be right. China does make its own locomotives, thousands of them, and they are much cheaper than GE's, but it turns out that GE's are the most energy efficient in the world, with the lowest emissions of CO_2, traditional soot particles, and nitrogen oxide, and they get the best fuel mileage per ton pulled. That's why China buys them. The EVO's new twelve-cylinder engine produces the same horsepower as its sixteen-cylinder predecessor. Best of all is that these locomotives are reliable. "They don't stop on the tracks," says Dineen.

One of the key factors driving GE Transportation to design the EVO the way it did was the U.S. Environmental Protection Agency's Tier II emissions standards for locomotives and other transportation vehicles. The new standards were issued in 2004 and required big reductions in the emissions of both nitrogen oxide and particulates. GE had no choice but to meet the new baselines, but the big question was how. Whenever a company making locomotives faces a standards issue like this, it can choose to trade off different variables. It can make its engine cleaner, for instance, at the expense of miles per gallon or miles per hour or reliability. GE's chairman, Jeffrey Immelt, decided that instead of just tweaking the company's existing locomotive engine, which met the Tier I standard, so that it could meet Tier II, they would simply start over.

"We knew we had to lower emissions," recalled Dineen. "If we wanted, we [also] knew we could trade things off on fuel efficiency and reliability, but we made a bet instead to advance all three through technology by redoing the whole engine . . . When you want to move all the variables in the right direction at the same time, you need to start with a clean blackboard. We went to a larger, more robust engine that could handle higher firing pressures in the cylinders, with new materials, new designs, and new pistons. We went for better reliability, lower emissions, *and* more miles per gallon—all at the same time." Yes, ultimately it was GE's engineers who figured out how to do this, and GE influenced the EPA on where to strike the balance. But the spark was definitely the 2004 Tier II emissions standard, said Dineen. "The EPA can be credited with instigating the need to drive new technologies into these locomotives."

Carbon emissions are directly correlated to a diesel locomotive's miles per gallon; as mpg goes up, emissions go down. So when GE decided to build a new engine that not only met the new Tier II EPA standards for nitrogen oxide, but would also get better mileage per ton pulled, it was able to reduce both the nitrogen oxide emissions of the EVO and its CO_2 emissions.

Back in 2004, this latter improvement seemed like just a nice added touch. CO_2 reductions were not part of the EPA Tier II agenda. But in the past two years, carbon emissions, especially for a country like China, became a huge issue, and China's government-owned railroads and a lot of other customers suddenly became eager to buy a locomotive that got better fuel efficiency and produced lower nitrogen oxide pollution *and lower CO_2 emissions*. "We were not sure the Chinese would be interested in lower emissions, but they are," said Dineen. Actually, given the fact that China in 2008 overtook the United States as the world's leading carbon emitter, with all the opprobrium that entails, it is not surprising that big state-owned Chinese companies would be eager to improve their emissions in a cost-effective way. The key, though, was to make lower emissions almost a free add-on that China's railroad companies could afford. When CO_2 emission reductions come through reductions in fuel consumption, said Dineen, "we see very quick adoption rates, not only in the U.S. market but in international markets that do not have government mandates."

The carbon emissions issue, added Dineen, "came up on us faster than we ever could have imagined . . . We got out in front of it, because of our own regulations. Regulations pushed us out there, we were early, and by the time others were interested, we had an advantage in this area."

The new EVO was 5 percent more fuel efficient than its predecessor. What's 5 percent? Over the twenty-year life cycle of the locomotive, it saves approximately 300,000 gallons of diesel fuel and the corresponding carbon emissions. And when one railroad buys hundreds of these loco-motives at a time, that can add up to a lot of fuel and carbon saved.

"Now we're already deep into discussions about Tier III and IV stan-dards," said Dineen. "The more carbon gets taxed, and fuel prices increase, the more it will push us to become more fuel efficient. GE and the EPA have recognized the lesson from Tier II and are looking for technology solutions that reduce traditional pollutants like nitrogen oxide, while improving fuel efficiency and carbon emissions. And, by the way, the higher the standards, and the more technology necessary to achieve them, the smarter the engineers we need to hire."

Indeed, GE Transportation has a huge appetite for talented engi-neers, but the Erie school system was struggling to keep up in its ability to teach math and science. So the GE Foundation put $15 million into improving the math and science programs in the local schools. It is not that GE is hiring high school grads from Erie to be its engineers, but if it wants to attract quality engineers to Erie and keep them there, it needs to help maintain a quality school system.

"This is western Pennsylvania," said Dineen. "This is not Silicon Val-ley. I spend a lot of time with the local government trying to get the lead-ers to recognize that our competitive advantage is rooted in technology, and not low-cost welding. So we are challenging this town to make sure we are constantly improving math and science education."

In short, companies like to locate where the engineers are the best and most plentiful and where the standards are constantly pushing them higher. Everything is connected: Higher climate and emissions stan-dards demand smarter products, smarter products demand smarter work-ers, and smarter workers like to live in clean environments with good schools, so they end up demanding still higher standards. If America wants to thrive in the Energy-Climate Era, the federal, state, and local governments all need to be driving that virtuous circle all the time.

Probably the most oft-cited theory about the relationship between environmental regulation and innovation is the Porter hypothesis, first expounded by the Harvard Business School professor Michael Porter in 1991. He asserted that "appropriately planned environmental regulations will stimulate technological innovation, leading to reduc-tions in expenses and improvements in quality. As a result, domestic businesses may attain a superior competitive position in the international marketplace, and industrial productivity may improve as well."

Another way of putting it, Porter explained to me, is that pollution is simply waste: wasted resources, wasted energy, wasted materials. Companies that eliminate such waste will be using their capital, technology, and raw materials more productively to generate maximum value and, therefore, will become more competitive. So, properly crafted environmental regulations give a kind of two-for-one kick—they can improve both the environment *and* the competitiveness of a firm and a nation.

Once regulations and standards are in place for energy efficiency, the message to everyone is: "Get your lawyers and lobbyists off the case and your engineers on the case." That point is well illustrated by the story of the Bush administration and the stunt it tried to pull concerning air conditioner efficiency standards. The Clinton administration, late in its second term, ordered that the air conditioner energy-efficiency standard be raised from SEER 10 to SEER 13, which, once implemented, constituted about a 30 percent improvement: more cooling for less electricity. (SEER stands for "seasonal energy efficiency ratio," which is defined as the total cooling output in British thermal units—BTUs—provided by an air conditioner during its normal annual usage period divided by its total energy input, in watt-hours, during the same period.)

But as Andrew Leonard, the always incisive technology columnist at Salon.com, wrote in a September 17, 2007, essay, citing research by the UCLA law professor Ann Carlson, SEER was turned into a political football: Shortly after the Bush administration took office, it decided to roll the standard back to SEER 12, only about a 20 percent improvement. The Bush team made this decision despite the position of its own Environmental Protection Agency that the proposed rollback was based on an analysis that both overstated the costs to manufacturers of the SEER 13 standard and underestimated the savings it would bring.

The Natural Resources Defense Council and ten states sued to reverse the Bush administration's action and won. In 2004, the U.S. Court of Appeals for the Second Circuit directed the U.S. Department of Energy to reinstate the SEER 13 standard for central air conditioners, and on January 1, 2007, about six years later, the original standard sought by the Clinton team came into force.

"What's the difference between a 20 percent and a 30 percent air conditioner energy-efficiency standard?" Salon's Leonard asked. "Only about twelve 400-megawatt power plants."

Steven Nadel, executive director of the American Council for an Energy-Efficient Economy, which had worked hard for the SEER 13 standard during the Clinton years, issued a statement after the appeals court decision elaborating on its impact: "This important ruling will save consumers money, reduce the risk of blackouts, and cut emissions of air pollutants and greenhouse gases . . . ACEEE analysis shows that American consumers will save 250 billion kilowatt hours and $21 billion in electricity bills through 2030. Over the same period, utilities will avoid building 20,000 megawatts of peak power capacity, saving billions of dollars in capital costs and reducing future electric rates. The energy saved will prevent the emission of over 50 million metric tons of carbon—the equivalent of taking 34 million cars off the road for one year."

I am sure that some in the air-conditioning industry lobbied heavily against the increased efficiency standards, but the benefits to the nation and to the atmosphere were so obviously great, at a time of rising energy prices, that it is a travesty President Bush fiddled with this.

I cite this case because it underscores how just a tiny shift in a regulation, one or two notches, can have a huge impact on energy generation, efficiency, and greenhouse gas emissions when scaled over a whole economy. I also cite it to highlight one of the most common shenanigans used in the energy debates—how those who oppose improving efficiency standards very often overstate the costs of the change and underestimate the benefits. This was artfully documented by Roland Hwang of the Natural Resources Defense Council and Matt Peak of CALSTART (which works on clean transportation solutions) in their April 2006 study on the relationship between regulation and innovation.

They asked a very simple but critical question: Before certain environmental regulations were imposed by the state of California on the auto industry, what did the industries say about those regulations—and how hard they would be to meet—and what, in the end, was the actual impact of those regulations on both prices and innovation? What Hwang and Peak found was that the target industries dramatically and consistently overestimated the costs that the regulations would impose on them and dramatically underestimated the innovations they would inspire.

In the mid-1970s, automakers strongly opposed the introduction of catalytic converters to reduce the toxicity of engine emissions. "Automobile executives claimed the regulations were not technically feasible and would cause severe economic hardship for their industry," noted Hwang and Peak.

For instance, during a 1972 congressional testimony, General Motors vice president Earnest Starkman declared that if automakers were forced to introduce catalytic converters on 1975 models, "It is conceivable that complete stoppage of the entire production could occur, with the obvious tremendous loss to the company, shareholders, employees, suppliers, and communities." Ford president Lee Iacocca claimed that "If the U.S. Environmental Protection Agency does not suspend the catalytic converter rule, it will cause Ford to shut down and would result in: (1) reduction of gross national product by $17 billion; (2) increased unemployment of 800,000; and (3) decreased tax receipts of $5 billion at all levels of government so that some local governments would become insolvent." Despite these claims, California implemented the regulations . . . requiring the first catalytic converters in 1975 and the first 3-way catalytic converters in 1977 . . . Chrysler claimed it would cost $1,300 more [per car] to comply with the proposed 1975 federal pollution standards. In today's dollars, this is equivalent to $2,770. Ford estimated that the cost of compliance for a Pinto would be $1,000 (equal to $2,130 in 2004 dollars.) However, a 1972 report by the White House Science Office estimated the cost would be $755 (equal to about $1,600 in 2004 dollars). The actual cost to comply with the standard, which was delayed until 1981, is estimated to have been $875 to $1,350 in 2002 dollars.

Meanwhile, the reduction in air pollution was enormous, the sky did not fall, and the U.S. economy did not, as predicted, grind to a halt.

Hwang and Peak show the same pattern over and over again with other environmental regulations: Industry, and often even regulators, vastly overestimate the costs to the economy of meeting the higher standards. To some degree, this is no doubt intentional, but to some degree, the authors note, it is because the industry and regulators underestimate the role of "unanticipated innovation."

A review of the history of automotive regulation, they write,

indicates that manufacturers very often utilize technologies and implement compliance paths different from initial predictions, resulting in lower than predicted costs. A clear theme also emerges from the study of the history of air pollution regulation, that a strong regulation spurs innovation. A strong regulation eliminates regulatory uncertainty and provides a powerful competitive incentive for automakers and their suppliers to innovate to sometimes radically reduce costs.

Clear price signals and clear regulations always create an environment much more conducive to innovation.

For example, note Hwang and Peak, before 1969 it was commonly thought that the only way to reduce automobile pollution was by using end-of-pipe technology, such as catalytic converters. "Yet, as California emission standards came into effect, influenced national policy, and culminated nationally in the 90 percent reduction in auto emissions as required by the Federal Clean Air Act of 1970, one automobile manufacturer, Honda, pursued alternative methods of pollution reduction," the authors note.

The company's founder, Soichiro Honda, instructed his engineers to "try to clean up the exhaust gases inside the engine itself, without relying on catalytic converters." These engineers proceeded by combining existing technologies in a new way to achieve a cleaner burn. Their efforts resulted in the "Compound Vortex Controlled Combustion" (CVCC) engine that was designed with a small "pre-burn" chamber upstream of the cylinders. Honda discovered that by pre-burning the gasoline/air mixture, more impurities were removed before they reached the tailpipe. This technology allowed Honda to meet the 1970s Clean Air Act standards without the use of catalytic converters. It also proved beneficial to Honda as Detroit manufacturers, who initially scoffed at Honda's accomplishments, each licensed the technology from Honda in 1973. The implementation of CVCC technology on the Honda Civic in the 1970s disproved Detroit's claim that meeting emissions and fuel economy standards simultaneously was impossible, as the EPA ranked the Civic first in fuel economy among all models.

George W. Bush and his presidential administration claimed that they were protecting American companies by not imposing tougher efficiency standards, such as those proposed for more efficient cooling by air conditioners or better mileage performance by American cars. It was an understandable reflex from an administration that considered itself business friendly. It was also dumb. When you are the most innovative country, with the best research universities, the best national laboratories, and the highest technological base, you should want higher standards—*because your companies can meet them while weaker ones cannot.* Why would an American air conditioner company lobby to weaken our standards, which would only enable lower-efficiency, lower-cost Chinese air conditioners to better compete in America?

But that reflex to fight standards runs so deep, particularly among industrial elites, that they lose sight of the larger battle, says the MIT professor Kenneth Oye, an expert on the politics of regulation and innovation. "Typically," Oye explained, "firms often fail to recognize the ways that more stringent regulations on energy efficiency and fuel standards actually benefit them—and therefore they don't mobilize to change policies to provide them with an advantage. Exxon Mobil would be the biggest beneficiary from really high clean fuel standards, if most other oil companies got knocked out because they didn't have the technology or innovative skills to meet them. But companies just get used to fighting regulations—instead of seeing them as a way to knock out their competition. They are used to seeing regulations only in terms of the costs imposed on their plants, not in terms of the differential effects that regulations can have in terms of your costs, and the quality of your technology, relative to your competitors."

It is impossible to stress how important improving energy efficiency is and how great an impact it can have on mitigating climate change and reducing our energy bills—now. It is truly "the first fuel"—the energy source that costs the least to install, has no emissions, is in infinite supply, and can be generated immediately with just the flick of a finger—also known as turning off the lights. As Dan Reicher, the top energy expert at Google.org, likes to say of energy efficiency: "This is low-hanging fruit that keeps growing back." What he means is that the minute industry meets one efficiency standard, the government can set another one, just a little bit higher. "We have to hit efficiency harder than ever," added Mike Davis, the Pacific Northwest National Laboratory scientist. "We need another thirty to fifty years to solve the supply problems for clean electrons, but on the demand side we can get way down the field right now."

Energy efficiency was always the quickest, cheapest, most effective way to create clean power, because the best form of power is the power that doesn't have to be generated at all because you eliminated demand for it. But when flat meets crowded, that becomes even more true. Why? Because anything we want to build by way of expanding clean power generation—wind turbines, solar panels, geothermal systems, solar thermal, or nuclear—is getting more expensive by the day. Every raw material input for every system—from the steel to make the towers for wind turbines, to the composite materials to make the blades, to the silicon for the solar panels, to the special equipment for nuclear plants or new transmission lines—is now in shortage, so there are long backlogs. Even if you can get the materials, the big contracting firms are often overbooked. And prices for everything are going up. So saving electrons in one place so that you can use them in another, without having to generate additional ones, becomes more valuable every day.

In a comprehensive 2009 report on energy efficiency entitled "Unlocking Energy Efficiency in the U.S. Economy," the McKinsey consulting firm concluded that if America truly focused on improving energy efficiency it could dramatically reduce existing carbon emissions and save the American public and businesses substantial sums of money at the same time. For instance, McKinsey found that electricity consumption in residential buildings in the United States in 2020 could be reduced by more than a third if compact fluorescent lightbulbs were adopted, along with higher efficiency standards for refrigerators, water heaters, kitchen appliances, windows, and room insulation. "Energy efficiency," wrote McKinsey, "offers a vast, low-cost energy resource for the U.S. economy—but only if the nation can craft a comprehensive and innovative approach to unlock it. Significant and persistent barriers will need to be addressed at multiple levels to stimulate demand for energy efficiency and manage its delivery across more than 100 million buildings and literally billions of devices. If executed at scale, a holistic approach would yield gross energy savings worth more than $1.2 trillion, well above the $520 billion needed through 2020 for upfront investment in efficiency measures (not including program costs). Such a program is estimated to reduce end-use energy consumption in 2020 by 9.1 quadrillion BTUs, roughly 23 percent of projected demand, potentially abating up to 1.1 gigatons of greenhouse gases annually." In a 2008 study on the same subject, McKinsey concluded that the amount of energy that could be saved from a comprehensive energy efficiency strategy would be equivalent to the production from 110 new coal-fired 600-megawatt power plants. Some experts argue that these statistics are overstated, but, even if they are, directionally they are right. We could accomplish so much just by setting higher standards for how homes are sealed to hold heat and cooling and for how much energy air conditioners and refrigerators can consume—and, yes, just by turning off the lights when we don't need them in our homes and offices. "If we do enough to scale energy efficiency, the money we save would be enough to pay to clean up—to decarbonize—the remaining supply of electrons and fuels so we could power our economy in a way that is consistent with containing climate change," said Rick Duke, director for the Center for Market Innovation at the Natural Resources Defense Council. We are likely going to need the next thirty to fifty years to scale renewable energy and carbon capture and storage technologies to a point where they can provide enough clean, reasonably priced electrons to power our entire economy. We can fill that gap in one of two ways. We could create "an efficiency surge," said Duke, that could actually soak up all the growth in energy demand for the next two decades—without adding a single molecule of carbon—or we will likely have to resort to filling that gap with more energy from dirty fuels.

We *know* this works. After the 1973–74 oil price shock, California began instituting the highest efficiency standards of any state in the country for buildings and appliances, like refrigerators and air conditioners. The net result: Per capita electricity consumption in California has stayed almost flat for the past thirty years, even though the state's economy has vastly expanded. The per capita electricity consumption in the rest of the country during this same period is up 50 percent, according to a study by NRDC. If California's energy use had grown at the same rate as that of the rest of America's, says NRDC, about 25,000 additional megawatts' worth of new generating stations would have been needed—roughly equivalent to fifty large 500-megawatt power plants.

A 2005 study by the Stanford University scholar Walter Reid and professional staff from the São Paulo, Brazil, Department of the Environment—commissioned by the William and Flora Hewlett Foundation—found that smart energy efficiency policies in California and São Paulo have both reduced the per capita emissions of greenhouse gas pollution over the last two decades and profited consumers.

According to the December 1, 2005, summary by the Hewlett Foundation, each Californian produces less than half the greenhouse-gas emissions as his or her fellow American. This is due in large part to state policies encouraging the use of natural gas and renewable resources over coal, as well as the aggressive promotion of energy efficiency. The state's per capita emissions have dropped nearly one-third since 1975, while the nation's per capita emissions have stayed flat. The study notes that each Californian typically saved about $1,000 per year between 1975 and 1995 [on electricity bills], just through efficiency standards for buildings and appliances. Energy efficiency has helped the economy grow an extra 3 percent—a $31 billion gain—compared to business as usual. The job growth created by the energy-efficiency industry will generate an $8 billion payroll over the next twelve years.

What this implies, then, is if one wants to have an impact on the environment, the first and most important thing one can do is learn the rules around energy efficiency and emissions and how they get made. That is what the fossil fuel giants do. They know the difference between a chat room and cloakroom. They don't waste a lot of time play-lobbying in online chat rooms; they focus on twisting real arms in real cloakrooms adjacent to the halls of Congress or in state legislature hallways or in regulatory boardrooms so as to influence who writes the rules—because the people who write the rules define how the game is played and wind up getting the gold.

One of my favorite stories in this regard is told by Frances Beinecke, the president of NRDC, about the "famous" bureaucrat Noah Horowitz:

One of our true rock stars at NRDC is a tireless engineer by the name of Noah Horowitz, who works in our San Francisco office. Not many people know his name. But Noah's fingerprints are everywhere. Take the humble vending machine. A few years ago, Noah noticed that they were popping up in more and more places: supermarkets, gas stations, hospitals, schools, even playgrounds. As it turns out, there is now one soda machine for every hundred Americans. Something like three million of them out there humming away, twenty-four hours a day, seven days a week. What's more, these things were using up to ten times more energy than the average household refrigerator. Not just to cool the soda, but also to light up the signs and run the change maker. Mainly, it never occurred to anybody to try and build them better. Noah went to the beverage companies. But they weren't interested in talking to some bearded environmentalist. And besides, they weren't paying the bills for these machines. That burden falls on shopowners, school boards, and others whose walls they are plugged into. So that's who Noah went to see. He said, "Why don't we work together on this?" They said yes. And that got the big soda companies' attention. They agreed to meet and to start looking for solutions. Things like more efficient compressors and fans and improved lighting. They also rethought some of the simplest things, like not having outdoor machines running all night in the middle of winter. The result was new machines that use half the energy of the old ones. Once Coke and Pepsi finish phasing in the new designs, we expect to save five *billion* kilowatt-hours a year. That's enough to run the refrigerators in ten million homes.

He also worked with manufacturers to tighten performance standards for computer monitors. By 2010, EPA estimates this agreement will save $14 *billion* in electricity costs, and keep almost forty billion pounds of carbon dioxide out of the sky. Noah Horowitz is one of my personal heroes.

It's the Design, Stupid

So one day a few years back your boss calls you and says, "Have I got a deal for you! We're deciding where to build our next wafer fabrication facility for producing leading-edge microprocessors. China, Taiwan, and Singapore have all offered tempting subsidies and tax breaks if we build it in one of their countries. But we'd like to stay here in the Dallas area, near our microchip design center and other facilities. Wherever this building goes, though, you—the building team—need to erect the new plant in 2005 for $180 million less than we built its predecessor for in 1998."

"Oh, yeah, right," you say. "Build a new building for $180 million less than its predecessor cost seven years earlier. Who does that?"

Sounds crazy, but that is exactly the challenge that the leadership of Texas Instruments laid down to its building team in the early 2000s, and here's what's really crazy: The building team went and did it. And here's what's even crazier: The cost-saving strategy the building team adopted was to make the building as green and as energy efficient as possible—and that is how they hit their target. Designing green *was how they saved money*, and therein lies an important tale.

Besides making homes and cars more energy efficient, there is a mother lode of energy efficiency waiting to be exploited in commercial buildings through building design—illustrated by the Texas Instruments wafer factory in Richardson, Texas. And the key to it is the realization that a properly designed energy-efficient building can not only be cheaper to operate, it can be cheaper to build than a conventional building. Buildings use roughly 40 percent of the total energy consumed in the United States and 70 percent of total electricity. When the general public comes to believe that green is the cheapest way to *build and operate*, the revolution is really under way.

I visited the new TI wafer factory in 2006 while making a documentary on energy for the Discovery Times channel. (By the way, what is a wafer? According to the technology dictionary Webopedia.com, it is a thin, round slice of semiconductor material, usually silicon, from which microchips are made. The silicon is processed into large cylindrical ingots, sliced into ultrathin wafers, and then implanted with transistors before being cut into smaller semiconductor chips.) Wafer factories always had a minimum of three floors, because of the complicated cooling systems and support equipment that had to surround the manufacturing line. The TI design team came up with a way to build the 1.1.-million-square-foot Richardson factory with just two floors—a huge savings in square footage and all the mass and energy needed to support it. TI also consulted with Amory Lovins and the green building experts at the Rocky Mountain Institute to design other parts of the plant in a way that would lower its resource consumption, a savings that, over the life of the factory, can exceed construction outlays. Together, TI engineers and the RMI team designed big water pipes and air-conditioning ducts with fewer elbows, which reduced friction loss and let them use smaller, energy-saving pumps. To bring down cooling costs in sun-baked Texas, engineers designed a plastic membrane that reflects 85 percent of the sun's radiation from the roof. In addition, the windows in the administrative wing were designed with special shelves that reflect light deep into room interiors, reducing the need for artificial lighting. Recycled water was used to run cooling equipment and irrigate outdoor landscaping—whose environmental impact the designers minimized by using native plants. These moves, together with innovations in how air is circulated, cooled, and recovered naturally, reduced total heat so much that TI was able to get by with one less huge industrial air conditioner than would normally have been required.

"We needed seven chillers instead of eight," said Paul Westbrook, who oversees sustainable design and development for TI's worldwide building team and helped turn TI leaders on to green building by taking them to tour his solar home. "Those chillers are about 1,600 tons each and cost about $1 million each to buy and install." Green building is not necessarily about producing your own power with windmills and solar panels, he added; "it's about addressing the consumption side with really creative design and engineering to eliminate waste and reduce energy usage. It's the next industrial revolution. Green building added some cost, but overall, we built a green building for 30 percent less per square foot than our previous facility six miles away."

The key to pulling that off, explained Westbrook, was making the TI factory in Richardson "the Prius of wafer factories." How so? "We didn't just take the old design and try to tweak it to save a little money here and there. We took out a blank piece of paper, we looked at how everything interacted with everything else, and we came up with a whole new design that turned out to be not only cheaper to build but cheaper to operate."

The main lesson of this, said Westbrook, is that if you rethink every process and all the connections between each process—for instance, how waste heat from one system can be used to power another, rather than just cooled with another air conditioner, or the way the Prius used braking to generate electricity to charge the batteries—you can actually take two goals that everyone thought had to be in opposition (saving money and building and operating green) and accomplish them together.

It is not easy, though. You need to put a lot more thought into the original design. You have to think of a house or building not just as walls, windows, and floors, with lights, heating, and cooling, but as a system of systems, and then rethink how they all interact. Historically, the heating and air-conditioning never talked to the windows. The windows never talked to the lighting. The lighting never talked to the doorways. So everything was usually on all the time and nothing talked to anything, let alone to the grid or to the energy market. With an intelligent building, with occupancy sensors in every room, you could have the auditorium, classroom, or office heated and lit only when it is in use. But more than that, smart windows can let in more light and heat when it is cold and dark and keep out more when it is hot and sunny, and these windows can be constantly talking to both the overhead lights and the heating and air-conditioning systems. Solar walls can be used to light up the school or power the battery of the school bus. When you start to think of a building as system of systems, not a block of bricks, all kinds of things become possible. And just imagine all these highly efficient smart buildings being integrated into an intelligent Energy Internet, where each building's flexibility is used to serve the needs of other buildings, not just its own.

Although completed by 2006, the TI factory has been delayed from going into operation by a downturn in the chip business. But the building is ready to go and all the systems have tested out. The tests indicated that when it is fully humming "we should see about $1 million a year in utility savings in the first year and around $4 million a year in lower utility bills when fully running," given current electricity prices, Westbrook said. That is about a 20 percent savings on electricity and a 35 percent savings on water from its predecessor, he added. "When we do start production, it will ramp up over a number of years—and our savings will ramp up with it."

Texas Instruments was proud "to prove you can [be] green and energy-sensitive and reduce costs and increase profits," Shaunna Black, TI's vice president for worldwide facilities, said to me back in 2006, when the building was just being finished. "Amazing things happen when people claim responsibility for creating the impossible."

That is the challenge we need to lay down across America—taking responsibility for creating the impossible. If I could wave a magic wand and impose one regulation to hasten achieving that goal, it would be a law requiring every first-year drafting, engineering, and architectural student to take a course in LEED (Leadership in Energy and Environmental Design) building and system design. The LEED Green Building Rating System encourages the adoption of sustainable green building practices by creating a recognized benchmark for the design, construction, and operation of high-performance green buildings. LEED, which was spearheaded in the mid-1990s by Rob Watson, the eco-consultant, is managed today by the U.S. Green Building Council. It gives out basic, silver, gold, and platinum certifications to buildings based on five criteria— sustainable site development, water savings, energy efficiency, materials selection, and indoor environmental quality. The TI facility in Richard-son is LEED Silver.

LEED is a perfect example of an energy/environmental standard that did not come from the government down, but from society up, as society has come to value more sustainable workplaces. The standard has spread virally, so far, so fast, and so compellingly that studies now show that oc-cupancy, rental rates, and sale prices are higher in LEED-certified build-ings than in conventional ones.

There is nothing more important for America's energy future than making every structure more energy efficient and every new building net-zero—a building that generates as much energy as it consumes. Nearly half the energy in America goes to buildings. Forty percent goes into building operations, such as heating, cooling, lighting, and power-ing appliances, and another 12 percent goes into making the cement, steel, glass, aluminum, drywall, and bricks. "If we could make the built environment energy net-zero," said Marc Porat, chairman of Serious Materials, "everything we do on the supply side would become that much easier. A negawatt is always cheaper than a megawatt. A watt saved is always cheaper than a watt produced." There is simply no way we ad-dress the five big problems ailing the world today without moving all new buildings to net-zero as fast as we can. And we now have the building sci-ence to do that—design breakthroughs that we did not have available as recently as three years ago.

"We now have the know-how to ensure that new buildings are de-signed and built to need two-thirds less energy, thanks to good designs and good materials, from the get-go," said Porat, who also founded ZETA Communities, which builds net-zero homes, and CalStar Products, which sells bricks produced with 85 percent less energy and CO_2 emis-sion than conventional bricks. "Once you have reduced the demand for electrons by two-thirds, then you can supply the rest with solar, wind, passive lighting, and geothermal. Ideally, in the future, buildings will be net-plus and actually make more electrons than they use, and the surplus will go into their electric cars."

We also need to attack existing buildings. The technology is available right now that, at a reasonable cost, can reduce energy demand in the av-erage existing building by 50 percent, by adding insulation, high effi-ciency windows and doors, efficient heating and cooling, new lighting (preferably LED), and new appliances, said Porat. This process is called "deep energy retrofitting" and a whole new industry is now emerging around this. "If we just do six million homes a year—there are 126 million homes in America—then we could transform all of America's homes in twenty years," said Porat. "At an average cost of $20,000 a home, that would make it a $120 billion a year industry employing over one million people. Then we do the same for offices, schools, and hospitals." Up to now, there has been too much emphasis on inventing the whiz-bang renewable breakthrough and too little on how to make windows that simply keep more of the heat or cooling in your home. There is no way that we can produce clean, renewable energy as fast or as inexpensively as we can reduce the dirty and wasted energy consumed by our built environment.

But we cannot just depend on volunteerism to make this happen. Landlords chronically underinvest in energy-efficient designs, building construction, and appliances, because their tenants pay the electric bills. When the tenant pays, the landlord doesn't care about forward operating costs, so he will minimize all upfront capital expenditures. When the landlord pays, the tenants don't care about efficiency and will not look to optimize and minimize ongoing energy consumption. And often, people just don't know that this lightbulb or that dishwasher is better than another in terms of energy efficiency, so they will not make the right choices, even if they are economically incentivized to care. That is why you want the government to step in and guide the marketplace.

This can be done in many ways, including outlawing certain kinds of energy-greedy lightbulbs or mandating performance standards for cars, buildings, and appliances—so people don't have any choice but to be energy efficient. As the Stanford climatologist Stephen Schneider put it in an interview with Katherine Ellison, on Salon.com (July 2, 2007): "Volunteerism doesn't work. I've said this about 85,000 times. It's about as effective as voluntary speed limits. No cops, no judges: road carnage. No rules, no fines: greenhouse gases. We're going to triple or quadruple the CO_2 in the atmosphere with no policy."

The European Union is already on the case, and America needs to leapfrog the EU. In 2009, the EU announced that all new buildings in all member states built after 2018 must be net-zero energy! They will have to produce all the energy they consume onsite, using solar panels, heat pumps, and other technology. The EU defines zero-energy buildings as buildings "where, as a result of the very high level of energy efficiency of the building, the overall annual primary energy consumption is equal to or less than the energy production from renewable energy sources on site."

As important as new regulations can be for stimulating technical innovations for more efficient appliances and buildings, their greatest potential is to stimulate financial innovations in one of our oldest, stodgiest, but most important industries—regulated power utilities. While it is true that we cannot afford to replace our utilities with some radically different entity—they have too much embedded infrastructure—we also can't afford to let our regulated utilities continue to sell power as they have in the past, like $5 all-you-can-eat electron buffets. The United States as a whole has to rewrite the basic social and economic compact between utilities, regulators, and customers to transform utilities into engines that optimize energy efficiency on the consumption end of the grid and drive the generation of clean electrons on the production end of the grid.

As I noted when discussing the Energy Internet, utilities were paid on the basis of how much power they sold and how many more power plants they built. As more customers started to turn off their lights when they left a room or installed energy-efficient appliances, the utility was hurt by lost sales and the deferral of new capital investments upon which the utility could earn a return. So the utilities had a fundamental interest in all of us gorging on electrons. Your mother and father were right when they said to you after you forgot to turn the lights off in your bedroom, "Hey, do you own stock in the electric company or something?" It was good for the utility when you left your lights on.

"There was always this fundamental tension between the customers' interests in lowering their bills by using less energy and the interests of the utility and its shareholders in raising more revenue by having people consume more energy," said Ralph Cavanagh, the utilities expert at NRDC. "It was like driving with one foot on the brake and one on the accelerator." But that's exactly what we've been doing. That has to change. We can't ask utilities to sell something—efficiency—that in the current business model only cuts into their profits, any more than we could ask Nike to go out and urge people not to buy tennis shoes. We have to make selling energy efficiency how a utility gets rich, not poor.

How do we do that? The place to start is by introducing a new regulation called, in industry jargon, "decoupling plus," which is now in place for electric utilities in California, Idaho, and other states. The basic idea is to break the notion that the only way a utility can make a profit and earn back its investments is by selling more electricity and natural gas. Profits and rising sales have to be "decoupled." Rather than pay the utility based exclusively on how much more energy it sells and how many new power plants or transmission lines it builds, decoupling would work like this: At the end of every year, regulators would compare a utility's actual energy sales with its predicted sales, and an independent auditor would determine the net dollar savings delivered to customers by the utility's conservation programs. If the utility's sales dropped unexpectedly, regulators would act to reimburse the utility for any out-of-pocket losses, while adding a reward in proportion to reductions in customer costs delivered by the utility's energy conservation programs. The amount of the reward would be determined by the independent auditor, who would tell the regulator what it believed were the net savings in dollars as a result of the utility's energy efficiency programs. Poor performance would result in a penalty, and if utility sales rose unexpectedly, the company would have to give the extra net revenues back in the form of lower future rate hikes. As a result, the utility's management focus would shift from boosting its customers' energy use to improving their energy productivity.

For instance, a utility might help a customer purchase a more energy-efficient air conditioner or subsidize a commercial building designer to reduce the energy consumption in a new building—to cut it well beyond what even the state "green" building code requires. The auditor would then figure out how much those conservation measures cost and how much they saved by way of power that did not have to be generated. Say the new, more efficient air conditioner would cost $500 more than the standard model, but over its life would save the utility $1,000 in kilowatt-hours that it would not have to generate. You are actually substituting conservation that cost only $500 up front for generation that would have cost $1,000 over time. That total savings of $500 would then be split between the utility and the customer.

In 2007, California utilities spent about $1 billion on programs promoting energy efficiency rather than new generation. California's goal is to meet at least half of its projected growth in electricity demand between now and 2020 by improving efficiency rather than building new power plants.

"This system removes the utilities' old incentives to want to sell more power, and to resist efficiency standards for appliances or buildings because they were injured by every new efficiency breakthrough," said Cavanagh. "Instead, this makes them allies in looking for every way possible to generate energy efficiency, because they will get a cut. You want to give the utilities performance-based incentives so they are motivated to deliver measurable reductions in their retail energy sales. That is when the utility will go out and say to the commercial building designers: 'We will pay you an extra $2 per square foot if you beat the minimum performance standard in the building code for energy efficiency by at least 30 percent.'"

That is also when the utilities will pay homeowners to get rid of their old energy-sucking refrigerators and buy new energy-efficient ones. Homeowners generally have no idea how much energy their refrigerators are using and whether it would make any economic sense for them to buy new energy-efficient models. Utilities do understand and can readily calculate the cost-benefit values associated with this proposition. When utilities are motivated to use this understanding to benefit both their customers and their own shareholders, things can really change. That is when the utility will invest in a smart grid and smart meters and smart appliances in every customer's home to stimulate and track efficiency gains.

It is why Jim Rogers, CEO of Duke Energy, calls energy efficiency "the fifth fuel—after coal, gas, renewables, and nuclear." "When there is a fight in 2040 and 2050 for resources around the world," says Rogers, "our energy efficiency will allow us to maintain our standard of living and will allow us to continue to grow."

John Bryson, chairman and CEO of Edison International, the parent company of Southern California Edison, told me his company estimates that the average cost of saving a kilowatt-hour through efficiency is 1.7 cents per kilowatt-hour; the cost of generating any new kilowatt-hour of electricity today would be over 10 cents per kilowatt-hour—so the cost savings generated through energy efficiency are spectacular. Energy efficiency "is a business we want to be in," said Bryson.

Larry Kellerman, one of the nation's top utilities experts, who works for Goldman Sachs and runs its power generation subsidiary, Cogentrix Energy, says he would put a "big piece of cheese" out there in the form of higher rates in the future to incentivize utilities to drive efficiency improvements. The ideal situation is that the utility makes more money by pushing you to save more electricity—so the utility's total profits go up and the customer's total bills actually go down, because the energy savings more than offset higher energy costs. If you have an energy ecosystem that produces societal value (lower CO_2 emissions and energy efficiency) but not business value (great savings for customers and profits for utilities), it will not scale. It has to produce both. Too many people for too long have gotten rich in the energy business doing the wrong things. I would be happy to see them get rich doing the right things.

We also need to use cheese, and lots of it, to drive other efficiency gains in the generation sector. Kellerman suggests having a regulator instruct its utilities that if they want to build another conventional, non-CO_2-sequestered coal-fired power plant, they're on their own to raise the capital. The regulator will not allow them to include the cost of the new plant in their rate base—which means there is no guarantee they will recover their costs. But if they want to invest in plants using solar, wind, hydro, geothermal, or nuclear power, or in fossil fuel generation that meets or exceeds predetermined standards for efficiency, CO_2 emissions, and other variables, the regulator will ensure they receive an extra-generous return on equity—an extra-large slice of cheese.

The utilities themselves would not have to build all these new solar or wind farms. There are plenty of independents who are already jumping into the clean energy generation business. You want to incentivize the utility to go out and contract with these independents, to build the smart transmission lines that could connect all these new clean power suppliers to one another, and then both sign them up and play them off against each other via competitive negotiations—so that consumers get the lowest price for clean power. The independent generators need access to the utility grid to get to customers and the utility has an interest in accessing more of their sources of clean power.

Kellerman also believes regulators should be empowered to drive efficiency in older technologies in more creative ways. They should be able to tell utilities: "You have all kinds of power plants—coal, natural gas, nuclear, wind. Here is the CO_2 emissions target for your whole fleet. If you continue to perform on emissions at your existing level, we will give you your standard rate of return. If you achieve a big reduction—by burning your coal more efficiently and losing less energy as you push it through your boilers and turbines—we will give you an extra return."

Half of all the electricity generated in America comes from coal. Put in these incentives across the whole coal fleet and the utilities will try to generate a lot more megawatts with less coal and therefore less CO_2.

I would also create incentives for all utilities to help their customers buy and even install distributed solar or wind power for their homes, offices, roofs, and parking lots, particularly at the stressed points on the power grid where those sources of energy will do the most good. If we can target more homes and offices—at those points on the grid that are most congested or hard to reach—to install their own wind and solar generation, it can take pressure off the grid. And as solar and wind technologies improve and move down in price, there is no reason utilities cannot be distributing and connecting them as part of their service.

"Today I look out on the rooftops of my customers and I see future power plant sites," said Duke Energy's Jim Rogers, who has suggested that utilities could install solar panels on the rooftops of customers and wrap that outlay into the overall cost of their existing power generation—if the regulators will allow his company to include those costs in its rate base.

But this has to be done in a smart and judicious manner. For now, given the current level of technology, centrally generated clean power is still more efficient for most homeowners.

"The amount of resources and incentives applied in facilitating customer-owned, on-premise generation needs to be tempered by the economic reality that small-scale distributed generation is typically much more costly, on a per-kilowatt-hour basis, than economy of scale central station generation," noted Kellerman. "A five-kilowatt solar photovoltaic array aesthetically placed on the rooftop of a Beverly Hills mansion costs much more, per kilowatt, to install and service than a hundred-megawatt solar thermal trough system installed in Death Valley. Add the fact that the amount of energy produced in the desert per installed kilowatt is dramatically higher due to the fact that the sun shines more there, with greater intensity, at a higher elevation and with little humidity to diffuse the energy received from the sun, and it is clear that society's resources should dominantly be focused on applying technology where it produces the energy most efficiently and therefore most cheaply."

Another regulatory innovation would be to incentivize utilities to contribute to the design and passage of better energy efficiency laws for buildings and appliances at state or national levels. "If Southern California Edison or Pacific Gas & Electric can show that it contributed substantially to the adoption of higher energy efficiency standards for buildings or appliances that deliver energy savings to customers, it should [also] be rewarded for that by regulators," said Cavanagh.

But to get the most efficiency gains and to make the Energy Internet–smart grid complete requires that one more big piece of the puzzle be put into place—electrifying transportation, and moving as many cars, trucks, buses, and trains away from exclusively combustion engines and into plug-in electric hybrids or plug-in all-electric cars. Plug-in electric cars, which run on the direct current stored in onboard batteries, and gasoline-electric hybrids, which generate and store their own electricity or can be plugged in, have the potential to make a huge impact in lowering energy demand, promoting renewable energy, and reducing carbon emissions.

A few facts: Roughly 30 percent of our greenhouse gas emissions come from the transportation sector, so weaning our vehicles off gasoline could make a big difference, if the electricity that would replace gasoline came from clean electrons. But right now about half of America's electricity comes from burning coal, 20 percent from nuclear power, 15 percent from burning natural gas, 3 percent from burning oil, 7 percent from hydropower, and 2 percent from burning wood and geothermal, solar, and wind sources. France obtains about 75 percent of its electricity from nuclear power plants. (America actually produces twice as much electricity from nuclear power as France does, but with our bigger economy it represents a smaller share of our total.) A barrel of crude oil is forty-two gallons. America consumes over twenty-one million barrels of crude oil per day, with more than half of that imported. About fourteen million of the twenty-one million goes to cars, trucks, planes, buses, and trains. The remaining seven million barrels go into heating buildings and manufacturing chemicals and plastics.

As noted, today's hybrid cars use a combination of a gasoline engine, a storage battery, and a power-generating system that converts energy normally wasted during coasting and braking into electricity, which is stored in a battery until needed by the electric motor. Because these cars run part of the time off the power generated and stored in the battery and part of the time off the power from combusting gasoline, they travel more miles on less gas—and therefore give off less CO_2 per mile traveled. That is how they lower emissions. The next great leap forward comes when we displace the combustion engine altogether and move to all-electric plug-ins with large enough batteries that they can be powered entirely by electricity from the grid.

That car would be even cleaner than today's hybrids because electric miles produce lower CO_2 emissions than gasoline miles, even when much of that electricity coming out of the wall and going into the car is generated from coal. That's right—it is cleaner and greener, as well as being much cheaper, to generate electricity even from coal and convert that electricity into the motive force necessary to propel your car than to combust gasoline in the vehicle's internal combustion engine. The reason is that, from well to wheels, an electricity-powered system has far fewer energy losses along the way than a gasoline-fueled system, when you include all the losses in the gasoline system from oil extraction, transportation, refining, and distribution of the gas—plus the lower efficiency of an internal combustion engine.

"Unlike gasoline-powered cars, the cleaner our grid gets, the cleaner plug-in electric cars will get," noted Felix Kramer, who heads the California Cars Initiative (Calcars.org), which promotes plug-in hybrids. "But this is just the beginning. What we need and are moving toward is the electrification of all transportation. That is critical, because it will combine two large industrial sectors—transportation and power generation. It gives the utilities what they have never had—the potential for distributed energy storage, using all of our car batteries—and it helps make both industries cheaper, more efficient, and cleaner."

Over 40 percent of the electricity generating capacity in the United States now sits idle or operates at a reduced load and at less than optimal efficiency overnight, which is when most plug-in electric cars would be charged. That means tens of millions of plug-in cars could be charged every night without the need for us to build additional electric generation capacity, and using plug-ins would actually enable this existing generation of plants to operate more cost-effectively. (We need to remember that a lot of that nighttime power, though, still comes from aging coal-fired power plants, so the sooner we clean up those plants or retire them, the quicker we get more benefits from electrifying transportation.) A study by Pacific Northwest National Laboratory found that 73 percent of our cars, trucks, and SUVs could be replaced with plug-in hybrids without any need to build new generating plants or transmission lines, because they would be charged at night with plentiful off-peak nighttime power. The PNNL study indicated that this change could reduce our foreign oil imports by 52 percent and reduce greenhouse gas emissions in every city by 27 percent on average. PNNL's Mike Davis estimates that if our whole car fleet were electric vehicles, with batteries that gave them a thirty-mile range, it could produce enough power to sustain the whole nation's transmission grid for six to eight hours, if we had a smart grid and utilities could use all those car batteries as a backup. John Bryson of Edison International explained to me: "Our prices of electricity at off-peak are 25 to 50 percent the price of gasoline, per mile."

For electrification of vehicles to work, and be integrated with a smart home and smart grid, we would need regulations to standardize the whole system. That means that whatever chip is in your GE washing machine has to operate with the same communications and transmission protocols as the one in your Whirlpool dryer and as the one in your Honeywell temperature controls system and as the one in the battery in your electric car—so that they can all speak to the Smart Black Box, or smart grid gateway in your home, and through that to the utility's supercomputer—to take orders when to go on, when to go off, when to recharge, and when to operate at lower power levels, and to communicate back when these devices might want to charge themselves or sell power to the grid.

Utilities will also have to invest in the deployment of more devices like phasor sensors—which measure voltage characteristics at different points in the grid's transmission lines with extremely high accuracy, much the way a meter would measure water pressure or temperature in a pipe—so the utility knows every thirty to sixty seconds exactly how much transmission capacity is available on every mile of its transmission grid. Right now, few utilities have that capability.

In addition to common standards between all the devices communicating with the utility, we will also need common standards for electric car plugs, chargers, and batteries—so if I drive my electric car from Washington to Minneapolis, I can charge it up at any motel or filling station along the way and, if I want to, sell electrons back to their grids and utilities. "There are over three thousand utilities in North America and there are fourteen smart grid groups trying to set standards," said John Bryson. "You are not going to get consensus. The government needs to come in and provide clarity."

The information technology revolution, particularly the PC, the Internet, and the World Wide Web, took off only after common transmission protocols and language standards emerged for sending e-mail and documents. Bits and bytes could then flow freely. The Energy Internet will require the same thing for electrons to flow freely. Once you have a common platform, consumers will be much more empowered to write energy efficiency programs, the way they now write software programs, and share them around the world. "It is going to require a lot of 'collaborative innovation,'" said Joel Cawley, one of IBM's top strategists. "Government's job will be to organize pilots that will allow all the different parties to participate where their exposure is minimized and their investment is manageable and their learning returns are ensured and abundant."

Which is why that African proverb Al Gore is fond of quoting is really appropriate to this clean power challenge: "If you want to go quickly, go alone. If you want to go far, go together."

Make the Word "Green" Go Away

The purpose of all these price signals and regulatory changes is, indeed, to go far. Their purpose is to both enable the building of an Energy Internet and enable utilities to move from just selling dumb electrons at $5 all-you-can-eat buffets to earning their profits by optimizing every aspect of this new network—from building out the smart grid, to helping more clean power flow at the lowest prices to more homes, businesses, and cars and back to the grid, to driving energy efficiency to higher and higher levels in more and more different ways. How will we know we have done it right? We will know that we have created a Clean Energy System when we wake up, look around, and notice three new things.

First, we will have created enough of a new incentive system for utilities, and enough competition—on both the generation side of the grid and the energy efficiency side—that the utilities and big energy companies will finally feel they have to *change or die*. In the IT revolution, because it was based on bits and bytes and innovation came fast and furious, companies either learned to master the inherent power of the information technology revolution and harnessed it to drive their own businesses past their competitors', or they were roadkill. Everyone in the jungle was either a lion or a gazelle, who each know only one thing. The lion knows that if it cannot outrun the slowest gazelle, it will starve, and the gazelle knows that if it cannot outrun the fastest lion, it will be breakfast. So when the sun rises every morning, they both know they had better start running. That kind of psychology has never existed in the traditional energy business and will come about only if government uses its power to set prices, regulations, and standards to reshape the energy market and force utilities and other big players to either innovate or die.

"The bullet that kills you never takes you between the eyes," said Jeff Wacker, the EDS futurist. "It always hits you in the temple. You never see it coming, because you're looking in the wrong direction." The traditional energy companies have never had to worry about a bullet coming out of the blue. When you see a few of them lying by the side of the road with bullets in their temples, you will know that we have finally created a change-or-die world in the energy business—and somebody didn't change.

Second, you'll know we're doing it right when you get your electricity bill at the end of the month and notice that the cost per kilowatt-hour of electricity has gone up—to pay for making your grid smarter and for incentivizing your utility to move to cleaner power—but your overall bill is either the same or lower. That will be an indication that the energy efficiency touching your home and life has reached such a level of systemic optimization that it is *saving you both energy and dollars*.

What would that look like? I could show you, but you'd have to go to Japan. Consider this article from Tokyo by Martin Fackler in *The New York Times* (January 6, 2007):

In many countries, higher oil prices have hurt pocketbooks and led to worries about economic slowdowns. But here in Japan, Kiminobu Kimura, an architect, says he has not felt the pinch. In fact, his monthly energy bill is lower than a year ago . . . Energy-efficient appliances abound in the many corners of his cramped home. There is the refrigerator that beeps when left open and the dishwasher that is compact enough to sit on the kitchen counter. In some homes, room heaters have a sensor that directs heat only toward occupants; there are "energy navigators" that track a home's energy use. And then Mr. Kimura, 48, says there are the little things that his family of four does to squeeze fuel bills, like reusing warm bath water to wash laundry and bicycling to buy groceries . . . Japan is the most energy-efficient developed country on earth, according to most specialists, who say it is much better prepared than the United States to prosper in an era of higher global energy prices . . . Its population and economy are each about 40 percent as large as that of the United States, yet in 2004 it consumed less than a quarter as much energy as America did, according to the International Energy Agency, which is based in Paris.

Japan's obsession with conservation stems from an acute sense of insecurity in a resource-poor nation that imports most of its energy from the volatile Middle East, a fact driven home here by the 1970s shocks. The guiding hand of government has also played a role, forcing households and companies to conserve by raising the cost of gasoline and electricity far above global levels. Taxes and price controls make a gallon of gasoline in Japan currently cost . . . twice America's more market-based prices. The government in turn has used these tax revenues to help Japan seize the lead in renewable energies like solar power, and more recently home fuel cells . . . Higher energy prices have also created strong domestic demand in Japan for more conventional and new energy-saving products of all sorts. That has spurred the invention and development of things like low-energy washing machines and televisions and high-mileage cars and hybrid vehicles, experts say. Japanese factories also learned how to cut energy use and become among the most efficient in the world. Companies like Mitsubishi Heavy Industries are now reaping the benefits in booming overseas sales of their highly efficient electric turbines, steel blast furnaces and other industrial machinery, particularly in the United States. The environment ministry forecasts that exports will help turn energy conservation into a $7.9 billion industry in Japan by 2020, about 10 times its size in 2000.

Japan, the article noted, has also encouraged development of energy-saving appliances with its Top Runner program,

which has set goals for reducing energy use. Products that meet the goals are awarded a green sticker, while those that fail get an orange sticker. Japan's trade and industry ministry says consumers heed the stickers, pushing manufacturers to raise the energy efficiency. The average air-conditioner now uses two-thirds less electricity than in 1997, and the average freezer 23 percent less, the ministry said. The savings add up. The average household here used 4,177 kilowatt-hours of electricity in 2001, the most recent figure, according to the Jyukankyo Research Institute in Tokyo. In the same year, the average American household consumed more than twice that, or 10,655 kilowatt hours, according to the Energy Department.

The final and most important sign that we are succeeding will be that the term "green" blessedly disappears. There will be no such thing as a green building, a green car, a green home, a green appliance, a green window, or even green energy. All those things will simply be the norm, because the ecosystem of prices, regulations, and performance standards will demand it. Therefore, you won't legally or financially be able to build anything that isn't green—anything that doesn't have the highest performance standards for energy efficiency and clean power designed in it from inception. Every new car will be green, every new office building will be green, every new home will be green, every new appliance will be green. Green will be the standard. It will be the new normal—nothing else will be available, nothing else will be possible.

"The term 'green' will go the way of the term 'civil rights,'" said David Edwards, an energy expert with VantagePoint Venture Partners. The civil rights movement was eventually so effective that civil rights is barely discussed today, except as an exception. We speak about the civil rights movement as something that happened in our past. Today it is the norm that people are not discriminated against because of the color of their skin, and the only time we read about civil rights issues in the newspaper now are the exceptions—the cases of blatant discrimination. Discrimination is now the news, not the norm. The green movement will have succeeded when energy inefficiency, carbon excesses, and a dependence on dirty fuels are the news, not the norm—when people who engage in those activities are looked upon the way someone who lights up a cigarette on an airplane would be looked at today.

So when you wake up one day and power companies are competing to make you more energy efficient, the way phone companies compete today for your long-distance business; when parking garages are paying you to park there because they will sell you solar power from their roof and share in your sale of that power to the grid; when your electricity is more costly but your bills have shrunk; and when green is the standard, not an option—you'll know that we're having a green revolution and not just a green party.

FIFTEEN

A Million Noahs, a Million Arks

Nature is an infinite sphere of which the center is everywhere and the circumference is nowhere.

— Blaise Pascal, French mathematician and philosopher

In December 2007, the UN held its big climate-change conference in Bali, and I decided to go both to observe the debate about what the world should do to confront global warming and to write about Indonesia's environmental challenges, the cutting down of its rain forests in particular. As I was coming from the Persian Gulf, I flew to Bali via Abu Dhabi, the capital of the United Arab Emirates. When I went to board the Etihad Airways flight at 2:30 a.m. in Abu Dhabi's teeming airport, the gate agent told me to take a seat, because my section was boarding last. So I sat down by the window and watched as about two hundred young Indonesian women, not one of whom was much more than five feet tall, boarded the plane, all carrying purses and wearing backpacks overflowing with clothing, shoes, and electronic equipment. They were obviously returning home after some kind of lengthy stay and were bringing back gifts and "stuff" in every pocket and bag.

"What do all these girls do?" I asked the well-dressed Indian businessman seated next to me. "They're all maids," he answered. He and I then fell into conversation. It turned out that he was a management consultant and was in the Gulf advising governments on how to improve productivity. We chatted about the impact of globalization on the region. Before long, we were comparing India and Indonesia, and finally, he turned back to that long line of Indonesian maids snaking past us onto the plane.

"Indonesia exports raw labor, not brains," he mused. What the country should be doing, he added, is educating its people better, so more of them could secure better jobs at home, and fewer of them would have to sell their manual labor abroad.

I made a mental note of our conversation and filed it away for my next book on globalization. But shortly after arriving in Jakarta, I realized that those maids had a lot in common with Indonesia's trees—and that exporting raw labor and exporting raw trees were, at root, different manifestations of the same problem.

I learned that from Barnabas Suebu, the governor of Indonesia's forest-rich province of Papua. We were talking about trees, but we just as well could have been talking about maids. So many Indonesians in his province, he explained, have such low incomes and so little education that they are always tempted to chop down a tree in one of Papua's tropical forests and sell it to a local middleman for a few hundred dollars, so that local middleman can export it to China or Vietnam for a few hundred more dollars, so a manufacturer in China or Vietnam can make it into finished furniture products for a few thousand dollars, so a furniture store in Tokyo, Los Angeles, or London can sell it for a few more thousand dollars. Unless his people can get the education that will enable them to bring more knowledge and value-added skills to their work—so that they can produce $10,000 worth of products from just one tree rather than sell a hundred trees for $100 each—the illegal logging of Indonesia's rain forests will likely continue, no matter how many police you put on the case. "We have to make sure we get a lot more value out of every tree we cut," said Suebu.

Trees, maids, education, governance, economic development: They're all interconnected. And that is the point of this chapter: Just as we need to develop a system for clean energy *generation*—to get more growth from abundant, clean, reliable, and cheap electrons—we also need to develop a global strategy for the *preservation* of our forests, oceans, rivers, and endangered biodiversity hot spots, to enable smart growth that doesn't destroy our natural world. That strategy for preservation has to include legal, financial, and educational components, and we cannot get it up and running fast enough, especially in places like Indonesia. Strategies for *generation* and *preservation* go together—they both are necessary if we want growth to be sustainable in a world that is hot, flat, and crowded.

While China's pollution has garnered much attention, we should be just as concerned about environmental degradation in Indonesia—and not just because of its big human population (237 million and growing). Indonesia is the second-richest country in the world in terms of terrestrial biodiversity, after Brazil, and first in terms of marine biodiversity. Though covering only 1.3 percent of the earth's land surface, Indonesia's forests represent 10 percent of all the world's tropical forest cover and are home to 20 percent of all the world's species of flora and fauna, 17 percent of the world's bird species, and more than 25 percent of the world's fish species. Just ten hectares in the Indonesian island of Borneo contains more different tree species than are found in all of North America—not to mention a raft of plants, insects, and animals that don't exist anywhere else on earth. In fact, little Borneo, with less than 1 percent of the earth's land surface, reportedly holds 6 percent of the world's total bird species, mammal species, and flowering plant species. The whole Caribbean has only about one-tenth the marine biodiversity of Indonesia, which sits at the confluence of the Indian Ocean, the South China Sea, and the Pacific Ocean, and is nourished by all three.

But much of this biodiversity in Indonesia is now under threat. Shortly after I arrived in Jakarta, my friend Alfred Nakatsuma, who runs the biodiversity preservation programs for the United States Agency for International Development in Indonesia, remarked to me that Indonesia had been entered into *Guinness World Records* for having the fastest rate of deforestation in the world. Indonesia is now losing tropical forests the size of Maryland every year, and the carbon released by the cutting and clearing of all these trees—much of it done illegally—has made Indonesia the third-largest source of greenhouse gas emissions in the world, after the United States and China. Brazil is number four for the same reason. We tend to think of the climate issue as purely an energy problem—how do we reduce the number of gasoline cars we drive and the amount of coal we burn? But in Indonesia, climate is a forest problem. We think of the problem as being too many cars. They think of it as being too few trees. More than 70 percent of CO_2 emissions from Indonesia come from the cutting and clearing of forests. According to Conservation International, a forest area the size of three hundred soccer fields is cut down in Indonesia *every hour*. Illegal logging from national forests costs the Indonesian government $3 billion in lost state revenues each year, but even what is legal involves extensive deforestation as Indonesia tries to grow its economy by, understandably, selling forest products.

Unfortunately, the trouble doesn't stop at the water's edge. The waters around the 17,000 islands of the Indonesian archipelago hold 14 percent of the earth's coral reefs and more than 2,000 coral reef fish species. "Corals are people too," joked Mark Erdmann, the marine biologist and senior adviser to Conservation International in Indonesia. We often forget that "corals are both plants and animals," he added, "and the main thing they provide is shelter and structure and substrate, like trees in the forest—no more trees: no more leopards or orangutans; no more corals: no more fish." But runaway development and both dynamite and cyanide fishing have imperiled many of Indonesia's coral reefs, which provide the critical habitat for fish and other reef animals. A Western diplomat in Jakarta who follows biodiversity issues told me that one Indonesian fishing fleet company had informed him that in the year 2000, 8 percent of its catch from the waters around Indonesia were small baby fish, and by 2004 that number was 34 percent. As this diplomat put it, "When you are into one-third babies, the end is near."

Imagine a world without forests. Imagine a world without coral. Imagine a world without fish. Imagine a world where rivers run only in the rainy season. Not only is that possible in more and more places, it is possible in our lifetime—if we don't develop a *system* for preservation of biodiversity and natural resources that is as smart, comprehensive, and effective as the system we are trying to develop for clean power generation.

Of course, lots of people offer quick-fix plans for how to stem the tide of biodiversity degradation, but in countries like Indonesia, plans are rarely implemented as intended. While attending the Bali climate-change conference, I came across an article in *The Jakarta Post* (December 11, 2007) that described what usually happens instead. The author, Andrio Adiwibowo, a lecturer in environmental management at the University of Indonesia, wrote about a smart plan to protect the mangrove forests around coastal Jakarta:

> Even for many biologists, mangrove forests are still viewed as wastelands. Yet, the tidal flood late last month in Jakarta reminds

us that if we don't respect these salt-water tolerant plant communities, it can turn our backyards into the wasteland. Approximately 14 years ago, a team from the ecology laboratory at the
Biology Department, School of Mathematical and Natural Sciences, University of Indonesia, made environmental assessments
on the coastal areas of Jakarta and warned of the possibility of tidal
floods. The suggested solution was first to maintain mangroves as
the core zone, and second to provide a buffer zone. Based on
forestry regulations and conservation laws, the vegetation in this
buffer zone should consist 60 percent of native mangrove plants,
and the rest plants that can be utilized by the surrounding people . . . If the plan is implemented, a repeat of the recent floods
can be avoided. Nevertheless, the plan was not implemented. Instead of providing a buffer zone, development encroached into
the core zone, which was covered over by concrete.

Nevertheless, the plan was not implemented. That is such a common
refrain when it comes to preservation of species, coral reefs, fish, mangroves, and our tropical forests. Governor Suebu of Papua seemed to be
well aware of this tendency. His own motto, he told me, was "Think big,
start small, act now." But act how? Now that we know the world's biodiversity is under greater threat than ever in a world that is hot, flat, and
crowded, what is the comprehensive strategy, not just a one-off plan, that
can work for preservation?

The short answer: We need a million Noahs and a million arks.

In our whole existence as a species, we have had the luxury of assuming
that the earth's plant and animal bounty was inexhaustible, but since
the 1992 Earth Summit in Rio de Janeiro, there has been a growing
global consensus that the earth's changing climate, our patterns of resource consumption, and our soaring population are combining to
threaten the very web of biodiversity that sustains all species, including,
and especially, our own, and therefore we need to redefine our relationship with the natural world.

As I have argued in the previous chapters, energy use, economic
growth, species loss, deforestation, petropolitics, and global warming are
all interconnected. Rapid economic growth and population expansion—

flat meets crowded—is driving the destruction of forests and other ecosystems at an unprecedented rate. The destruction of these forests and biodiversity-rich environments, in turn, contributes to climate change—flat and crowded meet hot and make it hotter—by releasing more carbon into the atmosphere. Moreover, this destruction of forests and other natural habitats, like coral reefs, makes us more vulnerable as humans, because the trees in the forests soak up that clean rainwater and store it beneath the surface in roots and aquifers and manage the water's release into rivers and streams, and because coral reefs and mangroves buffer coastal areas against tropical storms. In other words, the further we get into the Energy-Climate Era, the more we need natural habitats— forests that can hold the soil in place and provide homes for endangered species, and healthy reefs to protect coastal areas from being swamped by sea level rise and to nourish the fishing stocks that provide so much food for coastal peoples.

Generating abundant, clean, reliable, and cheap electrons would certainly help to take pressure off the world's most endangered ecosystems, but it would not be sufficient. We also need a comprehensive strategy to stimulate preservation at scale—to ensure that more plants, animals, and people have the resources they need to survive. And that strategy needs to be driven and maintained, first and foremost, by the people who live in and around our most valuable natural resources. It takes an ecosystem of the right government policies, the right invest- ments, and the right actors to save an ecosystem of plants, animals, and forests.

Each of these ecosystems for preservation will be different, depend- ing on the country and the place that needs protection. And each one I call an "ark." Noah had one ark to save the world's biodiversity in his day, and we need a million of them to save the biodiversity in ours. Each ark has to include the following components: (1) A national government policy to set aside certain protected areas that are off-limits for exploita- tion, conversion, or development because of their biodiversity impor- tance, while at the same time delineating other areas that can be developed for economic growth and managed carefully to protect endan- gered species, water quality, and other ecological values. (2) Economic opportunities for the local community that enable it to thrive without harming the area's biodiversity. (3) Private sector investors, be they hote- liers, energy or mining companies, agribusinesses, tourism developers, or others who have an interest in keeping the area's biodiversity intact and can attract global investment in projects that can make a profit, respect the natural world, and help raise local living standards all at once. (4) A local government that is able and willing to preserve protected areas and not sell them off to the highest bidders or allow itself to be corrupted by logging or mining interests. (5) Local or international experts who know how to do proper biodiversity assessments and land use planning to determine precisely which areas need to be protected and which can be developed with proper environmental safeguards. (6) Initiatives to improve primary and secondary education, so young people develop knowledge skills that make it less necessary for them to plunder the natural world around them.

While the elements of each ark need to be tailored to each setting, in every case the governments, companies, NGOs, and villagers involved in each ark have to understand that keeping the local ecosystem intact is in their interest. They have to be invested in preserving the protected areas and the overall biodiversity of the region; if any one of them is missing in action, the odds of success will be much lower.

But there is no ark without a Noah. In every instance you need a Noah who is able to pull together this coalition, this ecosystem, by helping everyone see his or her self-interest in its preservation. These Noahs can be local government officials, conservationists, or leaders in businesses or nongovernmental organizations; they can and should come in all shapes and sizes and personality types—as different and varied as the different environmental problems and the different economic interests that need to be addressed and pulled together in each ecosystem. That's why if we are going to preserve our natural world in the age of hot, flat, and crowded, we are going to need a million Noahs and a million arks.

There are many discussions going on today at the United Nations and the World Bank about how developed countries can transfer money to developing countries to, in effect, pay them not to chop down their tropical forests. Many hope that such a mechanism will be part of the next post-Kyoto treaty to govern climate change. Such global initiatives, while well intended, in my view will not work without these local arks. Anyone who thinks they will does not understand the complexity of biodiversity preservation. If I've learned anything about ecology in researching this book, it is this: *All conservation is local.*

That is, global treaties and financing mechanisms are necessary, but by themselves, they won't even come close to solving the problem. You need coalitions on the ground bound together by an interlocking web of self-interests to preserve a certain pristine region or forest. We need to spend as much time and effort helping developing countries nurture these ecosystems on the ground as we do negotiating what treaty provisions should stipulate. Every global dollar is only as valuable and useful in preserving biodiversity as the quality of the Noah and the strength of his or her ark on the ground.

Some say the key to solving our energy problem is just one really smart Thomas Edison—one inventor who can come up with that magic breakthrough to generate abundant, clean, reliable, cheap power. Maybe. But the key to solving our biodiversity problem is one million Noahs, with one million arks.

What does an ark actually look like? I visited one in March 2008. It looks like a meeting in a ramshackle wooden schoolhouse in a remote village on the edge of a tropical forest in North Sumatra, Indonesia. The village is called Aek Nabara, and it is located next to the Batang Toru tropical forest—375,000 acres of trees and wildlife, much of which the government in Jakarta had auctioned off as a logging concession to the highest bidder. The villagers were worried about what was going to happen to the forest, which has been a source of both spiritual and material livelihood to the people of the area for as far back as they could remember. These villagers did not have college degrees, but they knew their interests—though they didn't always know how to defend them. The day I visited, with a team from Conservation International and the U.S. ambassador to Indonesia, Cameron R. Hume, the entire village turned out to tell their story. Men and boys, women in batiks with babies wrapped to their hips, young and old, all gathered in the village square for an impromptu town hall meeting.

Only men, though, were actually allowed into the schoolhouse to a session chaired by the village's four leaders—three of whom were wearing traditional Indonesian Peci caps, the kind President Suharto made famous. Seated next to these elders, though, was a bearded younger man, wearing a green Australian bush hat. But what made him memorable was not his hat. It was the fact that on his shoulder he had a tiny eight-month-old rust-furred orangutan, which he was feeding from a baby bottle. It wasn't the sort of thing you usually see in the front row of a town hall meeting . . .

It turns out, I soon discovered, that that baby orangutan, an orphan that had been found in the forest next to the village a week earlier, was the key to the whole story.

That's because the Noah of Batang Toru is Dr. Jatna Supriatna, a fifty-five-year-old bespectacled professor of bioanthropology at the University of Indonesia who runs Conservation International's Indonesia programs. One of Supriatna's specialties is the endangered orangutan — the species of great apes found today only in the Indonesian tropical forests of Sumatra and Borneo and distinguished by their great intelligence, rusty orange hair, and long swinging arms. Those long arms come in handy, as the orangutan is the largest tree-dwelling mammal in the world, and they use both legs and arms to swing, like Tarzan, from tree to tree in the forest. According to zoology books, the word "orangutan" is derived from the Indonesian and Malaysian words for person, "orang," and forest, "hutan," and means "person of the forest." A century ago, there were over 300,000 orangutans living in the wilds of Indonesia and Malaysia. Since then, more than 90 percent of the population has been wiped out, many in the last decade and a half.

In 2004, Supriatna persuaded one of his students to write her master's thesis on the question of whether there were actually any orangutans left at all in the southern part of the province of North Sumatra. There had been rumors of an orangutan sighting in the Batang Toru tropical forest, adjacent to Aek Nabara, but they had not been confirmed. The forest is also home to Sumatran tigers and pythons, and to avoid them the Sumatran orangutans almost never walk on the forest floor, making them difficult to spot.

His student, explained Supriatna, "spent six months in Batang Toru and concluded that there were twelve orangutans living in the tropical forest there. So I started thinking: 'How do we save these animals?' There are only 4,000–5,000 Sumatran orangutans left." The orangutans are important for keeping the forest healthy. They are voracious eaters of termites and fruit, particularly sugar palm, the seeds of which they spread across the forest floor, helping to keep it forested. By coincidence, Senator Patrick Leahy of Vermont had recently pushed through a budget increase to the United States Agency for International Development for the specific purpose of helping to save the endangered orangutans of Indonesia. So USAID granted Conservation International $1 million to hire scientists to survey Batang Toru to determine exactly how many orangutans were living there and to design a program for saving them. They started surveying in 2005.

"We eventually came up with 350 to 400—a big number in Batang Toru alone," said Supriatna. "We also used some of the money to start talking to [people in] communities on the edge of the jungle. We took them into the jungle and showed them how the orangutans were living next to them. They said, 'Wow, we didn't even know they were here.' They knew their grandparents had mentioned them, but they had never seen any their entire lives."

Next Supriatna studied how the villagers themselves regulated their use of the forest, and drew up an economic evaluation of how much money they made or could make from different activities if the forest was to remain intact—from growing and selling cocoa, cloves, cinnamon, and rubber, either on the edge of the forest or on the forest floor, and, most profitably, from selling the geothermal power, which the village had a claim to, that naturally bubbles on the forest hillsides from old volcanic formations.

"We basically concluded that if the orangutan was to survive, the tropical forest had to survive," Supriatna explained, and the only way that was going to happen was if the villagers understood how much they benefited from the forest—not to mention the rest of us.

Just a few words about these huge trees that sustain us all: All along the equator, stretching both north and south over land surfaces, is a wide belt of tropical forests. These range from rain forests, where it rains all year round, to seasonally moist forests, which get lots of rainfall but only in certain seasons, to drier woodland forests. "Although tropical forests cover only about 7 percent of the Earth's dry land, they probably harbor about half of all species on Earth," noted NASA's "Earth Observatory" report on tropical deforestation by Rebecca Lindsey (March 30, 2007). "Tropical forests are [also] home to millions of native (indigenous) people who make their livings through subsistence agriculture, hunting and gathering or through low-impact harvesting of forest products like rubber or nuts."

While oceans are still the primary "lungs" of the world, storing and exhaling CO_2, tropical forests also play a critical role in the carbon cycle and in moderating global warming. Carbon is abundantly present in the earth's atmosphere in the form of carbon dioxide. Although only a tiny portion of our overall atmosphere, this carbon dioxide is critical in supporting plant, animal, and human life. Plants live, grow, and thrive by taking sunlight and, through photosynthesis, converting carbon dioxide into carbohydrates, giving off oxygen in the process.

This process is most intense in younger forests, where trees are still shooting up to the sky. Plants and trees incorporate the associated carbon atoms into sugars and other molecules in order to grow. "Plants use some of these sugars to generate energy in a process called respiration, which returns carbon atoms back to the atmosphere in the form of CO_2," notes Safeclimate.net. So intact tropical forests both absorb and give off CO_2. However, much of the carbon absorbed remains locked up in the plants' biomass until decomposition, logging, or fires release it back to the atmosphere. Old-growth forests, in particular, store vast amounts of carbon while continuing to absorb CO_2, which is why maintaining these forests is so critical for combating climate change. In the Amazon alone, according to the NASA study, scientists estimate that the trees contain more carbon than ten years' worth of human-produced greenhouse gases from driving and manufacturing. It noted:

> When people clear the forests, usually with fire, carbon stored in the wood returns to the atmosphere, enhancing the greenhouse effect and global warming . . . In places such as Indonesia, the soils of swampy lowland forests are rich in partially decayed organic matter, known as peat. During extended droughts . . . the forests and the peat become flammable, especially if they have been degraded by logging or accidental fire. When they burn, they release huge volumes of carbon dioxide and other greenhouse gases.

Wanting to preserve the Batang Toru forest for the sake of biodiversity in general, the villagers, the orangutan, and the climate, Supriatna decided to organize separate workshops with all the stakeholders in and around this vast expanse of trees. So he met separately with the local mining company, the villagers, and the loggers who owned the forest concession, as well as a big energy investor who wanted to tap the area's geothermal pockets.

The energy investor was one of Indonesia's richest men, Arifin Panigoro, the founder of Medco Energi Internasional, a big local oil and gas drilling company and a very unlikely "green." He had leased the geothermal concession in the middle of the Batang Toru forest from the government in 2006.

When Supriatna came to see him, Panigoro told me, he was very wary. "I had never heard of Conservation International. I thought it was like Greenpeace. I said to myself: 'Who is this guy?'" It took a few conversations, but eventually Supriatna persuaded Panigoro that he had as much if not more of a stake in maintaining the forest as the villagers. Panigoro needed the forest in order to maintain the watershed—so that the water table required to sustain the geothermal wells would not fall so low that the hot rocks couldn't generate steam. Panigoro may not have been an environmentalist when he met Supriatna, but he was a savvy businessman who loved his country and realized that its natural resources were now being radically depleted. "Twenty years back, we didn't have these problems," he told me. "We had huge tropical forests, and they continued to cut the trees at the time. They considered it sustainable, but it wasn't."

Panigoro eventually agreed to join Conservation International's Indonesian advisory board and to use his resources to try to buy the logging concession for the Batang Toru tropical forest from the timber company that owned it and turn it into a protected area, free from development, except controlled agroforestry and his ongoing geothermal project. As of the writing of this book, he was still in negotiations—buying the concession will cost about $2 million—but the Indonesian logging company appeared amenable to a sale because most of this forest is on steep hillsides where it was finding it hard to cut and remove trees.

Once Panigoro has the forest under his control, he plans to go ahead with the geothermal energy project—he hopes to produce 330 megawatts—and look for ways to partner with the locals in controlled agriculture on the forest floor and maybe in ecotourism. The power will go to nearby towns in Sumatra. Supriatna's Conservation International team helped to broker a deal whereby the villagers will get a royalty from the geothermal plant, once it is up and running, to support their local school and infrastructure. Meanwhile, Shanghai-based GITI Tire, China's largest tire manufacturer, looking to voluntarily offset its carbon emissions, has agreed to plant rubber trees to create a buffer zone of sustainable agroforestry around the edge of the forest, which will protect the trees, produce rubber for tires, and provide additional livelihoods for the villagers, explained Enki Tan, a company director who is also a member of the Conservation International board. GITI Tire plans to feature this "eco-friendly rubber" in its tire ads.

Supriatna's team also worked with the indigenous villagers to revive their own traditional oral laws, called Adat, which put a high premium on protecting forests, rivers, and the whole natural environment, which in previous generations sustained these little communities. "They were resurrecting the values of their grandparents, which had gotten lost with the new generation watching too much television—even though they lived next to the forest," said Supriatna, who also trained a force of twenty-five men to form an "Orangutan Patrol," paying them a small stipend each month to tend to the animals and ward off any poachers.

The guy in the bush hat feeding the baby orangutan, which had been tossed out of the nest by its mother, was wearing the official shirt of the local Orangutan Patrol. At their presentation to the U.S. ambassador, the villagers seemed cautiously optimistic that their locally built "ark" would work. They proudly displayed jars full of products they were already growing on the rain forest floor—including cinnamon, cloves, and sugar palm. "One thing we learned from Conservation International," one of the villager elders explained in his presentation, "was how to manage which areas are good for [agroforestry] and which ones are not. We are cut off—we did not know how to make a better living."

Rather than coming in and lecturing the villagers on how and why they should save the orangutan—which wasn't going to make a big impression on people so poor they could barely save themselves—Supriatna started by working with them to make their village a better place to live and to see the forest around them as something they had a collective interest in preserving. Saving the orangutan was a by-product of that.

"We always start by looking at the local power structure," said Supriatna, "understanding the local communities, their cultures, their social and economic aspects, and the influence of the business sector—and [focusing on] what was in it for them and not just the orangutan." If the orangutan benefits and the community doesn't, "we lose the foundation for protecting the whole."

Supriatna said that lately his academic colleagues have started to ask him, "Are you becoming a political ecologist?" "They are worried that I am going away from hard-nosed biology," he said. "But I believe that conservation is not just about protecting the tigers and just looking at how they behave and their food and their predators. Conservation is also about dealing with people. We are the ones disturbing nature. You need to know the biology, but you can't stop with that and assume that it is all going to be fine."

A lot of government officials just look at a map, draw a protected area totally disconnected from the living reality, and assume that an ark of preservation will grow there just like the vegetation. It doesn't happen that way. No people, said Supriatna, no conservation.

Supriatna used a similar formula, beginning in 2003, to build a very different ark in the nearby Batang Gadis tropical forest, where he and his team were able to help get 270,000 acres set aside as a national park in 2004, by then Indonesian president Megawati Sukarnoputri. Supriatna's strategy there was to leverage the local Islamic school, the Mustaphawiya Madrassah, which had 7,500 students. He began by approaching the school's imam, its top spiritual leader, and explaining to him that the river running through his school property would get polluted with tailings if a proposed gold mine upstream in the Batang Gadis forest was to go ahead as planned; the river would also get clogged with silt if logging was allowed. The mine had been licensed to dig right into the water catchment area, and Supriatna and his team wanted to have it relocated. But they needed local allies. So he explained to the imam that the river that his students depended upon to wash themselves before prayer five times a day was about to get very, very dirty.

"It is not enough to just tell them the forest is nice," said Supriatna. "I told him you will not be able to do your ritual washing if this river is polluted." The imam was skeptical at first, recalled Supriatna: "He said to me, 'This is just your prediction . . . [The river] can't be polluted. We have been here fifty years.' I said, 'Do you know there is mining starting upstream?' and he said, 'It is far away.' So I said, 'Come with me. I will take you to the mine.' So I and my staff took him to the mine. He could see the impact with his own eyes. He came back and went straight to the bupati [the district head] and asked that the forest be protected." Added Supriatna: "If you influence the imam, he will influence all the kids and all the kids will tell all the parents."

It was the first time the bupati, whose name was Amru Daulay, had encountered a bottom-up environmental movement. "He looked at this movement and said, 'This is very powerful,'" recalled Supriatna. So Supriatna started to work on him for a bigger project—to help turn Batang Gadis into a national park that no one could touch. "The bupati asked me: 'How can we afford to turn it into a national park? And how do we compensate people who benefit from the logging and mining?'" Supriatna built his case around the river and the fact that its water irrigated 100,000 acres of rice paddies, all of which would be imperiled if the river was polluted by logging or mining.

By coincidence, at the time Indonesia was moving to devolution of power from the central government in Jakarta to the outlying regions. The bupati, who had originally been appointed by the central government in Jakarta to head the Madina district, was going to have to run for office for the first time. "I said to him, 'You can be a hero,'" recalled Supriatna. Amru Daulay did the political math and realized that if he sent the letter to the Ministry of Forestry asking to declare Batang Gadis a national park, it could serve him well in his first real election—which is exactly what he did.

Needless to say, it took a lot of other lobbying and negotiating by groups like Conservation International, the local Islamic leadership, and other Indonesian environmentalists before the government created the park; it is not something that just one district boss can engineer with one letter. But in the end it did get done, and Daulay did not hesitate to base his first campaign, in part, on having helped to get the forest protected and the mining company to relocate its operation outside the watershed. By the way, he won.

Alas, this is not always the pattern—to say the least. In Indonesia, the move to democracy and decentralization has had mixed effects on environmental conservation. In some parts of the country, provincial and even district governments have strengthened conservation—as Governor Suebu has done in Papua. But in other areas, newly empowered local governments, with no supervision anymore from Jakarta, have gorged themselves with opportunities to make quick money by selling permits to extract natural resources, thereby making formerly illegal extractors legal.

Supriatna told me that the coalitions he has helped to build around Batang Toru and Batang Gadis remind him of "a sandwich with so many layers—cheese, tomatoes, meat, potatoes, the government, the communities, the scientists, and the private sector. It has to be adapted to what the problems are . . . When you talk with the head of the government, your language is economic; when you talk to the communities, the language is welfare; when you talk to business, you talk about their future

profits; when you talk to other NGOs, the language is environment."
There have to be different arks and different Noahs for different regions
and different folks. There is simply no other way we can hope to achieve
success.

But no ecosystem to promote healthier forests will survive for long
without better educated people. The two go hand in hand. The village
elders who came out to speak to us in Aek Nabara boasted that they finally had opened a library. I stopped in to see it—a mound of dusty
books and magazines piled onto a table. It was sad. Ultimately, the most
sustainable way to save the forest is to create knowledge jobs. If you want
to save the forests, you have to save the people first, and in today's world
the only way to do that is with an education through which people can
learn service or manufacturing skills that do not involve plundering the
forest. At a minimum, you want people to leave the tropical forest alone,
and at a maximum you want them actively protecting it, either for touris-
tic or medicinal or sustainable agriculture purposes.

Unfortunately, Indonesia—one of my favorite countries in the world,
with an uncommonly likable people and a stunning landscape—has
never given education the priority it needs, probably because the country always had so many natural resources to tap. Although Indonesia has
237 million citizens, only 6,000 have Ph.D.'s—an extremely low percentage. It spends more money today subsidizing gasoline and cooking
oil products for its people (30 percent of the national budget) than providing them with an education (6 percent of the national budget). Not a
good trade.

So, if you go to Indonesia in ten years and see planeloads of young
women being shipped out to be maids, you can be sure that the trees will
be gone too.

While each of these arks has to be built locally, with local investment and local players and local self-interest, global financing is
critical, because with the power of the global economy today, the
amounts of money being put up for oil palm plantations and soy plantations and raw timber are so high that in too many places the forests are
obviously worth more (in the short term) cut down than standing. If you
just look at the price a villager or a logging company can get today for
chopping down a tree, as opposed to what they might earn protecting it,

it's easy to see why the forest loses. And when you think what a big logging company can get from clear-cutting a vast area, it's even more frightening. That is why these arks cannot exist in isolation, and why we cannot leave these Noahs to fend for themselves; rarely are there enough resources locally to generate the alternative incomes and to build the alternative investments to exploiting the forest. Ninety percent of the people living in extreme poverty around the world today are directly dependent upon forests for their food, fuel, shelter, freshwater, and fiber, noted Michael Totten, the Conservation International expert on climate, water, and ecosystems, and most of these people live in rural areas. Many of them are also indigenous peoples whose cultures will not survive if the forests don't survive. There has to be an international system to support whatever arks local communities build, whether via traditional foreign aid programs, like USAID, or other mechanisms that have been effective in providing the resources, technical expertise, and political pressure to launch these arks.

This is not just charity. It's also national security, noted Alfred Nakatsuma of USAID:

Many conflicts are created by the destruction of natural resources that are necessary for the livelihoods of people living in natural ecosystems. One recent USAID study indicated that within a six-kilometer radius of large-scale deforestation in Indonesia, 40 percent of the communities had natural-resource-based conflicts. Conflict over water is happening on an increasingly broad basis, and this often is created by mismanagement of aquifers, poor upstream forestry practices, and industrial-domestic pollution problems. So, good environmental practices also reduce conflict and security problems within nations and across their borders.

That is why proposals like REDD—which try to assign a value to the tropical forests for the environmental services they provide in order to compete with the value that the commodity markets assign to them—are so important. REDD stands for Reduced Emissions from Deforestation and Forest Degradation, and environmentalists want to see the concept included in the UN's successor treaty to Kyoto. Under the REDD proposal, wealthy developed countries would pay poor developing countries to keep their forests intact. In return, the developed nations would get carbon credits that they could count against their emissions-reduction requirements under any new climate treaty. Figuring out how to calculate these credits will be difficult, but even more difficult will be ensuring that this doesn't just end up with one government's central bank transferring money to another while the forests get cut down anyway. You need to be able to track every dollar from the first donor down to the last Noah and make sure those funds do not only go into government accounts but into credible arks, built one at a time. Otherwise we will end up with a lot of leaky arks and continued deforestation and rising carbon dioxide emissions.

All conservation is local—but all our locals are increasingly connected. The palm oil that fried up your French fries today may have come from a chopped-down tropical forest in Indonesia, which in turn helped to contribute to climate change that is intensifying the drought in your backyard. That is why deforestation is everyone's problem and investing in abating it is potentially to everyone's benefit.

"The world's long-term health depends on healthy ecosystems," said Glenn Prickett of Conservation International. "The future will not be secure if we just find clean electrons and get rid of molecules of CO_2. We need healthy forests and clean rivers and productive soils just as much. We need to care for them in their own right and invest in them directly."

In the Dirty Fuels System, people simply took it for granted that economic growth was a trade-off between the health of the ecosystem and the economic health of a community, and that the extinction of species like the orangutan was an inevitable but necessary by-product—"an externality," in the language of economics. Under a Clean Energy System, we will understand that healthy ecosystems and healthy economies have to go together—otherwise the growth itself will be undermined by degraded or insufficient natural resources. "The survival of the orangutan is not just a nice by-product; it is the sign that your model is successful," said Prickett.

But at some point we also need to get beyond these economic and even practical arguments and get back in touch with the deepest truth of all: Green is a value that needs to be preserved in and of itself, not because it is going to make your bank account richer but because it makes life richer and always has. At the end of the day, that is what an "ethic of conservation" is also about. An ethic of conservation declares that maintaining our natural world is a value that is impossible to quantify but also impossible to ignore, because of the sheer beauty, wonder, joy, and magic that nature brings to being alive.

Clean electrons are necessary. Dramatic improvements in energy efficiency are necessary. But the preservation of nature can't be asked to compete with them on simple economic grounds. It must be appreciated, revered, and preserved as a value apart and above all things economic and practical. If we do not nurture this green value in our children, then the cleaner our economies get, and the more energy efficient they become, the more effectively and efficiently we will rape the natural world. There will be no hard walls to stop it. People don't preserve what they don't respect or revere.

"We still don't have an ethic of respect for nature," said Carol Browner, President Obama's energy policy coordinator and a former head of the Environmental Protection Agency. "We teach 'environmentalism' as 'recycling'"—not as the key to appreciating all the wonders, and services, of nature.

That's why I believe strongly in programs like "No Child Left Indoors," sponsored by the Ecological Society of America, the nation's premier organization of ecological scientists. The idea behind it is to develop a greater awareness among schoolchildren and their families of the web of nature right out their back doors and to encourage them to learn how to be good stewards of their larger "home"—planet earth. The ESA Web site, Esa.org, notes that "statistics show that visits to national and state parks have fallen off by as much as 25 percent in the last decade," as kids remain indoors watching TV and playing computer games. "A recent scientific study," it noted, "found that more children knew the characters of Pokémon [a popular children's game] than could recognize an oak tree or an otter. Science education—especially ecology and Earth-based sciences—in America is falling behind that of other countries. Biological, health, and economic data indicate that children who connect with nature perform better in school, have higher SAT scores, exhibit fewer behavioral challenges, and experience fewer attention-deficit disorders."

All you need to do is see young children exploring a garden or a riverbank to know that we are hardwired to enjoy and revere nature, but, in modern times, that instinct tends to get buried the older we get. That's probably what Mahatma Gandhi had in mind when he observed: "To forget how to dig the earth and to tend the soil is to forget ourselves." That's the spirit we have to reawaken if we want and expect that people will vote with their money, their voices, and their ballots to preserve the natural world. As my adventure-travel partner Glenn Prickett always says to me: "You have to see it to save it." Once you've seen a tropical rain forest in Sumatra framed by lush green rice paddies and garlanded by trumpet flowers, which look just like their name—pink flowers shaped like trumpets hanging down from every branch of a large bush—you'll want to save it. Once you've seen the sun rise on the Masai Mara in Kenya and a parade of giraffes walking single file by your camp at dawn, as you shave in the mirror, you'll want to save it. Once you've tramped through the Amazonian rain forests of Peru, dodged wild boar, and fed macaws from your shoulder at your breakfast table, you'll want to save it.

I was at a seminar once where the environmental pioneer Amory Lovins was asked by a member of the audience: "What is the single most important thing an environmentalist can do today?" He answered with two words: "Pay attention." Because when you really see it, you'll want to save it. In 2006, when our family was touring the Peruvian rain forest, we had a remarkable indigenous guide named Gilbert. He always led the way. He carried no phone. No binoculars. No iPod. No radio. He did not suffer from that disease of the modern age, "continuous partial attention"—always trying to do ten tasks at once. Just the opposite. He was always and only paying attention to what was happening around him. He heard every chirp, whistle, howl, or crackle in the rain forest and would stop us in our tracks and immediately identify what bird, insect, or animal it was. He also had incredible vision and never missed a spider's web, a butterfly, toucan, or column of marching termites. He was totally disconnected from the Web, but totally in touch with the incredible web of life around him.

I always felt there was a lesson there. At the end of the day, no amount of investing, no amount of clean electrons, no amount of energy efficiency will save the natural world if we are not paying attention to it—if we are not paying attention to all the things that nature gives us for free: clean air, clean water, breathtaking vistas, mountains for skiing, rivers for fishing, oceans for sailing, sunsets for poets, and landscapes for painters. What good is it to have wind-powered lights to brighten the night if you can't see anything green in the day? Just because we can't sell shares in nature doesn't mean it has no value.

Without an ethic of conservation we will lose that which is priceless but has no price tag.

SIXTEEN

Outgreening al-Qaeda
(or, Buy One, Get Four Free)

When we leave Iraq, it will be the biggest transfer of air conditioners ever known to mankind.

—Dan Nolan, energy consultant to the U.S. Army

Whoever heard of a "green hawk" before—a tough-minded army or marine officer who's as green an advocate of solar power as any sandal-wearing, bicycle-riding, yogurt-eating flower child in Berkeley? Green hawks, though, are just one of the new forces emerging in the Energy-Climate Era, as a wide variety of different groups come to understand that green is not simply a strategy for producing cleaner power, energy efficiency, and conservation, as important as those things are. It's also a strategy for winning in many different contexts. In the coming years, people are going to discover that they can "outgreen" their competition in the marketplace, on the battlefield, in the design studio, and even in the struggle against poverty. It won't be long before "outgreen" will be found in the dictionary, somewhere between "outflank" and "outmaneuver."

I first realized that outgreening could be a military strategy after I learned about the "green hawks" movement in the U.S. military. This informal group of like-minded officers emerged in 2006, after a U.S. Marine general in Iraq's Anbar Province, Major General Richard C. Zilmer, began to complain to the Pentagon that he needed some alternatives to diesel fuel to power his outposts on the Syrian border. One of the most dangerous tasks for marines in that area was driving trucks loaded with ten-gallon tanks of diesel out to isolated observation posts to run the mobile generators that were powering their air conditioners, radios, and other equipment. Either there was no electricity grid or it was not functioning in these remote areas, and the fuel convoys had become big fat delicious targets for Iraqi insurgents with roadside bombs. At the time, the Pentagon was already working with Amory Lovins of the Rocky Mountain Institute to find more energy-efficient ways to operate generally, but the demand from the field, said Lovins, created much greater urgency for the U.S. military to figure out ways to "eat its tail"—that is, to shorten its energy supply lines by finding renewable and distributed sources of power.

"It started with a single commander in Anbar," explained Dan Nolan, who headed the Power Surety Task Force for the U.S. Army's Rapid Equipping Force—which deals with energy logistics—when the request from General Zilmer came up the chain. "When we began the analysis of his request, it was really about the fact that his soldiers were being attacked on the roads, bringing fuel and water." So eating their tail, said Nolan, meant trying to satisfy the energy needs of far-flung outposts with renewable power and energy efficiency that could be generated on site, rather than from diesel fuel trucked in from afar.

Thus began the army's first comprehensive attempt at what I would call "outgreening al-Qaeda"—trying to take away al-Qaeda's advantage of being a very distributed, low-energy guerrilla force against a concentrated, high-energy-consuming conventional army, by looking for a green solution.

Nothing—and I mean *nothing*—will make you a believer in distributed solar power faster than having responsibility for trucking fuel across Iraq. I met two soldiers at the sprawling U.S. military base in Balad, Iraq, fifty miles north of Baghdad, who had undergone that conversion. Their unit was responsible for supplying DF2 diesel fuel to smaller outposts all over the northern Iraqi battle space to keep their generators running. The day I visited, August 25, 2007, the temperature hit 121 degrees Fahrenheit. Air-conditioning a tent in the desert when it is 121 degrees outside takes *a lot* of energy, which is why, at the time, about 70 percent of the U.S. Central Command's energy budget was being spent just moving fuel from one base to another. Even in the best of times and in the most temperate conditions, wars are a huge energy drain, and military equipment, in the past at least, has rarely been designed with energy efficiency in mind.

Before they came to Iraq, the only thing green about Sergeant Major Mike Wevodau and Sergeant Major Stacey Davis would have been their uniforms. But months of managing fuel and food convoys, as well as "route clearance"—sweeping the roads of IEDs, improvised explosive devices, before they blew up a convoy about to pass—had made the two of them advocates of any kind of distributed energy that would diminish the number of fuel trucks that needed to be escorted and roads that needed to be cleared.

Because the electricity system in Iraq is so decrepit and so vulnerable, explained Sergeant Major Davis, "we don't rely on the Iraqi grid at all. Everything is run off generators. You can't walk a hundred feet without running into a generator here, and they run 24/7 until they run out [of fuel]." If the army had distributed solar or wind power, Sergeant Major Wevodau told me, "it would eliminate putting soldiers on the road, and that is the most dangerous thing we do. Keeping people off the roads is the most important thing we can do . . . Why can't we have solar and wind [turbines] out here? I see them every time I drive on the Pennsylvania Turnpike; why don't I see them here?"

It took a while after General Zilmer first raised the issue for the Pentagon to realize that the best way to try to win the fight against IEDs was not just by adding armor, but by greening the army, said Department of Defense energy consultant Linton Wells II. "If a couple of 155 mm mortar rounds buried in a road can flip an Abrams tank, you can make yourself more safe with more armor—but not safe enough," said Wells. "We want to have a zero-casualty war and that leads you to sixty-ton vehicles that won't fit on an airlifter. The only answer is more distributed energy." The best way to beat an IED, he added, "is to not be there when it goes off."

Distributed energy puts fewer people at risk and requires less equipment than diesel does. It would also mean fewer grainy videos on al-Qaeda Web sites of U.S. military vehicles being dramatically blown apart, and lower energy costs for the military, so it could buy other equipment more useful to the fight. "Energy independence is not an economic issue," said Nolan, a retired army colonel who was assigned with his group to come up with energy-saving solutions for the Iraqi battlefront. "It's not a resource issue. It's a national security issue. It's the right business for us to be in."

It certainly is when you're involved in something as complicated as occupying another country, as we have done in Iraq, said Nolan. The United States "does not want to give the wrong impression to the local population. So it tries to put up temporary structures—so people don't think we are about a permanent occupation," he explained. What that means, though, is that the army relies on a lot of tents. "The army tent is our standard temporary structure," said Nolan. "To ensure the soldiers can get sleep and that the electronics inside the office tents will work right, you have to air-condition these temporary structures. Generally speaking, there are some places we could tie into the local grid in Iraq, but you have to ask yourself: 'Should we be taking energy away from the local community?'" That also makes you more vulnerable when some-one cuts one line and your whole army base goes black. "So more often than not, we bring in our own tactical generators," said Nolan, but these need to be fueled with diesel, trucked in from outside, usually Kuwait, but also Turkey and Jordan.

Nolan and his team attacked the problem by first visiting forward op-erating bases in Iraq. "Our survey found that in just one small forward operating base we were bringing in about 10,000 gallons a day of diesel—this was a small base—and 9,000 gallons were used for genera-tors and the rest for mobility. And 95 percent of that generator power was used to air-condition tents."

After analyzing all the battlefield data, Nolan and his team sat back and asked themselves: Where can we have the biggest impact that will not compromise military capability? "You had to take a holistic view and think about it as an energy system," said Nolan. "If I tell a tactical com-mander: 'I am going to give you solar mirrors and windmills,' his reaction will not be positive. But if I tell him that I have a system for supplement-ing his conventional power with renewables that will give him more tac-tical flexibility, he will be more comfortable with that idea."

Nolan's project happened to dovetail with work that the Pentagon had already been doing, work based on a February 2008 Defense Sci-ence Board report called "More Fight—Less Fuel." The report noted that the need to deliver high volumes of fuel to operational forces creates a large logistics tail, which is vulnerable to attack by insurgent forces and difficult to protect, and that as a result fuel delivered this way costs a lot more money than it does at your corner gas station. The Defense Sci-ence Board first recognized this issue in 2001 and coined the concept "the fully burdened cost of fuel." As Tom Morehouse, a former air force officer and another member of the informal green hawks brigade at the Pentagon, explained to me, the U.S. military was not making decisions about weapons systems based on the fully burdened cost of fuel—which is the commodity price of the fuel plus the cost to deliver that fuel to the end user plus the cost of the contractors and trucks that drive that fuel plus the cost of protecting that fuel all along the way plus the cost of tending to casualties from transporting that fuel. When the army started looking at this holistically, it found that the fully burdened cost of delivering a gallon of fuel in the Iraqi military theater "was at least $20 a gallon, and for many missions went upwards of hundreds of dollars per gallon for ground forces," explained Morehouse. Fuel delivered by airborne tanker aircraft actually costs the air force $42 per gallon. That got people's attention.

The first initiative Nolan and his team focused on was improving energy efficiency. They worked with suppliers to develop a technique for the exterior insulation of tents. "We sprayed commercially available foam insulation on the outside of the tents, creating an air barrier capability to that structure, which lowered the requirements for air-conditioning by 40 to 75 percent," he explained. "You have to get as much savings as you can at the front end from efficiency, so the amount of [renewable] energy you have to generate at the back end is as little as possible and will go much farther. If I have a base that is demanding 2 megawatts of electricity every day, trying to provide all that with solar or wind or other alternatives is impossible. But if I can take the demand down through efficiency savings to 500 kilowatts a day, then my alternative energy can work."

The army liked this approach enough to buy sufficient foam to insulate thousands of tents and containerized living units in Iraq. It was so cost-effective—achieving those 40 to 75 percent reductions in air-conditioning, which meant a huge reduction in fuel costs—that Nolan and his team were encouraged to explore a more advanced version of this technology. In this iteration, a large domed temporary structure was insulated with foam from the outside and then covered from the inside with a thin layer of concrete. This tent can sleep forty soldiers (four times the average tent), has more ballistic protection thanks to the concrete, and, Nolan says, with two mobile wind turbines and two sun-tracking solar panels (plus an emergency backup propane generator) it can produce enough energy to air-condition and power the whole living space—and have some left over to give to the nearby village! The U.S. Army is now working to perfect this system so it can be deployed in Iraq or Afghanistan at scale.

This is typical of what happens when you try to solve a problem by outgreening the competition—you buy one and you get four free. In Nolan's case, you save lives by getting convoys off the road, save money by lowering fuel costs, and maybe have some power left over to give to the local mosque's imam so his community might even toss a flower at you one day, rather than a grenade.

There is one more, less visible benefit, from Nolan's point of view: Soldiers see this kind of solution applied to their base in Iraq and then come back to America and demand the same thing for their community or from their factory. When the army desegregated, the country really desegregated; if the army could go green, the country could really go green. Just as the army showed blacks and whites that they could work together, the army can be the laboratory that shows people how to go green together. "That kind of thing starts to change the whole culture," said Nolan. "If we can get this out to Iraq, soldiers are going to come back and say, 'Why can't I have this at home?'"

Nolan, a broad-shouldered veteran who looks more like Patton than a tree hugger, concluded: "When we think about green, we have to think about it differently than how we thought about it in the past. And we have to change our perspective. It has tremendous tactical relevance to us."

I couldn't help but ask, "Is anybody in the military saying, 'Oh gosh, poor Dan has gone green—has he gone girly-man on us now?'"

Answered Nolan with a big laugh: "I'm OK with that."

I am OK with that, too, because I believe that we are on the cusp of an era when outgreening will become a strategy for achieving competitive advantage in a variety of fields. The term "outgreen" was coined by my friends Maria and Dov Seidman over a breakfast we had one morning. The main idea of Dov's book *How* is that in today's totally wired world, you are set apart by "how" you conduct yourself. Everyone is so much more transparent and connected than ever before. As a result, so many more people can now see more deeply into what you do and into your company's operations and tell so many more other people about it via the Internet—without any editor or any filter.

While all this connectivity can be a liability, it can also be an asset for an individual or business. Today, whatever product you make or service you offer can quickly and easily be copied and sold by everyone any-where. But "how" you do your business, argued Dov, an ethics consultant to companies, "how" you keep your promises, and "how" you relate to cus-tomers, colleagues, suppliers, and the communities in which you operate are much more difficult to copy if you are doing them well. That creates an opportunity for sustainable differentiation. "When it comes to human conduct, there is tremendous variation, and where a broad spectrum of variation exists, opportunity exists," he explained. The tapestry of human behavior is so varied, so rich, and so globally diverse, he added, that it presents a rare opportunity—"the opportunity to *outbehave* the competi-tion." How can you outbehave the competition? In Michigan, Dov noted, one hospital taught its doctors to apologize when they made mis-takes, and dramatically cut malpractice claims. That's *how*.

But now you can also *outgreen* the competition and you can *outgreen* your enemies. In a world of seemingly limitless abundance—in a world that was not hot, flat, and crowded—the natural strategy was to try to out-produce or outspend the competition, said Dov. So a country with a lot of agricultural land could outgrow the competition. A country with a lot of forests could outcut the competition. A country with a lot of mines could outstrip the competition. A country with a lot of oil could out-pump the competition. A country with a lot of raw materials could outsell the competition.

"That's why the dictionary is full of words like 'outspend' or 'out-produce,'" added Dov. "Because these were deeply ingrained habits of thought and behavior when resources were abundant—and you had the capital or resources and your competition didn't." This mind-set was im-mortalized in the climactic scene of the movie *There Will Be Blood*, when Daniel Plainview, the greedy oil baron, explains to a naive-seeming preacher, Eli Sunday, who is offering Plainview a lease for oil drilling, that he doesn't need his lease. He has already exploited the preacher's land. He just drilled diagonally from his property over to the preacher's property and sucked out all his oil.

PLAINVIEW: That land has been had. Nothing you can do about it. It's gone. It's had. You lose.
ELI SUNDAY: If you would just take this lease, Daniel . . .
PLAINVIEW: Drainage! Drainage, Eli, you boy. Drained dry. I'm so sorry. Here, if you have a milkshake, and I have a milkshake,

and I have a straw. There it is, that's a straw, you see? You watching? And my straw reaches acrooooooooss the room, and starts to drink your milkshake . . . I . . . drink . . . your . . . milkshake! [*sucking sound*] I drink it up!

In today's increasingly resource-constrained world, it is not so easy anymore to drink someone else's milkshake—and that is why outgreening is going to become more and more important. As noted earlier, in a world that is hot, flat, and crowded, either the market, your society, the global community, or Mother Nature is going to make you pay the true fully burdened cost to the planet for whatever you do and however you do it—for whatever you own, whatever you make, whatever you transport, and however you choose to live. A strategy that depends on outmining, outdrilling, outconsuming, outexploiting your own resources or a global commons—without having to pay any of the externalities—is not going to offer a sustainable competitive advantage any longer.

Instead, as society, the market, and Mother Nature increasingly impose the true costs of how we use energy and natural resources—through carbon taxes, gasoline taxes, regulation, and public opinion, or by simply changing the weather in ways that become dangerously destabilizing—the greenest, cleanest, and most efficient manufacturers, institutions, products, countries, schools, communities, and families will thrive the most, for the longest.

But outgreening requires a wholly different mind-set. It is not just about taking, making, or mining more. Instead of digging or drilling deeper into the ground, you have to dig and drill deeper into yourself, your company, or your community. Instead of mining the environment, you have to create a different kind of environment—a collaborative environment in which you, your company, and your community are constantly thinking about how to generate more growth, more mobility, more housing, more comfort, more security, more enjoyment, and more packaging from the most innovative use of the cleanest electrons and fewest resources.

When you start to drill inside yourself or your own company or your own community for more sustainable ways to power your future, all kinds of good things start to happen—as the U.S. Army discovered. You lower your energy bills. You raise your innovation capacities, because it is impossible to make a product greener without also making it smarter—smarter materials, smarter designs, or smarter software. You develop export products that will be in global demand. You get cleaner air and water. And you will have a better handle on your costs.

Solar and wind power may be more expensive to install today, but the price of the fuel—sun and wind—are fixed. They will be free forever. Fossil fuel systems may be cheaper to install today, but the prices of these fuels—coal, oil, and natural gas—are constantly fluctuating, and with carbon taxes of one kind or another part of the future and demand for these fuels steadily rising, in America and elsewhere, they are clearly heading upward in price.

"Uncertainty costs money," says David Edwards of VantagePoint Venture Partners, and it is now the fossil fuels that have increasingly *uncertain* prices attached to them (and prices that are trending upward), and it is the renewables that have increasingly *certain* prices attached to them (and prices that are trending downward). Here's the story in a nutshell, says Edwards:

"For many years, the developed world thrived by maximizing what seemed like free resources—fossil fuels, basic commodities, land, and water. Today, with the developing world building ever-expanding economies, we are now discovering that those resources that we built on for so long are either finite or no longer nearly free." So, with demand increasing and costs increasing, if you are in an economy that is reliant on fossil fuels, you can be nearly certain that your energy costs will be consistently higher in the future. This is not the 1970s. That oil shortage was driven by geopolitics; this shortage is driven by geology and demography. If you are in an economy that is reliant on clean technologies, though, said Edwards, the long-term economics are going to be very different. "If you install a wind turbine or solar panel or geothermal plant today," he said, "you know what the cost will be to deliver energy from that source for ten or twenty years. We also know that the technology underlying those renewable energy sources is reducing the cost to install new solar panels or wind turbines every year.

"Therefore, the economy with the largest percentage of clean energy sources will have the most certainty around its future energy costs—much more than an economy that is entirely dependent on fossil fuels. In the long run, being cheapest means being greenest," said Edwards.

That is why outgreening is going to be a source of competitive advantage. And that is why America should see itself in a worldwide race to build a clean energy infrastructure. "If I am correct that clean energy will be the cheapest source of energy," said Edwards, "we should be racing to build the cheapest clean energy faster than any other nation. If we win that race, we will have a major advantage over other nations that are saddled with the high costs of fossil energy." We will have a major advantage in energy-intensive manufacturing industries. And we will become a destination for international investment to take advantage of our energy infrastructure.

Moreover, the more you are seen as outgreening your competition, the more people will want to work for your firm—because green as a value will increasingly be something everyone (young people especially) will want to associate with, and therefore the greenest companies, countries, schools, and cities will attract the most talent.

When your mind-set shifts to outgreening, said Dov Seidman, "you stop thinking about accumulating more than someone else and you start thinking about innovation."

That's why it drives me nuts to hear companies or institutions talking about becoming "carbon neutral." That's crazy. In a world that is hot, flat, and crowded, why would anyone want to settle for being just carbon neutral, when there is so much to be gained from having a "carbon advantage"? Is your company striving to be "information neutral"? Do half your employees use computers and half use paper, pencils, and abacuses?

I learned this from David Douglas, vice president for eco responsibility for Sun Microsystems, who first raised the issue in an essay on BusinessWeek.com (January 2, 2008): "Carbon neutrality misses the point. Why pay money for someone else to plant trees to make up for your carbon excesses? It's good for companies to invest in others' good deeds, but right now it's absolutely critical that companies invest in creating more sustainable versions of themselves," said Douglas. Companies whose environmental strategy is defined by trying to be carbon neutral are generally doing some efficiency projects here, purchasing some green energy there, and offsetting the rest.

"Is this bad to do?" asked Douglas. "Of course not. Their efficiency gains help them and the atmosphere, their green energy purchases help grow the investment in even more green energy, and if they bought quality offsets, those should spur further [greenhouse gas] reductions somewhere in the economy. These are all good things—we're doing them too—but I personally don't believe they'll get us where we need to get to. We need companies that view climate change not as a threat but as an opportunity—and are pursuing it with the enthusiasm that big opportunities engender. We need companies to go beyond carbon neutrality to something I call 'carbon advantage.'"

Seeking carbon advantage is a strategy for outgreening.

"You can create a carbon advantage for your company in two ways," explained Douglas: "First, you can use efficiency and resource reduction to provide a fundamental cost advantage in your operations and products. Second, you can use innovation in green products and services to offer customers a competitive advantage, thus differentiating your offerings . . . Companies that have created more eco-friendly goods—such as carmaker Toyota Motor and carpet maker Interface—are increasing their market share and improving their business performance. But more important, there's increasing evidence we're on the edge of a new, virtuous business cycle: Companies seeking sustainability look for sustainable products and services, which provides further opportunities for sustainable companies. As a result, products and services that can help customers improve their own sustainability will be in increasing demand, creating the opportunity for major shifts in market share and net reduction in business impact on the environment.

"If Toyota uses their environmental efforts solely toward carbon neutrality, they never build a Prius," added Douglas. They don't dig inside themselves and "think about how to create a whole new level of efficiency that can get an edge on the competition."

I am struck by the myriad ways people are already trying to outgreen their competition. Let me give a couple of real-world examples, starting with New York City.

Cities compete in the age of globalization more than ever. They compete for talent to move in, start companies, and generate income and tax revenues. They compete for tourists. They compete for company headquarters and capital investments. They compete to keep young people from fleeing to the suburbs or elsewhere. In 2005, David Yassky, a New York City Council member, sat down with one of his supporters, Jack Hidary, a technology entrepreneur, to brainstorm about how New

York City could make itself more livable, and outgreen competing cities, by making New York's taxi fleet less toxic.

Yassky and Hidary started by checking with the Taxi and Limousine Commission to see what it would take to replace the gas-guzzling Ford Crown Victoria yellow cabs, which got only around 10 miles per gallon, with better mileage, low-emission hybrids. It sounded like a great idea, but it turned out to be *illegal*, thanks to some old regulations mandating how big a taxi had to be—regulations designed to favor Crown Vics and their manufacturer, Ford.

Recalled Hidary: "When they first told me, I said, 'Are you serious? Illegal?'" Hidary's response was to go out and form a nonprofit called SmartTransportation.org to help Yassky persuade others on the City Council to change the laws to permit hybrid taxis. In order to broaden their base of support, they went beyond the simple issue of pollution and exposed what a health issue dirty air had become for New York City children, with the help of Louise Vetter, CEO of the American Lung Association of the City of New York.

"New York City has [some of] the dirtiest air in the U.S.," Ms. Vetter explained to me. "When it comes to ozone and particulate matter, New Yorkers are breathing very unhealthy air. Most of it is tailpipe emissions. And in New York City, where asthma rates are among the highest in the nation, the high ozone levels create very serious threats, especially for kids who spend a lot of time outdoors. Converting cabs from yellow to green would be a great gift to the city's children."

Matt Daus, who heads the taxi commission, was initially dubious. He was typical of many leaders—not hostile, just not really aware that green could be better. But once he was persuaded of the health and other benefits of hybrid vehicles, he joined forces with Yassky and Hidary, and the measure passed the City Council by fifty votes to zero on June 30, 2005. Today, more than a thousand of New York City's 13,000 taxis are hybrids—mostly Ford Escapes, but also Toyota Highlanders and Priuses, and others.

On May 22, 2007, Mayor Michael Bloomberg, one of the most environmentally conscientious mayors in America, decided to push even further, proposing a new law, which the taxi commission eventually approved, that would not just permit *but require* all cabs to be hybrids or other low-emission vehicles that get at least 30 miles per gallon, within five years.

"When it comes to health and safety and environmental issues, government should be setting standards," the mayor said. "What you need are leaders who are willing to push for standards that are in society's long-term interest." When the citizens see the progress, Mr. Bloomberg added, "then they start to lead." And this encourages leaders to seek even higher standards.

In the summer of 2007, I asked Evgeny Friedman, a top New York City fleet operator, how he liked the hybrids: "Absolutely fabulous! We started out with eighteen, and now we have over two hundred . . . Now we only put hybrids out there," he said. "The drivers are demanding them and the public is demanding them. It has been great economically. With gas prices as they are [then around $3 per gallon], the drivers are saving $30 a shift." He said drivers who were getting 7 to 10 miles per gallon from their Crown Vics—and buying their own gas out of fares and tips—were getting 25 to 30 from their hybrids. The cost of shifting to these hybrids, he added, has not been onerous.

Having begun to green the taxi fleet, Hidary, Bloomberg, and Rohit Aggarwala, the mayor's top adviser on sustainability, turned their attention to an even worse problem: the 12,000 or so Lincoln Town Cars and other black limousines that are also huge polluters—especially when they sit idling on the doorsteps of Manhattan's top law firms and investment banks, waiting for their clients to get out of meetings. This was a harder problem to solve, because there was no obsolescence law covering limos, unlike taxis. You could keep one of those big black boats on the road as long as you wanted. Hidary started this campaign by taking pictures of the black Town Cars lined up outside the offices of the major New York City law firms and investment banks.

"I then FedExed a letter to the CEOs of each organization, with a picture, pointing out that all these idling Town Cars in front of their offices was a problem," said Hidary, a man who knows how to get things done. "A car that is idling produces twenty times the pollution that a car going 30 miles an hour does, because a car is made to move, not to idle." So this car idling with the heater or air-conditioning running full blast, because the client wants to walk into a perfect environment, "was producing a tremendous amount of pollution, and the largest corporations and law firms were directly responsible."

Hidary said he was surprised by how quickly the operation heads of all these firms got back to him. "Not only were they positively inclined to try to do something," he said, "but the number-one thing that came out was the retention issue."

Say what?

"They saw going green as a way of attracting and retaining young talent," Hidary explained. Hotshot young lawyers and bankers would rather be whisked around town in hybrids than in Town Cars! "There is only so much of an arms race you can do [by offering] dollars and salary or better food in the cafeteria. They immediately saw this as a differentiator." My law firm is greener than yours!

Most of the banks and law firms quickly called their limousine companies asking when they planned to introduce hybrids. The limousine companies quickly saw which way the wind was blowing and asked the mayor to pass a new regulation, so there would be a level playing field and no one could avoid making the new investment in cleaner vehicles. Bloomberg quickly accommodated. On February 28, 2008, Bloomberg announced that beginning in 2009 all "black cars" will have to become green. They will have to get at least 25 miles per gallon and, by 2010, 30 miles per gallon—emissions and mileage standards that can be met by Town Car–sized vehicles only if they are hybrids.

As *The Christian Science Monitor* noted the morning after the announcement: "Goodbye, Town Car (15 miles per gallon); hello, Toyota Camry hybrid (34 mpg)." Although hybrids cost $7,000 to $10,000 more than the typical Town Car, Hidary said the owners were expected to save $5,000 a year on fuel, or about half of what they spend today. Deutsche Bank Americas, Merrill Lynch, and Lehman Brothers set up financing mechanisms to help the Town Car drivers, who are mostly independent operators, finance new vehicles. The whole process is also spurring technical innovation. On February 20, 2008, New York City announced that it was working with automobile design firms to come up with new performance standards for the "taxi of tomorrow."

Don't assume because the driver behind the wheel of a cab or a limousine speaks with a foreign accent that he or she "doesn't want a healthier sustainable lifestyle for their kids," says Hidary. "Why do you think they came here in the first place? So their families could have a better quality of life. Go to any cabbie in New York and they'll say they can't wait to get a hybrid."

When the Big Apple becomes the Green Apple, when New York tries to outgreen Chicago, Beijing, or Detroit by greening its cab fleets, only good things happen, starting with the more than 45 million visitors coming through New York City every year, taking at least one hybrid taxi ride and going back home to their cities and asking: "Why don't we have hybrid cabs?"

Buy one—cleaner air from cleaner taxis and limos—and get four free: happier drivers, a better image for your city, smaller vehicles on your roads, and more innovation around hybrid vehicles.

Hug Shareholders, Not Just Trees

As chief sustainability officer for Sun, David Douglas does outgreening for a living. He is the first person to tell you that the best outgreening ideas often come from below—from those closest to the action. "One day I got an e-mail from one of the staff in our documentation group," he explained. "She writes to me with an idea for how to cut the amount of paper we're sending with our products to customers. What we were doing was sending a complete set of instructions and manuals with every server we sold. If a company ordered ten servers, they got ten manuals, and our large customers were ordering hundreds, so they got hundreds of manuals! So instead we made the manuals a separate option that customers could request. As a result, we cut 60 percent of the paper used and saved hundreds of thousands of dollars, because most companies just needed a couple manuals for each data center . . . Similarly, we recently decided not to print our annual shareholder report, and we put it on the Web instead. We saved ninety-nine million sheets of paper, all of which would be thrown away, roughly 12,000 trees, nine million gallons of fresh water—and the best part: $600,000."

It is amazing the changes in behavior we can produce when we just start to pay attention to our energy and resource productivity. Marcy Lynn, Sun's corporate social responsibility program manager, based at the company's headquarters in Santa Clara, California, told me this story: "We were running a pilot project on our team, because we were trying to see how much energy people use at work, at a time when many people were working at home a lot. I work full-time in an office, so as part of this pilot project they mailed us extension cords that had this thing on the end called a Kill A Watt, which monitors how you are using electricity. So I plug in everything in my office, except the lights, into this extension power strip and then I plug that into the Kill A Watt and then into the wall. Each day we would get an e-mail from this lady reminding us that we have to report what was the starting reading on the Kill A Watt and what was the ending reading and how many hours. It was fascinating. We use Sun Rays, not PCs, and it is amazing how little energy they burn.

"But here was the problem: My office is really cold because it is near a server room and the server room has to be air-conditioned all the time. I remember one day in particular I had the space heater running, and I was shocked [at how much energy it consumed], and I had to report these numbers. If you're going to count, you have to count. I was embarrassed to the point that it was behavior-changing—I waited until my fingers got blue! I didn't want this lady to know [how much electricity I was using] because I was on the eco-team. Now I keep a blanket in my office!"

Marcy Lynn reached for a new blanket because that was the only option available to her, but Sun eventually reached for *a new system*, because what was happening to Marcy Lynn was happening on a much bigger scale to all its customers: It was getting too expensive to air-condition all those servers and, as a result, Sun found that it needed to save energy to save its business—and it couldn't just give out blankets. Outgreening became a survival strategy. If Sun could not outgreen its competition—by offering more and more computing power for less energy—its business was literally going to brown out.

A little background: While the Internet and World Wide Web may seem invisible, residing somewhere out in the ether, in fact they reside in a network of interconnected data centers, also known as server farms. These data centers usually hold thousands of computer servers, jam-packed on racks, one on top of the other, which store and transmit the data and Web pages available on the Internet. Sun makes these servers, among other things. This is a big part of its business. Together, all of these servers in all of these data centers are known as the "cloud," and today more and more of what you do when you fire up your computer doesn't happen on the little hard drive under your desk, but actually happens out there in the network cloud.

Every time you punch out a text message on your cell phone or make a call, it is being processed by servers and routed by servers, and the billing information stored and sent out to you by servers. If you pay your phone bill online, that is processed by servers as well. Every time you search on Google or send an e-mail through Yahoo or use online "live" software from Microsoft or store a document on AOL or add to your Facebook page or upload a video onto YouTube or buy a book from Amazon.com or add to a Wikipedia page or fiddle around with the Linux operating system, you are actually working not on your home computer or PDA but through them to the data centers that make up the cloud. And as a report by the American Technology CEO Council entitled "A Smarter Shade of Green" (February 2008) noted, today "it can cost more to power and cool a server over its lifetime than it does to buy the server—and information technology facilities are running out of cooling capacity and power." All the servers in America today would take about six or seven 1-gigawatt nuclear power plants to keep running 24/7, with that number going up every year.

And that was the start of a new wave of problems for Sun and the computing industry generally. Starting in 2006, said Douglas, customers in the business districts of New York and London started coming to Sun and saying, "I can't get more electricity to cool my data center, so I can't buy anything new from you unless I turn something else off." In Tokyo, the full nightmare came true—the price for just powering and air-conditioning a server over its three-year lifetime started to exceed the price of a standard industry server, about $5,000.

"Unless we could make a more energy-efficient server, we couldn't sell more servers," said Douglas. And because customers also needed more and more computing power to run all these new applications, as more and more people started to do their work in the cloud, Sun concluded that it needed a solution offering more brain power from less electric power.

In a carbon-and-energy-constrained world, Sun needed to outgreen itself and the competition. Sun quickly understood, said Douglas, that "if we didn't become the most energy-efficient company, we would not be in business. But if we could make more energy-efficient servers than our competitors, we could take market share."

So in 2002, Sun began developing a new processing chip, code-named Niagara. Sun's bet in designing Niagara was that for many of today's applications, the most important thing was the ability to do many tasks at once, but none of them individually at Porsche speed. This was a departure from the industry tradition of focusing on peak speed, which enabled chips to do one or two things at a time very quickly. Sun's observation was that even though the top speed of a 260-mph Porsche sounds very cool, if the task at hand is to get sixty people from one place to another, a bus can do it both faster and more energy efficiently. The Niagara processing chip allowed Sun, for example, to process many eBay bids at one time on each server, "which allows us to get more total work done with less total power than something built purely for peak speed," according to Douglas.

Today, Sun's Niagara-based server line is one of the fastest-growing parts of Sun's business—going from zero to a billion dollars in just two years—and Sun is now applying the same principle to all its computer components. (Niagara has certainly helped Sun's balance sheet at a time when other parts of its business have been weak.) Sun figures that an official tax on carbon, once it arrives, will drive more customers to this kind of processing solution—so it is trying to get ahead of the curve. Not only is Sun helping its customers with their computing, but it is also helping them with their image, because more and more of Sun's customers are telling their customers that they are going green, and Sun is giving them the basis to make that claim.

"Most corporate responsibility is defensive," explained Douglas. "'Let's not get caught using underage workers in Burma.' You never really thought you could make a lot more money by being more corporately responsible." Not anymore. Now the whole energy frontier may become a source of competitive advantage, he explained: "We are making our costs lower and selling more energy-efficient products and then deploying them internally and making ourselves more efficient. This means we get to play offense on corporate social responsibility, and playing offense is always a lot more fun."

Only a company, or a country, whose chief executive officer is also a chief energy officer—someone who is thinking holistically about all the costs and benefits—will be able to outgreen the competition. Why? Because most companies in the world operated the way the U.S. military did—they never looked at the total cost of ownership in making their energy decisions. Often the people who designed or purchased products inside a company, and the people who used those products, and the people who paid the electricity or fuel bills for those products, were all different people. So the vice president for equipment buys the lowest-cost machine to make his budget look good. But the vice president for accounting, who pays the electric bills, is on his back every day because that same low-cost machine was the one that sucked up the most energy when electricity prices started to soar, and, when electricity prices went through the roof, that cheap machine actually cost the company over its life cycle far more than the expensive super-energy-efficient model would have. Because no one had a bird's-eye view of all the costs and benefits of energy decisions, money and resources were continually wasted.

"If you see green only from your silo, you only see increased costs," explained Jeff Wacker, the futurist for EDS. "You don't see the trade-offs, you don't see the decrease somewhere else, because it's not in your silo where that something else happens." So you need the CEO who can say, Let's go for an initially more expensive but low-heat, low-energy lighting system, because that will allow us to design and install and operate fewer air conditioners. Only if you look at it systemically "can you measure all the savings," said Wacker. "Once you start to measure, you recognize the benefits for the whole system."

Which is why, I suspect, in the Energy-Climate Era, if you don't run your company, or country, like a *chief energy officer*, you're not going to be very effective as a *chief executive officer*. You are never going to optimize all the assets under your control. If your thinking is limited to your silo, you will buy one and get less than one back. If your thinking stretches across your whole system, you will buy one and get four or five more for free—and that's how you get an edge on the competition.

About going green, remarked Douglas, "I don't remember who said it, but they sure were right: 'It's like there was all this money lying all over the floor, and we finally decided to have our employees reach down and pick it up.'"

Code Green for me, though, has never been just a business or a geopolitical strategy, as important as those are. This book makes a larger claim—that the best way to re-energize America, rebuild its self-confidence and moral authority, and propel it forward as a society is also by focusing on a green agenda. Therefore, outgreening has to be a strategy not only for beating the company, army, or city next door, but also for beating poverty at our back door. Code Green has to prove that it can offer something to the very lowest rungs of the economic ladder, not just to upper-middle-class people. If all Americans can't see outgreening as a strategy that could improve their lives, it will never generate the momentum and scale that it needs to succeed.

That may sound like a stretch, but it's not. Ask Van Jones. He's good at stretching. I met him at a conference in Dalian, China, when he stretched out an arm to introduce himself—as he was going down an escalator and I was going up the other side. Jones is a rare bird. At the time he was a black social activist in Oakland and as green an environmentalist as they come. He really gets passionate, and funny, when he talks about what it's like to be black and green.

"Try this experiment," he said to me. "Go knock on someone's door in West Oakland, Watts, or Newark and say, 'We got a really big problem!' They say, 'We do? We do?' 'Yeah, we got a really big problem!' 'We do? We do?' 'Yeah, we gotta save the polar bears! You may not make it out of this neighborhood alive, but we gotta save the polar bears!'"

Jones then just shakes his head. If you try that approach on people without jobs, who live in neighborhoods where they've got a lot better chance of getting killed by a passing shooter than a melting glacier, you're going to get nowhere—and if you don't bring America's underclass into the green movement, this movement's full potential will never be realized. "We need a different on-ramp" for people from disadvantaged communities, says Jones. "The leaders of the climate establishment came in through one door and now they want to squeeze everyone through that same door. It's not going to work. If we want to have a broad-based environmental movement, we need more entry points."

The big question, Jones told me in an interview, is this: "How do you use the green economy to deliver work, wealth, and health for communities who have had too little of all three? How do you connect the people who most need work with the work that most needs to be done, and, if you do it right, beat pollution and poverty at the same time?"

Can we really outgreen poverty and pollution at the same time? Jones makes a strong and impassioned case that we can—and he has been trying to prove it in some of the poorest neighborhoods in America. Thirty-nine years old and a Yale Law School grad, he exudes enough energy to light up a few buildings on his own. He founded the Ella Baker Center for Human Rights in Oakland, which helps kids get out of jail and into jobs, but he moved in 2008 to run Green for All, a new national organization working to build an inclusive green economy with a specific focus on creating "green-collar" jobs for underprivileged young people. Again, it all starts with a world that is getting hot, flat, and crowded. The more these trends intensify, the more federal, state, and local governments will require buildings to be energy efficient and the more work there will be retrofitting buildings all across America with solar panels, insulation, and other weatherizing materials. Those are jobs that can't be outsourced.

"You can't take a building you want to weatherize, put it on a ship to China, and then have them do it and send it back," said Jones. "So we are going to have to put people to work in this country—weatherizing millions of buildings, putting up solar panels, constructing wind farms. Those green-collar jobs can provide a pathway out of poverty for someone who has not gone to college." Let's tell our disaffected youth, he says, "You can make more money if you put down that handgun and pick up a caulk gun." Remember, adds Jones, "a big chunk of the African-American community is economically stranded. The blue-collar, stepping-stone manufacturing jobs are becoming fewer and fewer. And they're not being replaced by anything, except higher skilled jobs. So you have this whole generation of young blacks who are basically in economic free fall." Green-collar retrofitting jobs are a way to catch some of them.

To this end, Jones helped create the Oakland Apollo Alliance, a coalition of labor unions, environmental organizations, and community groups. In 2007, that coalition helped to raise $250,000 from the city government to create Oakland Green Jobs Corps, a union-supported training program to teach young people in Oakland how to put up solar panels and weatherize buildings. That was the beginning of the Green for All campaign (Greenforall.org) that Jones, backed by other environmental activists from around the country, like Majora Carter from Sustainable South Bronx, used to persuade Congress to pass the Green Jobs Act of 2007, which authorized $125 million per year from the federal government to create an "Energy Efficiency and Renewable Energy Worker Training Program" to prepare workers and people just entering the job market for jobs in a range of green industries.

"The big problem with the job training is that too often it is all about throwing certificates at people, whether they get a job or not," said Jones. "[But] more often than not they come to some school or an institute, get a certificate, and there is no job on the other side." The beauty of a green jobs program is that there is no question whatsoever, as building codes change and green technologies make retrofitting your home a no-brainer, that green-collar jobs will be there waiting for anyone who gets trained to do them. And the beauty of this initiative, if it can be made to work, is that like other forms of outgreening, you buy one and you get four others for free.

The more we make tax incentives available for retrofitting homes to make them more energy efficient and to encourage use of solar technologies, the more we strengthen the ability of poor people to stay in their homes and secure their neighborhoods. I'll let Jones explain:

"There is a category of very vulnerable poor people who own their own homes, but tend to be older and on fixed incomes," he says. "They are very vulnerable to soaring energy prices." If the government, he added, put in place a program that said: "We're going to send teams in to find out where your home is leaking energy and then install the insulation, weatherization, and a few solar panels," we could create jobs for underprivileged youth, lower energy bills for lower-income families, and add value into the homes of the most economically vulnerable sector of the population. For a lot of underprivileged people, greening their homes may be the only way to keep them in their homes, as fuel prices continue to soar. Those homeowners are the most stable pillars of any neighborhood.

"Make their homes energy-secure and their kids' jobs secure and you stabilize the neighborhood," said Jones. "And you get cleaner air to boot. You fix social problems and ecology problems at the same time. You help Grandma and the polar bears stay at home."

This is an industry that is ready to take off. "If we can get these youth in on the ground floor of the solar industry now, where they can be installers today, they'll become managers in five years and owners in ten—and then become inventors," argued Jones. "The entry-level rung is low enough, but the ladder reaches to the sun." If you green the ghetto first, he added, "and spend $7,000 training Pookey and giving him a life skill, it is a lot better than warehousing Pookey in a prison for $500,000. Save a watt, save a life—it's all the same principle. In a green economy, you don't just count what you spend, you count what you save."

One thing spurring him in this project, added Jones, was the way that the big oil companies bought ads in black-owned newspapers in California in 2006 to help bring out black votes—by dishonestly scaring people about higher gasoline prices—to defeat Proposition 87. Proposition 87 proposed a tax on oil companies drilling in California, the money from which would have gone to develop alternative energy programs. "The polluters were able to stampede poor people into their camp," said Jones. "I never want to see an NAACP leader on the wrong side of an environment issue again."

Not surprisingly, some of the worst polluting factories, power plants, and toxic waste dumps are located in poor neighborhoods, where people have little power to defend themselves against such projects.

What I find most compelling about Jones's argument is something that goes to the core thesis of this book: It used to be that the greener you were, the further away you were from ordinary Americans. Green was all about yoga mats, Birkenstock sandals, tofu, and individual lifestyle choices that often separated greens from average Americans. When you start to redefine green in the way Jones does, you come closer to ordinary Americans' concerns.

"In a real green economy," said Jones, "you don't have any throwaway resources—you don't have throwaway species and you don't have throwaway neighborhoods and you don't have throwaway kids either . . . I have not met a white person who would not support [this kind of approach] if they thought it could work. A green agenda brings us all together again, because the hope at the core nourishes everybody."

The last time someone said "I have a dream" in America, it was a dream about people, said Jones. "This is a dream about people and the planet. We need to put the two together, because the moral power of that will give us *our* dream."

For all these reasons, even though outgreening is not a word yet, I hope it will be soon—in every language. Because this is not a zero-sum competition. I can outgreen your company, country, or community in one area, and you can outgreen me in another. I can outgreen you today, and you can outgreen me tomorrow, and we will all be better off. But whoever outgreens and keeps outgreening will be the best off for the longest time, because the best employees are going to say: "That is the company I want to work for." The best students are going to say: "That is the school I want to attend." The most global citizens are going to say: "That is the country I want to follow."

India and China may take away a few American jobs with cheaper labor, but those are transient advantages. However, if one of these countries consistently outgreens America, they will be seizing a sustainable advantage. In the Energy-Climate Era, you cannot be the leader of the world without being the world's leader in conceptualizing, designing, manufacturing, deploying, and inspiring clean power solutions. Period. Full stop. Over and out.

PART IV

China

SEVENTEEN

Can Red China Become Green China?

I've visited China regularly since 1990, and, looking back, here's what strikes me most: Each time I go there, China's people seem to speak with greater ease and breathe with greater difficulty.

Yes, you can now have strikingly frank talks with officials and journalists in China. But when I walked out of my hotel room heading for an interview the last time I visited Shanghai, in November 2006, the air was so smoky—from the burning of farm fields after the harvest—that for a moment I honestly thought my hotel was on fire. For some three decades now, China's economy has grown at around 10 percent per year, based on low-cost labor and little regard for the waste and pollution it pumped into its rivers and the air. For many years, when you asked about pollution, officials and business leaders in China would say they will clean up when China gets rich enough to afford to clean up. I would argue that now that we are entering the Energy-Climate Era, China can get rich *only if it cleans up*. Unless Red China becomes Green China, the Communist Party leadership will not be able to deliver to all the Chinese people the rising standard of living it has promised.

China cannot afford to do what the West did: Grow now, clean up later. I know that this strikes many Chinese as unfair, which is why global warming is perceived by more than a few Chinese as a "conspiracy" concocted by the West to slow China's growth. It *is* unfair, if you consider how much CO_2 the Western industrialized countries blithely pumped into the atmosphere, long before the Chinese industrial dragon ever started huffing and puffing—and how the West has shipped its dirtiest manufacturing industries to China. But Mother Nature isn't into fair. All she knows is hard science and raw math: If China were to try to grow now and clean up later, the unprecedented pace and scale of its development would lead to an environmental disaster.

It's all in the numbers: China is one-fifth of humanity; it's now the world's biggest carbon emitter; it is the world's second-largest importer of oil, after the United States; and, according to a report in *The Times* of London (January 28, 2008), it is already the world's largest importer of nickel, copper, aluminum, steel, coal, and iron ore. Timber is certainly up there as well. It is not an exaggeration to say: As goes China, so goes planet earth. If China can make a stable transition to clean power and an energy-and-resource-efficient economy, we as a planet have a chance to mitigate climate change, energy poverty, petrodictatorship, and biodiversity loss in significant ways. If China can't, China's emissions and appetites will nullify everything everyone else does to save the earth, and the Energy-Climate Era will careen toward the unmanageable. So for me, the crucial question of this book is actually two questions: "Can America really lead a real green revolution?" and "Can China really follow?" Everything else is just commentary . . .

To put it in the local vernacular, Deng Xiaoping once famously said of China's economy: "Black cat, white cat, all that matters is that it catches mice"—that is, forget about Communist ideology, all that matters is that China grows. Not anymore. Now, if that cat isn't green, neither it nor the mice, nor any of the rest of us, are going to make it.

So how's China doing? The best short answer I've heard comes from the longtime Asia-watcher Nayan Chanda, the former editor of the *Far Eastern Economic Review* and now editor of *YaleGlobal Online*. When I asked Chanda for his views on China's energy and environment performance, he answered with barely a pause: "Go rent the movie *Speed*."

That 1994 thriller stars Keanu Reeves, Dennis Hopper, and Sandra Bullock. Reeves plays Jack Traven, an LAPD SWAT team specialist who is sent to defuse a bomb that Howard Payne, a revenge-driven extortionist (Dennis Hopper), has planted on a bus. But here's the rub: The bomb has been rigged to explode the second the speed of the bus falls below 50 miles per hour. So Jack and Annie Porter, a passenger played by Sandra Bullock, must keep the bus hurtling through the streets of Los Angeles at more than 50 miles per hour—or they, the bomb, and everything around them will go up in flames.

"China is that bus," said Chanda.

"It has to grow at a minimum of 8 percent a year or it will explode," he added, "because it will have so much unemployment and discontent, the population will erupt." The implicit ruling bargain that the Chinese Communist Party has offered the people of China has been very clear ever since the end of Mao's era. It goes like this: "We are replacing Communism with GDPism. GDPism says: We get to rule. You, the people, get to become prosperous. You accept our rule. We guarantee your rising prosperity." Without a steadily rising Gross Domestic Product—without that China bus going 50 miles per hour—that ruling bargain would unravel.

But my own regular visits to China over the past two decades have taught me that while this remains the ruling bargain, China's leaders, who are very shrewd, have come to understand that in a world that is becoming hot, flat, and crowded, China cannot sustain this ruling bargain any longer—without adding a footnote in fine print. And the fine print now says: "This ruling bargain is subject to limitations that China will soon have to impose on itself—because the environmental, energy, and biodiversity implications of China's largely coal-powered growth will, if unrestrained, end up killing Chinese, irredeemably polluting China's environment, sapping its economy, and alienating the rest of the world. If the rest of the world, particularly the United States, moves in the next few years to some form of carbon tax, or if Mother Nature imposes even harsher punishments in her own way, China will have to move away from cheap and dirty fuels; otherwise it will face a boycott of its goods. Therefore, the Communist Party reserves the right to slow down growth in the name of cleaning up the economy."

China's leaders may not have spelled out that footnote to themselves or their people in so many words, but it is the logic driving where they need to go and have already started moving. That is why, when you add it all up, there is no avoiding the conclusion that China's leadership is engaged in one of the most daring political high-wire acts ever attempted on the world stage. As Chanda put it: "China's leaders are trying to replace the motor in that Chinese bus from a gas-guzzling polluter to a superefficient hybrid—but they're trying to do it while the bus is still going 50 miles an hour."

This could be the greatest show on earth.

The drama unfolding in China is so compelling because the same Communist Party that three decades ago replaced Communism with

GDPism is now trying to replace GDPism with "Green GDPism." And what's most fascinating about this show is how the Chinese leadership has decided, after a lot of trial and error, to go about it. The bus driver has turned around, told the passengers that the engine needs to be changed—without specifying exactly how it's to be done—and even started allowing some of the passengers to jump into the engine well and tinker. China's leaders have come to understand that they can't change this engine alone.

At first, as mounting pollution became an issue in the 1990s, China's leaders tried to engineer Green GDPism the same way they did the Cultural Revolution and the Great Leap Forward: by just ordering it from the top down. But that didn't work. Plain old GDPism—growth at any price—had too much momentum. So now they are trying a more top-down-plus-bottom-up approach that involves allowing the Chinese press to spotlight environmental polluters, passing progressive energy efficiency laws, encouraging investments in clean power research and technology, and granting China's civil society some of the legal tools to bring violators to trial. I would not describe it as a system yet; it is often one step forward and two steps back. And sometimes the same local leader or businessman acts like a pure GDPist in the morning and as a Green GDPist in the afternoon. In real life, especially in societies in transition, people often have multiple identities. But *it is happening*, and it appears to be China's strategy for switching from dirty capitalism to *relatively* clean capitalism without having to slow down the bus too much.

"We tend to think in grand systematic ways, but in fact, if you look back, China's leadership moved from a Communist centrally planned system to a capitalist market society without having a grand plan," said Edward S. Steinfeld, a China specialist at MIT and the author of *Forging Reform in China: The Fate of State-Owned Industry*. "It was done in an incremental, nonsystematic way, and the same thing seems to be happening with environmentalism. Some in the leadership are recognizing the dire costs of growth. They are not flipping a switch to turn it off, but they are empowering forces in society and the media to do something about it. It produces this kind of whirlpool of competing claims and impulses, but it is moving in a certain direction."

This strategy raises several fundamental questions, and they are the focus of this chapter. What exactly got China's leaders to move from GDPism to Green GDPism? Are they moving fast enough? What role can the United States play in supporting China's Green Leap Forward? And, maybe most important, by granting more power to the Chinese people so they can protect their *freedom to breathe*, will China's Communist Party leadership unleash political forces that, over time, will give the Chinese people much more *freedom to speak*? Could this turn out to be the first big democracy movement that starts as an environmental movement?

"Could a movement that begins with people being empowered to pursue their right to breathe, their right to drink clean water, and their right to see the stars in the sky at night," asks Chanda, "end with people securing their right to speak, because you cannot do one without the other?" Could a battle "over the right to inhale," added Chanda, "end with more rights to exhale?"

Most China experts would tell you the answer is no, but when you look at the scope and scale of what China is going to need to do to wrestle its pollution problems to the ground, you see that it could end up requiring and stimulating more political change than anyone now realizes.

What got the Chinese leadership to move toward Green GDPism? Probably nothing more than looking out the window. It's not like they could miss the problem, even riding in a limousine with tinted glass. An American friend in Beijing tells me that every morning he gets up and does his own air quality test—as many Beijing residents do: He looks out his twenty-fourth-story window and checks how far he can see. On a rare pristine day, when the wind has swept Beijing clean, he can see the Fragrant Mountain rising to the northwest. On a "good" pollution day, he can see the China World building four blocks away. On a bad day, he can't see the building next door. Those are the days when Beijing is enveloped by a film of pollution from exhaust given off by the thousand new cars a day, on top of the three million existing cars, that hit the road there, mixed with emissions from coal-burning power plants and factories, as well as dust from construction sites, from off the deserts, and from cement plants running full out. (It's almost too much to have asked, but China should have learned from America's mistake, skipped cars altogether, and gone directly to the world's best mass transit system, because to fuel all these vehicles for a burgeoning Chinese middle class is going to be an endless economic drain and an environmental nightmare.)

The problem of conventional pollution reached a degree of critical-ity in recent years that not only made it inescapable but made future trend lines terrifying for the Chinese leadership, if they took no action. As the deputy minister of China's State Environmental Protection Agency, Pan Yue, said in a famously candid interview with *Der Spiegel* (March 7, 2005):

> Many factors are coming together here: Our raw materials are scarce, we don't have enough land, and our population is con-stantly growing. Currently, there are 1.3 billion people living in China, that's twice as many as 50 years ago. In 2020, there will be 1.5 billion people in China. Cities are growing but desert areas are expanding at the same time; habitable and usable land has been halved over the past 50 years . . . The environment can no longer keep pace. Acid rain is falling on one third of the Chinese territory, half of the water in our seven largest rivers is completely useless, while one fourth of our citizens does not have access to clean drinking water. One third of the urban population is breath-ing polluted air, and less than 20 percent of the trash in cities is treated and processed in an environmentally sustainable manner. Finally, five of the ten most polluted cities worldwide are in China . . . Because air and water are polluted, we are losing be-tween 8 and 15 percent of our gross domestic product. And that doesn't include the costs for health. Then there's the human suf-fering: In Beijing alone, 70 to 80 percent of all deadly cancer cases are related to the environment. Lung cancer has emerged as the No. 1 cause of death.

No, those are not problems any government could ignore—let alone the rest of us. The U.S. Environmental Protection Agency reports that on some days almost 25 percent of the polluting matter in the air above Los Angeles originated in China.

One of the most famous pictures to ever come out of China was Chairman Mao swimming in the Yangtze River. But as Andreas Lorenz observed in a *Der Spiegel* essay (November 28, 2005) on the toxic pollution that has now poisoned so many of China's rivers and lakes: "Nowadays . . . chairman Mao Zedong's legendary swimming outing in the Yangtze River in 1966 would no longer be seen as evidence of his strength, but more as a suicide attempt."

Beyond this general trend toward environmental degradation, China's leadership was clearly alarmed by a sudden surge in energy use in recent years. As the team of experts who follow China's environment at the Lawrence Berkeley National Laboratory explained to me, between 1980 and 2000 China's GDP quadrupled, but its total energy usage only doubled—a sign of good energy and resource efficiency and tight government controls.

Post-2001, however, the new government in Beijing loosened monetary policy, and China's entry into the World Trade Organization dramatically increased foreign investment in the country, particularly for manufacturing, and this turbocharged China's exports. In the process, China fell off the wagon in terms of energy efficiency, alarming the leadership. Between 2001 and 2005, growth in energy usage in China outpaced growth of its GDP—in 2005 it was 40 percent faster—as the Chinese at once embarked on a massive and energy-intensive buildup of its nationwide physical infrastructure, took on the dirty industries being shed by the West, and just began to live more comfortably, in bigger apartments with air-conditioning, TVs, and computers.

Finally, China's leadership began to act because of climate change. In just the past two years, China's leaders, like many others around the world, have come to realize that climate change is not only real but appears to be changing China's own climate in potentially disastrous ways much faster than anyone had anticipated. "China's average temperature in 2007 was 10.3 degrees centigrade [50.5 degrees Fahrenheit], which made 2007 the warmest year since the establishment of a national climate-observation network in 1951," the *Beijing Review* reported (January 4, 2008). "This record-high temperature, which marked the 11th year in a row that the national average temperature has been higher than in a normal year, was remarkably higher than the second highest figure of 9.9 degrees centigrade [50 degrees Fahrenheit] in 2006."

In December 2006, China's government issued its first official report on climate change. It noted that glaciers in the nation's northwest had decreased by 21 percent since the 1950s, and that all of China's major rivers had shrunk over the past five decades. "Global climate change has an impact on the nation's ability to develop further," said the Ministry of Science and Technology, one of twelve government departments that prepared the report.

Lu Xuedu, deputy director of the Global Environmental Affairs Office of the Ministry of Science and Technology, told China's Xinhua

News Agency (October 4, 2007) that "climate change has begun to take its toll in China in recent years, and we shouldn't wait till it is too late to take action." In China's National Climate Change Program (June 4, 2007), the government pledged to restructure the economy, promote clean energy technologies, and improve energy efficiency. China is the world's biggest producer and consumer of coal, using coal-fired power to meet 80 percent of its vast energy needs; it adds roughly 1 gigawatt of coal-fired power every two weeks.

Lu told Xinhua that if climate change remains unchecked, the yield of China's major crops (including wheat, rice, and corn) will drop by up to 37 percent in the second half of this century. "Global warming will also reduce the river levels, and lead to more droughts and floods. And water supply in western China will fall short of demand by up to 20 billion cubic meters from 2010 to 2030," he said. Climate change also presents a major threat to ecologically vulnerable areas such as the Qinghai-Tibet Plateau, which is the water tower of China, the Xinhua report noted. Less water in the rivers is not only bad for farmers, but will also significantly decrease hydro power, which will make China even more dependent on coal than it is now.

But recognizing the problem and its urgency is only half the battle for China's leadership. Getting the whole system to respond—from cities to provinces to the central government, and from the public sector to the private sector—is another matter.

In September 2007, I visited Beijing in the middle of an Indian summer. Every time I went to interview a Chinese official in his office, I found myself loosening my tie and exclaiming: "Hey, is it a little warm in here, or is it just me?"

No, I was told, it wasn't just me. In June 2007, China's State Council had ordered—in the way only China could—that all government agencies, associations, companies, and private owners in public buildings must set their air-conditioning thermostats no lower than 26 degrees Celsius, or 79 degrees Fahrenheit. Air-conditioning consumes one-third of the electricity demand in China in summer. And you could definitely feel the difference in public offices.

A few days later, I was reading some reports from China's English-language newspapers and I came across an item from the *Shanghai*

Daily. It said the municipality had sent out teams to see who was comply-
ing with the government's air-conditioning edict, and they found that
"more than half of the city's public buildings have failed to obey power-
saving rules setting air-conditioning at 26 degrees Celsius, according to
local energy authorities."

That in a nutshell is the good news, the bad news, and the interesting
news from China today. The good news is that the government has
decided to step in and take over people's thermostats in public buildings. That is an indication of seriousness. The bad news is that in the
provinces and cities outside Beijing, and even inside Beijing, local officials are not afraid to ignore the State Council's environmental edicts. As
the old Chinese saying goes: "The sky is high and the emperor is far
away."

But the interesting news is that someone ordered the *Shanghai
Daily*, a state-run newspaper, to expose those city buildings and officials
who were ignoring the air-conditioning order—something I'm not sure
would have happened five years ago. (And the really, really interesting
news is that maybe nobody ordered the *Shanghai Daily* to write this
story. Instead, maybe entrepreneurial journalists, sensing a relevant
space in which they could report like real journalists and effect social
change, and have political cover to boot, went out and did the reporting
on their own. That's the new China.)

In many ways, it is these three trends that are fighting it out in China
today: a leadership that understands the problem and is taking serious
measures, a system that is so big and diffuse and has so much momentum for growth that slowing it down is extremely difficult (even for an authoritarian government), and the first tentative steps to enlist civil society
and media in China on the side of environmentalism. It is not clear
which trend is going to win.

Certainly, China's initial effort to green its GDP from the top down
has met with enormous resistance from the capitalist system unleashed
in the early 1970s, as ad hoc coalitions of local government and business
officials who benefited from cowboy capitalism eluded whatever edicts
came down from Beijing—sometimes in cahoots with high officials
there.

China is "a veritable unstoppable growth machine," wrote the China
experts Elizabeth C. Economy and Kenneth Lieberthal in their *Harvard
Business Review* essay (June 2007) on China's environmental problems,

"Scorched Earth: Will Environmental Risks in China Overwhelm the Opportunities?" The fact that the Communist Party's legitimacy depended on maintaining economic growth, they noted, meant that any environmental regulations that got in the way of growth tended to be ignored or watered down one way or the other.

China's political system is built on five layers: national, provincial, municipal, county, and township, explained Economy and Lieberthal—with the Communist Party sitting atop all five. For officials who are trying to move up the system, "success is rewarded in two ways," they noted. "Formally, annual performance evaluations are pegged primarily to GDP growth in each jurisdiction. Informally, local officials personally benefit financially from that growth by investing in or holding positions in key firms, by assigning relatives to management positions, by engaging in plain vanilla corruption, and so on." This system has unleashed so many official entrepreneurs, said Economy and Lieberthal, that if the Chinese Communist Party were aptly named, it would really be called the "China Bureaucratic Capitalist Party." Party leaders at all levels, they added, "are entrepreneurial tigers hell-bent on using political power directly, in league with local public and private enterprises, to spur rapid GDP growth in their own bailiwicks."

The whole system enabled "local officials to protect their enterprises from meaningful implementation of environmental laws and regulations," added Economy and Lieberthal. "Indeed, officials often require that enterprises in their jurisdictions ignore such laws and regulations in their quest for ongoing GDP growth. Then, in an effort to offset any fines the companies may have to pay for environmental transgressions, officials cover up the resulting problems in their reports to higher levels, interfere in local courts to prevent adverse rulings, and bestow tax breaks, bank loans, and other financial support on affected enterprises."

It was for all these reasons that Beijing's Green GDP initiative in 2005 and 2006—which promised to judge Chinese officials on how well they protected their environment and deduct points for environmental degradation from their GDP growth numbers—never had any impact. It was difficult to calculate and measure uniformly, and local officials resisted implementing such a green yardstick. So the initiative died an early death. So too did some early goals. China's tenth Five-Year Plan, which began in 2001, called for a 10 percent reduction in sulfur dioxide in China's air—and when that plan concluded in 2005, sulfur dioxide pollution in China had *increased* by 27 percent.

What China's leaders apparently realized from that tenth Five-Year Plan—their first serious foray into green policy—was that taking China from Communism to capitalism was actually easier than trying to take it from dirty capitalism to clean capitalism. Because going from Communism to state-directed capitalism, while by no means easy, involved taking the lid off a people who were yearning to be entrepreneurial, wildcatting capitalists. It involved unleashing something long suppressed in the Chinese culture—and the results of all that unleashed energy are apparent everywhere.

But going from Dirty GDPism to Green GDPism is about restraining and redirecting all that natural energy—and to do that effectively requires a system with some judicial independence, so that courts can discipline government-owned factories and power plants. It requires a freer press that can report on polluters without restraint, even if they are government-owned businesses. It requires more transparent laws and regulations, so citizen-activists know their rights and can feel free to confront polluters, no matter how powerful. And most of all, it requires growth based on sustainable energy productivity—not growth based on dirty energy productivity.

Although China's leadership underestimated how hard it would be to change the engine on their bus from a dirty combustion engine going at full throttle to a hybrid, here's what's interesting: They have not backed off. There were more than a few signs in 2007 and 2008 that they've actually decided to double their green bets—and that is going to make the early-twenty-first century politically very interesting in China.

It is almost as if a light went on in the Chinese politburo. The leadership realized that if it did not tackle this environment-energy-climate problem, dirty air, as much as slower growth, would undermine the stability and legitimacy of the Communist Party. Therefore, finding a way to grow green was becoming an imperative, not an option. It was a survival strategy. In that sense, China's leadership is becoming like those of many other governments around the world in the Energy-Climate Era—shifting the basis of its legitimacy from the ability to defend China's borders, which is now taken as a given, to the ability to deliver a higher living standard and to protect the nation from environmental degradation and energy and climate disruptions.

So what we've started seeing with the eleventh Five-Year Plan—2006 to 2010—is Beijing pushing with one hand even more extensive green laws from the top and, with the other hand, opening things up a little to enable more change from the bottom: fitfully giving more power to its citizens and newspapers to expose environmental crimes and to bring pressure to bear on those local officials and factories that want to continue exploiting the old, cheap-coal-based system. And, with a third hand, the Chinese leadership is pushing the bureaucracy and the private sector to pursue the enormous economic opportunities inherent in clean power and energy efficiency, telling them in effect: "To get green is glorious."

China's eleventh Five-Year Plan includes a goal of reducing energy intensity—energy consumption per unit of GDP—by 20 percent below 2005 levels across the whole economy by 2010. It's estimated that this would result in about 1.5 billion tons of avoided CO_2 emissions. That target is five times as ambitious as the commitment announced by the European nations under the Kyoto Protocol. China's National Development and Reform Commission, which oversees all these energy programs, has spread out the target reductions among provinces and industrial sectors. And this time the leadership expressly made meeting these goals part of every government official's personnel assessment. This gives it teeth. Individuals are now accountable for meeting key energy efficiency and environment goals. In 2006 and 2007, however, China fell short of the annual 4 percent goal in energy efficiency that it needs to reach the 20 percent improvement by 2010. Until I see a major governor, or industry manager, sacked for realizing his or her GDP goals but failing to meet their green targets, I will remain skeptical. But it is, at least on paper, a much more serious approach than any China has ever had.

Unfortunately, the challenge China's leaders face today is much more serious as well. The sheer scale and scope of urbanization is staggering: By 2020 the urban population is expected to increase from 42 to 60 percent, equivalent to tens of millions of new urban residents and hundreds of new satellite cities, notes Jiang Lin, senior vice president of the China Sustainable Energy Program, in his May 2008 report. "Accompanying urban population growth has been skyrocketing demand for the energy-intensive materials of which new buildings, roads, power plants, and factories are built." This is, he added, "the largest migration in human history."

To give the government more muscle, in March 2008 China's politburo also elevated the status of the State Environmental Protection

Agency, a famously toothless watchdog agency, into a full-fledged Cabinet ministry, with more staff and a bigger budget.

"China has adopted several world-class policies in just the past two years, and they are working on more. In a couple of areas they are now actually leading the United States," notes David Moskovitz, director and cofounder of the Regulatory Assistance Project, a U.S. nonprofit research group that works on conservation issues in many countries, including China.

On January 1, 2006, China instituted a national renewable energy mandate—of the sort the U.S. Congress rejected in 2007—that requires China's provincial governments to develop and adopt renewable energy for their localities. China's target is to increase renewable energy—particularly wind, hydro, and biomass—to 16 percent of its total energy production by 2020. Today it is 7 percent. China also adopted world-class mileage standards for its cars.

In October 2007, Moskovitz pointed out, China also imposed a new rule on power plants, which said that instead of burning the cheapest fuel first, such as coal, they had to use the cleanest fuel first—natural gas, solar, or wind, if it is available. "It drives demand for cleaner fuels and on a day-to-day basis has had an immediate effect on emissions," said Moskovitz. "If we adopted it [in America], it would make a huge difference." In an effort to weed out polluting and energy-intensive industries, China has also instituted a differential pricing system, whereby state power companies now charge higher electricity prices to the least efficient industrial concerns and lower prices to the more efficient ones, in an effort to reward the most efficient producers and force the least efficient to either change or shut down.

"So the most efficient steel mill wins in two ways, by having lower energy use and lower energy prices, and the least efficient loses in two ways—having higher energy use and prices and therefore higher production costs," said Moskovitz. "We can't get our power companies to even think about doing that." China is now in the midst of a program of shutting down its most inefficient small power plants, totaling around 50 gigawatts (or 8 percent of China's total generating capacity), by 2010. Most important, while every American energy bill is just the sum of all lobbies, with very little long-term strategic thinking, in 2006 China began drafting a comprehensive national energy law that will provide a long-term strategy for the whole country, and the leadership has been cir-

culating it to experts for comments to get it right rather than just promul-
gating it from on high.

The proof will be in the breathing. China still has a long, long way to
go to even get close to America's environmental profile, considering that
its energy consumption is growing at about 15 percent a year, while in
America consumption is growing at 1 or 2 percent. "They are not efficient," said Moskovitz, "but they are becoming more efficient quickly,
because with their growth they are bringing in a lot of new plants, so their
average efficiency level is improving."

The more China's leadership pushes to make green growth real, the
more it is staking its credibility on this goal. Therefore, one has to
wonder whether the leadership can afford *not* to empower China's civil
society and unleash it as a green watchdog that can buttress these new
regulations being passed from the top, so they actually get implemented
this time. China's citizens are the leadership's only ally against the bureaucratic and private sector Dirty GDPists. This is the dynamic I am
tracking most closely.

Green movements historically have started as grassroots movements
in democratic societies. They start from the bottom up, usually as a society achieves a certain level of economic growth and develops a large and
secure middle class that cares about these issues. Many countries, including China and America, have wonderful environmental laws on the
books, but without civil society groups to monitor compliance and bring
lawsuits against local governments or companies that try to skirt the rules
or violate them outright, those laws will always be vulnerable.

I got a tutorial on this subject right after returning from China in September 2007 at the Sierra Club's annual meeting in San Francisco,
where I was being given a journalism award. It was one of two dozen
awards that the Sierra Club presented that night, and the longer I sat
through the awards ceremony, the more I thought about China. Almost
every award the Sierra Club handed out that evening went to local citizens or small Sierra Club chapters or legislators who had, on their own,
used America's courts or regulatory bodies to expose or halt some egre-
gious attack on the environment.

What struck me as I watched these activists come up to accept their
scrolls was how *ordinary* they were, in the very best sense of that word.

They were just ordinary citizens who cared deeply about the environment and had exercised their rights of free speech, assembly, and petition to take on huge companies or local governments—and won!

Here's just a sample: Congressman Mike Thompson, who represented California's first congressional district, won the Sierra Club's Edgar Wayburn Award for helping to pass national legislation in 2006 that guaranteed protection for 431 square miles of wilderness in Northern California. A Special Achievement Award went to the Illinois chapter of the Sierra Club for leading a statewide campaign to approve new regulations on mercury pollution. The Walter A. Starr Award went to Ted Snyder of Walhalla, South Carolina, for spending more than thirty-five years fighting a proposed thirty-seven-mile road through the Smoky Mountains National Park that would have sliced through the largest roadless tract of mountain land in the east. The William O. Douglas Award went to Richard Duncan of Minneapolis, for his handling of critical pieces of litigation in the Sierra Club's fight to protect the Boundary Waters.

I am convinced that China's leaders are slowly realizing that they have to create a similar model, now that they have staked their own reputations on a greener economy. They will never say so, but I do not think they can go green without, over time, going at least a little orange—à la the Orange Revolution in Ukraine in 2004—and loosening the reins on civil society.

Tim Shriver, chairman of Special Olympics, once said to me something about how China deals with people with disabilities that also applies to how it will have to deal with the environment. "My question is whether or not China has any understanding of the one phenomenon that many consider the most unique and politically significant American contribution to social and political life: the engaged citizen," said Shriver. "It is our least noticed export and yet is also, in my humble opinion, our most valuable one. Engaged citizens help each other, organize around issues they believe in, and hold officials accountable for actions whenever they can. They are the economic engine of a free press . . . So the question raised by globalization and the increasing economic and political integration of China isn't just about the extent to which big-time bosses will allow political dissent, or the extent to which they can fight internal corruption, or the extent to which they can manage the yuan. It is also [about] the extent to which they understand and allow one of the key precursors to all of these: citizens organizing themselves. The best enforcers are engaged citizens. The only reason a social change law gets enforced, in the end, is because citizens become engaged in making the change themselves. The state alone can't do it. And the common ground of all these movements trying to effect social change agendas is that they depend on citizens actually caring—otherwise the state passes a law, puts it on the books, and everyone just goes home."

There are certainly signs in the media from China that "ordinary citizens" there wanted to be empowered, and indeed are demanding to be empowered, on the environmental front—while the state cannot quite make up its mind. But the more Chinese citizens obtain the tools of the flat world—cell phones, the Internet, PDAs, and so on—the more their voices can and will be heard. Here is just a sample of the environmental stories I came across from China in the months while I was finishing this book, which illustrate what is percolating there:

Residents took to the streets of a provincial capital over the weekend to protest a multibillion-dollar petrochemical plant backed by China's leading state-run oil company, in the latest instance of popular discontent over an environmental threat in a major city. The protest, against a $5.5 billion ethylene plant under construction by PetroChina in Chengdu, the capital of Sichuan Province, reflected a surge in environmental awareness by urban, middle-class Chinese determined to protect their health and the value of their property. A similar protest last year, against a Taiwanese-financed petrochemical venture in Xiamen, in China's southeast, left that project in limbo. The recent protest, which was peaceful, was organized through Web sites, blogs and cellphone text messages, illustrating how some Chinese are using digital technology to start civic movements, which are usually banned by the police. Organizers also used text messages to publicize their cause nationally. The protesters walked calmly through downtown Chengdu for several hours on Sunday afternoon to criticize the building of a combined ethylene plant and oil refinery in Pengzhou, 18 miles northwest of the city center. Some protesters wore white masks over their mouths to evoke the dangers of pollution. About 400 to 500 protesters took part in the march, witnesses said. Organizers circumvented a national law that requires protesters to apply for a permit by saying they were only out for a "stroll." [*The New York Times*, May 6, 2008]

Polluters along two of China's main rivers have defied a decade-old clean-up effort, leaving much of the water unfit to touch, let alone drink, and a risk to a sixth of the population, state media said on Monday. Half the check points along the Huai River and its tributaries in central and eastern China showed pollution of "Grade 5" or worse—the top of the dial in key toxins, meaning that the water was unfit for human contact and may not be fit even for irrigation, national legislators were told. Years of crackdowns and waste treatment investment have reined in some of the worst damage to the Huai and Liao Rivers, but industrial pollution remained far too high, Mao Rubai, chairman of the National People's Congress environment and resources protection committee, said in a report delivered on Sunday. The rivers posed a "threat to the water safety of one sixth of the country's 1.3 billion population," the *China Daily* said. [Reuters, August 27, 2007]

China has ordered provincial governments to replace 50 million traditional incandescent lamps with heavily-subsidized energy-efficient lights this year. This is part of a campaign launched by the Ministry of Finance and the NDRC in January with the goal to use 150 million energy-efficient light bulbs over the next 5 years. Several provinces received specific targets of 2 or 3 million bulbs, including a 2-million bulb target for Beijing. China produced at least 80% of the world's energy-efficient light bulbs, with 2.4 billion bulbs made in 2006, compared with only 200 million in 1997. China would save 60 billion kilowatt hours of power each year, or 22 million tons of coal equivalent each year, if all its incandescent lamps were replaced with CFLs, reducing emission of carbon dioxide by 60 million tons. [Xinhua News Agency, May 14, 2008]

In the past 15 years, more than 80,000 journalists have taken part in the All-China Environmental Protection Century Tour, one of China's largest nationwide environmental protection campaigns.

Since 1993, more than 200,000 news reports have been filed to raise the public's awareness about energy and the environment. Their reports have helped overhaul China's polluting mining industry and also initiated investigations to protect the Yellow and Yangtze Rivers. The theme of the campaign changes every year; for 2007, it focused on reducing energy consumption and pollutant emissions. "A public opinion survey released in Beijing found that 60.7 percent of respondents were concerned about food safety. It also found that 66.9 percent of respondents felt that environmental problems were very serious in China. However, despite rising concern over pollution, 49.7 percent of people believed their involvement in environmental-protection campaigns made no difference." [Xinhua News Agency, January 8, 2008]

"Sustainability issues are inducing what I believe are extraordinary sociopolitical changes in China today," said MIT's Ed Steinfeld. "While many of us, including myself, tend to view these changes in purely oppositional terms—citizen versus state—the changes are obviously more complicated, involving emerging civic groups, blurring of the boundaries between state and civic actors, growing political consciousness among citizens, and growing policy activism by political entrepreneurs within the state. Kevin O'Brien and Liangjiang Li, writing primarily on rural anti-tax protests, get at this sort of political change in their book, *Rightful Resistance in Rural China*. They really hit that dynamic of the policy entrepreneurs in the central state pushing a variety of citizen-focused weapons—legal measures, state media reports on targeted issues like taxation or pollution—[and] citizens then picking up those weapons and running with them by protesting against wayward local officials, all in the name of legitimate central policies and laws, and then local officials hitting back. Plus, you have elite activists—younger technocrats at the central level, leading academics, leading journalists—all of whom are tied to the state and party, the establishment in effect—often getting into the act by pushing the passage of progressive laws or even directly encouraging protest at the local level."

People at the grass roots witness this, see the new laws passed, get information from establishment media outlets, often get direct encouragement from some of those establishment activists, and then go out and do things themselves—like bring a lawsuit against the local government the next time it tries to build a chemical plant, added Steinfeld. "Sometimes the citizens win, sometimes they don't. More tragically, sometimes they end up getting beaten up by local thugs or thrown in jail. The point isn't that the system is just, but rather that this dynamic of 'rightful' or 'legitimate' protest has been unleashed . . . There are many reasons to dislike what goes on in China. But it is a mistake to believe that this system is stuck in the past, incapable of change, or willing to change only on its own terms. I'm actually optimistic."

And now there is a new factor: the emergence of a clean-tech industry in China, which has an acute economic interest in promoting greener laws and regulations so that it can sell more of its products around China, build its strength and cut its costs using China's big domestic market, and then leverage all that to grow globally. China's leadership is aggressively pushing clean tech because it is a way to make GDP and Green GDP compatible. As China looks for technology fixes to its own pollution problems, it wants to create an export industry.

One need only sit down with a mayor like Xia Deren, the longtime mayor of Dalian, to understand how big a push China is making into clean tech. Mayor Xia is renowned for having taken great care to both preserve and expand the parks in his coastal city of six million people—my favorite city in China—knowing that, as the nation's software capital, it has to attract knowledge workers, and such workers are highly mobile and prefer healthy cities.

When I interviewed him in September 2007, the first thing Mayor Xia said to me was: "The biggest challenge we have is how to balance economic growth with the energy needs and environment . . . We are increasingly aware that resources in both China and the world are limited. For example, Dalian is scarce in fresh water, so we have to develop water-saving industries. And second, Dalian is scarce in coal, and that means we have to develop a lot of energy-saving industries . . . If we want to achieve the balance between the environment and energy and growth, we have to develop those industries that are energy saving and environmentally friendly, like software . . . Currently in China there is a concept of the recycling economy—to reuse everything. However, we know that it is really difficult to translate this concept into practice in a short period of time, so we have to do it in a step-by-step way. But, anyway, we have to move forward and start now. We have a strict policy on environmental protection and energy consumption. For example, we don't have such plants as steel-making here, because it adds pollution to the air and is highly energy consuming. We have also relocated more than a hundred industries to the industrial park, where there will be centralized pollution treatment. In the last year, we closed thirty-one large cement plants because of their pollution. And this year we plan to close nineteen small-sized cement plants . . . We are constantly focused first on the percentage of energy consumption per unit of GDP and second on reducing pollution and waste."

He then went on to explain that Dalian's massive new convention center was using a cutting-edge clean-tech heat pump technology, which recovers thermal energy from seawater and then uses that thermal energy to cool and heat the building in a totally renewable way. "We can save 30 percent on our energy costs," he remarked proudly.

When I asked the mayor how he was managing his time these days, he said: "In terms of my economic work, about one-fourth to one-third of my time is now devoted to cutting emissions and cutting energy usage. I think of myself as developing an energy-efficient city . . . We set our environmental standards to those of developed countries. We have set our auto-emission standards to European levels and our air quality can reach the standard of European countries."

Dalian, he added, had just won the national competition to host China's top energy research laboratory. I have interviewed Mayor Xia several times since 2000. I'd never had a conversation with him like this before.

And I also never had an interview quite like the one I had with Shi Zhengrong—who, when I sat down with him in 2006, was ranked as the seventh-richest man in China by *Forbes* magazine. His fortune then: $2.2 billion. Guess what Shi does. Real estate? No. Banking? No. Manufacturing for Walmart? No. Construction? No. Shi is China's leading maker of silicon photovoltaic solar cells, which convert sunlight into electricity.

Yes, one of China's richest men today is a green entrepreneur! It should only happen in America. Shi thinks that clean power is going to be the growth industry of the twenty-first century, and he wants to make sure that China and his company, Suntech Power Holdings, are the industry leaders. Only forty-five years old and full of energy himself, Shi told me he would like to do for solar energy what China did for tennis shoes: drive down the cost, so that millions of people who cannot afford solar photovoltaic panels will be able to do so. I visited him at his office in Shanghai, which gave us both a laugh because we were atop a sky-scraper and could barely see through the pollution haze that day, *while talking about solar power*.

Shi founded Suntech in Wuxi, China, near Shanghai, after earning a Ph.D. in engineering in Australia in 1992. As *The Wall Street Journal* put it in a profile, Suntech combines "first world technology and developing world prices"—so effectively that it has become one of the world's top four solar manufacturers, along with Sharp and Kyocera of Japan and BP of England. The key to his business, Shi explained to me, is that he uses low-cost Chinese labor, rather than high-tech machines, to make his so-lar modules and handle the fragile silicon, and he takes advantage of the subsidies offered by different Chinese provinces, whose officials are ea-ger for him to open a Suntech factory in their region. Roughly 90 per-cent of his business today is abroad, he explained. But as he brings the price of his solar cells down, the China market is opening up. Shi expects to use that combination of price and market size to gain greater scale and drive the price of his cells down further, giving him a real cost advantage with which to attack his global competitors.

"If we have a market here, we feel confident we will be a cost leader," he says. Thanks to Suntech's success, "now there is a rush of [Chinese] businesspeople entering this sector, even though we still don't have a market here," said Shi. "Many government people now say, 'This is an industry!'"

And it is not the only renewable one. China's wind energy industry is also experiencing dramatic growth: Installed wind capacity grew by nearly 100 percent between 2005 and 2007. China achieved its 2010 wind development target of 5,000 megawatts by the end of 2007. At this pace, in five years, China will become a major player in global wind gen-eration and manufacturing.

Just when you think the Chinese could never possibly replace that dirty diesel engine in their bus with a clean plug-in hybrid while keeping the bus moving at 50 miles per hour, you get an e-mail like the one I got from Jon Wellinghoff, a member of the U.S. Federal Energy Regulatory Commission, after he returned from China in April 2008: "The most in-teresting thing of the entire trip was discovering that in the course of less than ten years they have literally turned over their entire stock of two-stroke scooters and mopeds into all-electric vehicles. There are now forty million electric scooters and bicycles in China. I was blown away. And they all take their little batteries upstairs at night to charge up and bring them back down in the morning and plug them back into their scooters and off they go. So electrification of the transportation sector is possible and being done in China today. And even going to coal-based electrification of transportation lowers CO_2 as well as dramatically lowering urban pollution. The two days I was in Beijing there were actually blue skies."

Bottom line: When it comes to clean energy technologies, "China is just beginning to move from copying to creating," said Rob Watson, the energy consultant. "The last time they were in full creative mode they invented paper, the compass, and gunpowder."

For all these reasons, the Green China story is definitely a work in progress that bears careful scrutiny. There are so many trends and countertrends, hopeful signs and signs of an environmental apocalypse, that I certainly wouldn't predict how it will all play out. Of all the indices I will be watching closely, the one I believe will be most decisive in determining whether Red China becomes Green China is how the Chinese deal with their new buildings challenge. As I noted above, China is expected to erect hundreds of new cities and smaller towns in the next twenty years. It will have to build new homes and offices for over 300 million people who will be moving from the countryside to urban areas, and it will have to build homes for another 250 million people it wants to keep living in villages, and not move to the cities. The world has never seen such a building project before, and much of China's future is riding on how it proceeds. If China's leaders do it the "American way," with big energy-consuming structures, it will give birth to a giant pig that will eventually eat China out of house and home—out of coal, oil, and gas— in the coming decades. Remember, buildings generally account for roughly 40 percent of national energy consumption, and once they start eating energy and water, they don't stop for thirty or forty years. If, instead of following America's already outdated practices, the Chinese decide to leapfrog us and go straight to "net-zero" buildings—buildings with passive lighting, solar exteriors, or wind turbines that can generate their own energy during the day and take from the grid only at night so that they are net-zero energy consumers—they have a chance to avoid the worst crisis. But today's Chinese leaders need to be as serious about this as their predecessors were about the one-child policy. Just as the one-child policy has probably saved China from a population calamity, net-zero buildings might save China—and therefore the rest of us as well—from an energy and environmental calamity.

"America today has 300 billion square feet of real estate—commercial buildings and private homes—and by 2030 we will have 400 billion square feet," said Marc Porat, the chairman of Serious Materials. "China, in the next twenty years, will build 550 billion square feet. So round that up to 600 billion and you could say China will build two Americas in the next twenty years. If they do it like us, they will run into a wall. China is facing an energy-driven recession because of peak coal. They will run out. That means they will have to try to maintain a 'harmonious society' in the middle of an energy-driven recession." The only way around that is for China to adopt net-zero buildings to go along with its one-child population policies—and it can. China's leaders have a much cleaner slate to work with at the national, provincial, and city levels. They actually could drive the concept of net-zero right through their whole system—if they choose to.

Getting this right is going to be a real challenge for China's Communist Party leadership, as will be figuring out how much to unleash China's civil society to help expose, reduce, and monitor pollution, as will be determining how quickly and how much to slow down growth in dirty areas while trying to stimulate it in clean areas, and how to do all of them in a way that maintains social stability and continues to narrow income gaps. Precisely because doing all those things together is so hard and the stakes are so high, China's leadership may be tempted to be tentative—to sit on the fence at times, to settle for less, to fiddle with numbers. But China can't afford that. The world can't afford that.

In short, China is purposively trying to become something different tomorrow from what it is today, and we have to do all we can to ensure that the "New China" has a green face. Because that is not a sure thing, America has a decisive role to play. We can help tip China in the right direction, but only if we go first. Leadership is not about "after you." It's about "follow me." We are the ones who put into the atmosphere the lion's share of the CO_2 that is slowly warming the world. We are the ones with the resources that should enable us to take the lead in inventing a clean power system. The greatest thing that America could do today for itself, China, and the world is become an example of a country that grows prosperous, secure, innovative, and respected by becoming the greenest, most energy-efficient, and most energy productive country there is.

I would even take it a step further and say that the greatest thing that the United States could do today for itself, for China, and the world is to publicly state its intention to "outgreen China"—to let the Chinese know every day in every way that we are going to try to clean their clock in the next great global industry: clean power. Just as we and the Soviets had a space race, a competition to see who could put a man on the moon first—a competition that greatly strengthened our own society, from education to infrastructure—we, the European Union, and the Chinese need to have a similar race today. Only instead of a race to put a man on the moon, it has to be a race to preserve humankind on earth. In the Cold War there was a winner and a loser, but in the earth race either we will all win or we will all lose, because if China's speeding bus were to explode—economically or environmentally—it would be a disaster for everyone.

If America decisively embarked on building a Clean Energy System and the technologies to drive it, China would have no choice but to move decisively in the same direction. Because staying dirty would not just mean that a billion and a half Chinese will continue to breathe dirty air. It would mean that China lags behind in the next great global industry. But we cannot even begin to suggest that the Chinese do the hard work of greening their society until we do some hard work ourselves. (It is truly galling to the Chinese that we've raided Mother Nature's buffet and that now, when they're getting to the leftovers, we're accusing them of gluttony.) "The most frequent and difficult question we get in China with every policy initiative we put forward," said David Moskovitz, "is this: 'If it is so good, why aren't you doing it?' It's hard to answer—and somewhat embarrassing. So we point to good examples that some American states, or cities, or companies are implementing—but not to the federal government. We can't point to America."

China's collective "societal raison d'être has been utterly tied up with a process of linking China to a global system and getting China onto a 'global track,'" said MIT's Ed Steinfeld. "If advanced industrial societies 'go green,' China isn't somehow going to see this as an opportunity to break the rules and undercut us all on pricing. Just the opposite—it's going to feel intense pressure societally and politically to go green as well. Political legitimacy and national identity in China are deeply tied up with the mission of modernizing China. Modernity, for better or worse, is represented by us. That's in part why, even at great cost, China ultimately pushed for WTO accession. It's also, in part, why the state establishment in China is interested in pushing certain attributes of modern democracy—rule of law, civil society, accountability, limited elections—even as it resists any hint of a multiparty system . . . If we build it, they will come—just as they have done consistently, if fitfully and unexpectedly, in every other case of global institutional change over the past twenty years."

We are still the city on the hill for many Chinese, even though they hate what we've done at times at the top of the hill. When we live dirty, it is justification for them to live dirty. And when we live big, they want to live big—big houses, big skyscrapers, big cars. "And if we live a sustainability story," added Steinfeld, "that will get translated into China as a benchmark of modernity and what being world-class is all about."

If America assumes leadership on the clean power issue, and China feels impelled to follow, this cannot help but encourage China's leadership to empower more of its citizens and media to speak out on environmental excesses and to act as watchdogs on local governments and businesses. Therefore, the more and the faster we, America, inspire, shame, provoke, induce, and lead China down a greener path, the sooner we not only make the world a cleaner place but also help strengthen the rule of law in China and encourage its civil society groups. It won't happen overnight, and I am not suggesting that it alone will lead China to become a multiparty democracy anytime soon. But I am saying that the Chinese Communist Party will not be able to deliver on its promise to its people of the freedom to breathe unless it gradually but steadily starts to grant more of them the freedom to speak.

A year after writing the above lines for the hardcover edition of this book, I've started to wonder: Who is going to clean whose clock? Who is going to outgreen whom? And who is going to shame whom? Could it be that China will leap ahead of America in the earth race and in dominating the ET industry?

Why do I ask? In part, because for America going green remains a matter of choice, and the U.S. Congress and the Obama administration have not yet demonstrated that they really are ready to put in place the price signals and the big investments we need to develop a Clean Energy System in America. Well, we delay at our peril: I believe China may be only five years away from deciding that it has to go green no matter what America does, because too many of its people simply cannot breathe its air, because too many of its rivers are too polluted to drink from, because too many of its lakes are too polluted to fish from or swim in, because too many of its forests have been cut back to the bone, and because climate change is already affecting China in the form of prolonged droughts and more frequent dust storms. I believe China may soon go green not because enough Chinese saw Al Gore's movie and were persuaded, but because the grim realities of daily life are persuading China's leaders that they have no other choice. They will realize that China must go green out of necessity. And there is one thing we know about necessity: It is the mother of invention. A green China will invent the wind, solar, nuclear, and carbon-capture-and-sequestration power systems at a price that can, first and foremost, scale in China. And once China has perfected all those clean power systems, it will sell them to us. So you won't just be buying your toys and plastic salad shooters from China; you will be buying your next car, solar panels, wind turbines, refrigerator, microwave, and home heating and cooling system from China. And they will clean *our* clocks in the next great global industry, ET.

Think I am exaggerating? Think again. On May 4, 2009, the Chinese news Web site Caijing.com.cn translated a story from the *Shanghai Securities News*, which quoted Shi Dinghuan, a State Council adviser and head of the Chinese Renewable Energy Association, as stating that "China's central government will soon release a plan to support the country's renewable energy industry. It will be a blueprint for driving the new energy industry's development in China." The newspaper said that Shi made the remarks at the launch of EI DuPont de Nemours & Co.'s photovoltaic technology research center in Shanghai. Wang Mengjie, from the Chinese Academy of Sciences, was also quoted by the newspaper as saying that the National Development and Reform Commission had completed a draft of the plan following discussions by ministers in April. Wang said the new plan would raise existing targets for renewable energy development to a much higher level. Under the long-term industry plan released in 2007, the government vowed to speed up construction of renewable energy power plants and, by 2020, to reach installed electricity generating capacity of 300 million kilowatts from hydropower,

30 million kilowatts from wind power, 30 million kilowatts from biomass power, and 1.8 million kilowatts from solar power. The latest industry plan will raise those targets, the Shanghai newspaper reported, citing wind power expert Shi Pengfei. The 30 million kilowatt target for wind power, for example, will be raised to 100 or 150 million kilowatts because the original goal is likely to be reached by 2011, Shi said.

A few weeks later (May 27, 2009), Keith Bradsher, the *New York Times* Hong Kong bureau chief, broke this story: "Worried about heavy reliance on imported oil, Chinese officials have drafted automotive fuel economy standards that are even more stringent than those outlined by President Obama last week, Chinese experts with a detailed knowledge of the plans said on Wednesday. The new plan would require automakers in China to improve fuel economy by an additional 18 percent by 2015, said An Feng, a leading architect of China's existing fuel economy regulations who is now the president of the Innovation Center for Energy and Transportation, a nonprofit group in Beijing. The plan is going through the interagency approval process, with comments sought from automakers, and is scheduled for release early next year, he said . . . Mr. An estimated that the average new car, minivan or sport utility vehicle in China already gets the equivalent of 35.8 miles a gallon this year based on the American measurement system of corporate averages and will be required to get 42.2 miles a gallon in 2015. By comparison, President Obama announced last week that each automaker will be required to reach a corporate average of 35.5 miles per gallon by 2016."

One last data point: In Copenhagen in August 2008, I interviewed Ditlev Engel, the president of Vestas—Denmark's (and the world's) biggest wind turbine company. He told me that he simply did not understand why the U.S. Congress was not doing more to stimulate the ET industry in the United States. After all, he pointed out, in the last eighteen months "we've had thirty-five new competitors coming out of China . . . and not one out of the U.S."

We can lead or we can follow. Just don't think that we can stand still—or that China will.

PART V

America

EIGHTEEN

China for a Day (but Not for Two)

[Presidential candidate George W.] Bush said today that if he was president, he would bring down gasoline prices through sheer force of personality, by creating enough political goodwill with oil-producing nations that they would increase their supply of crude.

"I would work with our friends in OPEC to convince them to open up the spigot, to increase the supply ... Use the capital that my administration will earn, with the Kuwaitis or the Saudis, and convince them to open up the spigot."

Implicit in his comments was a criticism of the Clinton Administration as failing to take advantage of the goodwill that the United States built with Kuwait and Saudi Arabia during the Persian Gulf war in 1991. Also implicit was that as the son of the president who built the coalition that drove the Iraqis out of Kuwait, Mr. Bush would be able to establish ties on a personal level that would persuade oil-producing nations that they owed the United States something in return.

—*The New York Times*, June 28, 2000. Crude oil was selling for $28 a barrel that day.

In January 2007, as part of the research for this book, I sat down for an interview with General Electric chairman and CEO Jeffrey Immelt, who has been responsible for refocusing GE's product line around clean power technologies, under the brand of "Ecomagination." Immelt and I talked about different forms of energy generation and bandied about the question of what would be the ideal set of regulations, incentives, taxes, and infrastructure that the federal government could put in place to stimulate the market and drive clean power, energy efficiency, and conservation to scale. The answers seemed obvious, so obvious that Immelt eventually lamented with a mix of exasperation and passion:

Why doesn't America have a government that can just put all the right policies in place to shape the energy market?

"What doesn't exist today in the energy business is the hand of God," said Immelt. "I think if you asked the utilities and big manufacturers in this business what they would most like, it would be for the president to stand up and say: 'By 2025 we are going to produce this much coal, this much natural gas, this much wind, this much solar, this much nuclear, and nothing is going to stand in the way.' Well, you'd have about thirty days of complaining and crying, and then people across the whole energy industry would just stand up and say, 'Thank you, Mr. President, now let's go do it.' And we would go out and do it."

Why would such a clear set of directives from the top down make such a big difference? Because once the business community had a clear, durable, and long-term price signal for carbon, a clear sense of what the national market would be for clean power sources like wind and solar, and a clear set of regulations and incentives in place across the country to encourage utilities to help their customers do more energy saving than energy consuming, said Immelt, the market opportunities would be obvious to everyone. We would finally have some long-term clarity for investors to make big bets. And at that point, all of America's tremendous assets—our universities, national laboratories, individual inventors, risk takers, venture capitalists, free markets, and multinationals, like GE and DuPont, which drive their own research and understand how to commercialize innovation—would get fully in gear, go "all in" on renewable energy, and the whole clean power ecosystem would just take off.

That night I thought a lot about our conversation. I replayed it several times in my head, and eventually a mischievous thought occurred to me: If only . . . If only America could be China for a day—just one day. *Just one day!*

As far as I am concerned, China's system of government is inferior to ours in every respect—except one. That is the ability of China's current generation of leaders—if they want—to cut through all their legacy industries, all the pleading special interests, all the bureaucratic obstacles, all the worries of a voter backlash, and simply order top-down the sweeping changes in prices, regulations, standards, education, and infrastructure that reflect China's long-term strategic national interests—changes that would normally take Western democracies years or decades to debate and implement. That is such an asset when it comes to trying to engineer a sweeping change, like the green revolution, where you are competing against deeply embedded, well-funded, entrenched interests, and where you have to motivate the public to accept certain short-term sacrifices, including higher energy prices, for long-term gains. For Washington to be able to order all the right changes and set up the ideal market conditions for innovation, and then get out of the way and let the natural energy of the American capitalist system work—that would be a dream.

What would be so bad? China? Just for one short day?

Consider this: One morning in late 2007 China's shopkeepers woke up and found that the State Council had announced that beginning June 1, 2008, all supermarkets, department stores, and shops would be prohibited from giving out free plastic bags, in order to discourage the use of these petroleum-based products. In the future, stores would have to charge customers for them. "Stores must clearly mark the price of plastic shopping bags and are banned from tacking that price onto products," the Associated Press reported (January 9, 2008). China also banned outright the production, sale, and use of ultrathin plastic bags—those thinner than 0.025 millimeters—in order to get shoppers to use recyclable baskets and cloth satchels.

Bam! Just like that—1.3 billion people, theoretically, will stop using thin plastic bags. Millions of barrels of petroleum will be saved, and mountains of garbage avoided. America started the process of removing lead from gasoline in 1973, and it took until 1995 until all gasoline sold in our country was unleaded. China decided to go lead-free in 1998; the new standard was partially implemented in Beijing in 1999, and by 2000 the entire country's gasoline was lead-free. America took roughly thirty-two years between its first major effort to raise fuel economy standards for cars, in 1975, and its second major effort in 2007. Meanwhile, in 2003, China began to put in place a major fuel economy initiative for its cars and trucks and sent proposed new standards to the State Council for approval. They were adopted in 2004 and went into effect in 2005. Now all new cars and trucks must meet the new standard.

I am keenly aware that China's leadership often issues directives from the top down that are ignored or are only partially implemented by local governments or state companies there. That's why I wish we could be China for one day—but only one day. In the United States, unlike in China, once our government passes a law or issues a regulation, it gets implemented—because if it is ignored by companies or local governments, a dozen public interest groups, led by the Sierra Club and the

Natural Resources Defense Council, will sue the violators (including the federal government) all the way to the Supreme Court. That is why being China for a day—imposing all the right taxes, regulations, and standards needed to launch a clean power system in one day—would be so much more valuable to Washington than to Beijing. Because once the directives are given from above, we would be overcoming the worst part of our democracy (the inability to make big decisions in peacetime), and the next day we would be able to enjoy the best part of our democracy (the power of our civil society to make government rules stick and the power of our markets to take advantage of them).

Big in Big Things?

In my view, we cannot do this a moment too soon. Our economy depends on our technological leadership more than we realize. Imagine, say energy experts, if Microsoft were a Japanese company, Apple a British company, Google a Chinese company, IBM a German company, Intel a Russian company, and Oracle a French company. What would our standard of living be if we were not the leaders in IT? Take away all those exports, all those good jobs, and all the taxes they generate, and you are looking at a much less prosperous America. Well, that is exactly where we are heading on ET. Remember Jeffrey Immelt's line: If you want to be big, you have to be big in big things, and the way we are heading we are not going to be big in the next big thing: ET.

Consider this paragraph from the 2009 report by President Obama's Economic Recovery Advisory Board, based on a study by the Lazard Frères investment bank of the top ten companies in the world, as measured by market capitalization, in the wind, solar, and battery industries: "If the U.S. fails to adopt an economy-wide carbon abatement program, we will continue to cede leadership in energy technology to other nations. The U.S. is now home to only two of the ten largest solar photovoltaic producers in the world, two of the top ten wind turbine producers and one of the top ten advanced battery manufacturers. That is, only one-sixth of the top renewable energy manufacturers are based in the United States."

These numbers should worry every American. To lose our advantage in technologies that were pioneered in the U.S. may cost us dearly in terms of our standard of living if the trend is not reversed—and soon.

Solar PV Suppliers: Top 10 by Market Capitalization

Company Name	Market Cap	Domicile
Kyocera	$12,224	Japan
First Solar	10,834	United States
Sharp	8,853	Japan
Sanyo	2,738	Japan
Q-Cells	2,215	Germany
SunPower	2,045	United States
Suntech	1,821	China
Yingli Green Energy	764	China
Motech	714	Taiwan
JA Solar	566	China

Wind Turbine Manufacturers: Top 10 by Market Capitalization

Company Name	Market Cap	Domicile
GE	$106,853	United States
Siemens	49,568	Germany
Mitsubishi	22,024	Japan
Vestas	8,131	Denmark
Acciona	6,385	Spain
Goldwind	5,875	China
Gamesa	3,088	Spain
Suzlon	1,253	India
Nordex	862	Germany
Clipper	127	United Kingdom

Advanced Battery Manufacturers: Top 10 by Market Capitalization

Company Name	Market Cap	Domicile
Panasonic	$22,372	Japan
Mitsubishi	22,024	Japan
Sumitomo	10,650	Japan
Hitachi	8,936	Japan
Toshiba	8,306	Japan
Johnson Controls	7,131	United States
NGK	4,970	Japan
BYD	3,777	China
Sanyo	2,738	Japan
GS Yuasa	1,796	Japan

Source: Lazard Frères (April 2009)

Innovations in solar, wind, nuclear, and other clean power systems and in electric vehicles, the report added,

> will, in the view of many on our board, drive the future global economy. We can either invest in policies to build U.S. leadership in these new industries and jobs today, or we can continue with business as usual and buy windmills from Europe, batteries from Japan and solar panels from Asia. The new green economy could be transformational for our country. Compare it to the internet. Fifteen years ago there was no web browser. There was no internet at your fingertips, no ecommerce, no search engines. Now, the internet has transformed our lives: how we learn and inform, how we entertain and communicate, how we buy and sell goods. Today, the internet economy is estimated at $1 trillion with 1.5 billion internet users worldwide—and growing. The new green economy has greater potential. Energy is a $6 trillion market with 4 billion users of electricity—and usage doubling in 25 years. It is perhaps the largest economic opportunity of the 21st century. With the right policies driving innovation and investment, America can retake the lead in energy technology and create millions of new green jobs and industries, preserve millions of indirect jobs and repower our economy.

America needs to be a leading player, if not the leading player, in the emerging wind, solar, and battery industries, not to mention nuclear, which are sure to be major sources of jobs and revenues in the first half of this century. But we are not and we will not be unless we change course now. As the report concluded:

> The U.S. suffers from our dependence on foreign oil and long ago lost worldwide leadership in automobiles; we *cannot afford to trade an addiction to Middle Eastern oil for an addiction to Asian batteries* [italics mine]. Only with the right policies driving innovation and investment can America retake the lead in energy technology and create millions of new green jobs and industries, preserve millions of indirect jobs and repower our economy. This is a defining moment in American history and in our lives as individuals and as political and business leaders.

And it is not clear that our politicians or political system is up to it. Oh, if only we could be China for a day . . .

W here in the world did *that* come from? China for a day? How could I, a lifelong believer in liberal democracy, ever even day-dream about the benefits of America being China for a day?

Where it came from was enormous frustration born of traveling from one end of this country to the other over the past four years, looking at al-most every conceivable form of energy generation, and meeting all sorts of wacky, wild, and wonderful energy innovators, entrepreneurs, and venture capitalists—from garage mechanics to directors of our premier research institutes—and coming away feeling that we are really primed for a green takeoff, that we have all the necessary ingredients for a real Code Green revolution, but our government has not shaped the market to capitalize on what is naturally bubbling up from below.

Let me offer an example. One day in December 2007, I visited the MIT campus to participate in a seminar on its open-university program. Before I arrived, two different MIT student energy clubs invited me to peel away from the open-university program and come hear what they were doing. One simply blew me away. It was called the Vehicle Design Summit group—a global, open-source, collaborative effort managed by MIT students that had brought together twenty-five college teams around the world, including groups from India and China, to design and build a plug-in electric hybrid. Each team was contributing a different set of parts or designs. And I thought writing for my college newspaper was cool—these kids were building a hyperefficient car! Their aim was to demonstrate that they could build a car with a 95 percent reduction in embodied energy, materials, and toxicity from cradle to grave and pro-vide the energy equivalency of 200 miles per gallon. That's right: 200 miles per gallon. It's the Linux of cars! Their other goal, they explained on their Web site—Vds.mit.edu—was "to identify the key characteristics of events like the race to the moon and then transpose this energy, pas-sion, focus, and urgency" into catalyzing a global team to build a clean car. Their tagline? "We are the people we have been waiting for."

Again, I came away from this encounter just shaking my head: All the human energy and talent is here, ready to launch. Yes, it can go a long way on its own, as the MIT students demonstrate. But it will never go to the scale we need as long as our national energy policy remains so ad hoc, uncoordinated, inconsistent, and unsustained—so that the market never fully exploits our natural advantages. We will always be less than the sum of our parts. Immelt compares us to a team that has made it all the way to the Super Bowl but is still sitting in the locker room and won't, or can't, take the field.

A different image comes to my mind when I visit places like MIT. It is the image of a space shuttle taking off. That's what America looks like to me. We still have all this tremendous thrust coming from below, from a society that is still enormously idealistic, experimental, and full of energy. But the booster rocket of our space shuttle (the political system we have now) is leaking fuel, and in the cockpit (Washington, D.C.) the pilots are fighting over the flight plan. As a result, we cannot generate the escape velocity—the direction and focus we need to reach the next frontier, fully seize the opportunities there, and fully meet the challenges of the Energy-Climate Era.

What is our problem? If the right things to do—most notably raising the gasoline tax and putting a fixed, durable, long-term price on carbon—are so obvious to the people who know the most about the energy business, why can't we put them in place?

First and foremost are the legacy industries from the Dirty Fuels System, which want to protect their turf and preserve their dominance in the American energy infrastructure. In the best cases, these are just executives, employees, and supportive politicians trying to protect jobs and communities, and give the country the cheapest power for the most growth. In the worst cases, they are greedy companies looking to protect their mother lodes, even though they know their products are as harmful to society and the planet as cigarette smoking. Either way, they have helped to rig the game when it comes to energy policy-making. In too many cases, they have distorted facts, placed misleading ads in many newspapers and television markets, and bought out politicians—all this in order to preserve the Dirty Fuels System. The money from this "energy-industrial complex"—auto companies, coal companies, certain unenlightened utilities, and oil and gas companies—has obscured our ability to tell the ecological truth about the situation we are in and has undermined our ability to engineer the smart policies (at scale) that are needed for us to put an Energy Internet in place.

Their cumulative impact on decision-making is this: Rather than having a national energy strategy, we have instead what the energy expert Gal Luft called "the sum of all lobbies." Whichever lobby generates the most campaign cash wins. To put it another way, "We have *energy politics*, not *energy policy*," said Nate Lewis of Caltech. And energy politics is like gender politics or race politics or regional politics. It means that the politics of the issues (that is, who will benefit specifically) drive the policy priorities (what is really best for the country as a whole), not the other way around. It is very difficult to produce a coherent and viable long-term strategy in such an environment.

At election time, said Lewis, he likes to ask people this question: "Name five political swing states. People often say, 'Florida, Ohio, Pennsylvania, Tennessee, and West Virginia.' Then I say, 'Step back and eliminate Florida and say those states again: Ohio, Pennsylvania, Tennessee, West Virginia—what do they all have in common? Coal, coal, coal, coal.' You simply cannot say anything bad about coal and become president of the United States. Then add Iowa and the Midwest and biofuels and pretty soon you have no discussion" about renewable energy at all. What you have instead is a lot of blather about "clean coal" and a lot of money pouring into corn ethanol programs, out of all proportion to what makes national sense.

In the heat of the 2008 presidential primary campaign, *The Washington Post* (January 18, 2008) reported that "a group backed by the coal industry and its utility allies is waging a $35 million campaign in primary and caucus states to rally public support for coal-fired electricity and to fuel opposition to legislation that Congress is crafting to slow climate change. The group, called Americans for Balanced Energy Choices, has spent $1.3 million on billboard, newspaper, television and radio ads in Iowa, Nevada and South Carolina"—all key primary states. One of the ads, the article noted, depicted "a power cord being plugged into a lump of coal, which it calls 'an American resource that will help us with vital energy security' and 'the fuel that powers our way of life.'"

Coal has powered America's growth for almost two centuries. We are going to need to burn coal for the next few decades, at least, absent a surprise breakthrough. We need to do all we can to make that process cleaner by installing supercritical and ultrasupercritical technologies that result in a much more efficient burning process and lower emissions than in traditional coal-fired power generation. But let's not confuse what is necessary with what is preferable, and let's not call a pig a rabbit.

Coal is never going to be a clean fuel in CO_2 terms. It is preferable that we transition away from coal as fully as possible, as alternatives become cost-effective.

Jeff Biggers, author of *The United States of Appalachia*, wrote an essay in *The Washington Post* (March 2, 2008) that seemed to be a direct refutation of the plug-into-coal advertisement:

> Clean coal: Never was there an oxymoron more insidious, or more dangerous to our public health. Invoked as often by the Democratic Presidential candidates as by the Republicans . . . this slogan has blindsided any meaningful progress toward a sustainable energy policy . . . Here's the hog-killing reality . . . No matter how "cap 'n trade" schemes pan out in the distant future for coal-fired plants, strip mining and underground coal mining remain the dirtiest and most destructive ways of making energy. Coal ain't clean. Coal is deadly.

On November 7, 2006, California put Proposition 87 on the ballot, an initiative to establish a $4 billion Clean Alternative Energy Program to reduce California's oil and gasoline consumption by 25 percent through incentives for alternative energy, education, and training. It was to be funded by a small per-barrel fee on oil that was drilled within California—a standard practice in other states, which oil companies in California, through their collective clout, had managed to evade up until that time. This Proposition 87 would have funded rebates encouraging consumers to buy cleaner, cheaper operating vehicles that use hybrid technology and would have increased deployment of solar, wind, and other renewable energy technologies. The initiative lost after oil companies got together and launched an advertising campaign that deliberately misled California voters into thinking that if they voted for this bill, their gasoline prices at their local pumps would rise drastically— an absurd claim, considering that the gasoline prices in any state have nothing to do with the cost of extracting oil there, but are set by global or national supply and demand balances and refining capacity. That's why the price of gasoline at the pump in California has gone up steadily, even though Proposition 87 was killed: because global prices have gone up. In total, the oil companies and their allies reportedly spent close to $100 million on ads and lobbying to kill Proposition 87. That is almost as much as Bill Clinton spent to become president in 1992.

The production tax incentives designed to stimulate innovation and long-term investment in solar, wind, wave, geothermal, and biomass energy, which were aimed at enabling these industries to grow competitive with dirty fuels, were not going to be renewed by Congress either after they were scheduled to expire at the end of 2008. It took the Great Recession of 2008, and the $700 billion stimulus bill that followed, to finally get the House and the Senate to renew the federal tax credits for renewable technologies—including wind, geothermal, and solar power both from large-scale solar plants and rooftop solar photovoltaic and solar hot water systems—in late 2008. These tax incentives were the most obvious thing in the world to put in place. Everyone knew how much the wind and solar industries depended on them. Yet throughout 2007 the House and Senate dithered over extending them—due in part to lobbying by the oil and gas industry. The solar tax credit allows homeowners and businesses to write off 30 percent of the cost of installing a solar power system on a residence or commercial building. The production tax credit for wind is 1.8 cents for every kilowatt-hour generated. These credits are critical because they ensure that if oil prices are low, investments in wind and solar power will still be profitable. That's how you launch a new energy technology and help it go to scale so it can eventually compete without subsidies. It is crazy that it took a near financial meltdown to spur friendly legislators to insert them into the stimulus. Specifically, on October 3, 2008, Congress passed the Emergency Economic Stabilization Act of 2008, which extended the 30 percent federal tax credit for solar energy systems through 2016 and extended the production tax credit for wind projects, as well as geothermal, biomass, hydropower, landfill gas, and trash combustion facilities until 2010. Until the Great Recession forced Congress's hand, our representatives counted pennies when it came to building new clean industries, as if the money for wind, solar, and biomass were coming out of their own children's piggy banks, and yet threw money out the window like a house full of drunken sailors when it came to the old, established, well-capitalized oil, coal, and gas industries—let alone the agriculture lobby.

In the past fifty years, tens of billions of dollars in annual subsidies (which never expire, and so are not subject to congressional review) have been extended to the fossil fuel and nuclear industries. A scathing article in the *National Review*, entitled "Oil Subsidies in the Dock" (January 17, 2007), listed a few of the tax breaks given just to the oil and gas industry. They include preferential tax treatment for afforded intangible domestic drilling expenses (primarily labor and material costs associated with finding and exploiting oil and gas fields), the accelerated depletion allowance provided to small oil producers, preferential expensing for equipment used to refine liquid fuels, accelerated depreciation for natural-gas distribution pipelines, accelerated depreciation for expenditures on dry holes, and the exemption from passive loss limitation for owners of working interests in oil and gas properties. Don't understand all this mumbo jumbo? Neither do I. But you can bet that the lobbyists who crafted these tax breaks know exactly—to the penny—how much they are worth to Exxon Mobil and ConocoPhillips.

We have paid a huge price for the stop-and-start way our government uses tax credits to support the renewable energy industry. As investors in these renewable energy systems will tell you, short-term tax credit extensions can have very harmful effects on emerging industries, which are trying to attract patient capital in order to scale up manufacturing, system assembly, and delivery of equipment and services. These are large projects that require big, long-term investments, and therefore a long-term, stable tax structure—like the one enjoyed by the oil and gas industry, which still receives tax incentives that were put in place decades ago.

Michael Polsky, founder of Invenergy, one of the biggest wind developers in America, says Congress has no appreciation of the impact it has on a company such as his when it fails to extend the production tax credit on wind. "It's a disaster," says Polsky. "Wind is a very capital-intensive industry and financial institutions are not ready to take 'congressional risk.' They say, If you don't get the [production tax credit] we will not lend you the money to buy turbines and build projects."

It is really sad to think, says Rhone Resch, president of the Solar Energy Industries Association, that in 1997 the United States was the leader in solar energy technology, with 40 percent of global solar production. "Last year we were less than 8 percent, and even most of that was manufacturing for overseas markets."

When I spoke with Resch in April 2008, he told me about a conversation he'd just had with a European solar manufacturer who was looking to outsource production of his solar panels to America. They would do all the innovation in Europe, he said, but would do the blue-collar assembly in America, where the cheap dollar had made everything half price for companies with foreign currency to spend.

"He told me," said Resch, "'You are the new India.' It sent a chill down my spine."

For all the talk in magazines and by politicians about the energy issue, if you look at our walk and not at our talk, you would have to conclude that the United States has no sense of urgency when it comes to energy research. It's as if Sputnik has gone up, the nation has been challenged again to reinvent itself, this time in regard to energy, but we're sleepwalking into the future—still quietly hoping that it's all just a bad dream from which we'll soon wake up again, able to fill our tanks with dollar-a-gallon gasoline and drive off with Green Stamps and a set of NFL-logo glasses.

We need to get back to basics. Government's job is to seed the research that will produce the sorts of fundamental breakthroughs in chemistry, materials science, biology, physics, and nanotechnology that open the way for whole new approaches to solving energy problems, approaches that create new building blocks for energy and easier ways for innovators to put them together. Venture capitalists can then pick off the most promising ideas and try to commercialize them. But to find one really good idea, a green Google, you need thousands of scientists and postdocs experimenting with different options.

"That is what basic research funding is for," explained Nate Lewis of Caltech. "Basic energy science asks the question: 'How do we make new things out of new materials in new ways?' What we try to establish in our labs is the fundamental science engineering that says: 'Here is a new way to do it. It can be done.'" Then the venture capitalists come in and put up money to see if it can be done cheaply and at scale. Often it can't. "But you need the precompetitive research to seed this garden," he said. "You need to fund a hundred ideas because you know ninety-nine are not going to work and one will be the next Google. When someone asked Linus Pauling, the two-time Nobel laureate, why he has so many good ideas, he answered: 'Because I have a lot of ideas.'"

No one should be under the illusion that the venture capital community can replace massive government funding at the level of basic scientific research. The venture capitalist's job is to pick the flowers that are blooming and see if he or she can transplant them so they turn into crops that can scale. But if no one is planting seeds and fertilizing the soil with new scientific breakthroughs—from which new flowers will grow—there will not be much to pick from.

The reason there's a shortage of VC investing in green is that there has been a shortage of federal funding from the Department of Energy in renewable research, explained George P. Shultz, the former treasury secretary and secretary of state, who since leaving government has taken a great interest in clean energy tech in his role as chair of the Energy Task Force at Stanford's Hoover Institution. The market does not naturally support basic research, he said, because venture capital firms cannot firmly capture the benefits of basic research—they want to pluck flowers that come from the soil of basic research. Therefore, added Shultz, "non-market sources of support for basic research are needed. Government, along with private foundations, needs to take primary responsibility for basic research. This is probably the most important undertaking of any prospective energy policy and needs to be pursued in a generous and sustained manner. This will be the source of the truly game-changing innovations."

John Doerr, one of the country's most successful venture capitalists, who, with his partners at the legendary firm Kleiner Perkins Caufield & Byers, helped launch Google, Amazon, Sun, and Netscape, agrees with Shultz. "With few exceptions," Doerr said, "VCs don't, knowingly, fund basic research—though at Kleiner Perkins we've done so accidentally on occasions."

Even an extra $1 billion to $2 billion investment by the federal government in basic science research could make an enormous difference. "The amount of money going into this area for research is a fraction of what is needed," said Paul Alivisatos, the deputy director of the Lawrence Berkeley National Laboratory. "These days, if you meet a student working in chemistry, physics, or biology and you tell them you want them to work on a solar energy project, their eyes light up. This is what they really want to work on. There are thousands of students who want to work on this problem, but we cannot find the fellowships to support and enable them to do the work that is needed."

But what about those who say scientists always want more funding and always complain the government isn't supporting enough research?

"There can be some truth to that statement, and sometimes it is hard to prioritize—and we're an entrepreneurial bunch," said Alivisatos. "But let's just remember what happened in the latest budget cycle: Seven hundred research proposals for working on solar energy were turned down for fiscal 2008. The [Department of Energy] put out a call for proposals, the response was overwhelming, scientists all over the U.S. responded with research proposals, and the money did not materialize. The DOE is really trying. They thought they would have $35 million to spend on basic solar research. We got $5 million for our project, and we were one of the few to get funded. Think about that potential—think about how many scientists and how many postdoc [students] were ready to work on this problem, and they were all basically turned away. Thousands of scientists who want to work on the energy problem are not able to work on it today."

Numbers matter, because we need to be thinking about energy innovation in a much more strategic way than we have in the past, explained Steve Chu, the Nobel laureate who ran the Lawrence Berkeley National Laboratory when I interviewed him in 2008 and has since become President Obama's secretary of energy. Chu revamped the energy research at the lab, breaking down all the traditional silos between physics, biology, materials science, chemistry, and nanotechnology and merging experts in each of these fields into collaborative teams, where each specialty can nurture the other. In his view, the real breakthroughs are going to be found in the intersections of all these specialties, so you want a lot of people in a lot of disciplines working on this problem.

"We need to be supporting the energy research community more broadly, but we also need to be focusing on a few large-scale research centers which have critical mass—where there are enough different scientists working a lot of different projects, so you have lots of different possibilities for collaboration," said Chu. "When I joined Bell Labs as a young scientist, it was a life-changing experience. You walked into a building with thousands of world-class scientists—working in teams on the same problem. While much of the innovative research will come from our universities, we need a few places with that amount of intellectual firepower working the energy problem under one roof . . . This problem doesn't have a simple solution. We have not found the answers yet.

"What makes me really optimistic, though," Chu told me, "is when I go and hang out with my own students, and talk to students all around the country. They want to work on this problem. They see that the energy problem has become both a national and international crisis, and want to join up to solve it. Sadly, with the almost flat funding in basic energy research, our students are lining up to enlist, but the recruiting stations remain closed."

Indeed, prior to President Obama's coming to office and reenergizing the federal government's commitment to energy research, we were clearly falling behind in very dangerous ways. Before 2009, if you added up all the federal dollars going into energy research—and that would include research on oil, gas, and coal as well as solar—said Daniel M. Kammen, the University of California, Berkeley, energy policy expert, the total would be about $3 billion in government money and about $5 billion in private sector and venture funds, which was about equal to the cost of "nine days of fighting in Iraq" at the height of the war. Energy is a $1 trillion a year industry in America, and that means reinvesting about $8 billion in R & D constituted 0.8 percent of revenues. But even that paltry 0.8 percent of revenues being reinvested in energy R & D had been going up and down like a roller coaster since the first oil shock in the 1970s, and this had wreaked havoc on the energy research world. "No researcher can build a lab and hire the best graduate students when the money is going up and down every year," said Kammen. "A really good student would be dumb to work in this area, as opposed to biotech or information technology, where they know resources will be there to finish their projects, and where they can also be assured to get a job afterward."

Compare this with health care, noted Kammen. The national health budget went through a planned expansion that from 1982 to 1990 essentially doubled the budget of the National Institutes of Health. The NIH budget has stayed high ever since—so it is possible—and there wasn't even a specific health care crisis. "When the federal budget in that area increased, the private sector R & D budget went up by a factor of fourteen to fifteen," said Kammen, "which changed the whole landscape. Business saw that we were serious and they invested, and now we tout our biotech revolution as a great success."

Jeffrey Immelt of GE, which has a huge health care equipment business, estimates that the difference in R & D spending between the health care and energy industries over the last twenty years has been about $50 billion in favor of health care. To look at the problem another way, as of 2003 nuclear energy had received 56 percent of total energy research and development funding from the Department of Energy since 1948. Fossil fuels—coal, oil, and gas—had received 24 percent of the total, renewable energy 11 percent, and energy efficiency 9 percent, according to the Congressional Research Service study "Renewable Energy" (May 25, 2005).

Fortunately, this lackadaisical approach to energy research has changed lately, thanks to the Obama administration and the economic crisis. In his first year, President Obama has done more to advance clean power technologies and renewable energy than any president in history. His Environmental Protection Agency took a bold, historic step by declaring carbon dioxide and other heat-trapping gases pollutants that threaten public health. Soon afterward the EPA made another unprecedented move—acting to impose the first-ever limits on greenhouse gas emissions from cars and trucks, a move that will drive further improvements in fuel economy. The American Recovery and Reinvestment Act, President Obama's initial stimulus package to help the economy recover from the Great Recession, injected more than $60 billion into clean energy investments. These included $11 billion for a bigger, better, and smarter power grid that will move renewable energy from the rural places where it is produced to the energy-hungry cities, as well as for the installation of forty million smart meters in American homes; $5 billion to weatherize homes in low-income neighborhoods, to capture wasted energy; $4.5 billion to green federal buildings and slash the nation's energy bill; $6.3 billion for state and local renewable energy and energy efficiency efforts; $600 million in green job training programs; and $2 billion in competitive grants to develop the next generation of batteries to store energy.

"It is now possible to discuss in terms of the realities of the 2010 and 2011 budgets real and sustained increases in federal energy spending of a factor of three, five, or even ten," said Kammen. "So, now we have the moment of investment that the science of climate change and the need for an economic reinvention both demand. Can we evolve this moment from short-term excitement to long-term strategy? It took the health and biotechnology community a decade of discussion and lobbying to argue for, and achieve, a doubling of the federal medical research budget via the National Institutes of Health. Arguably, the key to achieving this increase—*and, far more importantly, to making relatively good use of it*— was the rapid growth of private sector investment in medical and biotechnology R & D."

There is no doubt that the generally higher prices of crude oil over the past three years have stimulated more investments in solar, wind, and biofuels by traditional fossil-fuel energy giants, venture capitalists, and start-ups. "For the current run-up to matter long-term, though," concluded Kammen, "this trend must not only continue, but actually grow,

with green energy programs, offices, and divisions the norm across commercial ventures large and small."

And for that to happen—for the private sector to leverage the public
sector's investments in clean energy research and development and
bring them to market—there has to be a meaningful, fixed, long-term
price signal. All this investment into energy research, which is so important, will barely make a dent without a steadily rising price on carbon and
on gasoline. We must not fool ourselves, as we have done for so many
years: Price matters, as I argued earlier. Without a fixed, rising, long-term,
durable price on carbon, none of the Obama clean-tech initiatives will
achieve the scale needed for them to have an effect on climate change or
make America the leader it must be in energy technology. And it still is
not clear whether the U.S. Congress will impose such a meaningful
price signal, even indirectly through the cap-and-trade legislation. There
is no sustained ET market without the price signals that drive consumers
to choose the most energy-efficient options and the clear-cut rewards to
investors to engage in continuous funding of innovation and deployment
of emissions-free electrons. You may get a lot of innovation, but you will
not get a lot of commercialization at the scale and variety we need, and
ultimately getting innovation to market is what matters.

As David Hawkins, director of climate programs at the Natural Resources Defense Council, put it in congressional testimony (July 7,
2009): "The primary barrier to a clean energy economy is not a shortage
of American ingenuity or even a shortage of financial resources to apply
to the task; it is the lack of a powerful and sustained set of predictable
market rewards that are needed to motivate private sector innovators to
invest in bringing low-carbon options to market rather than products and
services where the carbon footprint is ignored."

Only such a market-based system will enable us to quickly turn over
our capital stock and displace inefficient homes, vehicles, factories,
power systems, and lightbulbs with those using much less energy and
emitting much less CO_2. That is the only way for the United States to
grow sustainably. Although we keep looking for an easy out, there is no
way around it: No serious price on carbon means no serious green revolution. Because you will not have consumers demanding these new technologies and therefore you will not have producers who have a consistent
set of incentives to provide them. What you will have instead is a lot of
companies focusing on using all the new government incentives to make

money from renewable energy. They won't really be looking at the consumer; they will be looking at the incentives. Some will make money, new technologies will emerge—but they will not scale without a meaningful and long-term price signal. Politically, though, this still seems to be a nonstarter for both Democrats and Republicans.

Now you understand why I fantasize about being China for a day. Just one day . . .

The only silver lining, when you compare how much we are investing in health care research to how little we are investing in energy research, said Joseph Romm, who served as a senior official in the Department of Energy during the Clinton administration, is this: "At least people will live long enough to see how badly we've screwed things up."

To be sure, the last time our leadership did make a significant investment in energy, upping the federal research budget $2.5 billion to over $6 billion from 1977 to 1980, some programs got funded that were not that great, said Kammen. "You don't always make the right bets, but there have been some spectacular successes. Solar energy science and technology advanced in leaps and bounds as a result of that money. Much of the solar energy technology being deployed today in what has been a boom in the industry was developed during that period." But the flip side of our lack of steadfastness has been that many of these innovations went into American companies that, lacking domestic market support, were eventually bought by Japanese or European solar companies. So American taxpayers in effect ended up funding other countries' R & D.

How could this happen? "Ever since 1945, the U.S. economy has had to reinvent itself every ten to fifteen years to keep jobs growing," said Kammen. "Big new job growth comes from waves of technological innovation—like IT and biotech. The next boom in technology is going to be clean energy, but it just has not penetrated through our macroeconomic policy analysis. Higher economic growth goes to the places that innovate. If you are not building these new [clean power] technologies for export, you are losing out on the next big economic boom—no matter what you say. India and China and Indonesia are all installing new power plants today." We need to be selling them the next generation—solar, wind, solar thermal, geothermal, and other cutting-edge technologies—which we have an advantage in designing and building.

We are not going to remake a $1 trillion energy industry in one generation, though, by spending less than 1 percent of revenues on R & D, when the norm in other industries is 8 to 10 percent.

In case you don't think this attitude has consequences, let me tell you the story of First Solar Inc., probably America's premier solar company. Warning: This story will make you cry . . .

First Solar started in Toledo, Ohio. Unlike firms that use silicon to make solar cells, First Solar generates electricity from thin films of cadmium telluride (a semiconductor made from cadmium and tellurium) coated onto glass. These cadmium telluride solar cells are currently not as efficient as silicon solar cells, but they are cheaper and can operate in more varied climates and light conditions, and they easily blend into a building's facade. The company's CEO, Mike Ahearn, picks up the story:

"We started in 1992, when a small group of scientists and engineers came together to develop a technology that could deposit thin films of semiconductor material onto sheets of glass, much like flat panel TV screens, and process these sheets into solar panels capable of absorbing sunlight and converting it to electricity. Their dream was to dramatically reduce the cost of solar electricity, to the point that it could be used to meet much of the daytime electricity needs of the industrialized world and begin providing affordable power to the millions of people on our planet who live today with little or no electricity. For twelve years, our associates struggled to transform patented technology into a workable manufacturing process, enduring technical failures, funding crises, employee attrition, and a host of other start-up problems along the way. When it looked like we were going to have to shut down because of a lack of funds, John Walton, of the Walton Walmart family fortune, who was a First Solar investor, stuck by us through some really difficult times as we perfected the process. It wasn't until late 2004, after a total investment of over $150 million, that the first small manufacturing line became fully operational."

This factory line, using a lot of machinery that First Solar initially designed and built on its own, can stamp very high volumes of solar cells and can be replicated anywhere in the world—not an easy trick in the solar business.

"During the three years since completing that first manufacturing line, we've increased our annual production rate by over 800 percent, to become one of the largest solar module manufacturers in the world," said Ahearn. "Our annual revenues have grown from $6 million to over $500 million by the end of 2007, and we've cut the cost of solar modules from nearly $3 per watt in 2004 to $1.12 per watt as of the end of 2007, which brings our founding vision into range and shows you the power of combining semiconductor technology with production scale. In November 2007, we became a public company and today have a market capitalization approaching $20 billion. When I was discussing this story with a friend, he remarked, 'Only in America.' And it's true that our story at first glance does seem to have many of the hallmarks of the classic American dream. But in fact First Solar is to a large extent a German success story."

How could that be? "In 2003," explained Ahearn, "we began initial production and we started looking around for markets that would give us the scale that we needed, that would drive big volumes, so we could get more efficient. At the time, Japan had the world's first solar incentive program, dating to around 1990, based on residential systems. It was a highly coordinated effort by the Ministry of Economy, Trade and Industry, which had promoted Sharp and Kyocera and Sanyo and Mitsubishi to be the leaders of the global solar market. And Sharp had a dominant share of the Japanese market. You could see how they got their supply chain, production, and distribution channels all forged into an efficient scalable model that made them the low-cost solar manufacturer in the industry. That Japanese market was bigger than the rest of the world combined and of course was effectively closed to non-Japanese companies.

"So we said, 'We need our "Japan" if we are going to expand and reduce costs,'" said Ahearn. "Where are we going to find a sponsor to scale us up? Here we had invented this incredible technology, it is starting to look like it is going to work, and our scientists and engineers are saying to me: 'Where are we going to find a market for 25 megawatts?,' which was our annual production target. And I just kept telling them: 'You solve the technical problems, we'll sell the product.' But then I started looking around and asking myself, 'Where *are* we going to sell this?' We needed to find a way to get high volumes of our product into the marketplace cost-effectively so that we could begin to drive the price to the levels we think are needed to open large markets, close to the average U.S. retail energy price, which was 8 to 10 cents a kilowatt-hour. That meant that we had to eventually sell our solar panel at $1 to $1.25 per watt. At the time, in 2003, our manufacturing costs were over $3 per watt, so we had a long way to go. We really needed somewhere to get some volume going."

Naturally, this American company, headquartered in Arizona and with its main factory in Ohio, wanted to exploit the American solar market. The problem was—there was no American solar market, and no one in Washington or anywhere else was particularly interested in creating one, even though jobs in the solar industry are pure manufacturing jobs: You don't mine, you don't strip, you don't dig, you don't drill—you just build stuff while wearing a blue collar.

"We came to Washington and then went to many states in the southwest," Ahearn recalled. "We said to a couple of American utilities, 'We will lose money to just get going,' because we knew that as we scaled, the costs would go down. And we still could not get any takers. At that time we had a hundred employees . . . We talked to Arizona and Ohio congressmen. They were all opposed to taxpayer subsidies. We did not get a lot of traction. With the backing of John Walton, we told them, 'We'll take the risks, just tell us you'll buy the power.' We got lower-level guys who would agree, but by the time it worked up to the top, it got nowhere . . .

"That was when we decided to go to Germany.

"In 1990," explained Ahearn, "the year of reunification, the German government had created and passed the first feed-in law for solar electricity. The feed-in law is a demand incentive program that has been widely copied by countries outside the U.S. and expanded within Germany to make Germany the world's largest market for solar products. It started small, but in 2004 the Germans said to themselves: 'How do we really engage the private sector to get some scale in financing and real investment in technology and equipment?' They decided to go all the way to the end user—the home or the business—and say to them: 'What level of feed-in tariff would make you just jump into this?' So in 2004, they changed their feed-in rates. They told every German consumer: If you build a solar system on your home or office or farmland or landfills—if you build a system anywhere—the local utility has to interconnect it and pay you for the kilowatt-hours your solar system feeds into the grid at a price fixed by national law for twenty years. *For twenty years!* That is a no-brainer."

Every year—and this was really smart—new solar projects coming on line in Germany have a feed-in tariff that is 5 percent lower than the previous year's tariff to account for, and to stimulate, improvements in efficiency. Research around learning curves says that when sales double, you usually get a roughly 20 percent reduction in price. So volume matters here. The more volume, the quicker and further you move down the learning curve toward the price that will scale in China and India.

"After we made the initial market test in Germany, we realized that the feed-in program will create a market that will allow us to scale. Also, we realized that their program had created a center of technological excellence, with a lot of budding innovators," said Ahearn. "So we ended up employing or partnering with a number of these German scientists and engineers, and their contributions have been critical to our success. Today we purchase over half of the equipment used in our production lines from German manufacturers and count suppliers in eastern Germany as among our most important business partners."

Meanwhile, back home: "The American market was totally fragmented—you could not imagine scaling a business here," said Ahearn. "Not only had Germany created its own surge in demand in 2004 that got us launched, but Spain, Italy, France, Greece, and Portugal all adopted very similar feed-in tariff markets. And this produced a big inflow of capital into the whole value chain across Europe. Unlike in America, where government incentive programs stop and start every couple of years and you never know when the subsidies might come on and off, the German program has no time limits and the incentives on existing solar generation projects are guaranteed for at least twenty years. So there was no cliffhanging out there. We had our original production line in Ohio, and then added two more, and then we had to build our next plant. Where should we put it? We decided to build it in eastern Germany—in the city of Frankfurt Oder—540 jobs, good paying jobs. We knew if we built a factory that comes on line in two years in Germany that the market would still be there. If you built it somewhere in the United States you could not be sure of that. Then we went to our German customers and signed long-term contracts with progressive pricing so we knew we could repay the plant investment. You could plan your whole cash flow . . ."

Because the German market was so developed, thanks to the feed-in law, "a broad network developed there of solar distributors and system integrators, with strong technical abilities, who could help us bring the new product to market efficiently," said Ahearn. "We formed a German sales and marketing subsidiary and built a sales and technical support team in Mainz that today serves as our global sales and marketing base. We continue to generate well over half of our revenues from Germany . . . In fact, the 800 percent increase in production that I mentioned comes predominantly from our factory in Frankfurt Oder. It is the largest thin-film solar factory in the world and represents one of the largest foreign direct investments ever made in the solar industry."

That factory could have and should have been built in Ohio, but "we wanted to be close to our business partners and demonstrate to the German government that we were prepared to provide an economic return to the region based on the investment that the government made in creating the market," said Ahearn. "Also, eastern Germany is a good place to manufacture. It possesses well-trained people, good manufacturing infrastructure, a stable economy, and good social and political infrastructures. We were also able to obtain financial incentives provided by the European Union and the German government . . . The German government gave us a shot and we thought we needed to demonstrate a payback to them. They took the first step and wrote a check to validate our theory. So we made ourselves a German company."

The world—most of the world—took notice, Ahearn told me. "Countries all over the world are now contacting us to build our next factory there, but so far no one has called from the U.S. . . ."

Between 2006 and 2008, First Solar's market capitalization went from $1.5 billion to $20 billion. You would think that would get the attention of Ohio's lawmakers. But it didn't. When the 2007 energy bill came up for debate, and the question was whether or not to include a national renewable energy portfolio standard, which would have really grown the U.S. market for solar, and to extend the investment tax credit of 30 percent for building solar energy, Ohio's Republican senator, George Voinovich, voted against both. No Michigan lawmaker dared vote against the car companies, even though they'd been swimming in red ink (and laying off Michigan workers) for years. But when it comes to launching a whole new industry that is creating real jobs, big profits, and new technologies, Republican senators from solar states do not hesitate to vote with their party and against the real interests of critically important local companies.

What did those senators tell you? I asked Ahearn. "What we have consistently heard," he answered, "is that there is a lot of support for renewable energy but it just got caught up in political maneuvering. At a minimum, there is a leadership void where this kind of petty politics can stand in the way of launching a whole new industry."

I understand politics. I am not naive. But I also understand a crisis and an opportunity. As my friend the former Stanford economist Paul Romer likes to say, "A crisis is a terrible thing to waste." But we are well on our way.

Are you crying yet?

Blowin' in the Wind

When we aren't shooting ourselves in both feet, the simple fact remains that remaking our Dirty Fuels System into a Clean Energy System is really hard—even with the best of intentions. It is not only the science that is hard. Once we have a clean-technology breakthrough, building the transmission lines that can be integrated into a smart grid can be excruciatingly difficult. Just ask the folks at Southern California Edison, who have more renewable power in their arsenal than any utility in the world. What is it like, I asked their leadership team, to add just one wind farm to their power mix? It sounds great, right? Let's add some wind. One little wind farm. No problem.

Do you have eleven years?

Here's the story: Thanks to California's renewable energy mandate, lots of people have invested in wind power in that state. The only problem is that the places where the wind blows the hardest and longest, and where you can put the wind turbines while disturbing the fewest people, are far away from major cities. Because SoCalEd wanted to buy wind in bulk, it had to erect a new $2 billion power transmission line from the big new wind farms in the Tehachapi Pass north of Edwards Air Force Base over to Los Angeles. Distance: 275 miles of power lines. The first hurdle was transmission planning, which is known as the "interconnection study process." This process includes a "finding of need" for the new line, what route it will take, and, most important, who will pay for it. In SoCalEd's case, the process triggered a fight over how much of the new line was really for carrying renewable wind power and how much was just to improve the reliability of the grid and who should pay for each piece. Everyone got a chop at this process—including the Federal Energy Regulatory Commission and the California Independent System

Operator, a not-for-profit public-benefit corporation charged with operating the majority of California's high-voltage wholesale power grid. This review was an open process, and all the wind owners came forward with their maps of where the transmission line should run and how much they should pay.

After months of that fight, said Ron Litzinger, senior vice president for transmission and distribution for Southern California Edison, "we finally said, 'Look, we'll pay for it all, as public policy support will likely ensure investment recovery. Would everyone now please put their pencils down so that we can proceed?'"

Then the fun starts.

"It takes you two years to get through the study process," said Litzinger. "Then you have a year to do an environmental survey along the route to study what vegetation grows there and what endangered species you might run into. Then you have one and a half to two years with the Public Utilities Commission. They reconfirm the finding of need and review our environmental assessment and hire another contractor to do an independent environmental review. We also have to go through some federal land, and that is always a problem, because then you have to get a separate permit from the particular federal land agency. State and federal law are not in sync on this, so the National Forest person says, 'I don't want a transmission line going through my forest.' We had to work that out, too . . . Then we had to present an environmental mitigation plan for how we intended to mitigate the damage along the route. Only after that was accepted could the whole thing go ahead. On a good day, a transmission line will take five years from the start of the process until you have the permit and the route in hand."

All these reviews are important—you can't be an environmentalist and disdain them—but you can't be an environmentalist anymore, either, without wanting to find a way to streamline them so the right projects get built in real time.

The construction itself takes only two years—less than half the time it takes to get the permits. "We have about 4,500 megawatts in Tehachapi we can draw on," said Litzinger. "We started the project in 2002, and today [February 25, 2008] we have permits for one-third of the project in hand. We started construction on January 3, 2008, and we hope to be delivering some power, about 700 megawatts, to homes in the Los Angeles basin by 2009. The whole thing will be permitted and constructed and fully operational by 2013—eleven years in the making."

Eleven years to fully connect one wind farm. I don't think that timetable is going to cut it in a world where every two weeks China opens new coal-fired power plants big enough to serve all the households in my hometown of Minneapolis. Yes, you say, it's relatively easy to build dirty coal plants—and you are right. It's much more difficult to build power plants that are clean and superefficient. Right now China is mainly putting up dirty ones. But soon they will be putting up wind farms, solar facilities, and nuclear plants with the same relentless efficiency. You can bet your house on it. It will take time, but they will eventually try to outgreen us. They'll have to, or they won't be able to breathe.

And what about us? Will we step up our game? We can't be China for a day, and we should not have to and we should not want to. But it is a measure of how incoherent, ad hoc, and asystematic American energy policy is right now that such fantasies flash into your mind. If we cannot find a way to overcome all these weaknesses and chart an intelligently de-signed energy strategy, our generation had better brace itself for a rocky retirement—and some really unpleasant questions from our kids.

"I have always believed," said Jeffrey Immelt, "that every generation looks back at the generation before it and has one big question about something they did or did not do. For our generation, the big question to the generation before us was 'How could good people be so prejudiced against blacks or women?' I am convinced that when our kids are fifty, and they look back at us, they are going ask us: 'What were you thinking? You were the richest country in the world. You had the technology to really make a difference on things like global warming. Why were you so slow to do the right things?' They are going to say, 'Gosh, what were you doing?'"

NINETEEN

A Democratic China, or
a Banana Republic?

There is a story about the advice a Chinese gardener gave to his employer. When the landowner asked, "What is the best time to plant an oak tree?," the gardener replied, "A hundred years ago, but the second best time is today." For climate protection perhaps the best time to enact a comprehensive program to fight global warming was thirty years ago, but the second best time is this year.

—David Hawkins, director of climate programs at the Natural Resources Defense Council

So what *were* we doing to change the world in the years when we were the world's unrivaled superpower? Actually, that's a question our children are already asking. They have been asking it for a while. In July 2007, I took part in a green technology conference in Colorado that brought together some of the world's top energy innovators and scientists under the auspices of Kleiner Perkins Caufield & Byers, the venture capital firm. It was a stimulating, often deeply technical discussion led by climate and energy experts. At the close of the conference, our hosts said they wanted to show an old news clip. Up on the screen came a slightly grainy video from the 1992 Earth Summit in Rio de Janeiro, Brazil. A twelve-year-old girl from Canada named Severn Suzuki was addressing the plenary session of the Rio summit. The camera would occasionally pan to the audience of environment ministers from all over the world, who could be seen listening to her every word with rapt attention—as we did. Suzuki's speech is one of the most eloquent statements I have ever heard about both the strategic and the moral purpose of a real green revolution at the dawn of the Energy-Climate Era—from anyone of any age. It reads as well as it was delivered. Here is an excerpt:

> Hello, I'm Severn Suzuki, speaking for ECO—the Environmental Children's Organization. We are a group of twelve- and thirteen-year-olds trying to make a difference: Vanessa Suttie, Morgan Geisler, Michelle Quigg and me. We raised all the money to come here five thousand miles to tell you adults you must change your ways. Coming up here today, I have no hidden agenda. I am fighting for my future. Losing my future is not like losing an election or a few points on the stock market. I am here to speak for all generations to come. I am here to speak on behalf of the starving children around the world whose cries go unheard. I am here to speak for the countless animals dying across this planet because they have nowhere left to go. I am afraid to go out in the sun now because of the holes in the ozone. I am afraid to breathe the air because I don't know what chemicals are in it. I used to go fishing in Vancouver, my home, with my dad until just a few years ago we found the fish full of cancers. And now we hear of animals and plants going extinct every day—vanishing forever. In my life, I have dreamt of seeing the great herds of wild animals, jungles and rain forests full of birds and butterflies, but now I wonder if they will even exist for my children to see. Did you have to worry about these things when you were my age? All this is happening before our eyes and yet we act as if we have all the time we want and all the solutions. I'm only a child and I don't have all the solutions, but I want you to realize, neither do you . . . You don't know how to bring the salmon back up a dead stream. You don't know how to bring back an animal now extinct. And you can't bring back the forests that once grew where there is now desert. If you don't know how to fix it, please stop breaking it! . . .
>
> At school, even in kindergarten, you teach us how to behave in the world. You teach us: not to fight with others, to work things out, to respect others, to clean up our mess, not to hurt other creatures, to share—not be greedy. Then why do you go out and do the things you tell us not to do? Do not forget why you're attending these conferences, who you're doing this for—we are your

own children. You are deciding what kind of world we are growing up in. Parents should be able to comfort their children by saying "everything's going to be all right," "it's not the end of the
world," and "we're doing the best we can." But I don't think you
can say that to us anymore. Are we even on your list of priorities?

My dad always says, "You are what you do, not what you say."
Well, what you do makes me cry at night. You grown-ups say you
love us, but I challenge you. Please make your actions reflect your
words. Thank you.

Every time I listen to that speech, I get a little chill—especially from
the line: *You are what you do, not what you say.* For me, the beauty,
power, and virtue of Suzuki's words is in their raw reminder of what a real
green revolution is all about. It is not about Earth Day concerts. It is not
about special green issues of magazines. It is not about 205 easy ways to
go green. It is not just the latest dot-com gold rush or marketing fad,
either. It is a survival strategy. It is about what we do in response to the
truly massive challenge that we face to preserve the natural world that
has been bequeathed to us. Somewhere along the way, that larger purpose has gotten lost. Too often and in too many ways, "green" has become a license to feel good without doing good, to raise awareness
without actually changing our behavior.

People often ask: I want to be green—how can I make a difference?
My answer is always twofold. First, pay attention and personally lead as
environmentally sustainable a life as you can. Nobody is perfect; I'm
sure not. But just make sure your own environmental awareness and behavior is always a work in progress. That is vitally necessary, but it is not
sufficient.

Personal commitments alone, though, will not solve scale problems
like the one we face around clean energy and climate. Whatever personal commitments you, your kids, or your neighbors make, we as a society must translate them into national and international commitments, by
institutionalizing them in laws, regulations, and treaties. That is the only
way to achieve scale. And that leads to my other answer: It is much more
important to change your leaders than your lightbulbs.

Why? Because elected national, state, and local leaders—our lawmakers and the regulators who work for them—write the rules and regulations, and establish the price signals, that shape markets and change

the behavior of millions of people. They create the incentives for thousands of investors and regulate the performance of billions of machines, devices, and vehicles—all at once. Elected officials write the laws for just how efficient your lightbulbs have to be, whether you turn the lights on or remember to shut them off; they write the laws for how many miles your car has to get per gallon, whether you buy a Prius or a Hummer; they write the laws for how much clean power your utility has to buy, whether its CEO is a progressive or a Neanderthal; they write the laws for how efficient your air conditioner has to be, whether you can afford to run it or not; they write the laws for whether a transmission line for clean power can run across your property or can be held up in legal battles for a decade; they write the laws about what tax incentives Congress will offer—or not—to developers of wind, biomass, and solar power; they write the laws for what price will be assessed for carbon emissions in any cap-and-trade system; they write regulations (or don't) for gasoline taxes; they write the regulations that ban plastic shopping bags, lower speed limits, restrict where biofuel crops can be planted, determine whether utilities are compensated for encouraging you to consume electricity or to save it, and require companies and consumers to pay for all of nature's services that they use.

But how do we as a society produce national, state, and local leaders who will write the right laws, rules, and regulations in ways that will truly shape the market to produce a real green revolution? The green revolution could learn from two precedents: the civil rights movement and America's mobilization to fight World War II.

The civil rights movement forced white Americans to treat black Americans the way they themselves would want to be treated. But that movement was not just about asking people to be nice to a new African-American neighbor or to voluntarily open up the membership of the local swimming club. Ultimately, it was about changing laws, so that no one had an option to discriminate, and it was those laws that ultimately changed the behavior and attitudes of tens of millions of people. But the civil rights movement started with citizen activism—the black activists who were ready to sit down at the whites-only lunch counter, the ones who refused to go to the back of the bus or give up their seats to white people, the ones who defied racists and walked through the front gates of Ole Miss and the University of Georgia. Their example and courage inspired others. And eventually, on August 28, 1963, that movement reached a crescendo, as a million people gathered on the National Mall to listen to Martin Luther King, Jr., deliver the "I Have a Dream" speech from the steps of the Lincoln Memorial. Thanks to this combination of civic activism and inspiration, the country had become aware that something had to be done—that the status quo was no longer tolerable because it would no longer be tolerated.

Eventually, these protests (and the sheer number of protesters) attracted the attention of local, state, and federal lawmakers, many of whom, though long aware of segregation, and aware that the majority of the country didn't like it, had taken the view that changing things would be more trouble than keeping the status quo. But seeing that mass movement visibly calling for change on the National Mall, along with many other protests in many other places, changed their minds—and so altered the political landscape. It made the painful task of changing the race laws preferable to the pain of doing nothing. It made the painful task of changing the race laws a political imperative. Yes, it was disruptive—very disruptive—and would be for two decades. But no reasonable person would now say that it was not the right thing to do for our country. As Senator John F. Kerry wrote in an essay in *Newsweek* (April 28, 2008), "Real change comes only when people form a movement so large that Washington has no choice but to listen . . . It's the only way to change the nation."

Amen. And that is the next step the green revolution has to take. Despite all the ink and hot air that it gets, the green movement in America has not yet made its agenda unignorable to a sufficient number of politicians to produce the sorts of changes in rules and prices that would actually affect the climate at the scale that is required. Green is still more option than necessity. The civil rights movement for African-Americans is that rare cause that managed to make itself both a moral imperative and a political imperative. That is where the green agenda wants to be. While it is easy to argue that greening the planet is a moral imperative, an economic imperative, an innovation imperative, and a strategic imperative, even President Barack Obama has not yet made it a political imperative. He will only have done that, in my view, when he has fought for a significant price signal on carbon, no matter what the political cost.

What that means, of course, is that if the green movement were really behaving like the civil rights movement, really trying to encourage, or indeed force, the politicians to do the right thing, we would see a million people on the Mall demanding a price signal—a high carbon tax, or a stringent cap-and-trade regime, or a gasoline tax and a credible national renewable energy mandate. These would be the green equivalents of civil rights laws. As Stanford's Larry Diamond once put it to me: "A price signal is to the green movement what the Voting Rights Act was to the civil rights movement. It is the pivot point for changing reality." Once the Voting Rights Act was passed, and millions of African-Americans were guaranteed the right to vote, and the government was prepared to send troops to ensure that it happened, everything changed. The same would happen with a real price on carbon. A price signal would trigger innovation and consumer demand at scale. And once that happens, you will see green products arriving much faster, and at much lower prices, than anyone now anticipates.

Alas, though, it is a lot easier to get a million people on the Mall asking for equal rights, especially for parts of the country and neighborhoods where they don't reside, than to get them there asking for a carbon tax, which might have tangible effects only in their children's generation. But unless politicians believe that the public is willing to accept the price and regulatory changes needed to launch the clean energy revolution, they will continue to take the view that maintaining the status quo, or minimizing the price signal, is easier than butting heads with oil, coal, and gas companies—and possibly losing their campaign donations. As long as the public indicates to the politicians that it is only interested in the 205 easy ways to go green, no one is going to propose the one or two hard ways that could actually make a difference.

Getting a million people on the Mall demanding a real price on carbon is really hard, though, without a Pearl Harbor. Our parents and grandparents rose to the challenge of freedom in their day—World War II—only after it became a visible, immediate, and inescapable threat to their way of life. We applied all our economic resources and human effort to solving the problem, and we did not stop until we won—because we understood that our way of life was at stake. Everyone had to sacrifice and everyone had to participate—from "Rosie the Riveter" to your grandparents in their victory garden to General Motors being told by Franklin Roosevelt that it had to make tanks instead of cars. We need a similar mobilization to launch a real Clean Energy System—but we have to do it to *prevent* a Pearl Harbor that we think will happen rather than respond to one that has. Because once the climate Pearl Harbor happens, and the threat is inescapably obvious, escaping from it will be well-nigh impossible.

The big challenge we have today in energizing a real green revolution is that the people most affected by any climate change are not likely to be "us." The people who will be most affected by energy and natural resources supply and demand, petrodictatorship, climate change, energy poverty, and biodiversity loss don't get to vote—because they haven't been born yet. They are the next generation. Historically, political reform movements emerge when the have-nots, the people who are negatively affected or aggrieved by some policy or situation, become numerous enough to bring their weight to bear in a democratic system. But this green issue, particularly climate change, "doesn't pit haves versus have-nots," says the Johns Hopkins University foreign policy expert Michael Mandelbaum. It pits "the present versus the future—today's generation versus its kids and unborn grandchildren. The problem is, the future can't organize. Workers organize to get worker rights. Old people organize to get health care. But how can the future get organized? It can't lobby. It can't protest."

In our model of democracy, policy is the product of the clash of interest groups. But the green interest group has not fully formed yet. When it does—if a few more Hurricane Katrinas hit a few more cities—"it will be the biggest interest group in history," added Mandelbaum, "but by then it could be too late."

An unusual situation like this calls for that ethic of stewardship: what parents do for their kids—looking over the horizon, thinking about the long term, so they can have a better future. Of course, it is much easier to get families to look out for their descendants than whole societies. Yet that is our challenge—and it is a challenge for political leaders, business leaders, and for the Re-Generation. All three have to step up in a new way. I see positive signs in all three areas.

In the leadership area, President Obama has understood that the green revolution cannot just be presented as a necessity, without which we are all going to die as a result of climate change. It also has to be framed as an opportunity and in our case as the most important opportunity for American renewal. It is very difficult to tell people that a greenhouse gas that they cannot see, touch, or smell is going to destroy the world in a hundred years and get them to act. It just cuts against human nature. That is one reason why throughout this book I have tried to stress that meeting the challenge of the Energy-Climate Era is not just about facing a new set of dangers; it is also about rising to *a new set of opportunities*—opportunities that would make America more prosperous, healthy, inspiring, and secure. World War II was not really an "opportunity." It was purely an obligation. The Energy-Climate Era is both: the obligation to make sure there is a stable planet for all species—and an opportunity for America to renew and regenerate itself.

But there is no getting around the fact that transitioning to a real green revolution will involve sacrifice, the same way that fighting World War II or the Cold War did, and the president will have to make the case to the American people for that level of sacrifice—including a serious price signal on carbon—because it will produce a stronger America and preserve a livable planet. There is no escaping that. If the president is not ready to make that case to the people, it will not happen. Or it will only happen after five more Katrinas.

Whenever you face a big challenge, like ending segregation or fighting a world war, the quality of leadership is often the deciding factor. In the case of the Energy-Climate Era, we need leaders who can shape the issues so that people understand why ignoring them is such a threat and why rising to them is such an opportunity. We also need leaders who not only understand the importance of dealing with this problem in a systemic way, but who can actually generate the vision and authority to pull that system together.

To get that level of leadership without a climate 9/11, though, we will need both industry and the public to demand action to a degree we have never seen before. Leaders don't just grow on trees. We have to help birth them.

When it comes to industry, well, we know that nothing moves politicians these days more than the prospect of campaign donations. And what is interesting about the titans of American industry is the degree to which a split is emerging between those who want to do nothing—and argue that any carbon price signal will cause a loss of jobs and shrinking of profits—and those businesses who understand that the green revolution truly is an economic opportunity to invent new products, build new markets, and create shareholder value.

In other words, the good news is that many industries can be moved today on the green issue, because they have already started moving themselves, understanding that outgreening represents a competitive opportunity, not a burden. These companies are becoming more and more numerous and vocal. They still cannot override the Chamber of Commerce, the hydrocarbon lobby, and the National Association of Manu-

facturers, who want to slow down any green revolution, but they can and
are increasingly acting on their own and playing hardball to boot.

Look at the impact Walmart has had by promoting energy-efficient
lightbulbs. "Last year, Wal-Mart announced an ambitious goal—they
wanted to sell 100 million compact fluorescent light bulbs in one year,"
wrote TreeHugger.com (October 23, 2007). "Now the company has announced that they've already achieved that goal. Wal-Mart estimates that
these energy-saving bulbs will have the effect of taking 700,000 cars off
the road, or conserving the energy needed to power 450,000 single-
family homes." Walmart is also well on its way to meeting its 2005 stated
goal of making its fleet of 7,200 tractor-trailer trucks 25 percent more fuel
efficient by the end of 2008—which would be equal to taking almost
68,000 cars off the road—and 100 percent more efficient by 2015. Obviously every new Walmart store is a new energy sink, but in the absence
of a freeze on expansion, it's important that Walmart 's growth be as
green as possible—not only for itself, but for how much it will drive technological improvements for everyone.

Dan Becker, a former Sierra Club lobbyist in Washington and now a
private environmental consultant, shared with me a story that highlighted the division that is now emerging between green and ungreen
U.S. industries. In 2007, as the House and Senate debated whether and
how much to raise gas mileage standards for cars sold in America, there
was a split among the car companies. Some were prepared to go for a
new mileage standard of 35 miles per gallon by 2020. But the Detroit Big
Three—GM, Ford, and Chrysler—opposed any significant changes in
the mileage standard, and only when they saw which way the wind was
blowing did they reluctantly propose 32 mpg by 2022 as a weaker compromise. Nissan USA, which knew it could easily meet the higher standards, was in the group that supported 35 mpg by 2020. Nissan's
American manufacturing plants are mainly in the South, in states such
as Mississippi. Nissan's representatives told the senators from those states
how it hoped they would vote—including Republican heavyweight Senator Trent Lott of Mississippi.

"I have been working environmental issues in Congress for many
years, but I had never met Trent Lott before," said Becker. "His voting
record on environmental issues was probably the worst in Congress. But
there is a Nissan plant in Mississippi now . . . I was lobbying hard to help
win passage for the tougher mileage standards. Nissan was our ally. I was

standing off the Senate floor one day during this debate, and Trent Lott walks out. I went over and introduced myself to him and was getting ready to make my case. I had this sort of plain, run-down suit on. And he says to me, 'Dan, didn't y'all get the memo? It's seersucker day.' Then he keeps walking, gets in the elevator, and says, 'I'm with y'all.' And the elevator door closes and he is gone."

In short, the tougher mileage standards passed not by the power of logic but through the balance of power in the lobby. "The Sierra Club could not have gotten Trent Lott. Nissan had to deliver Trent Lott and Ted Stevens [the senator from Alaska who typically voted with the oil industry], and we never would have won without them," Becker said. "They brought all these extremely conservative senators who had Nissan in their states . . . There are environmentalists in Mississippi, but Trent Lott knows they did not vote for him."

It was Nissan that moved Trent Lott to get a little green—at least for a day—but it was Nissan's customers who helped to turn Nissan green. It always comes back to what we do more than what we say.

The Re-Generation, Again

And that brings me to why I am so off Earth Day. We do not need our consciousness raised anymore by rock bands whose electricity usage is erased by carbon offsets. I was invited to be a speaker at the Earth Day concert/rally on the Mall in 2008. When I accepted the invitation, I wondered if a political leader would show up to lead a mass rally the way Martin Luther King did in 1963. It was a rainy day, and when I was summoned to address the crowd for ten minutes, a rock band was tuning up behind me. I thought I would avoid the rah-rah stuff and speak about something practical—how this crowd might use its influence and size to get the solar and wind tax credits, which had been stuck in Congress for almost a year, finally passed into law. But I quickly figured out that a lot of people were there to listen to the band, not to listen to a political strategy.

As it happened, a lightning bolt forced the organizers to shut down the rally abruptly, and I never got to finish my remarks. I trudged through the rain and took the Metro home. Several other attendees were in the same subway car that I was in, and one of them came up to talk. He was in his late twenties and said he worked for the USAID contracting firm Development Alternatives Inc. "I liked what you were trying to say," he began. "I am sorry you didn't get to finish. A lot of the people were just there for the music." Yes, I agreed, maybe it wasn't the right time for a serious speech on how to lobby Congress.

But when is? If the Re-Generation really wants to have an impact, it has to get those million people on the Mall—or find a moral and political equivalent—not to listen to bands but to tell the politicians that they are ready for a serious price signal. And they have to do it without a Pearl Harbor or a 9/11. For starters, that requires understanding how the energy game is played and focusing pressure on the key actors. That means learning how Congress works, how campaign finance gets done, how utilities get rate increases, and how major firms lobby the government. Exxon Mobil, Peabody Energy, and General Motors know the difference between a Facebook group and a blocking coalition in Congress. They are not on Facebook, but they are in the faces of those lawmakers who stand in their way. When their interests are threatened, they are not in the chat room blogging about it; they are in the cloakroom twisting arms and buying votes. If the Re-Generation wants to play in this game, it has to get out of Facebook and into somebody's face. It needs to get out of the chat room and into the cloakroom, where the rules get written. The people who run and benefit from the Dirty Fuels System do not attend Earth Day concerts.

Beyond that, though, the job of the Re-Generation is to work student by student, school by school, teacher by teacher, neighborhood by neighborhood, to change the culture around green, making it not only "hip" but also more central to how we regenerate our country. The green revolution is still not where it needs to be. For too many politicians, Code Green is still just a box to check, not a governing philosophy.

The easy sound bite now is for politicians to say that we need a "Manhattan Project" for inventing clean energy that would parallel the Manhattan Project that invented the atomic bombs that ended World War II. But as I hope I have demonstrated, that's just a cop-out—a substitute for thinking seriously and systemically about the whole problem. "Yes, we needed the bomb to end the war," said Michael Mandelbaum, "but we would not have gotten to that point, on the verge of victory, without a huge army, a draft, D-day, and all the people back home who sacrificed." We won the war thanks to the combined efforts of our armed forces (and let's not forget our allies), but those combined efforts were made possible by the combined efforts of the American people.

That is the real energy shortage in America today: a shortage of the energy we need to get serious about a big goal like a Clean Energy System and to stick with that goal until we achieve it—at both the citizen level and the political level.

Again, Michael Maniates, a professor of political science and environmental science at Allegheny College, in his *Washington Post* essay (November 22, 2007), said it best:

> Throughout our history it has been the knotty, vexing challenges, and leaders who speak frankly about them, that have fired our individual and communal imagination, creativity and commitment. Paul Revere didn't race through the streets of Middlesex County hawking a book on "The Lazy Revolutionary." Franklin Roosevelt didn't mobilize the country's energies by listing 10 easy ways to oppose fascism. And it's unlikely that Martin Luther King Jr.'s drafts of his "I Have a Dream" speech or his "Letter from Birmingham Jail" imagined a practical politics of change rooted in individualistic, consumer-centered actions . . . The greatest environmental problem confronting us isn't melting ice, faltering rain, or flattening oil supplies and rising gasoline prices. Rather, it's that when Americans ask, "What can I do to make a difference?" we're treated like children by environmental elites and political leaders too timid to call forth the best in us or too blind to that which has made us a great nation.

Alas, though, with all the money in politics, all the gerrymandering of districts, the twenty-four-hour cable news cycle, the blogosphere, and our nearly permanent reelection campaigns—one has to wonder whether we are capable of producing leaders able to solve a problem of this magnitude: a multigenerational, multifaceted, multitrillion-dollar problem. I always keep in mind a story that the Stanford climatologist Stephen Schneider tells. "Can democracy survive complexity?" he asks. "That is what this [energy-environment] problem represents. It is so difficult. It is multiscale, multidisciplinary, with large certainty in some areas and small certainty in others. It is irreversible and reversible and we won't know how we did until it is over. We will only know forty years later. That is why climate complexity is a challenge to democracy. Democracy is short term. In 1974, I [was working] in the Old Executive Office Building. I was twenty-nine years old and was working at the time for NCAR, the National Center for Atmospheric Research, [based] in Boulder. It was the Nixon administration, and I was talking to White House executive branch agencies interested in climate and security. It was arranged by the CIA. I did not know that at the time. And there was me and one other senior guy. I was talking about 'irreversibility'—and about eleven- and twenty-two-year drought cycles. And this guy in the back of the room, wearing a crumpled jacket and a little string tie twisted backward, shouted out, 'Kiddo, you do not understand. Around here, the only cycles that count are the two-, four-, and six-year cycles.' I met him afterward. He was from the CIA. He saw it straight."

And so must we. We are going to be either a democratic China or a banana republic. Either we are going to generate, through our democratic system and its elected leaders, the will, focus, legitimacy, authority, and persistence to look beyond the latest news cycle and do whatever it takes to design and deploy a Clean Energy System to take our country to the next level—which is what China is trying to do through more authoritarian means—or we are going to end up as a banana republic.

No, no—not that kind of banana. When I say "banana republic," I am not referring to a sort of Latin American dictatorship out of the 1960s. I am using the term "banana" the way utilities experts use it. You've heard the acronym NIMBY—"not in my backyard," as in: "I love wind turbines, but just not in my backyard"?

Well, BANANA is a broader variant of that. It stands for "build absolutely nothing anywhere near anything."

As a democracy, we in America have increasingly become that kind of banana republic, an unserious place when it comes to transformational change. We need more nuclear power, but no one wants the waste stored near them. We think wind turbines could provide a huge boost to our power grid, but please don't put any off Hyannis Port, Massachusetts, where they might mar my view of the ocean. Solar—yes, solar is the answer, but don't even think about running the high-voltage transmission line you need to get solar energy from where it can be generated at scale in the deserts of Arizona all the way over to Los Angeles, where it is most needed. Maybe natural gas is superior to coal for generating electricity, but don't you dare build a liquefied natural gas terminal (which would allow us to import more natural gas) in any American coastal community. OK, fine, let's rely on coal with carbon sequestration, but if you sequester the carbon dioxide from that coal in underground caverns and it starts leaking and coming up my toilet, I just want you to know one thing: I will sue your ass off—so don't go storing any of it near me. As for tidal-wave power—yes, it's OK, as long as you don't go putting one of those big tidal generators near my favorite beach.

For all these reasons, if we are going to summon the will, focus, and authority to push through a real green revolution, we will need a president who isn't afraid to do whatever it takes to lead it. To win the Civil War, Abraham Lincoln had to democratically take authority away from the states and invest it in a federal government that he made bigger and stronger than any America had seen since its founding. He even suspended the writ of habeas corpus. Franklin Roosevelt had to transform a weak, thin federal government into the massive institution it is today in order to overcome the Great Depression and win World War II.

Any president who wants to build a new clean energy and conservation system is going to have to do the same thing: to claim, democratically, the authority to forge a more integrated national energy system from the patchwork we have now. It was no accident that President Teddy Roosevelt was once heard to remark: "Oh, if I could only be President and Congress too for just ten minutes." Most presidents would say the same thing after they were briefed on the hydra-headed and hydra-armed monster that is today's American energy "system."

Indeed, hydra-headed understates the reality. Here's a snapshot. Local and regional utilities provide the electricity and natural gas for most Americans, but they are regulated by the states, which determine what prices they can charge for the power they generate and the transmission lines they build. The Environmental Protection Agency oversees air quality, water quality, and fuel quality standards. The Department of Transportation, though, is responsible for setting auto and truck mileage standards. The Department of Energy's Office of Science is the biggest source of funds in the country for energy research. And the DOE has responsibility for setting efficiency standards for appliances and the national model building code. The Department of Agriculture has a big say in ethanol production. The U.S. Army Corps of Engineers oversees the building and maintenance of many of our hydroelectric dams, while the Federal Energy Regulatory Commission oversees interstate electricity transmission lines and the Nuclear Regulatory Commission regulates the building and operation of nuclear plants. It's the president's Council of Economic Advisers that rules on the economic viability of any energy initiative. Meanwhile, senators, members of the House of Representatives, and governors are all lobbying every one of these agencies to protect or enhance the use of the particular form of power generated in their state, sometimes with the help of private sector investors and sometimes in opposition to them. When lobbyists don't like what one agency is doing on their issue, they will block them by going to another agency—and that is how you get an administration to work against itself.

This "system" was largely put in place after World War II on the assumption that the price of natural gas was $2 per million metric BTUs, and always would be, and that the price of crude oil floated between $10 and $24 a barrel and always would—save for occasional wars or political crises. Therefore, no single agency in the U.S. government had to be tasked with envisaging and implementing a clean energy revolution. We never thought we would need one. The whole system was "designed to make inaction easy and transformational action almost impossible," said Dan Becker, the environmental consultant. And therefore there was, and is, no master strategy, no single person or department seeing the whole board or thinking about how to get all the parts working together. "It is as if we [were] fighting World War II with only captains and colonels—and no generals," said Glenn Prickett of Conservation International. "Everyone just marching off in their own direction."

President Obama has been changing that. He has created his own green cabinet, comprising the key energy and environment officials in his administration. And, most important, he is trying to become that CEO—a chief energy officer—who uses democratic means to establish authority over this American energy beast that is shouting and pulling in so many different directions, and refocus it on the single priority of innovating and generating clean power, energy efficiency, and conservation through a smart system.

President Obama has accomplished an enormous amount in his first year, showing a real desire to become not only America's first black president but its first green president, and putting in place through his stimulus package and regulatory actions the real foundations for a green revolution. But whether that revolution actually takes shape will depend on his willingness and ability to sell Americans on doing something hard, something that will hurt for a while, but something that will make all the difference and leave us a better country with a more livable planet—a significantly higher price on carbon that really changes what consumers demand from the energy-using products in their lives. My hope is that he will rise to this occasion. My fear is that the economic mess he inherited will prevent him from doing so, and that therefore nothing less than an environmental Pearl Harbor or a climate 9/11 will be required to get it done. Let us hope not.

In the summer of 2007, in Basalt, Colorado, I took part in the twenty-fifth anniversary of the Rocky Mountain Institute, one of the country's great centers of environmental innovation. Before the dinner began, inside a huge private horse arena magically converted into a gala ballroom, I fell into conversation about environmentalism in Colorado with my friend Auden Schendler, the community and environmental affairs officer for the Aspen Skiing Company. When we finished speaking, I asked Schendler for his business card so I could stay in touch.

"I just changed my card," he said to me. Oh, have you moved? I asked. No, Schendler explained, he hadn't moved or changed jobs. He had his business cards reprinted because he wanted to change the quote that he had on the bottom of each card.

"My old business card used to have a quote from [the biologist and environmentalist] René Dubos that said: 'Trend is not destiny.' Then one day I said to myself, 'Guess what? Trend just might be destiny when it comes to the climate. There is nothing stopping us from doubling the amount of CO_2 in the atmosphere.' So I changed my business card. It now has a quote from [the late author] Charles Bukowski, who was this hard-drinking barroom brawler. It is the title of his book of poetry: 'What matters most is how well you walk through the fire.' We have not begun to fight on this issue. I am going to do it, even if I think the odds are long. I am thirty-seven, and I have a feeling of regret about what we have done so far. I want to live to see us win this. I want to see how this plays out. I used to say this is our children's problem. But the fact is, we've got about ten years to make a difference, so it is actually *our* problem."

Schendler is right. It really is our problem. We are living at a hinge of history that is going to determine just which way this Energy-Climate Era will swing. If we are going to manage what is already unavoidable and avoid what will be truly unmanageable, we need to make sure everything we do from here on helps to build a real, sustainable, scalable solution. The clear and easy paths are all closed. All that matters now is how we walk through this fire.

Given the enormity of this task, how do we avoid the trap of easy optimism or easy pessimism? We have to walk the line between Auden Schendler's two business cards: the line between a can-do optimism and a keen awareness that the hour is late and the scale of the problems practically overwhelming.

People need hope to undertake a challenge this big, this long-term, and this daunting. You can't stimulate and sustain a broad political movement without it. If you tell people, "Look, let's face it, we're cooked. If you just add up the numbers—the amount of CO_2 that is already in the atmosphere and the tons more certain to get lodged there—the truth is that the only polar bears your grandchildren are going to ever see will be in the pages of an old *National Geographic*," then their natural reaction is "Well, if there is nothing we can really do to stop this train, let's party."

But if you tell people that the solutions are really at hand, or that with 205 easy ways to go green from your latest gardening magazine we can produce a whole new energy system and lick global warming, the attitude of many will also be "Well, if it's that easy, then let's party." I like the way George Monbiot put it in his book *Heat: How to Stop the Planet from Burning*. "To succumb to hope of this nature," he says, "is as dangerous as to succumb to despair."

So what am I? I guess I would call myself a sober optimist—I prefer to hold on to both of Auden Schendler's business cards. If you are not sober about the scale of the challenge, then you are not paying attention. But if you are not an optimist, you have no chance of generating the kind of mass movement it will take to achieve the needed scale.

A eulogy is no way to end a book, but the remarks that Amory Lovins delivered at the memorial service for Donella H. "Dana" Meadows expressed so many of my own hopes that I can't help but share part of it here. Meadows, the Dartmouth-based environmental expert and writer, inspired or taught many of my friends in the green movement. She died February 21, 2001, and Amory's remarks at her memorial service went like this:

A biologist, perhaps E. O. Wilson, noted that bees, ants, and termites, though not very smart individually, display high intelli-

gence collectively—and then he added, "People seem just the opposite." Dana was an exception. She was one of those promising
specimens that are turning up more and more often in the search
for intelligent life on earth—one of those much higher primates
whose love, logic, radical stubbornness, courage, and passion
awaken the rest of us to our ability and our responsibility to save
the world . . . She wrote three years ago, "By nature I'm an optimist; to me all glasses are half-full," yet she didn't shrink from reporting bad news, always blended with encouragement about
how to do better. She treated the future as choice, not fate, and
she defined with luminous clarity how to do (as one sometimes
must) what is necessary. She shared René Dubos's view that despair is a sin, so when asked if we have enough time to prevent
catastrophe, she'd always say that we have exactly enough time—
starting now. Two years ago, when e-mailing an unusually somber
column about events that made her weep, she appended the following note as counterpoint: "A CEO was having to babysit for his
young daughter. He was trying to read the paper but was totally
frustrated by the constant interruptions. When he came across a
full page of the NASA photo of the Earth from space, he got a brilliant idea. He ripped it up into small pieces and told his child to
try to put it back together. He then settled in for what he expected
to be a good half-hour of peace and quiet. But only a few minutes
had gone by before the child appeared at his side with a big grin
on her face. 'You've finished already?' he asked. 'Yep,' she replied.
'So how did you do it?' 'Well, I saw there was a picture of a person
on the other side, so when I put the person together, the Earth got
put together too . . .'"

There is so much to admire in that eulogy: the conviction that the future is our choice, not our fate, that when you put people together you
put the planet together, that there is nothing in the universe quite as powerful as six billion minds wrapping around one problem, and, most of all,
the best expression of sober optimism I've ever heard: *We have exactly
enough time—starting now.* So let me end this book where I began it—
with us, with America. John Dernbach, the environmental law expert,
once remarked to me that in the final analysis, "the decisions Americans
make about sustainable development are not technical decisions about

peripheral matters, and they are not simply decisions about the environment. They are decisions about who we are, what we value, what kind of
world we want to live in, and how we want to be remembered."

We are the first generation of Americans in the Energy-Climate Era.
And what we do about the challenges of energy and climate, conservation and preservation, will tell our kids who we really are. After all is said
and done, I am still an optimist that we will rise to this challenge. I am
certain that my children and grandchildren will live in a cleaner world
and a safer world and a more sustainable world. Why? Because technology today is allowing us to connect and leverage more and more brainpower than ever before. Whole swaths of the world that really could not
collaborate in solving problems are being brought into the discussion.
That is hugely important and the reason that I believe *we will figure this
out—we will learn as nations and individuals that we cannot afford to
grow the old-fashioned way—by just mining the global commons and
by thinking that the universe and nature revolve around us, and not the
other way around.* The only question is how soon—whether it is before
a climate Pearl Harbor or after. Ultimately that will depend on leadership—from politicians, scientists, and We the People—We the American
People.

The world expects us to lead, the world needs us to lead, and our ability to thrive as a country in the future requires us to lead. We need to redefine green and rediscover America, and, in so doing, renew, refresh,
and reengineer our country and what it means to be an American. It is a
daunting task, but also a quintessentially American one. We have done it
before, and now we must do it one more time.

We are all Pilgrims again. We are all sailing on the *Mayflower* anew.
We have not been to this shore before. If we fail to recognize that, we
will, indeed, become just one more endangered species. But if we rise to
this challenge, and truly become the Re-Generation—redefining green
and rediscovering, reviving, and regenerating America—we, and the
world, will not only survive but thrive in an age that is hot, flat, and
crowded.

ACKNOWLEDGMENTS

INDEX

Acknowledgments

When I think about what I hoped to accomplish in writing this book, I am reminded of something that Larry Summers, now the head of President Obama's Council of Economic Advisors, said about the time after his tenure as the president of Harvard, when he was trying to stimulate a new discussion about globalization and its impact on the middle classes: "I think one has to be prepared to accept long causal chains," Summers told a reporter for *The New York Times Magazine* (June 10, 2007). "That is, if you're trying to think about a problem and propose a solution, it does not happen the next day. But it affects the climate of opinion, and things go from being inconceivable to being inevitable." If this book contributes in any way to making a real green revolution, spearheaded by America, move from inconceivable to inevitable, I will consider it a success.

You can't write a book that covers this many varied topics and this much geography without a lot of good counsel. I have had the benefit of many generous tutors, teachers, and guides.

This is the fifth book I have written while on the staff of *The New York Times*. And, like the previous four, it would not have been possible without the support of the paper and the remarkable people there. In particular, I want to thank the publisher, Arthur Sulzberger, Jr., for giving me the column that has enabled me to see so much of this hot, flat, and crowded world, and for approving the leave that made it possible for me to write this book. I also want to thank Andrew Rosenthal, editor of the paper's editorial page, for enthusiastically backing this project and organizing my sabbatical.

As for the tutors and helpers, the list always starts with the Johns Hopkins University foreign policy expert Michael Mandelbaum. Our endless conversations about energy, politics, and foreign policy constantly served to sharpen my arguments.

My primary teacher when it comes to the issue of biodiversity has been Glenn Prickett. Glenn and I have traveled from the Atlantic rain forest in Brazil to Shangri-La in Chinese Tibet and from the wilds of southern Venezuela to the southern tip of Indonesia. A senior vice president of Conservation International, where my wife, Ann, is a board member, Glenn has forgotten more than I will ever know about the environment and biodiversity, but along the way he has taught me more than any other person has about these subjects. His passion for preserving our natural world is infectious. CI's leaders, Russell Mittermeier and Peter Seligmann, have also always been enthusiastic supporters of my work. Two of CI's biodiversity experts, T. M. Brooks and Michael Totten, took the time to read and advise me on critical sections of this book. Jatna Supriatna and Mark Erdmann of CI Indonesia were both compelling tour guides and offered great insight into the terrestrial and marine biodiversity of the Indonesian archipelago, as did Alfred Nakatsuma, who runs the USAID environmental programs in Jakarta.

Among the many people Glenn Prickett has introduced me to, none has been more important than Rob Watson, who inspired the LEED building rating system when he was at the Natural Resources Defense Council and now heads EcoTech International. Rob is a passionate but patient teacher, and his far-ranging insights are all over this book. Frances Beinecke, the president of NRDC, invited me to road test some of my ideas at a board retreat, and many NRDC staffers have enriched different sections of this book, particularly Rick Duke, Roland Huang, and most of all Ralph Cavanagh, NRDC's superstar utilities expert. Ralph educated me on the world of utilities and repeatedly read over those sections of the book, for which I am deeply grateful.

On the complex issue of climate change, I had the benefit of great teachers: Professor Nate Lewis of Caltech, and Professor John Holdren of Harvard, the Woods Hole Research Center in Massachusetts—and more recently the Obama administration. When I spoke at Caltech two years ago, Nate was assigned to be my host. It was my good fortune. His ability to explain abstruse scientific issues in language that nonexperts can understand is unparalleled. Our long lunches at the Caltech faculty club, which helped me connect so many dots in this book, are among my fondest memories of work on this project. I met John Holdren through Rob Watson. He too was such a patient tutor about the inner workings of climate change and took the time to carefully review some of my arguments. What a treat it was to bat around ideas with these two distinguished scientists!

Amory Lovins was one of the first people to turn me on to the geo-economic and geostrategic importance of clean power, and I am grateful for his friendship and tutelage. The same goes for my friend David Rothkopf of the Carnegie Endowment; our long-running dialogue about energy and geopolitics has been a source of great insight for me and has helped to enrich many aspects of this book.

I met Joseph Romm, formerly a senior official in the Clinton administration's Department of Energy, in the latter stages of the book, but I am glad I did, because I benefited greatly from his tough-minded critiques of some of the bad science around climate change. Joe also took the time to review many passages. Any mistakes that are still here are my own.

My appreciation of the climate issue was also greatly enhanced by Heidi Cullen, climatologist for the Weather Channel, who filled my notebook with her insights. Stephen Pacala from Princeton and Stephen Schneider from Stanford were also generous with their time.

Google.org's energy team, spearheaded by Larry Brilliant and Dan Reicher, was kind enough to give me an afternoon on the Google campus to share their assessment of the clean-tech opportunity, while Felix Kramer, who has made plug-in electric cars not only his passion but an imminent American reality, was always ready to take a query from me.

My understanding of China's energy challenge was greatly enhanced by David Moskovitz, director of the Regulatory Assistance Project, and by Edward S. Steinfeld, associate professor of political science at MIT. Professor Daniel M. Kammen at the University of California, Berkeley, kindly walked me through the thicket of information and misinformation surrounding the issue of energy research funding. Nobody has taught me more about oil than Philip K. Verleger, Jr., to whom I am also deeply grateful.

I made two documentaries on energy for the Discovery Channel with Ken Levis and Ann Derry. Ken's work in tracking down the right voices to portray America's energy challenge today enriched my understanding of this issue. Thanks, too, to Jonathan Rose for tutoring me on systems. Thanks also and always to Yaron Ezrahi—my teacher and friend.

No book of mine would be complete without the insights of my wise friend Michael Sandel, a political philosopher at Harvard, who helped me to think through the relationship between clean energy and an ethic of stewardship and conservation. Michael's Harvard colleague Edward O. Wilson, the great biologist, generously shared with me his views on today's threats to biodiversity. Spending time with him at his lab was a privilege. Steven Chu, now the secretary of energy, gave me an awesome display of the energy talent at the Lawrence Berkeley National Laboratory when he was director there, and I left with a mother lode of insights. Mike Davis, Robert Pratt, and Carl Imhoff did the same for me at the Northwest Pacific National Laboratory, and followed up with numerous conversations. What national treasures these institutions are.

Outside the environmental field, Curtis Carlson, president and CEO of SRI International, has been a delightful pen pal, sounding board, and adviser on every aspect of this book. Riley Bechtel kindly introduced me to his senior manager for renewable energy issues, Amos Avidan, who became both a friend and a tutor on the nuts and bolts of the energy business. Jeffrey Immelt, CEO of General Electric, and his whole team—Gary Sheffer, John Krenicki, John Dineen, and Lorraine Bolsinger—educated me about the intricacies of the power-generation business. Duke Energy's CEO, Jim Rogers, and Southern California Edison's CEO, John Bryson, generously took time to explain the economics of the utilities world and review parts of the book. For two guys in a boring business, they are both really interesting. Ron Litzinger, senior vice president for Southern California Edison, also schooled me on the issue of transmission lines. Peter Corsell and Louis Szablya from Grid-Point and Larry Kellerman from Goldman Sachs patiently walked me through the intricacies of the smart grid and reviewed my text about it. My conversations with the three of them opened my mind to so many aspects of the utilities business that I did not know about. The green business strategist Andrew Shapiro offered many great insights for this book, as part of a long-running conversation. Andrew also provided valuable comments on the text. Dov and Maria Seidman spawned the concept of "outgreening" over a long discussion at their breakfast table—one of many we have enjoyed together. I cherish their friendship. David Edwards, an energy expert at VantagePoint Venture Partners, kindly stopped by for regular chats about the book and to offer insights, as did Alan Waxman, an energy expert with Goldman Sachs. David Douglas, who oversees sustainability programs for Sun Microsystems, provided me with all

sorts of great ideas, as well as specific insights into the environmental implications of the computing business. Brian Silverstein, vice president
with the Bonneville Power Administration, walked me through the intricacies of the electric grid. Former Assistant Secretary for Energy Efficiency and Renewable Energy at the Department of Energy Andy
Karsner, whose breadth of knowledge on the financing of energy projects
is unrivaled, gave me valuable feedback at every stage of the writing. Jim
Connaughton, who was President Bush's top environmental adviser, got
stuck sitting next to me on a flight from Tokyo to Washington and was a
good sport about submitting to a thirteen-hour interview. Dan Nolan and
Tom Morehouse were hugely important tutors on the green hawk movement within the U.S. military. Kenneth Oye of MIT, Mamoun Fandy
from IISS, Larry Diamond from Stanford, the venture capitalist Jack
Hidary, the scientist Peter Gleick, the wind expert Michael Polsky, the social entrepreneur Van Jones, the military expert Linton Wells, and the
Shell Oil scenario team in The Hague, as well as John Ashton and Tom
Burke from London, all pitched in with their insights along the way. So
too did Joe Kahn, the former *New York Times* Beijing bureau chief. Diana Farrell from the McKinsey Global Institute and I have had a fifteen-
year running conversation about globalization, which continued, to my
benefit, with this book.

Bill Gates and Craig Mundie, from Microsoft, had me out for a
lengthy discussion about all aspects of the energy issue and the book in
general. You haven't had your ideas stress-tested until you've tested them
on those two! It was exhausting, but, as with *The World Is Flat*, it was
tremendously helpful in sharpening my arguments and stimulated the
chapter "Energy Poverty." Robert Freling, executive director of the Solar
Electric Light Fund, was also critical in shaping my thinking on energy
poverty. Nayan Chanda, who runs the *YaleGlobal Online* Web site,
helped me to break the code when it came to China's energy challenge
and its environmental implications. Nandan Nilekani, chairman of Infosys, who was so helpful in my previous book, was always generous in offering insights for this one as well.

John Doerr was a delightful traveling companion, from the rain
forests of Peru to the sugarcane fields of Brazil. John's personal commitment to mitigating climate change has been an inspiration, and his
generosity in introducing me to the entire network of clean energy
entrepreneurs that his venture firm has backed was invaluable. Of the

many people he introduced me to, none has been more helpful than K. R. Sridhar, founder of Bloom Energy. A more gentle and thoughtful soul on the issues of energy and environment does not exist.

I also want to thank for their advice: Carl Pope, executive director of the Sierra Club; consultant Dan Becker; and FERC commissioner Jon Wellinghof; as well as Volkert Doeksen; Margo Oge; Cherie and Enki Tan; Lois Quam; Jacqueline Novogratz; Rhone Resch; and, last but not least, the folks at IBM who hosted my first seminar about this book: Joel Cawley and his colleagues Martin Fleming and Ron Ambrosio. I am indebted to Chad Holliday and his team at DuPont for their generous assistance. I'd also like to thank my friend George Shultz for his wise counsel, and Jeff Wacker and Bill Ritz of EDS for all their insights.

A few important honorable mentions: Barbara Gross, general manager of the Garden Court Hotel, where I always stay in Palo Alto, made the ultimate sacrifice and gave me her personal laptop computer, after mine broke, and let me use it for three days of interviews and the flight back to Washington. That is full service. My golf pals Joel Finkelstein, Alan Kotz, and George Stevens, Jr., heard all about this book long before my publisher did. I am grateful for their companionship.

My little book publishing team—literary agent Esther Newberg, FSG's president Jonathan Galassi, marketing director Jeff Seroy, publicity director Sarita Varma, art director Susan Mitchell, sales director Spenser Lee, managing editor Debra Helfand, copy editor Don McConnell, fact-checker Jill Priluck, and my editor, Paul Elie—has been with me since the Creation. At least it feels that way. I am lucky to have their support and friendship. Paul made every single page of this book better; lucky is the author who gets such a smart and devoted editor. My assistant at *The New York Times*, Gwenn Gorman, has kept all the trains running on time—books, columns, and travel. For that, and for the conscientious way she does her job, I am very grateful.

My dear little mom, Margaret Friedman, died while I was writing this book. I told her I was working on it, but I am not sure it ever got through the haze. I missed being able to hand her the first edition. My mom's life spanned an incredible period. She was born in 1918, just in time to catch the tail end of World War I; she grew up in the Depression, enlisted in the navy after Pearl Harbor, served her country in World War II, and lived long enough to play bridge on the Internet with someone in Siberia. She left us just as the world started getting hot, flat, and crowded.

My daughters, Orly and Natalie, and their whole generation will inherit this challenge. I hope this book can be a helpful guide for them, especially given the light they have brought to my life.

When you write a book about energy and the environment, people rightly want to know how you live your own life. Like many people, I suppose, I would describe my own family's greening as a work in progress. I wrote this book as someone who was not thinking about his carbon footprint much before 2001, and who is thinking a lot about it now. Six years ago, my wife, Ann, and I bought one of the last large pieces of property in our Maryland neighborhood to prevent it from being redeveloped into a subdivision of a dozen or more houses. We had to outbid commercial developers to do so. We eventually built on it ourselves, erecting a large house on one end and turning the rest into a parklike green space. We preserved all the specimen trees that were already on the lot, and planted nearly two hundred new trees and thousands of flowering plants. It has become a refuge for deer, rabbits, birds, butterflies, and a fox or two. To reduce the energy footprint of our home, we installed a geothermal HVAC system and two large solar arrays that provide about 7 percent of our electricity, and we have covered the rest of our power needs with Green-e certified wind renewable energy credits from Juice Energy. Ann and I drive a hybrid car. Ann, as a Conservation International board member, has helped to fund CI's Center for Environmental Leadership in Business, which works on greening companies, and CI's operation in Peru, which is working to prevent deforestation caused by roads being built through ecologically sensitive rain forest areas. That's our work in progress. We won't be done until we are energy net-zero.

Ann, as always, shared intimately in this book as a work in progress as well. She edited and improved the first draft very early on, traveled with me to some exotic corners of Indonesia (among other places) to join in the research, and listened to the ideas evolve every step of the way. Her own commitment to preserving the environment, not to mention our own garden, is an inspiration. For that, and for so much more for so many years, this book is dedicated to her.

Thomas L. Friedman
Bethesda, Maryland
September 2009

Index

Page numbers in *italics* refer to charts and graphs.

BUSINESS

THE WORLD IS FLAT
THOMAS FRIEDMAN

Winner of the *Financial Times*/Goldman Sachs Business Book of the Year 2005

Three-times winner of the Pulitzer Prize

> The world is changing, the future is flat.

Thomas Friedman's international bestseller is the most up-to-date and exciting view yet of today's new era of globalization. He draws on this travels to India, China and the Middle East, and on the explosion of new technologies including blogging, online encyclopedias and podcasting, to show how knowledge and resources are connecting all over the planet as never before. This 'flattening' of our world, he argues, can be a force for good – for business, the environment and people everywhere.

'Truly amazing ... an essential read' A. C. Grayling

'A great book ... makes you see things in a new way' Joseph Stiglitz